T0215619

Dynamic SQL

Applications, Performance, and Security in Microsoft SQL Server

Second Edition

Edward Pollack

Apress®

Dynamic SQL: Applications, Performance, and Security in Microsoft SQL Server

Edward Pollack
Albany, NY, USA

ISBN-13 (pbk): 978-1-4842-4317-6   ISBN-13 (electronic): 978-1-4842-4318-3
https://doi.org/10.1007/978-1-4842-4318-3

Library of Congress Control Number: 2018967497

Managing Director, Apress Media LLC: Welmoed Spahr
Acquisitions Editor: Jonathan Gennick
Development Editor: Laura Berendson
Coordinating Editor: Jill Balzano

Cover image designed by Freepik (www.freepik.com)

Distributed to the book trade worldwide by Springer Science+Business Media New York, 233 Spring Street, 6th Floor, New York, NY 10013. Phone 1-800-SPRINGER, fax (201) 348-4505, e-mail orders-ny@springer-sbm.com, or visit www.springeronline.com. Apress Media, LLC is a California LLC and the sole member (owner) is Springer Science + Business Media Finance Inc (SSBM Finance Inc). SSBM Finance Inc is a **Delaware** corporation.

For information on translations, please e-mail rights@apress.com, or visit www.apress.com/rights-permissions.

Apress titles may be purchased in bulk for academic, corporate, or promotional use. eBook versions and licenses are also available for most titles. For more information, reference our Print and eBook Bulk Sales web page at www.apress.com/bulk-sales.

Any source code or other supplementary material referenced by the author in this book is available to readers on GitHub via the book's product page, located at www.apress.com/978-1-4842-4317-6. For more detailed information, please visit http://www.apress.com/source-code.

Printed on acid-free paper

To Theresa, Nolan, and Oliver: the best players 2-4 (aka: family)
I could ever have asked for!

Table of Contents

About the Author

Edward Pollack has over 18 years of experience in database and systems administration and architecture, developing a passion for performance optimization and making things go faster. He has spoken at many SQL Saturdays, 24 Hours of PASS, and PASS Summit. This led him to organize SQL Saturday Albany, which has become an annual event for New York's Capital Region.

In his free time, Ed enjoys video games, sci-fi & fantasy, traveling, and cooking exceptionally spicy foods. He lives in the subarctic icescape of Albany, NY with his wife Theresa, his sons Nolan and Oliver, and an impressive collection of video game-related plushies and figures.

About the Technical Reviewer

Kathi Kellenberger is the editor of Simple-Talk at Redgate Software, and Data Platform MVP with over 20 years experience working with SQL Server. She is the author of several books, including Beginning T-SQL, Beginning Reporting Services, and Expert T-SQL Window Functions. When she is not working, she enjoys spending time with friends and family, singing, and climbing the stairs of tall buildings.

Acknowledgments

The SQL Server community is vast, made up of user groups, companies, professionals, colleges, and organizations that create a network of like-minded individuals all looking to further their knowledge, while at the same time helping others.

My interest in database administration was borne of some masochistic curiousity, but the resources to learn, grow, and share that knowledge were made possible by more people than I can count, each of whom has volunteered countless hours for the betterment of others.

Thank you to the Professional Association of SQL Server; the Capital Area SQL Server Group and its founders, Dan Bowlin and Joe Barth; to Autotask, a company that has given me great amounts of professional freedom to explore database technologies in my free time; Matt Slocum for organizing and letting me be a part of SQL Saturday Rochester (the first I spoke at); APress for the opportunity to write and support throughout the process; SQL Shack for standing behind my writing for years; my friends, who are always there for me, no matter what life has thrown at us; to the many volunteers who organize, speak, write, blog, and otherwise improve the world in their free time; and to my family for having immense patience when I've come up with crazy ideas like this one.

Introduction

Dynamic SQL is a tool that is often described in bits and pieces, when a need for code arises and time is limited. This book is an opportuntiy to put as many of those fragments as possible together into a meaningful journey, from defining the technology to delving into its deepest and most complex aspects. This is a dive into many topics that are extremely important when working with any database. We will intentionally delve deeper into performance optimization, application development, and security than may seem necessary.

What is This Book?

This is meant to be a discussion of smart database design and architecture, with a focus on dynamic SQL. If any topic that is covered in an aside feels incomplete, it is because there simply isn't room in these pages for a thorough analysis of all of them without losing focus on why we are here. Dynamic SQL is a tool that is often underused, misused, or overused. The many tangents into other arenas of design and development serve as guides to keep us on track and emphasize the value of well-written database queries, as well as ensuring that we use dynamic SQL for the correct applications.

Each chapter delves into a specific topic and attempts to go into as much detail as possible, while also providing multiple examples to demonstrate it in the simplest way possible. If you have never written a line of dynamic SQL, this will be an opportunity to learn, practice, and immediately apply it. If you already have experience in writing and using dynamic SQL, this will be a chance to learn new applications while getting a refresher on those you have worked with in the past.

Most examples in this book will reference the Microsoft AdventureWorks sample database, which provides basic database structures that can be freely experimented with. Queries are compatible with any version of AdventureWorks, but were tested most heavily with AdventureWorks 2016.

Intended Audience

Anyone with a healthy interest in database administration or development can benefit from the topics covered within this book. Each chapter starts out with basic definitions and examples, providing an easy entry point for professionals with any level of experience. We transition into more advanced techniques, allowing you to not only learn the basics of an important subject, but also gain access to scripts and ideas that could be tested and used to solve problems you may face in your everyday experiences.

If you have a particular interest in database security or optimziation, then you will appreciate the focus on these topics in each chapter. SQL Injection gets an exhaustive review, with many different aspects and examples presented to ensure a thorough explanation of this important topic! Every chapter, regardless of topic, will reference performance whenever possible. It is an oft-made mistake that a database is designed with little data and few users, ignoring the possibility that it will one day grow into a behemoth. Reminders are placed throughout this book to consider query performance at all times, even when performance may seem "good enough."

Contacting the Author

We can only grow personally and professionally if we are willing to consider other viewpoints and revise our own to improve.

I love hearing from anyone who has ideas, questions, applications, video game recommendations, or criticism. Please contact me at `ed7@alum.rpi.edu` and let me know what I can do to improve the content of this book, or address any questions or problems you may have.

CHAPTER 1

What Is Dynamic SQL?

T-SQL is a scripting language that expands with each new release of SQL Server. Success in the world of database development and administration requires flexibility and the ability to adapt constantly to new situations, technologies, and demands. Many of the challenges we face are unknowns, or situations in which we cannot know exactly the data we will be working with until runtime. In order to find the optimal solution in the face of unknowns, one of the best tools at our disposal is dynamic SQL.

Understanding Dynamic SQL

Dynamic SQL is quite simple to understand, and once acquainted, the number of applications can become staggering. Dynamic SQL seeks to solve scenarios where we want to operate on one or many objects, but do not know all of the pertinent details as we write our code. Parameters can be passed into our code in order to persist sets of important values, but what do we do when the structure of our T-SQL is defined by these values?

A Simple Example

Starting with a very simple select statement, we will build a starting point for understanding dynamic SQL:

```
SELECT TOP(10) * FROM Person.Person;
```

This statement returns 10 rows from the table `Person.Person`, including all columns in the table. What if we wanted to select data from a table, but did not know the name of the table until runtime? How would we substitute the variable table name into our

E. Pollack, *Dynamic SQL*, https://doi.org/10.1007/978-1-4842-4318-3_1

1

T-SQL? Before answering that question, let's introduce dynamic SQL by simply rewriting the preceding query so that we are executing it as a character string, rather than standard T-SQL:

```
DECLARE @sql_command NVARCHAR(MAX);
SELECT @sql_command = 'SELECT TOP 10 * FROM Person.Person';
EXEC (@sql_command);
```

In this example, we have defined a character string called @sql_command that will be used to hold our dynamic SQL. What is the dynamic SQL? It's the string that we are building and then later executing. In this case, it is the same select statement from before, with no alterations. After we set the value of our @sql_command, it is then executed, providing the same results as before.

The EXEC Statement

EXEC is used to execute @sql_command. EXECUTE may also be used, as they are equivalent statements. Other ways to execute dynamic SQL will be presented later in this book, in response to the need for further flexibility or security. Remember to always put parentheses around the @sql_command string. Here's an example that omits the parentheses:

```
DECLARE @sql_command NVARCHAR(MAX);
SELECT @sql_command = 'SELECT TOP 10 * FROM Person.Person';
EXEC @sql_command;
```

Failure to do so will result in a somewhat odd error:

```
Msg 2812, Level 16, State 62, Line 11
Could not find stored procedure 'SELECT TOP 10 * FROM Person.Person'.
```

The dynamic SQL command string is treated by SQL Server as a stored procedure when parentheses are not included. Leave them out and you'll be unable to execute your SQL string, receiving an error similar to the preceding one.

Data Type to Use

Note that NVARCHAR(MAX) is used as the data type for our command string. While we could use VARCHAR, we would potentially be losing data if any extended Unicode characters were in any of the objects we work with. The size could also be shortened, but if our command string becomes larger than that size, it will be truncated and our dynamic SQL will become the source of confusing error messages or logical errors.

For consistency and reliability, use NVARCHAR(MAX) as the data type for your dynamic SQL command strings.

It may be tempting to use VARCHAR or use a smaller size string to save computing resources, but as these are scalar variables, the memory used is relatively small and very temporary. A 10,000 character NVARCHAR string would cost 20KB, whereas the VARCHAR version would cost 10KB. The difference is minimal and will not have an impact on any modern computing system. This logic should not be applied to tables, where computing resources are multiplied by row counts, and additional storage systems are involved.

Dynamic Execution Process

To understand how dynamic SQL works and the various ways in which it can be applied to the many problems we encounter, it is important to consider how dynamic SQL is built. In addition, becoming familiar with the execution process used by SQL Server in order to parse and run our string of T-SQL will make using dynamic SQL a much easier process.

All dynamic SQL follows 3 basic steps:

1. Create a string variable that will store our dynamic SQL.
   Any variable name may be used.

2. Build a command string and store it in this variable.

3. Execute our command string.

The benefit of storing our T-SQL command as a string is that we are free to use any string manipulation commands on it, building it in one or many steps. Now to tackle our original problem: how to select data from a table that is not defined until runtime. To accomplish this, we remove `Person.Person` from the string and replace it with a variable that we define as shown previously:

```
DECLARE @sql_command NVARCHAR(MAX);
DECLARE @table_name SYSNAME;
SELECT @table_name = 'Person.Person';
SELECT @sql_command = 'SELECT TOP 10 * FROM ' + @table_name;
EXEC (@sql_command);
```

The variable `@table_name` stores the name of the table we wish to query. Commonly, this would be passed in as a parameter, either from other stored procedures, or an application that calls this directly. By building it into `@sql_command`, we gain the flexibility of querying any table we wish, without hard-coding it ahead of time. While this is a trivial example (how often will we want to select data in this fashion?), it provides the basis for thousands of applications, each of which can save immense time, resources, and complexity. Before diving further into the details of dynamic SQL and its many uses, let's look at a more practical (and more complex) example of dynamic SQL in action.

Dynamic SQL in Action

A common maintenance need is to run T-SQL against many databases on a server. This maintenance could involve backing up databases, rebuilding indexes, reporting on critical data elements, or many other applications. If our database list never changes and no databases are ever renamed, we could hard-code names into each procedure and not need to worry about changing them in the future. This would work until the one day when we finally experience those inevitable changes, moving or renaming databases, ultimately breaking those valuable maintenance procedures. It's critical that our maintenance, monitoring, and reporting jobs operate with the highest level of reliability possible.

Listing 1-1 shows a common example of a statement that could be used to run a backup against a single database, storing it on a local drive.

Listing 1-1. Simple Backup Statement

```
BACKUP DATABASE AdventureWorks2014
TO DISK='E:\SQLBackups\AdventureWorks2014.bak'
WITH COMPRESSION;
```

This T-SQL will back up the AdventureWorks2014 database to the SQLBackups folder on the E drive, using compression. If we want to perform a custom database backup on a subset of databases that all begin with the text "AdventureWorks," we would need to build T-SQL that could adapt to collect a list of all databases with that name, and then perform backups on each of them separately. The following T-SQL shows one way that this could be accomplished, using dynamic SQL.

Listing 1-2. Dynamic SQL Built to Back Up All Databases Starting with "AdventureWorks"

```
DECLARE @database_list TABLE
      (database_name SYSNAME);

INSERT INTO @database_list
      (database_name)
SELECT
      name
FROM sys.databases
WHERE name LIKE 'AdventureWorks%';

DECLARE @sql_command NVARCHAR(MAX);
DECLARE @database_name SYSNAME;

DECLARE database_cursor CURSOR LOCAL FAST_FORWARD FOR
SELECT database_name FROM @database_list
OPEN database_cursor
FETCH NEXT FROM database_cursor INTO @database_name;

WHILE @@FETCH_STATUS = 0
BEGIN
      SELECT @sql_command = '
      BACKUP DATABASE [' + @database_name + ']
      TO DISK="E:\SQLBackups\' + @database_name + '.bak"
      WITH COMPRESSION;'
```

```
    EXEC (@sql_command);

    FETCH NEXT FROM database_cursor INTO @database_name;
END

CLOSE database_cursor;
DEALLOCATE database_cursor;
```

This T-SQL is certainly more complex than the first backup statement that we looked at. Let's break it apart in order to understand what is going on here, and why it works. We can then focus on the dynamic SQL that provides the backbone of this set of statements.

1. Populate a table variable with a list of database names.

2. Go through a loop, one time per database.

3. Build a dynamic SQL command string that takes into account the current database name.

4. Execute the dynamic backup statement.

5. Continue iterating through the loop until all relevant databases have been backed up.

We declare a number of variables here:

> **@database_list**: Contains all databases that match our search criteria. In this case, any database that starts with the word "AdventureWorks" will be included.

> **@sql_command**: This is the command string that will contain our dynamic SQL statement.

> **@database_name**: Holds the name of the database that is currently being backed up.

> **database_cursor**: A cursor that will be used to iterate through all databases named in @database_list.

Much of this example is setup for the loop. The critical portion is where we substitute the database name and backup file name with @database_name. This allows us to generate a backup statement that will not only back up each database, regardless of how many there are, but will name the backup file using that name. We could just as easily append additional information onto the file name, such as the date, time, or server name, if it were important.

Backups are a perfect use of dynamic SQL, as we can continue to customize and add time-saving functionality into our code, such as:

1. Whether to use compression

2. Determining if subfolders should be used (or not) for backup files

3. Should we perform a FULL, DIFF, or TLOG?

4. Should this backup be COPY_ONLY?

Advantages of Dynamic SQL

There are many reasons why we would want to incorporate dynamic SQL into our everyday arsenal of SQL Server tools. In addition, there are many specific challenges for which dynamic SQL is the optimal solution. Discussing these scenarios will highlight why an entire book can be written on this topic.

Optional or Customized Search Criteria

Search boxes are one of the most common tools used in the development of web pages or applications. For simple searches, we may only need to pass in a single variable for evaluation. In more powerful web searches, we may be able to choose between many criteria, of which each could be evaluated with AND or OR conditions. While we could write a very long SELECT statement with left joins to every possible table involved, we would likely end up with an immense, inefficient, and unwieldy pile of T-SQL. Dynamic SQL allows us to build up a select string that only queries the tables necessary to satisfy a given search.

Customizable Everything

Adding joins or WHERE clauses are only the beginning. With dynamic SQL, any statement can be customized to provide greater flexibility to your code. Want to group by a column based on a dynamic search? The solution is to write the GROUP BY clause as dynamic SQL, altering it as needed to fit the needs of each specific situation. Want to generate row numbers for a data set, but won't know which columns to partition by or order by until runtime? No problem!

Our preceding example illustrated how we could use dynamic SQL to customize a backup operation, and customize the name of the backup file. Any conceivable T-SQL statement can be altered to utilize dynamic SQL, and in doing so, allow for greater flexibility in any number of day-to-day challenges.

ORM (object-relational mapping) software can allow for similar levels of customization, but not all companies can (or want) to use software that automatically generates T-SQL, as performance and complexity can quickly become overwhelming. Like any querying application, choosing the correct tool is essential to scalability and performance.

Optimize SQL Performance

So far, dynamic SQL has appeared to make things more complicated, adding the need for temporary variables, loops, and command strings. Despite the seemingly added complexity, this framework can allow us to reduce the size of the SQL statements that we typically execute and improve performance.

Dynamic SQL provides an opportunity to customize our statements to match performance needs. Removing excess objects, adjusting joins and subqueries, and reducing the size of an SQL statement can result in faster executions times and reduce resource consumption.

While our scripts may have more lines of T-SQL, the queries that are ultimately executed by SQL Server will be simpler and perform more reliably.

Generate Large Amounts of T-SQL or Text, Fast!

Sometimes we need to execute large SQL statements that act on a set of many objects. Other times, we want to generate output text based on data stored in a specific set of tables. Perhaps we want to generate SELECT statements that will be used to gather reporting data from any number of sources.

Writing all of this T-SQL by hand could take a very long time, and lead to a significant opportunity for human error to occur, as we trudge through a time-consuming, boring task. If the SQL statements involved are to be run on a regular basis, then preparing them in advance may be impossible if the target tables or other objects involved can change on a regular basis.

Using dynamic SQL, we can generate any amount of commands or text without limit. SQL Server will not tire of this process, no matter how dull it may seem. This is an opportunity to automate tedious tasks and reduce operator intervention in those that would end up being busy work. The result is that our jobs become easier, more fun, and we can focus on more important tasks that demand our attention!

Execute SQL Statements on Other Servers or Databases

A common challenge occurs when you want to run queries against other entities, but do not know ahead of time what all of those entities are. If those objects can vary, or change at runtime, then dynamic SQL is a great solution for managing these operations without having to hard-code object names that are likely to change over time. This reduces the chances of an application breaking after a software release, configuration change, or hardware upgrade.

Similarly, in these scenarios, we may have an application with code that runs in many locations, with references to servers, databases, or other objects that vary based on environment. Writing slightly different code in each environment would be inefficient and would result in significantly higher maintenance needs over time. Far simpler would be to maintain configuration data and write code that processes those configurations, reading and writing to the database as needed. Dynamic SQL allows for that configuration data to be easily handled and acted upon, regardless of the complexity of the operations involved.

Do the Impossible!

Simply put, there are many tasks in SQL Server that would be extremely difficult, or seemingly impossible without dynamic SQL. Many common maintenance scenarios that need to iterate across database objects become trivially easy with dynamic SQL.

Have you ever tried to PIVOT or UNPIVOT across a dynamic column list? The command is powerful, but requires a definitive column list. If the list is not known until runtime, then the only way to get the data we need is to use dynamic SQL to insert our customized column list into the statement and then execute it.

We will have many examples of interesting, useful, and fun ways in which dynamic SQL can make very difficult tasks easy. Stay tuned and enjoy!

Dynamic SQL Considerations

As with any tool, dynamic SQL shouldn't be used everywhere blindly, nor is it the solution to every database problem you'll encounter. With a discussion of any tool, it is imperative that we consider its challenges, pitfalls, and complexities prior to implementing it.

Apostrophes Can Break Strings

As we build dynamic SQL commands, we incorporate other variables and strings into them. If any of these contain apostrophes, then our command string will be broken. The resulting command will, if we are lucky, throw an error and not run. SQL injection is the process of using the variables in dynamic SQL to intentionally close the string with an apostrophe, and then attempt to execute malicious code. If we do not cleanse all parameters and inputs prior to building our command statement, we risk introducing colossal security holes into our code.

Like in application code, it is imperative that we ensure that our inputs are clean and that unexpected symbols in our parameters will have no negative effect on the operation of our code. Failure to do so can result in broken code, unexpected behavior, or catastrophic security holes. Input cleansing is important in all components of an application, including the database!

NULL Can Break Strings

NULL is a complicated state of affairs. As an absence of value, any attempt to concatenate a string with NULL will result in NULL. If the dynamic SQL command string that we build is passed a parameter that is NULL, then our entire statement will become NULL. The result will likely be T-SQL that does absolutely nothing. This can lead to troubleshooting nightmares as it becomes unclear why an SQL statement appears to do nothing. Further, the search for the NULL parameter may be a daunting task if the statement in question has many inputs.

Difficult to Read and Debug

Dynamic SQL loses the benefits of color coding that exist in SQL Server Management Studio (and most text/code editor tools) that you get when you write standard SQL in the text editor. Within apostrophes, much of the text will be red, including keywords, strings, and variable names. In addition, the error checking that is performed as you type does not occur as effectively within a dynamic SQL string. A simple typo that would be underlined in red normally will not be as apparent when it is within a string.

In order to combat these challenges, we must devise very well-written T-SQL. In addition to writing very organized code, we have to be even more diligent when documenting our work. T-SQL that may normally be trivially easy to understand can be harder to grasp when written as part of a string. Extra time and care must be used in order to ensure that when we revisit this code in the future, it is still easy to read and meaningful.

Dynamic SQL *always* compiles correctly. To SQL Server, it is simply a character string. The contents of it are not checked for syntax or object validity until runtime. Effective testing and debugging are the key to ensuring that the T-SQL we write executes as we expect it to.

A positive side effect of this situation is that it encourages and trains us to write better code. We are more conscious of spacing, naming, and line breaks, allowing our code (dynamic SQL or otherwise) to be easier to read.

Permissions and Scope Are Different

Dynamic SQL statements are executed in their own scope. Variables defined within the string will not normally be available outside of it. In addition, dynamic SQL is executed with the permissions of the user executing the overall T-SQL code (stored procedure, job, etc...). It does not execute with the permissions of the owner of the stored procedure or the user that happened to be executing it recently.

To avoid unexpected errors, permissions conflicts, or other security concerns, it's important to consider what users will be running any code that includes dynamic SQL. If we need to save data from a dynamic SQL statement, or pass parameters in from outside, then that needs to be explicitly managed in order to get the desired effect.

Scoping in SQL Server is a feature whose purpose is to segregate objects in different sessions and benefits us by ensuring that different users cannot access data in-flight that they may not be allowed to see.

Dynamic SQL Cannot be used in Functions

Simply put, we can use dynamic SQL in stored procedures, ad hoc T-SQL, and jobs, but it is not allowed within functions. Any attempt to include dynamic SQL within functions will result in an error:

```
Msg 443, Level 16, State 14, Procedure fn_test, Line 72
Invalid use of a side-effecting operator 'EXECUTE STRING' within a
function.
```

SQL Server functions must be deterministic. Inputs and outputs must be in the form given in the function definition. Dynamic SQL by nature is nondeterministic, and therefore cannot be used within functions.

Dynamic SQL Style

Writing code that works is very important. Writing code that is easy to understand and maintainable is equally as important. As someone charged with the creation and upkeep of immense numbers of database objects, you must always consider how easy it will be to read, understand, troubleshoot, and upgrade these objects at any point in the future. Because dynamic SQL tends to be harder to read, extra care should be taken to ensure that our T-SQL is well written, effectively documented, and that objects/variables are named according to reasonable conventions. These design considerations will save your future self considerable time, as well as show your colleagues that you care about their well-being and the future of your organization.

These tips apply to all types of coding, but will be of particular benefit when writing T-SQL, and especially when implementing dynamic SQL.

The rules of good dynamic SQL design begin here, but will continue to be built upon throughout the rest of this book. Consider any efforts on your part to write maintainable code, whether it utilizes dynamic SQL or not.

Document Thoroughly

This is the mantra that is repeated to anyone who has ever written a line of code, a script, or a nontechnical process. Your documentation explains how your code works, why it is written as it is, and serves as a guide when changes will inevitably be made. T-SQL that may not normally warrant documentation will become harder to read when dynamic SQL is applied. Consider creating additional documentation to supplement this added complexity.

The first and simplest way to document your work is to include a header at the top of your file. This header provides basic information on who created this code, some revision notes, its purpose, and a quick overview of how it works. Understanding the reasons behind why a stored procedure was created can be as useful as knowing how it works. More importantly, it is possible to discern the function of code by reading through it and scratching one's head a bit. It isn't possible to figure out the original request that spurred the creation of that code without either having some existing application knowledge that others may not have or asking other developers for help.

Consider the following header for a simple backup script:

Listing 1-3. Header Comments, Documenting a Hypothetical Backup Script

```
/*     8/1/2018 Edward Pollack
       Backup routing for AdventureWorks databases

       As a result of ticket T1234, logged on 7/21/2018, it became necessary
       to selectively back up a limited set of AdventureWorks databases via a
       SQL Server Agent job.  The job can have its schedule adjusted as needed
       to fit the current needs of the business.

       Dynamic SQL is used to iterate through each database, performing the
       backup and naming the resulting file using the database name, date,
       time, and source server.     */
```

This header tells the reader the following:

1. The date that this code was written, to provide context into when it came about

2. The author, which allows future developers to know where to go with questions

3. Background into why this was written and the problem that was being addressed

4. A brief description of how it works and any special features that are used

This short documentation block answers most of the common questions that a developer may have about your code. The things we consider obvious while writing T-SQL may not be so obvious to someone else reading this years later. Our own code is always easier to read than that of others, and this is easy to forget when buried in development projects. As time passes, though, even our own code can be hard to understand as we become more detached from the details of how we wrote it.

When writing code that involves dynamic SQL, we must consider documenting thoroughly, but also not go overboard and explain every single line of T-SQL. Let's take our backup routine from earlier and add some meaningful documentation to it.

Listing 1-4. Backup Script Sample, with Documentation Added

```
-- This will temporarily store the list of databases that we will back up
   below.
DECLARE @database_list TABLE
      (database_name SYSNAME);

INSERT INTO @database_list
      (database_name)
SELECT
      name
FROM sys.databases
WHERE name LIKE 'AdventureWorks%';
-- This WHERE clause may be adjusted to back up other databases besides
   those starting with "AdventureWorks".

DECLARE @sql_command NVARCHAR(MAX);
DECLARE @database_name SYSNAME;
DECLARE @date_string VARCHAR(17) = CONVERT(VARCHAR, CURRENT_TIMESTAMP, 112) +
'_' + REPLACE(RIGHT(CONVERT(NVARCHAR, CURRENT_TIMESTAMP, 120), 8), ':', '');

-- Use a cursor to iterate through databases, one by one.
DECLARE database_cursor CURSOR FOR
SELECT database_name FROM @database_list
OPEN database_cursor
FETCH NEXT FROM database_cursor INTO @database_name;
```

```
WHILE @@FETCH_STATUS = 0 -- Continue looping until the cursor has reached
the end of the database list.
BEGIN
        -- Customize the backup file name to use the database name, as well
           as the date and time.
        SELECT @sql_command = '
        BACKUP DATABASE ' + @database_name + '
        TO DISK="E:\SQLBackups\' + @database_name + '_' + @date_string +
        '.bak" WITH COMPRESSION;'

        EXEC (@sql_command);

        FETCH NEXT FROM database_cursor INTO @database_name;
END

-- Clean up our cursor object.
CLOSE database_cursor;
DEALLOCATE database_cursor;
```

This example shows our backup script from earlier with the addition of a timestamp on the file name. Documentation is added to explain each section. Note that the comments are short, simple, and explain the parts that I think may benefit from them. We don't waste time with obvious comments that would take up extra space and distract from the task at hand. For example, I'd never include a comment like this, unless I was looking for some misplaced comic relief:

```
-- This variable holds the database name.
DECLARE @database_name SYSNAME;
```

While amusing, my addition tells us nothing new. Whether it annoys or amuses, it doesn't provide any useful information that wasn't already made obvious in the variable name.

Documentation is often like choosing pizza toppings. Everyone has their own style, and it would be foolish to try and settle on a single style that is appropriate in all environments for all objects. If you are writing more complex code, especially if it involves dynamic SQL, consider being as thorough as possible. Your bit of extra work now will save someone immense time in the future!

Debugging Dynamic SQL

Dynamic SQL benefits from debugging more than the standard queries that we write. Since SQL Server will always compile dynamic SQL statements successfully, it's important that we perform further testing on our code before executing it. Simple errors that would normally be obvious could easily be missed due to the lack of feedback in SQL Server Management Studio. In addition, our code will partially be obscured in a string, surrounded by apostrophes. The harder the code is to read, the harder it will be to debug and locate mistakes, whether they are syntax or logical mistakes.

The easiest and most effective way to test and debug dynamic SQL is to replace the EXEC with PRINT. When the T-SQL is executed, the command string will print out rather than be executed immediately. The printout can then be copied into another editor window and reviewed for syntax, logic, spelling, and any other considerations you may have. Many common dynamic SQL typos are the result of misplaced quotation marks, which become quickly apparent when moved into a new window. For example, consider the following short command string:

```
DECLARE @CMD NVARCHAR(MAX);
SELECT @CMD = 'SELLECT TOP 17 * FROM Person.Person';
EXEC (@CMD);
```

This statement will compile successfully, but throw the following error:

```
Msg 156, Level 15, State 1, Line 79
Incorrect syntax near the keyword 'TOP'.
```

The resulting error message is cryptic and tells us very little of what we did wrong. Print out the command string and paste it into an editor window, and the issue becomes obvious:

```
SELLECT TOP 17 * FROM Person.Person
```

SELECT is clearly misspelled, and in addition to being underlined in red in SQL Server Management Studio, it will not be highlighted blue as a reserved keyword normally would be.

For larger blocks of T-SQL, there is great value in adding a debug bit into the code. When @debug is 1, all statements will print rather than execute. When @debug is 0, then statements will execute. This allows you to control all blocks of code with a single bit that can easily be configured at the top. It is far easier to flip this one bit than to constantly write print statements and comment out execute statements whenever debugging becomes necessary. Once the code is reviewed and complete, the debug bit and PRINT statements can be removed.

Following is our backup script example from earlier, with a debug parameter added.

Listing 1-5. Backup Script Sample, with Debug Parameter Added

```
DECLARE @debug BIT = 1;

DECLARE @database_list TABLE
      (database_name SYSNAME);

INSERT INTO @database_list
      (database_name)
SELECT
      name
FROM sys.databases
WHERE name LIKE 'AdventureWorks%';
-- This WHERE clause may be adjusted to back up other databases besides
those starting with "AdventureWorks".

DECLARE @sql_command NVARCHAR(MAX);
DECLARE @database_name SYSNAME;
DECLARE @date_string VARCHAR(17) = CONVERT(VARCHAR, CURRENT_TIMESTAMP, 112) +
'_' + REPLACE(RIGHT(CONVERT(NVARCHAR, CURRENT_TIMESTAMP, 120), 8), ':', '');

-- Use a cursor to iterate through databases, one by one.
DECLARE database_cursor CURSOR FOR
SELECT database_name FROM @database_list
OPEN database_cursor
FETCH NEXT FROM database_cursor INTO @database_name;

WHILE @@FETCH_STATUS = 0 -- Continue looping until the cursor has reacdhed
the end of the database list.
BEGIN
      -- Customize the backup file name to use the database name, as well
        as the date and time.
      SELECT @sql_command = '
```

```
        BACKUP DATABASE ' + @database_name + '
        TO DISK="E:\SQLBackups\' + @database_name + '_' + @date_string + '.bak"
        WITH COMPRESSION;'

        IF @debug = 1
                PRINT @sql_command
        ELSE
                EXEC (@sql_command);

        FETCH NEXT FROM database_cursor INTO @database_name;
END
-- Clean up our cursor object.
CLOSE database_cursor;
DEALLOCATE database_cursor;
```

With the addition of four lines of T-SQL, we have allowed execution to be controlled by a single bit. By copying the print output into a new window and reviewing it, we can quickly confirm if it compiles successfully and looks correct.

Additionally, if the source of a problem is unclear, we can add PRINT statements into our code for some of our variables. For example, if we were unsure that the @date_ string was being populated correctly, we could print it out separately and verify that the value is what we expect:

```
PRINT '@date_string (line 20): ' + @date_string
```

This is a very simple debugging action, but by including the variable name and line number, we make understanding our code easier. If the results were still perplexing, we could split up the result further, printing the date and time portions of the variable separately. By breaking a problem into smaller, simpler pieces, debugging becomes a much easier task, and one that causes far less frustration along the way.

When writing new dynamic SQL, be sure to print the command string often, verifying that the resulting TQL is valid, both syntactically, and logically.

SELECT may be used instead of PRINT. This can allow command strings to be saved into a table or file for further review in the future. This removes the need to immediately review code in the results pane of a code editor.

Last, for any code that will take inputs from other applications (or an end user), remember to test all possibilities. Ensure that either the application or the T-SQL checks and validates inputs as needed. What happens if an input contains a special character? What if it has an apostrophe, underscore, or escape character? If a human is allowed to manually enter text, assume they will make mistakes, enter garbage, blanks, special characters, or in some way do the unexpected. Account for this and you will prevent untold numbers of potential errors, and greatly improve the security of your application.

Write Dynamic SQL Just Like Standard T-SQL

Just because your dynamic SQL is enclosed in a string does not mean that it should be written any differently than your usual statements. Whatever your normal standards are for capitalization, indentation, and spacing should be similarly applied here. Too often is a dynamic SQL statement written as one long line of code, with no spaces, new lines, capitalizations, or breaks. The result is often unintelligible, and far more prone to mistakes. If you were to copy the debug text from a PRINT statement into a new window, the result should look precisely like the T-SQL you would normally write.

Listing 1-6. Example of How to Annoy Future Developers with Poorly Formatted Dynamic SQL!

```
DECLARE @CMD NVARCHAR(MAX) = ''; -- This will hold the final SQL to execute.
DECLARE @first_name NVARCHAR(50) = 'Edward'; -- First name as entered in
                               search box.
SET @CMD = 'SELECT PERSON.FirstName,PERSON.LastName,PHONE.
PhoneNumber,PTYPE.Name FROM Person.Person PERSON INNER JOIN Person.
PersonPhone PHONE ON PERSON.BusinessEntityID = PHONE.BusinessEntityID INNER
JOIN Person.PhoneNumberType PTYPE ON PHONE.PhoneNumberTypeID = PTYPE.
PhoneNumberTypeID WHERE PERSON.FirstName = ''' + @first_name + '''';
PRINT @CMD;
EXEC (@CMD);
```

String Sizes and Truncation

When we attempt to store a string in a variable that is not large enough to hold it, the string will be automatically truncated. The result will be incomplete data that will likely cause us headaches later on in our code. Consider the following T-SQL, which generates a timestamp and stores it in a string:

Listing 1-7. Example of Truncation When Generating a Timestamp String

```
DECLARE @date_string VARCHAR(10) = CONVERT(VARCHAR, CURRENT_TIMESTAMP, 112) +
'_' + REPLACE(RIGHT(CONVERT(NVARCHAR, CURRENT_TIMESTAMP, 120), 8), ':', '');
PRINT @date_string;
```

We expect a timestamp with the date (MMDDYYYY) and time (HHMMSS). What we instead get is a string that is cut off at ten characters: *20150908_1*. Always declare variables that are large enough to hold any valid data that could be stored there. If you are unsure of the potential data size, erring on the side of caution and providing extra characters is not a bad decision. Seventeen characters are required to get the full text output expected in this example. What if we were considering adding milliseconds to the timestamp, but were not going to do so until a future software release? Make the @date_string larger now, and there will be no need to make further changes in the future in order to account for that change. The cost is tiny, and the potential for errors in the future is greatly reduced.

A more complex example of string truncation can occur when dynamic SQL gets very, very large. If you write a command string that is greater than 8192 characters, and are concatenating it with other strings (names, dates, input parameters, other dynamic SQL strings, etc…), there is an implicit, undocumented risk of truncation. SQL Server will automatically convert strings of different data types and sizes in an attempt to process them quickly and efficiently. The result will be a NVARCHAR(MAX) command string that seems to be truncated down to 8192 characters when executed. This truncation can be resolved in one of two ways:

1. Split the dynamic SQL statement into multiple statements, each less than 8192 characters.

2. Change all parameters and variables involved in the command string to NVARCHAR(MAX).

The first option can be difficult to guarantee. How do we split an extremely long command into pieces that are guaranteed to always be 8192 characters or less? The second option will always work when faced with this conundrum, and is an easy, inexpensive fix.

When working with very large dynamic SQL, consider using NVARCHAR(MAX) for all scalar parameters involved in the construction of the command string to avoid inadvertent string truncation.

Management Studio Text Display

An unrelated, but somewhat similar problem can occur when we print output directly to our text window. We will do this frequently, either to debug new T-SQL, or to manually execute dynamic SQL that we have generated. By default, the text limit in the output window of SQL Server Management Studio is set to 256 characters. Any text printed from any SQL statements will be truncated at 256 characters, which will often be inconvenient.

This limit only affects output that you PRINT to the results window and has no bearing on the string sizes when you execute a command string. The text limit has no effect on actual query execution. For the sake of debugging, it is advantageous to modify your SQL editor options to increase this limit to 8192 characters.

This setting can be found by navigating to Tools➤Options➤Query Results➤SQL Server➤Results to Text and modifying the Maximum number of characters displayed in each column. See Figure 1-1 for an example.

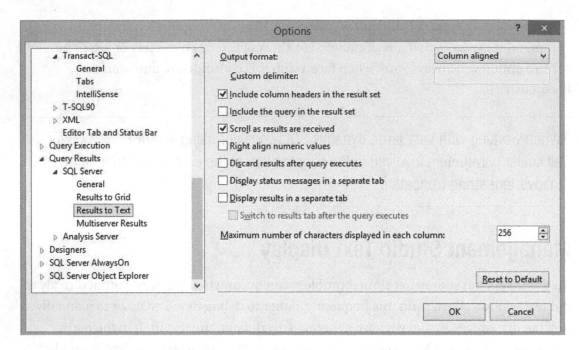

Figure 1-1. *Results to Text settings in SQL Server Management Studio*

Change 256 to 8192 and you'll have an easier time printing and debugging larger dynamic SQL statements in the future.

Sp_executesql

Thus far, all dynamic SQL statements have been executed using the EXEC keyword. This method of execution is simple, straightforward, and convenient for quick testing and debugging. EXEC comes with a number of limitations and security concerns that encourage us to find a better solution:

1. EXEC is far more vulnerable to SQL injection and the effects of unexpected input. Escape characters and apostrophes can easily wreck a dynamic SQL statement.

2. There is no built-in way to manage input or output variables with EXEC.

3. When using EXEC, it is unlikely that execution plans will be reused. This reuse of execution plans, known as parameter sniffing, is a useful feature and generally something we want to occur.

Each of these topics will be covered in extensive detail later in this book and can be addressed using the system stored procedure sp_executesql, instead of EXEC.

The syntax for sp_executesql is straightforward:

```
sp_executesql N'SELECT COUNT(*) FROM Person.Person';
```

Whatever T-SQL is provided in the string will be executed in the same way as our previous examples. The more common (and more useful) syntax is to store the command string in a variable and use EXEC in front of sp_executesql:

```
DECLARE @sql_command NVARCHAR(MAX) = 'SELECT COUNT(*) FROM Person.Person';
EXEC sp_executesql @sql_command;
```

For all examples going forward, we will use sp_executesql instead of EXEC. This is considered a best practice in SQL Server, and one that will improve the reliability, security, and performance of your dynamic SQL.

In the world of databases, we rarely use the words "always" or "never." Oftentimes, the answer to a question is "it depends," followed by quite a bit of discussion. This is one of those rare scenarios where "always" is the best answer. When writing dynamic SQL, always use sp_executesql, and never use EXEC. The benefits far outweigh any inconvenience that we may face from using this new stored procedure in our work.

Building Strings via Concatenation

There are two straightforward ways to combine strings in T-SQL. The first is to use the "+" operator, which has been the method used thus far in this book. This is simple, easy and quick to implement, and intuitive.

Remember our brief introduction to how NULL can break strings? When piecing many strings together, if any one of them happens to be NULL, then the entire string output will become NULL as well. NULL + 1 is treated by SQL Server in a similar manner that infinity + 1 is handled by mathematics. We can combat this by using ISNULL, COALESCE, or perform an explicit check of the variable for NULL and replace it as needed. Consider the following dynamic SQL queries.

Listing 1-8. Examples of String Concatenation Results When a Parameter is NULL

```
DECLARE @schema VARCHAR(25) = NULL;
DECLARE @table VARCHAR(25) = 'Person';
DECLARE @sql_command VARCHAR(MAX);
SELECT @sql_command = 'SELECT COUNT(*) ' + 'FROM ' +  @schema + '.'
                      + @table;
PRINT @sql_command;
SELECT @sql_command = 'SELECT COUNT(*) ' + 'FROM ' +  ISNULL(@schema,
                      'Person') + '.' + @table;
PRINT @sql_command;
SELECT @sql_command = 'SELECT COUNT(*) ' + 'FROM ' + CASE WHEN @schema IS
                      NULL THEN 'Person' ELSE @schema END + '.' + @table;
PRINT @sql_command;
```

The first query returns NULL. Since @schema is NULL, anything we concatenate with it will also become NULL. This will generally be undesired behavior, and we would immediately be confounded by a command string that does nothing or generates errors when executing.

The second query uses ISNULL to ensure that, if @schema is NULL, something will be returned in place of it. In this case, we hard-coded the Person schema, which produced the same results as we got before. This required the assumption that Person was an appropriate default schema. In the event that we do not have a default value, we may be better served by throwing an error, rather than making up a value that may not be accurate. Alternatively, we could simply never allow @schema to be NULL and exit immediately if it is.

The third query uses a CASE statement to replace NULL with the "Person" schema. This is the same result as our last query, though CASE provides some additional flexibility that we could utilize. If necessary, we could alter the structure of our query to account for missing variables, or have multiple code paths.

There is a second way to concatenate strings that can be beneficial under circumstances where the data types and values of our data are unpredictable. The built-in function CONCAT allows us to combine strings using the following syntax:

```
SELECT CONCAT('SELECT COUNT(*) ', 'FROM ', 'Person.', 'Person');
```

Variables may be passed into this function as parameters as well:

```
DECLARE @schema NVARCHAR(25) = 'Person';
DECLARE @table NVARCHAR(25)= 'Person';
DECLARE @sql_command NVARCHAR(MAX);
SELECT @sql_command = CONCAT ('SELECT COUNT(*) ', 'FROM ', @schema, '.',
                      @table);
PRINT @sql_command
```

The results of both of these SQL statements will be the same:

```
SELECT COUNT(*) FROM Person.Person
```

CONCAT offers several features:

1. NULL parameters are always converted into empty strings.

2. The data type of the result is intelligently determined based on
    the inputs. NVARCHAR parameters will yield NVARCHAR results,
    VARCHAR will yield VARCHAR, and MAX inputs will yield an
    output of MAX size.

3. If all inputs are NULL, then the output will be an empty string of
    type VARCHAR(1).

4. It will automatically attempt to convert different data types in
    the process of concatenation. This works on numeric values as
    well, which you may allow to convert for you, or introduce your
    own use of CAST/CONVERT to explicitly convert prior to the
    application of the CONCAT function.

Removing NULL may not be desired behavior, though! Oftentimes, if a parameter is
unintentionally NULL, we may very well prefer that an error be thrown by our code than
continue processing with dummy values. Utilize this feature only if removing NULLs is
advantageous to your application.

CONCAT is a viable alternative to using the "+" operator. There are many other
SQL Server string manipulation functions that are useful when generating dynamic
SQL. We'll continue to use "+" for the duration of this book, but it's worth the time to
quickly review a handful of useful string functions that may prove convenient.

LTRIM, RTRIM: Removes any whitespaces on the left (LTRIM) or right (RTRIM) of an expression. This can be useful when dealing with unpredictable inputs, or those that often have extra whitespaces attached to them:

```
DECLARE @string NVARCHAR(MAX) = '   This is a string with extra whitespaces';
SELECT @string;
SELECT LTRIM(@string);
SELECT RTRIM(@string);
SELECT TRIM(@string); -- Available in SQL Server 2017 and later.
```

The preceding T-SQL returns the following:

"This is a string with extra whitespaces"

"This is a string with extra whitespaces"

"This is a string with extra whitespaces"

"This is a string with extra whitespaces"

TRIM is available in SQL Server 2017 and later, but will save some typing by removing whitespaces from either end of a string, similar to applying both an RTRIM and an LTRIM.

CHARINDEX: This will return the first instance of a search expression within a string. For example, if we wanted to return the position of the first instance of "dinosaur" in a string, then this would do the trick:

```
DECLARE @string NVARCHAR(MAX) = 'The stegosaurus is my favorite dinosaur';
SELECT CHARINDEX('dinosaur', @string);
```

The result of this query would be 32, the starting character of the word dinosaur. An optional third parameter can specify where in the string to begin looking for the search string. CHARINDEX returns "0" if the search string isn't found.

STUFF: Allows you to insert a string into the middle of another string and optionally delete characters from the insert point. This has many uses, and can be a convenient way to combine SQL statements, text output, or input parameters in desired combinations. Here are a few examples of how to use STUFF:

```
DECLARE @string NVARCHAR(MAX) = 'The stegosaurus is my favorite dinosaur';
SELECT STUFF(@string, 5, 0, 'purple ');
SELECT STUFF(@string, 5, 11, 't-rex');
SELECT STUFF(@string, 32, 8, 'animal!');
```

The first parameter is the text to be modified, and the last is the string that is being inserted. The second is the insert point (what character position number within the string to insert into). The third parameter indicates how many characters will be deleted prior to the insertion (enter 0 if you don't want to delete any characters). The results of our queries are as follows:

```
"The purple stegosaurus is my favorite dinosaur"
"The t-rex is my favorite dinosaur"
"The stegosaurus is my favorite animal!"
```

REPLACE: Within a string, this will replace all occurrences of a text pattern with another. This is often useful for removing specific characters from a string, or for replacing undesirable parts of input strings with a standard or consistent segment of text. The behavior of REPLACE and STUFF can be very similar, so you can choose whichever is convenient for the task at hand:

```
DECLARE @string NVARCHAR(MAX) = CAST(CURRENT_TIMESTAMP AS NVARCHAR);
SELECT REPLACE(@string, ' ', '');
SELECT REPLACE(REPLACE(@string, ' ', ''), ':', '');
SELECT REPLACE(REPLACE(REPLACE(REPLACE(@string, ' ', ''), ':', ''), 'AM', ''),
'PM', '');
```

In these examples, we are stripping out a variety of characters from the current date/time string. A single REPLACE can be used to remove a specific character, or several can be used to remove additional characters as well. In the first example, we replace all spaces with empty strings, thereby removing them from the string. The second query also removes colons, and the final additionally removes "AM" or "PM" from the timestamp. This is a frequent tactic used when cleansing strings to be used in file names, labels, or a standard name for catalog data. The query results are as follows:

```
Sep1320152:40PM
Sep132015240PM
Sep132015240
```

TRANSLATE allows you to perform any number of REPLACE operations within a single statement. You supply a list of characters to replace, and the targets to replace with, and it does the work for you:

```
DECLARE @string NVARCHAR(MAX) = 'Text;with&extraneous(characters)';
SELECT TRANSLATE(@string, ';&()', '    ');
```

27

The result will be a string in which the various characters specified have been converted into spaces:

```
Text with extraneous characters
```

Note that this function is only available in SQL Server 2017 and later.

SUBSTRING returns a segment of a string, based on a starting point and the number of characters to return. This can also be used to remove characters from a string, to extract a specific portion, or return the beginning or end of a string.

```
DECLARE @string NVARCHAR(MAX) = CAST(CURRENT_TIMESTAMP AS NVARCHAR);
SELECT SUBSTRING(@string, 1, 3);
```

In this example, we return the three-letter month from the string:

```
Sep
```

REPLICATE repeats a string the number of times specified. This can be a quick way to generate a large volume of test text, or to create data when there are parts that are expected to repeat often.

```
SELECT 'Look, a robot' + REPLICATE('!', 50)
Look, a robot!!!!!!!!!!!!!!!!!!!!!!!!!!!!!!!!!!!!!!!!!!!!!!!!!!!
```

The example is simple (outputting lots of exclamation marks), but consider the following example, where serial numbers are entered into a system, but should all have 20 digits (with leading zeroes):

```
DECLARE @serial_number NVARCHAR(MAX) = '91542278';
SELECT REPLICATE(0, 20 - LEN(@serial_number)) + @serial_number;
```

In this example, LEN returns the number of characters in the serial number. By subtracting that from 20, we can determine how many additional characters we need to reach 20. By replicating zeroes this many times, we can quickly pad the serial number with the appropriate number of zeroes. This tactic is also useful with zip codes, identification numbers, or any numeric values represented as strings, where leading zeroes could be omitted.

REVERSE is also a simple function that takes a string and reverses the characters. This can be useful if we are looking to operate on the end of the string (in reverse order) or to manage a list, starting at the end.

```
DECLARE @string NVARCHAR(MAX) = '123456789';
SELECT REVERSE(@string);
```

In this quick example, we take a number string and reverse it, which returns the expected result:

```
987654321
```

Notes on Apostrophes

Because dynamic SQL is built within strings, it's important to carefully consider how to correctly use apostrophes when we build more complex string logic. For example, let's say we wanted to locate all people with a first name that started with Ed. Using dynamic SQL, we would need to include some extra apostrophes to ensure that our syntax is correct:

```
DECLARE @sql_command NVARCHAR(MAX);
DECLARE @first_name NVARCHAR(20) = 'Ed';
SELECT @sql_command = '
SELECT
      *
FROM Person.Person
WHERE FirstName LIKE "' + @first_name + '%"';
PRINT @sql_command;
EXEC sp_executesql @sql_command;
```

The resulting command string will look like this:

```
SELECT
      *
FROM Person.Person
WHERE FirstName LIKE 'Ed%'
```

Note that three apostrophes are used instead of one. Within a string, a pair of apostrophes is translated into a single apostrophe. Whenever you are working with strings within a dynamic SQL command string, be sure to debug and print often to ensure that you're building valid T-SQL and have not forgotten any string delimiters.

If there was a need to modify a string within a parameter within dynamic SQL, the result would be the need for six apostrophes instead of two. If this sounds complicated, then use that complexity as a caution against developing an application that is more difficult to understand and maintain than is necessary.

Conclusion

Dynamic SQL is a powerful tool that is capable of executing complex requests quickly and efficiently. There are many database queries and tasks that would be very difficult to accomplish without the ability to customize queries on the fly. We will soon delve into greater detail on dynamic SQL features, as well as provide many practical examples of how to effectively use it.

Before diving in, though, it is important to discuss security and the best practices for writing and maintaining dynamic SQL. As with any tool, it can be used and misused, and knowing how to effectively utilize it will not only improve the quality of development, but also help secure your existing applications and systems.

CHAPTER 2

Protecting Against SQL Injection

There are few SQL vulnerabilities as commonly exploited as SQL injection. This form of database attack has destroyed companies, ruined careers, and is a constant challenge for security officers. As database professionals, data is our greatest asset, and it is our responsibility to guard it above all else. SQL injection is not limited only to dynamic SQL, but is a technique that can be applied to many areas of SQL Server. Therefore, understanding and defending against it are among the most important priorities when considering SQL Server security.

What Is SQL Injection?

SQL injection is an attack where a hacker attempts to insert malicious T-SQL into the parameters used in dynamic SQL. Consider the example shown in Listing 2-1.

Listing 2-1. Dynamic SQL, Intro to SQL Injection

```
DECLARE @CMD NVARCHAR(MAX);
DECLARE @search_criteria NVARCHAR(1000);

SELECT @CMD = 'SELECT * FROM Person.Person
WHERE LastName = ''';
SELECT @search_criteria = 'Smith';
SELECT @CMD = @CMD + @search_criteria;
SELECT @CMD = @CMD + '''';
PRINT @CMD;
EXEC sp_executesql @CMD;
```

31

© Edward Pollack 2019
E. Pollack, *Dynamic SQL*, https://doi.org/10.1007/978-1-4842-4318-3_2

We perform a search of Person.Person for anyone who has a given last name. @search_criteria was passed into this code. The resulting command string appears exactly as we expect it to:

```
SELECT * FROM Person.Person
WHERE FirstName = 'Edward'
```

Over time, this search is used by many, many people and is expanded to also search for people by last name, middle initial, title, e-mail address, and more! Eventually, someone with the last name of "O'Brien" tries to search for their records.

Listing 2-2. Use of Input Value with an Apostrophe

```
DECLARE @CMD NVARCHAR(MAX);
DECLARE @search_criteria NVARCHAR(1000);

SELECT @CMD = 'SELECT * FROM Person.Person
WHERE LastName = "';
SELECT @search_criteria = 'O"Brien';
SELECT @CMD = @CMD + @search_criteria;
SELECT @CMD = @CMD + "";
EXEC sp_executesql @CMD;
```

The results are not what the user expected. Instead of getting their info, they get an SQL Server error instead:

```
Msg 102, Level 15, State 1, Line 322
Incorrect syntax near 'Brien'.
Msg 105, Level 15, State 1, Line 322
Unclosed quotation mark after the character string ".
```

We return to our command string and verify that it looks correct, and notice the following:

```
SELECT * FROM Person.Person
WHERE LastName = 'O'Brien'
```

The apostrophe within "O'Brien" broke our command string, closing the string after the "O" in "O'Brien." Instead of receiving the expected data, our friend O'Brien receives a cryptic error and contacts your help desk to determine why this web application is broken. This is a best-case scenario of what could happen: the user shrugs and submits an incident to your organization to fix this bug so they can search for their information without odd error messages.

Let's consider another example where the end user is more tech savvy and a bit more malicious. They enter a string with apostrophes and are returned an error message. Instead of reporting the error to you, a light bulb goes off and they begin writing some T-SQL of their own, as shown in Listing 2-3.

Listing 2-3. How a Hacker Can Begin to Use SQL Injection Against Unsecured Dynamic SQL

```
DECLARE @CMD NVARCHAR(MAX);
DECLARE @search_criteria NVARCHAR (1000);
SELECT @CMD = 'SELECT * FROM Person.Person
WHERE LastName = "';
SELECT @search_criteria = 'Smith" OR 1 = 1 AND "" = "';
SELECT @CMD = @CMD + @search_criteria;
SELECT @CMD = @CMD + "";
EXEC sp_executesql @CMD;
```

The sneaky user realized immediately that this site was vulnerable to SQL injection and began tinkering with search parameters until they found one that allowed them to extract all of the personal data from this table, not just theirs. By adding two apostrophes after "Smith," our uninvited guest has returned to the main T-SQL query and appended "OR 1 = 1" to the end. Finally, they added some additional apostrophes on to the end in order to complete the command string correctly and avoid syntactical errors. The resulting command string is as follows:

```
SELECT * FROM Person.Person
WHERE LastName = 'Smith' OR 1 = 1 AND " = "
```

The last name of "Smith" is irrelevant to the attack. By adding in a condition that is always true, they've effectively bypassed the WHERE clause and have gained access to all of the data in the table. In a single statement, they have stolen tens of thousands of rows of personal data and begun a data breach that would cause great harm to any organization targeted by it!

If a username and password prompt were managed via dynamic SQL, then a similar attack as the preceding scenario would result in someone gaining access to a software application that they were not authorized to use. Consider the dynamic SQL in Listing 2-4, which verifies a user's ID and password.

Listing 2-4. Dynamic SQL that Verifies a User/Password Combination

```
DECLARE @sql_command NVARCHAR(MAX);
DECLARE @id INT = 3;
DECLARE @password NVARCHAR(128) = ";

SELECT @sql_command = '
SELECT
      *
FROM Person.Password
WHERE BusinessEntityID = ' + CAST(@id AS NVARCHAR(25)) + '
AND PasswordHash = "' + @password + ""

EXEC (@sql_command)
```

Any guess of an incorrect password will result in a failed login, and no results are returned, but what if a hacker tries to use SQL injection to bypass the login validation altogether? The following string for @password would be all it would take to completely invalidate this security check:

```
"' OR 1 = 1 AND "" = "'
```

By including an OR in the conditional, a malicious user could find ways to log in using any user, even an administrator. Since these logins may appear legitimate from the perspective of the application, it's possible that this attack could go unnoticed until it is too late.

Similarly, UNION ALL can allow additional data to be selected without triggering any errors, as seen in Listing 2-5.

Listing 2-5. Use of UNION ALL via SQL Injection to Collect Additional Secure Data

```
DECLARE @sql_command NVARCHAR(MAX);
DECLARE @id INT = 3;
DECLARE @password NVARCHAR(128) = "' UNION ALL SELECT * FROM Person.
Password WHERE "" = "';

SELECT @sql_command = '
SELECT
       *
FROM Person.Password
WHERE BusinessEntityID = ' + CAST(@id AS NVARCHAR(25)) + '
AND PasswordHash = "' + @password + '""

EXEC (@sql_command)
```

In this example, the original query is allowed to execute with a blank password, but an additional SELECT statement is appended, which returns the entire contents of the Password table. The resulting command string looks like this:

```
SELECT
       *
FROM Person.Password
WHERE BusinessEntityID = 3
AND PasswordHash = " UNION ALL SELECT * FROM Person.Password WHERE " = "
```

This is a bit trickier to pull off, as both tables need to be of the same structure in order to prevent syntax errors when the columns from the first table do not match the second. Given time, though, a hacker can figure out ways around this, such as adding dummy columns to the appended table, choosing specific columns, or using COLLATE to ensure that language and localization settings match up. Guessing the names of tables in order to exploit them is a matter of trial and error here, but later on we will discuss ways in which a hacker can determine them through more covert means.

A similar attack involving a user name/password scenario would be to use comments to remove the remainder of the T-SQL so that the user name is validated but the password is not. This database schema is hypothetical, but the use case very common, as seen in Listing 2-6.

Listing 2-6. User/Password Verification Statement

```
DECLARE @sql_command NVARCHAR(MAX);
DECLARE @username NVARCHAR(128) = 'edward';
DECLARE @password NVARCHAR(128) = 'my_password';

SELECT @sql_command = 'SELECT
     *
FROM dbo.password
WHERE username = "' + @username + "' AND Password = "' + @password + "";

EXEC(@sql_command);
```

An attacker may see that SQL injection is possible here and try to remove the password from the equation altogether by entering the following for their user name:

```
'administrator" --'
```

The resulting command string shows that the remainder of the WHERE clause is commented out, therefore bypassing the password check:

```
SELECT
     *
FROM dbo.password
WHERE username = 'administrator' --' AND Password = 'my_password'
```

An open comment delimiter "/*" may be used in an attempt to bypass multiline queries, or those that have some precautions in place.

For a skilled hacker, this would only be the beginning. From here, they could begin testing the structure of your database, learning the names of tables, stored procedures, views, and the security permissions granted to the user that the application runs under. In order to do this, they would continue to rewrite their search box entry, in an attempt to learn more, as seen in Listing 2-7.

Listing 2-7. Closing a Dynamic SQL String from an Input Parameter to Probe Schema Objects

```
DECLARE @CMD NVARCHAR(MAX);
DECLARE @search_criteria NVARCHAR(1000);
```

```
SELECT @CMD = 'SELECT * FROM Person.Person
WHERE LastName = "';
SELECT @search_criteria = 'Smith"; SELECT * FROM sys.tables WHERE "" = "'
SELECT @CMD = @CMD + @search_criteria;
SELECT @CMD = @CMD + "";
EXEC sp_executesql @CMD;
```

After a bit of experimenting with apostrophes, the hacker has figured out how to close the search statement and start a new one of their own. By selecting data from sys. tables, they have now collected a list of all tables in the database. If they did not have access to system views, then guesswork would still yield some results, as most databases have somewhat predictable object names. More guessing would result in more risk, as many failed T-SQL statements or high activity from this search by a single user may eventually arouse suspicion. Unfortunately, most companies do not have the time or resources to vigilantly monitor and guard their web logs. Oftentimes these vulnerabilities are discovered too late, after data has been stolen.

Their next step would be to identify specific tables of interest: those with passwords, credit card numbers, or other valuable data. In addition, they can now run any SQL statements for which the application user has permissions without generating any further errors, as seen in Listing 2-8.

Listing 2-8. Using SQL Injection to Freely Gather Password Data

```
DECLARE @CMD NVARCHAR(MAX);
DECLARE @search_criteria NVARCHAR(1000);

SELECT @CMD = 'SELECT * FROM Person.Person
WHERE LastName = "';
SELECT @search_criteria = 'Smith"; SELECT * FROM Person.Password WHERE "" = "'
SELECT @CMD = @CMD + @search_criteria;
SELECT @CMD = @CMD + "";
EXEC sp_executesql @CMD;
```

At this point, the hacker can have whatever data they collect from the database. If you're lucky, then critical data will be encrypted, reducing their ability to immediately gain access to sensitive information. With this level of database access, though, they may be able to collect enough additional information to access other systems and eventually decrypt that data. This is an excellent example of why highly privileged accounts, such as sa, should never be used in the context of an application login. Doing so can allow a hacker who gains unauthorized access to an application to also gain extensive access to the database server as well. This access could span many databases, linked servers, or other entities that would comprise a data breach that could involve other applications than the one initially targeted.

There is a single worst-case scenario that has played out many times in recent history. If our hacker was feeling destructive, they could use their newly found database access to delete data, truncate or drop tables, or even delete backup files from disk. How could they access files on disk? If xp_cmdshell is enabled on your server, then they may be able to use it to access any data that is directly accessible from here. They could also potentially adjust server settings, change database and server security, add or remove users, and more. The limits at this point are only restricted by one's imagination.

Disable xp_cmdshell on all database servers that could be accessed from outside of your internal network. As an additional safety measure, disable it anywhere that it isn't absolutely needed!

In addition to xp_cmdshell, other system stored procedures should have their security limited. xp_regread, xp_regwrite, xp_servicecontrol, xp_loginconfig, sp_addextendedproc, and many others can provide far more access to the server and operating system than we would ever want. Be sure to limit access to these so that any user that doesn't need them doesn't have them. Other functions that can be dangerous include HOST_NAME(), OPENQUERY(), OPENROWSET(), SHUTDOWN, and KILL.

Another scenario that has added further insult to injury has been the desire of hackers to profit off of their escapades. They may try and blackmail your company in an attempt to profit off of their efforts: "Pay up, or watch your precious data go up in flames!" More complicated situations have arisen when our hacker attempts to cover their data theft by issuing a DDOS (distributed denial of service attack) attack. The influx of web/data requests overwhelm your web servers, and distract you from their true intentions.

Additional SQL injection attacks have been documented in which the hacker did not steal data, drop tables, or otherwise make their presence immediately known. Instead, they would use their newfound access to modify web page code, inserting links to viruses, malware, or other malicious code that could exploit anyone visiting this web page. This expands the scope of the attack greatly, and could result in significant damage until the target realizes what has happened, removes the malicious code, and patches the original SQL injection target.

The preceding scenario is scary but is far from a bedtime story gone wrong. We will spend the rest of this chapter discussing our aforementioned nightmare situation, and the steps we can take to alleviate each and every mistake that led to our database server being infiltrated by an outside party. This is not only a discussion of SQL injection, but also one of general security best practices.

Cleansing Inputs

The first step toward guarding against SQL injection is to ensure that all inputs are clean and that no invalid data can be passed in. This is a responsibility that is shared by application developers (via code), database administrators (via SQL), and web developers (via the web interface). In an ideal environment, inputs are cleansed at all stages of execution. The web page or application that initially prompts for inputs should make efforts to ensure that invalid entries are not allowed. Some common methods are:

1. Generate a custom error message for the user that indicates that invalid characters or text were entered.

2. Strip out the invalid characters and allow execution to proceed.

3. Define roles for input data and if the entry doesn't fit that specific format, throw an error to the user. For example, a birthdate could be in the form MMDDYYYY, and all other entries disallowed.

4. Implement a software framework that automatically handles the cleansing of inputs for you.

These efforts will greatly enhance security and ensure that end users receive immediate feedback regarding the data they input. A good application will implement at least one, but likely several, of these safeguards. A great application will implement all of them, regardless of those efforts seeming redundant or unnecessary. As database professionals, we want these protections but cannot rely on them. It is our responsibility to ensure that all parameters that are passed into our T-SQL are cleansed with the same level of diligence. Doing so on all layers of a software application ensures the highest level of protection in the event that mistakes are made.

SQL Server error messages should always be handled internally via code and never exposed to end users. Instead, provide them with a friendly error message and reporting instructions.

The simplest way to cleanse inputs is to directly address them at the start of our code. In an attempt to keep our sample code as easy to read as possible, we'll use stored procedures for any reusable code going forward. Using Listing 2-9, let's reconsider our search from earlier and add some basic input cleansing at the top.

Listing 2-9. Basic Input-Cleansing Search Procedure

```
CREATE PROCEDURE dbo.search_people
        (@search_criteria NVARCHAR(1000) = NULL) -- This comes from user
                                                      input.
AS
BEGIN
      SELECT @search_criteria = REPLACE(@search_criteria, "", """);

      DECLARE @CMD NVARCHAR(MAX);

      SELECT @CMD = 'SELECT * FROM Person.Person
      WHERE LastName = "';
      SELECT @CMD = @CMD + @search_criteria;
      SELECT @CMD = @CMD + "";
      PRINT @CMD;
      EXEC sp_executesql @CMD;
END
GO

EXEC dbo.search_people 'Smith';
EXEC dbo.search_people 'O"Brien';
EXEC dbo.search_people "' SELECT * FROM Person.Password; SELECT "';
```

The preceding stored procedure contains a single addition at the top: all instances of an apostrophe are replaced with a pair of apostrophes. This guarantees that if anyone enters apostrophes, they will not break the string and cause immediate errors or obvious SQL injection vulnerabilities. The queries generated by each of the three executions are as follows:

```
SELECT * FROM Person.Person
     WHERE LastName = 'Smith'
SELECT * FROM Person.Person
     WHERE LastName = 'O''Brien'
SELECT * FROM Person.Person
     WHERE LastName = '' SELECT * FROM Person.Password; SELECT '''
```

In the first example, "Smith" is entered and all people with the last name of Smith are returned as usual. When an O'Brien enters his last name, the apostrophe is doubled, his name is searched, and results are found normally, without any error messages. When our malicious user tries to access passwords within the database, they are given an empty result set. Since the apostrophes are doubled in all cases, this string of attempted SQL injection turns into a harmless string with no holes in it.

SQL Server has a built in function whose purpose is to ensure that string contents are correctly delimited. QUOTENAME takes two parameters: the string to be cleansed and the character that will be verified. The stored procedure in Listing 2-10 is similar to the one in Listing 2-9, but the REPLACE operation has been updated to use QUOTENAME instead.

Listing 2-10. Input-Cleansing Search Procedure, Implemented Using QUOTENAME

```
IF EXISTS (SELECT * FROM sys.procedures WHERE procedures.name = 'search_
people')
     DROP PROCEDURE search_people;
GO

CREATE PROCEDURE dbo.search_people
     (@search_criteria NVARCHAR(1000) = NULL) -- This comes from user input.
AS
BEGIN
     DECLARE @CMD NVARCHAR(MAX);
```

41

```
        SELECT @CMD = 'SELECT * FROM Person.Person
        WHERE LastName = ';
        SELECT @CMD = @CMD + QUOTENAME(@search_criteria, "");
        PRINT @CMD;
        EXEC sp_executesql @CMD;
END
GO
EXEC dbo.search_people 'Smith';
EXEC dbo.search_people 'O"Brien';
EXEC dbo.search_people "' SELECT * FROM Person.Password; SELECT "';
```

QUOTENAME handles the apostrophe cleansing for us, and as a result we no longer need to wrap the last name portion of our command string in additional apostrophes. The output of this stored procedure is exactly the same as in the last example. Each name is correctly delimited with apostrophes to ensure that the search criteria will not cause any opportunities for errors to occur. In addition to apostrophes, QUOTENAME can be used to delimit square brackets ([,]), as well as quotation marks ("").

Parameterizing Dynamic SQL

Manually cleansing inputs using REPLACE or QUOTENAME is leaps and bounds better than having no protection at all. This will help prevent the most common SQL injection attacks, but it's not perfect. Manual input cleansing ensures that certain character combinations are replaced with more desirable options, but they are still subject to our vigilance in escaping inputs everywhere they exist. This tends toward a manual process where the database developer must remember to correctly use REPLACE or QUOTENAME in conjunction with all dynamic SQL statements.

A more reliable choice is to shift the responsibility from the developer to sp_executesql. This versatile stored procedure can accept input parameters, and in the process of doing so, will cleanse them automatically. Consider the new version of our previous stored procedure, as seen in Listing 2-11.

Listing 2-11. Parameterized Search Procedure

```
IF EXISTS (SELECT * FROM sys.procedures WHERE procedures.name = 'search_
people')
      DROP PROCEDURE search_people;
GO
CREATE PROCEDURE dbo.search_people
      (@search_criteria NVARCHAR(50) = NULL) -- This comes from user input.
AS
BEGIN
      DECLARE @CMD NVARCHAR(MAX);

      SELECT @CMD = 'SELECT * FROM Person.Person
      WHERE LastName = @search_criteria';
      PRINT @CMD;
      EXEC sp_executesql @CMD, N'@search_criteria NVARCHAR(1000)',
      @search_criteria;
END
```

The syntax for parameterizing `sp_executesql` is broken into three parts:

1. The command string to execute (`@CMD`)

2. The parameter list, including data types for each (`N'@search_criteria NVARCHAR(1000)'`

3. The parameters that are being passed in from our stored procedure (`@search_criteria`)

The results of this stored procedure are identical to each of our previous input cleansing examples. In this case, `sp_executesql` will handle the cleansing itself, ensuring that the inputs are correctly delimited, without the need for any further instruction from us. The parameter list may be stored as a separate variable as well. This can prove useful when there are many parameters, when we want to modify this list prior to execution, or when we want the `sp_executesql` command to be as short and clean as possible. As a bonus, we do not need to manage clumps of apostrophes as we delimit strings within dynamic SQL.

Listing 2-12. Parameterized Search Procedure Using a Separate Parameter Variable

```
IF EXISTS (SELECT * FROM sys.procedures WHERE procedures.name = 'search_
people')
     DROP PROCEDURE search_people;
GO

CREATE PROCEDURE dbo.search_people
     (@search_criteria NVARCHAR(1000) = NULL) -- This comes from user input.
AS
BEGIN
     DECLARE @CMD NVARCHAR(MAX);
     DECLARE @parameter_list NVARCHAR(MAX) = N'@search_criteria
     NVARCHAR(1000)';

     SELECT @CMD = 'SELECT * FROM Person.Person
     WHERE LastName = @search_criteria';
     PRINT @CMD;
     EXEC sp_executesql @CMD, @parameter_list, @search_criteria;
END
```

Notice the addition of the variable @parameter_list, which provides a separate place in which to store the list of input parameters. Adding this parameter is optional, but can help improve the readability of your dynamic SQL execution statement.

Using sp_executesql and passing all parameters into it ensures that all inputs are properly delimited and that SQL injection will not be possible using those inputs

---

The parameter list string (@parameter_list) contains all of the parameter names that correspond to the text within the dynamic SQL command string. The input parameters (@search_criteria) correspond to the parameters that are being passed in from outside of the dynamic SQL, listed individually. The parameter names in each list may be different, and the naming convention used is up to you. Exercise consistency, though, so that future developers are not left guessing with each line of T-SQL.

How many parameters are allowed in an `sp_executesql` statement? The answer is based on the SQL Server built-in limit for parameters in a stored procedure. The limit for any stored procedure is 2100, but in the case of `sp_executesql`, the command string and parameter list count as parameters, leaving us with a 2098 parameter limit, which should be more than enough for even the wildest programmers among us!

We can even use string building and dynamic SQL in the construction of the search criteria and parameter list, if we want to. This can allow us further customization of what variables are important for a given application at a given time.

The preceding example illustrated a dynamic SQL statement with a single parameter. Listing 2-13 shows how this would look with many parameters, naming the internal and external names differently.

Listing 2-13. Search Procedure with Multiple Optional Parameters

```
IF EXISTS (SELECT * FROM sys.procedures WHERE procedures.name = 'search_
people')
     DROP PROCEDURE search_people;
GO

CREATE PROCEDURE dbo.search_people
     (@FirstName NVARCHAR(50) = NULL,
      @MiddleName NVARCHAR(50) = NULL,
      @LastName NVARCHAR(50) = NULL,
      @EmailPromotion INT = NULL)
AS
BEGIN
     DECLARE @CMD NVARCHAR(MAX);
     DECLARE @parameter_list NVARCHAR(MAX) = N'@FirstName NVARCHAR(50),
     @MiddleName NVARCHAR(50), @LastName NVARCHAR(50), @EmailPromotion INT';

     SELECT @CMD = 'SELECT * FROM Person.Person
     WHERE 1 = 1';
     IF @FirstName IS NOT NULL
          SELECT @CMD = @CMD + '
          AND FirstName = @FirstName'
     IF @MiddleName IS NOT NULL
          SELECT @CMD = @CMD + '
          AND MiddleName = @MiddleName'
```

```
    IF @LastName IS NOT NULL
        SELECT @CMD = @CMD + '
        AND LastName = @LastName'
    IF @EmailPromotion IS NOT NULL
        SELECT @CMD = @CMD + '
        AND EmailPromotion = @EmailPromotion';
    PRINT @CMD;
    EXEC sp_executesql @CMD, @parameter_list, @FirstName, @MiddleName,
    @LastName, @EmailPromotion;
END
```

There are a few interesting changes to our search proc here. First, there are now four parameters that are passed into our stored procedure. Note the syntax of the sp_executesql command: command string first, then the internal parameter list, and then each parameter passed in separately. It is important that the order of parameters in each list match, otherwise you risk passing a first name in as a last name or a string where an integer is expected.

The second significant change in this stored procedure is that all parameters are optional. In order to facilitate this, "WHERE 1 = 1" is the first WHERE clause, followed by each parameter. This ensures that if all parameters are NULL, we aren't left with a hanging WHERE keyword and no clauses following it, which would result in an error. Consider the following executions of the preceding stored procedure:

```
EXEC dbo.search_people 'Edward', 'H', 'Johnson', 1
EXEC dbo.search_people 'Edward', NULL, NULL, 1
EXEC dbo.search_people
```

The first example provides values for all parameters and will return a single row from Person.Person. The T-SQL command string will look like this:

```
SELECT * FROM Person.Person
    WHERE 1 = 1
        AND FirstName = @FirstName
        AND MiddleName = @MiddleName
        AND LastName = @LastName
        AND EmailPromotion = @EmailPromotion
```

The second example leaves the middle name and last name NULL, and the resulting command string is:

```
SELECT * FROM Person.Person
    WHERE 1 = 1
        AND FirstName = @FirstName
        AND EmailPromotion = @EmailPromotion
```

The final example provides no parameters, and illustrates the importance of the "WHERE 1 = 1" placeholder in order to maintain good syntax when we do not know what parameters (if any) will be supplied:

```
SELECT * FROM Person.Person
    WHERE 1 = 1
```

It is likely within any large application where the table we are searching contains thousands (or millions) of rows, that we would not want to allow an empty search like this. It is generally beneficial to require at least one search parameter, which prevents a user from blindly returning everything. It is also worthwhile to limit the rows returned by the database to some relatively small number. Limits of 10, 25, 50, and 100 are common defaults for many applications, which ensure that we never inadvertently allow a user to query a table for millions of rows at one time.

Using `sp_executesql` is not enough to ensure protection against SQL injection. All parameters must explicitly be passed into `sp_executesql` as shown in the last few examples. If parameters are concatenated directly to the command string without passing them into `sp_executesql`, then those inputs will be subject to SQL injection attacks by exploiting apostrophes as previously demonstrated, and as we will see in further examples to follow. Always verify that there is no opportunity for anyone to have their search text directly incorporated into a command string without the appropriate input sanitation first!

Schema Name and Square Brackets

This convention applies to writing standard SQL, as well as dynamic SQL. When querying against dynamically defined database schema, such as tables, views, columns, or stored procedures, we are unable to parameterize the database objects. Without this protection, our T-SQL is opened up to the potential for SQL injection attacks. Consider the following T-SQL search in Listing 2-14.

Listing 2-14. Dynamic Table Search with No SQL Injection Protection

```
DECLARE @table_name SYSNAME = 'ErrorLog';
DECLARE @CMD NVARCHAR(MAX);

SELECT @CMD = 'SELECT * FROM ' + @table_name;
PRINT @CMD;
EXEC sp_executesql @CMD;
```

When executed, this returns all rows in the table `ErrorLog`. As with our examples earlier, this search, which defines the table to be queried at runtime, can easily be targeted by SQL injection. The following sinister input for `@table_name` would result in the contents of `Person.Password` being returned to the user, in addition to `ErrorLog`:

```
'ErrorLog; SELECT * FROM Person.Password WHERE "" = ""';
```

An easy defense against this is to explicitly include the schema name, even if it is the default. In addition, include square brackets around all objects, which will further delimit the SQL statement and restrict its ability to be easily manipulated.

Listing 2-15. Dynamic Table Search with Added Schema and Brackets

```
DECLARE @table_name SYSNAME = 'ErrorLog; SELECT * FROM Person.Password
                              WHERE "" = ""';
DECLARE @CMD NVARCHAR(MAX);

SELECT @CMD = 'SELECT * FROM [dbo].[' + @table_name + ']';
PRINT @CMD;
EXEC sp_executesql @CMD;
```

Executing this new version will result in the following command string:

```
SELECT * FROM [dbo].[ErrorLog; SELECT * FROM Person.Password WHERE " = "]
```

Executing that T-SQL results in an error at runtime:

```
Msg 208, Level 16, State 1, Line 142
Invalid object name 'dbo.ErrorLog; SELECT * FROM Person.Password WHERE " = "'.
```

Adding the schema and delimiting brackets caused that simple SQL injection attempt to fail. Assuming that the error message is caught by an application, and a friendly error returned, then the user will not know for certain what happened. This, of course, isn't foolproof, and a very persistent hacker will continue entering attempts at command strings until they figure out the pattern and try this input:

```
'ErrorLog]; SELECT * FROM [Person].[Password'
```

By closing the square brackets, and then reopening them with their table name, they've defeated our attempts to secure this query. While we could take further measures to complicate the command string to thwart a potential hacker, there would still be a security risk involved.

As stated earlier, any command string where all inputs are not parameterized using sp_executesql will be potentially vulnerable to SQL injection attacks. In general, avoid using database objects as dynamic SQL parameters unless you are certain that there will be no external access to this system. Regardless of audience, use QUOTENAME in order to properly delimit your parameters. While they cannot be passed in to sp_executesql directly, this will at least ensure that they cannot be exploited as seen.

For internal procedures to be used exclusively by DBAs or developers, these sorts of dynamic SQL statements are reasonable, though caution should still be exercised. As soon as any unknown parties have access, such as nontechnical departments, end users, or the Internet as a whole, the level of risk increases immensely. Always consider your audience before making stored procedures available to outside parties in any form, and ensure there is no way for them to exploit your code. Even if those procedures are internal and deemed safe, it is still important to utilize every security precaution and T-SQL best practice. Seemingly unlikely events, such as rogue users, disgruntled employees, or social engineering attempts happen far too often to be considered irrelevant under any conditions.

Effective Spacing

The example in Listing 2-6 showed a scenario where an attacker used comments to remove the password check in a login script. The primary cause of this vulnerability was the lack of parameterization or input sanitation, but a secondary cause was that the entire WHERE clause was on a single line.

I am unsure what possesses anyone to write dynamic SQL mostly or all on a single line, but in addition to rendering it illegible, it also increases the ways in which SQL injection could be used to exploit a poorly written query. Writing dynamic SQL with the same formatting and care that standard SQL is given will not only make it more maintainable, but will also remove a very simple SQL injection attack method from a hacker's arsenal.

Properly Type Inputs

In addition to sanitizing inputs, it is important to always use the correct data type for inputs. SQL injection specifically targets string inputs, in which apostrophes and malicious SQL can be inserted. Nontext data types, such as BIT, INT, or DATETIME cannot be the target of SQL injection.

Some applications are written with all (or most) input parameters as strings, for convenience. When working with strings, there is no need to cast or convert them to strings when concatenating them with your dynamic SQL command string. While this may reduce development time slightly, it increases the number of inputs in which SQL injection is theoretically possible.

If any data type is being evaluated that is not inherently a string, ensure that it is stored as a nonstring at least until it has been passed into your stored procedure. Once execution has passed these parameters into T-SQL, they can then be cast as strings and used in dynamic SQL with no risk of SQL injection. If desired, string variables can be declared within a stored procedure, and then populated with the converted types from above. Since the conversion is internal to SQL Server and has no connection outside of the stored procedure, it too is safe from SQL injection.

Always ensure that data is properly typed. Storing values as nonstrings ensures that they cannot be the target of SQL injection.

Similarly, ensure that applications always verify inputs to ensure that they match the expected type. An integer that is passed into a T-SQL statement as a string may allow arithmetic to be embedded safely in the string. If a malicious user realizes that they can replace "5" with "5 + 1," then they will immediately begin to probe other nonstring inputs to determine if they are converted blindly to strings. A parameter should be typed correctly from the moment it is entered by a user until it is consumed by a stored procedure. This prevents any opportunities for manipulation, in addition to reducing complexity and the chance that mistakes may be made as a result of confusing data types.

Blind SQL Injection

Even if a hacker cannot gain complete access to the database server via SQL injection, they may still be able to use some query elements to slowly gain information about a server, its security settings, and data. This can be done through the SQL injection methods demonstrated previously, or by modifying URLs or other data that is passed directly to the application.

The simplest example of this attack is to modify an HTTP string in order to view data that would otherwise be inaccessible to the user, such as a user profile, personal pictures, or upcoming travel plans. This attack requires little or no T-SQL knowledge, and therefore it is very common and often one of the first attempts made against a web application. The defense against these attempts to steal data is to ensure that the web page itself does not allow URLs to be blindly modified. In addition, if user, client, or web browser data is verified with all requests to sensitive data, then denying unauthorized access becomes much easier.

If the hacker can gain some SQL Server access via dynamic SQL, but finds him or herself limited by security restrictions, they can use their limited access to poke at the server and slowly discover limitations, security settings, data elements, and more. They will send requests in the form of IF statements that evaluate to true or false. Alternatively, the malicious user could ask questions that lead to error messages, and therefore determine the results by which the statement throws an error or not. TRY/CATCH can be used to manage error messages, thereby reducing the impact of these queries on web or database logs. Delays can be used, as well, to help in diagnosing responses based on the time it takes for them to complete. Even if friendly errors are displayed, that information would confirm that they have enough access to query the server for information and succeed.

Listing 2-16 illustrates some simple examples of the sorts of blind SQL injection queries that might get targeted at a vulnerable server.

Listing 2-16. Example Queries that May be Used in Blind SQL Injection Attacks

```
IF CURRENT_USER = 'dbo' SELECT 1 ELSE SELECT 0;

IF @@VERSION LIKE '%12.0%' SELECT 1 ELSE SELECT 0;

IF (SELECT COUNT(*) FROM Person.Person WHERE FirstName = 'Edward' AND
LastName = 'Pollack') > 0
WAITFOR DELAY '00:00:05'
ELSE
WAITFOR DELAY '00:00:00';

BEGIN TRY
    DECLARE @sql_command NVARCHAR(MAX);
    SELECT @sql_command = 'SELECT COUNT(*) FROM dbo.password;'
    EXEC (@sql_command)
END TRY
BEGIN CATCH
    SELECT 0
END CATCH;
```

The first three examples use basic yes/no questions in an attempt to learn about the server. The last example is a bit sneakier, and involves creating additional dynamic SQL to probe database objects further without throwing database errors in the process. TRY/CATCH does not work if syntax errors are present, hence querying an invalid table would return error messages. Injecting or appending further dynamic SQL allows an attacker to verify the existence of tables without causing syntax or parsing errors.

Blind SQL injection is a slower attack method, but can, over time, reveal critical data about a system. Each query reveals a new piece of information, and with enough data, they may be able to alter/bypass security restrictions in order to execute queries in the same way as they would have if no security precautions were in place.

Detection and Prevention

Prevention is the optimal way to prevent SQL injection, but as with any large software system, there will be code that predates you and could contain security holes. How do we guard ourselves against existing threats, or those we have yet to identify?

Security Testing

It has become a regular security task for companies to have third party vendors run penetration tests against their applications. This provides an opportunity for an unbiased external source to probe your environments for any of the common signs of SQL injection (or other vulnerabilities). Alternatively, these tests can be run internally if you have your own set of tools that are up to the task. This is an excellent way to find uncommon, old, or hidden vulnerabilities.

This sort of testing is often required in order to meet compliance standards, for example, with HIPAA (Health Insurance Portability and Accountability Act). If you work for a company or industry where sensitive data is stored by your software, conduct the necessary research to ensure that your security testing and verification are meeting your industry's compliance standards. Additional compliance may be necessary if you are doing business with customers in other countries.

Similarly, the GDPR (General Data Protection Regulation) greatly increases the level of responsibility an organization must take with its data. Any breach or attack that results in access to personal data (even if not stolen or altered) requires notification within 72 hours of its discovery.

The most common methods for detecting SQL injection vulnerabilities involve blindly populating application inputs with a variety of injection statements, in an attempt to generate application errors or coax unusual HTTP responses from a web page. For example, a set of valid searches is performed and the response time measured. Next, SQL injection statements are supplied to the application. By comparing those response times, it is possible to determine if the injected SQL was executed or not.

Checking for error messages is also common. If a set of typical SQL injection statements can result in unusual application or SQL errors, then the possibility exists for further exploitation.

It is important to understand that while security companies possess a variety of tools as a method of defending you from SQL injection attacks, hackers also possess their own sets of similar tools. If any security vulnerability can be demonstrated, regardless of how improbable or obscure, it is likely that a hacker will also eventually discover and immediately take advantage of it (or already is!).

Scanning of Application Traffic

Lightweight monitors can be put in place that will scan incoming traffic for unusual data patterns. For example, are common SQL commands or syntax being sent to your database servers from applications where only text is expected? Searching for semicolons, apostrophes, comment delimiters (--, /*, */), or T-SQL keywords such as SELECT, WHERE, and FROM are effective ways to locate and manage the sources of hacking attempts.

While these scans can be very useful, their value is solely based on the ratio of valid information versus noise. The need to catch SQL injection attacks needs to be weighed against the potential that common SQL characters or keywords may be common among application traffic. Realistically, any application that is open to the Internet will be blindly targeted by hackers for common vulnerabilities.

If this is the case, then it is up to us to determine a baseline for an average day of traffic (without any actual attacks occurring). Once that is established, then we can limit alerts to scenarios where suspicious activity is high enough to make us want to investigate further.

Log Review

Similar to monitoring network, application, or database traffic, we can regularly scan our web logs, application logs, or database error logs to determine if anything unusual or concerning is taking place. Similar searches can be made as with application traffic, and the results can be trended over time to produce an overview of SQL injection attempts, common targets, and sources.

Using this data, we can review the most common targets and ensure they are not vulnerable to SQL injection. In addition, we can analyze the sources of attacks to determine if any patterns exist. Many companies will block web traffic from specific countries, domains, or IP ranges, in order to remove risks while not affecting legitimate end user activity.

Note that password change requests are not logged by default, as a security precaution so that details (such as the old or new passwords) are not stored anywhere that others could view. As a result, if injected T-SQL statements contain `sp_password`, they will evade the SQL Server logs (though they will still appear as normal in application or web logs). There are many available ways to audit password changes, a few of which will be covered in Chapter 4.

Many of the ideas presented here can be automated so that a human is not actively monitoring web traffic or SQL Server logs. By filtering suspicious or anomalous requests, we can regularly capture and store anything of interest to us and only alert an operator of those requests that are of concern to us.

Code Review

All new application code should follow a review process by which an experienced developer reviews it. Similarly, all T-SQL should reviewed by a DBA or developer with enough database experience to be able to sniff out security holes. If the database scripts include dynamic SQL, then that can be focused on, ensuring that no SQL injection vulnerabilities exist. Even if the review is quick and targeted, it is likely that any significant problems will be discovered and fixed. Even if only a single vulnerability were ever found, the process itself would be completely justified in its elimination.

For larger and older applications, a sequential review of existing code can provide an additional defense against attacks. While it may sound time consuming to review all existing code, we can greatly reduce the volume by filtering based on the presence of common mistakes. For example, for SQL injection review, specifically single out database scripts/objects and review only those that contain EXEC, `sp_executesql`, or `xp_cmdshell`.

Software Patching

Be sure to keep your servers up to date! In addition to SQL Server, stay current with service packs and patches for your operating system, application software, and any commonly used tools or frameworks. Vulnerabilities are discovered daily in many commonly used software products, and some could potentially allow unauthorized access to your data.

While SQL injection is typically associated with dynamic SQL, it has been discovered in the past as a vulnerability where seemingly legitimate HTTP or command strings are passed from the web or another application directly to yours. The most readily available defense against unexpected attacks such as these is to regularly review application patch notes, and if any relevant security holes are found, patch them immediately.

Limit URL Length

As mentioned previously, it's possible for malicious SQL or application requests to be passed into an application via an HTTP request. Some web servers will not log the complete URL if it is too long. This is one possible way in which a hacker can probe your system for vulnerabilities without their actions being immediately noticed. They can create an unusually long URL, with the hope that it will either be truncated, or not logged at all.

Most web servers allow you to set a limit on the allowable length of URL strings, and unless any applications require long URLs, setting that limit is beneficial. 2048 characters is a common limit, though any can be chosen. As with security, only allow as much as is required for your application to operate normally (including future growth).

For example, in Microsoft IIS, when this limit is set, a longer URL will return a 404 error to the client with no further detail. The server logs, though, will include additional information as to why the request was blocked, so that you can identify potential threats:

1. 404.10: Request Header Too Long

2. 404.13: Content Length Too Long

3. 404.14: URL Too Long

4. 404.15: Query String Too Long

These errors, when detected in bulk, should be a red flag when looking for potential attackers or software bugs. If the origin of the requests is dubious, then consider blocking them, otherwise research further to determine their cause and if they necessitate further research and development.

Use Views and/or Masking for Sensitive Data

In those scenarios where encrypted sensitive data needs to be accessed, such as passwords or credit card numbers, consider only supplying permissions to views that provide the fewest fields necessary to service those queries. Denying direct access to critical tables removes the ability of a hacker to access them, and therefore use SQL injection to infiltrate them.

For example, a password table may have a variety of information that could not only give away password hash details, but also password policies, user names, locked accounts, recent login times, and more. The application likely only needs access to the encrypted password (or hash) and positive identifying data (such as a user ID).

SQL Server 2016 includes a new security feature: Dynamic Data Masking. This can be extremely effective for any scenarios where part of sensitive data is needed, such as the last four digits of a social security number or credit card number. For users without the UNMASK permission, a predetermined segment of the sensitive data will be obscured. This added layer of data obfuscation provides an extra defense against an unauthorized user gaining the complete details of your important data.

Data masking, while convenient, is not intended to be a hardened security feature. In no way does data masking provide user-level security, and there are many documented ways to bypass this feature if a user has direct SQL Server access. Masking is exclusively a presentation feature that provides security to the end-user of the data. Anyone with direct access to SQL Server and the masked data can work around the masking in order to reveal the hidden characters.

Despite these limitations, Dynamic Data Masking is another lock on the vault that is critical data, and one that will either dissuade a hacker from proceeding, or slow them down enough that your security team has extra time to respond to the threat head-on. For scenarios where only data validation is needed, but not full access to that data, this is an excellent tool for providing only what is needed and nothing more.

Vendor Software

Not all software on our systems was written by us or a trusted industry leader. Many companies rely on additional applications to manage a variety of needs, such as:

- Payroll
- Vacation Time

- Help Desk

- E-mail/Calendars

- Reporting

- Expense Reports

- Hiring/Recruitment

Each of these applications has their own code, data storage, user interface, and security concerns. When we use vendor software, regardless of whether it is cloud-based or on-premises, we open ourselves up to any security vulnerabilities that software may have.

When researching SQL injection or performing security audits or penetration tests, be sure to include all software that your organization uses, regardless of its source. If the software is installed on-premises, then be sure to validate the security and access it has to local computing resources. Make sure that the application can in no way access data or systems aside from its own.

In addition, perform your tests on their software as well. We often take it for granted that the security of vendor software isn't our problem, but if they lose our data, we cannot simply blame them and move on.

Any client, regulatory, or industry standards that apply to our software must also apply to software we install, use, or trust from other vendors. Major companies suffer breaches regularly and lose social security numbers, credit card data, or personally identifiable information. If any of that data belongs to your clients, then that vendor's mistake becomes your headache.

Login Pages

Of all the text boxes we fill out in an application, none is more sensitive and more attacked than the login page. Validating user names and passwords is extremely important, and mistakes in doing so can render all of our other security precautions irrelevant.

Defending against SQL injection is important when managing login pages, but there is benefit in taking additional steps to improve security:

- Do not provide detailed feedback on failed logins. If a login is unsuccessful, report that fact and say nothing more. Indicating that a user name is invalid allows attackers to hammer a site to determine which login names are real or not. Reporting an incorrect password will validate the existence of a specific user name, also providing useful information to a hacker.

- Use two-factor authentication. Forcing a user to validate a new login attempt from another device greatly cuts down on garbage login attempts and allows users to take charge of their own security.

- Limit login attempts over a given time period. This stops an attacker after enough bad guesses and logs that fact to web logs that can be reviewed later.

- Account signup forms and password reset forms should be as vague as possible, not confirming or denying the existence of accounts, credentials, e-mail addresses, or previous login/signup attempts.

- Allow passwords to meet modern guidelines:

  - Allow very long passwords. This allows the use of hard-to-guess sentences or phrases. Force a minimum length, such as 8 or 12 characters.

  - Drop specific complexity requirements. They are confusing, hard to remember, and result in easy-to-guess passwords.

  - Block the use of common passwords that are too easy to guess, such as "Password" or "qwerty123."

  - Do not force frequent password resets, but do allow users to change passwords any time.

  - Do not use password hints. They are only effective in spreading users' personal information further by asking easy-to-research questions. Favorite sports teams or car models are easy to guess or confirm via social media.

Any place in an application where user security is validated should receive as much scrutiny as possible. If someone can gain unauthorized access to an account, then they can access important data without the need for further hacking or trickery. Worse, this access may be challenging to detect before it is too late.

Conclusion

SQL injection is one of the top vulnerabilities exploited throughout the entire process of application development. In fact, many government, corporate, and independent surveys have consistently ranked SQL injection as the #1 vulnerability in all of computing. This is clearly a very serious topic and one we must keep in mind on a regular basis as we design, develop, test, deploy, and maintain a software application.

The easiest and most effective way to protect against SQL injection is to be proactive and write both secure T-SQL and application code. Consider how user inputs will be integrated into search parameters and ultimately into database queries. Once those sensitive areas are located, address them with multiple levels of security. Implementing `sp_executesql` is a good start, but also adding input verification, parameterization, and explicit schema references will be even more effective. Depending on your application, take as many additional steps as are practical, as each will be another lock on the vault that is your data.

If the time and effort required for these additional steps is ever questioned by management, feel free to explain to them the vulnerabilities that you are addressing. List out the potential threats and the consequences of them being realized. Security is often seen as an inconvenience, but it is our responsibility as database professionals to justify its necessity and ensure that our data is as secure as possible. Never let doing the "right" thing with regard to security be entangled with release dates, efficiency, or resources. The consequences of disregarding what are relatively simple development steps are too high to shrug off.

In Chapter 4, we will discuss security in further detail. SQL injection is significant enough to warrant a separate and special place in the hierarchy of SQL Server security. Documenting your efforts and the threats they address will justify themselves in the long run.

CHAPTER 3

Large Scale Searching

One of the most common, versatile, and useful ways to implement dynamic SQL is when performing complex searches. Consider your favorite web sites and the search functionality provided in each. For some, the search may be simple: go to the single text box in the top-right corner, enter some text, and results are returned. For others, such as searching for a hotel, a flight, or a car rental, they can involve dozens (or more) of optional parameters. Dynamic SQL can allow us to pare down our search queries in order to only process what is needed. In addition, we can also greatly customize the search, as well as the data returned. We can even analyze the input to determine the correct course of action, based on its structure.

Why Use Dynamic Searches?

Let's say we want to search through a table of products, but need to join this data to other tables along the way. Depending on the application, the number of tables could be small, or they could be immense. For the hotel search, we may very well need to join fifty tables if we wanted to query on every single possible search parameter. Listing 3-1 is an example of a relatively small product search that could benefit from the use of dynamic SQL.

Listing 3-1. Search Stored Procedure, with Six Optional Parameters (No Dynamic SQL)

```
CREATE PROCEDURE dbo.search_products
@product_name NVARCHAR(50) = NULL, @product_number NVARCHAR(25) = NULL,
@product_model NVARCHAR(50) = NULL, @product_subcategory NVARCHAR(50) = NULL,
@product_sizemeasurecode NVARCHAR(50) = NULL, @product_weightunitmeasurecode
NVARCHAR(50) = NULL
```

© Edward Pollack 2019
E. Pollack, *Dynamic SQL*, https://doi.org/10.1007/978-1-4842-4318-3_3

```
AS
BEGIN
    SET NOCOUNT ON;

    SET @product_name = '%' + @product_name + '%';
    SET @product_number = '%' + @product_number + '%';
    SET @product_model = '%' + @product_model + '%';

    SELECT
            Product.Name AS product_name,
            Product.ProductNumber AS product_number,
            ProductModel.Name AS product_model_name,
            ProductSubcategory.Name AS product_subcategory_name,
            SizeUnitMeasureCode.Name AS size_unit_measure_code,
            WeightUnitMeasureCode.Name AS weight_unit_measure_code
    FROM Production.Product
    LEFT JOIN Production.ProductModel
    ON Product.ProductModelID = ProductModel.ProductModelID
    LEFT JOIN Production.ProductSubcategory
    ON Product.ProductSubcategoryID = ProductSubcategory.ProductSubcategoryID
    LEFT JOIN Production.UnitMeasure SizeUnitMeasureCode
    ON Product.SizeUnitMeasureCode = SizeUnitMeasureCode.UnitMeasureCode
    LEFT JOIN Production.UnitMeasure WeightUnitMeasureCode
    ON Product.WeightUnitMeasureCode = WeightUnitMeasureCode.
                                        UnitMeasureCode
    WHERE (Product.Name LIKE @product_name OR @product_name IS NULL)
    AND (Product.ProductNumber LIKE @product_number OR @product_number
    IS NULL)
    AND (ProductModel.Name LIKE @product_model OR @product_model IS NULL)
    AND (ProductSubcategory.Name = @product_subcategory OR @product_
                                        subcategory IS NULL)
    AND (SizeUnitMeasureCode.Name = @product_sizemeasurecode OR @product_
                                        sizemeasurecode IS NULL)
    AND (WeightUnitMeasureCode.Name = @product_weightunitmeasurecode OR
                                        @product_weightunitmeasurecode IS
                                        NULL);
END
```

This stored procedure will search for products, and has a variety of search options available for the user to choose from: product name, product number, product model, product subcategory, size measure, and weight measure may all be provided or omitted from the user's input. It is assumed for this specific example that product name, product number, and product model are wildcard searches; hence the addition of "%" to each parameter after it is passed in. The other parameters are assumed to be selected from a prepopulated menu, ensuring that any values passed in will be exact, and therefore there is no need to make those into wildcard searches.

In the case of this search, we will always return the same six columns, regardless of the parameters passed in. As a result, we will LEFT JOIN all participating tables to ensure that we get a row per product, even if any join criteria are NULL. To ensure that no results are omitted for unused parameters, an additional check is added to all WHERE clauses such that, if the input is NULL, it will evaluate to true. The resulting logic allows us to choose one of the following:

- A parameter is passed in from user input and should be evaluated against the appropriate column. The NULL check evaluates to FALSE, and has no bearing on this logic.

- A parameter is not passed in from the user, and therefore the comparison against it is irrelevant. Instead, the NULL check evaluates to true and therefore the entire WHERE clause evaluates to TRUE.

The following three examples illustrate how this works:

```
EXEC dbo.search_products @product_number = 'BK-M18', @product_model =
'Mountain', @product_subcategory = 'Mountain Bikes';
```

In this search, three parameters are provided and we will search for any product that has a product number that includes "BK-M18", a product model that includes the word "Mountain", and must be in the subcategory of "Mountain Bikes." The other three parameters do not participate in the WHERE clause and are evaluated against the second NULL check instead. Ten results are returned that fit these specifications.

```
EXEC dbo.search_products @product_name = 'Mountain-500 Black, 48';
```

Here, the user knows exactly what they are looking for, and enter a specific product name. All other parameters are NULL and are discarded from the search logic. A single row is returned with the product they were searching for.

```
EXEC dbo.search_products;
```

In this last example, the user enters no search criteria and simply runs an empty search. Our stored procedure allows this, and every product is returned. All inputs are NULL and therefore bypass the WHERE clause predicate.

In reviewing this stored procedure, we find it to be accurate, returning the expected results, but it is also somewhat lengthy and evaluates quite a few WHERE clause predicates in order to accomplish what it needs to. The T-SQL that is executed is very similar, regardless of what parameters are provided, which could be problematic in scenarios where we were evaluating many parameters.

As business logic grows and becomes more complex over time, it is a given that these queries will also grow and increase in size and complexity. A simple LEFT JOIN on one column may no longer be enough to handle this new logic. WHERE clauses may have additional options attached to them, such as the ability to be wildcard searches, equality searches, include AND/OR logic, and more. While this stored procedure may continue to grow over time to encompass all of these new requirements, we definitely do not want the resulting T-SQL that is executed to grow indefinitely. Performance will become problematic when we are joining dozens of tables, issuing subqueries, existence checks, and complex WHERE clauses. This is where dynamic SQL comes in! See Listing 3-2 for an example of using parameters to limit joins.

Listing 3-2. Search Stored Procedure, with Six Optional Parameters (Using Dynamic SQL)

```
IF EXISTS (SELECT * FROM sys.procedures WHERE procedures.name = 'search_
products')
BEGIN
      DROP PROCEDURE dbo.search_products;
END
GO

CREATE PROCEDURE dbo.search_products
      @product_name NVARCHAR(50) = NULL, @product_number NVARCHAR(25) =
      NULL, @product_model NVARCHAR(50) = NULL,
      @product_subcategory NVARCHAR(50) = NULL, @product_sizemeasurecode
      NVARCHAR(50) = NULL,
      @product_weightunitmeasurecode NVARCHAR(50) = NULL
```

```
AS
BEGIN
    SET NOCOUNT ON;

    SET @product_name = '%' + @product_name + '%';
    SET @product_number = '%' + @product_number + '%';
    SET @product_model = '%' + @product_model + '%';

    DECLARE @sql_command NVARCHAR(MAX);
    DECLARE @parameter_list NVARCHAR(MAX) = '@product_name NVARCHAR(50),
    @product_number NVARCHAR(25),
    @product_model NVARCHAR(50), @product_subcategory NVARCHAR(50),
    @product_sizemeasurecode NVARCHAR(50),
    @product_weightunitmeasurecode NVARCHAR(50)';

    SELECT @sql_command = '
    SELECT
        Product.Name AS product_name,
        Product.ProductNumber AS product_number,
        ProductModel.Name AS product_model_name,
        ProductSubcategory.Name AS product_subcategory_name,
        SizeUnitMeasureCode.Name AS size_unit_measure_code,
    WeightUnitMeasureCode.Name AS weight_unit_measure_code
    FROM Production.Product
    LEFT JOIN Production.ProductModel
    ON Product.ProductModelID = ProductModel.ProductModelID
    LEFT JOIN Production.ProductSubcategory
    ON Product.ProductSubcategoryID = ProductSubcategory.
    ProductSubcategoryID
    LEFT JOIN Production.UnitMeasure SizeUnitMeasureCode
    ON Product.SizeUnitMeasureCode = SizeUnitMeasureCode.UnitMeasureCode
    LEFT JOIN Production.UnitMeasure WeightUnitMeasureCode
    ON Product.WeightUnitMeasureCode = SizeUnitMeasureCode.
    UnitMeasureCode
    WHERE 1 = 1'
```

```
    IF @product_name IS NOT NULL
        SELECT @sql_command = @sql_command + '
        AND Product.Name LIKE @product_name'
    IF @product_number IS NOT NULL
        SELECT @sql_command = @sql_command + '
        AND Product.ProductNumber LIKE @product_number'
    IF @product_model IS NOT NULL
        SELECT @sql_command = @sql_command + '
        AND ProductModel.Name LIKE @product_model'
    IF @product_subcategory IS NOT NULL
        SELECT @sql_command = @sql_command + '
        AND ProductSubcategory.Name = @product_subcategory'
    IF @product_sizemeasurecode IS NOT NULL
        SELECT @sql_command = @sql_command + '
        AND SizeUnitMeasureCode.Name = @product_sizemeasurecode'
    IF @product_weightunitmeasurecode IS NOT NULL
        SELECT @sql_command = @sql_command + '
        AND WeightUnitMeasureCode.Name = @product_weightunitmeasurecode'

    PRINT @sql_command;
    EXEC sp_executesql @sql_command, @parameter_list, @product_name,
    @product_number,
    @product_model, @product_subcategory, @product_sizemeasurecode,
    @product_weightunitmeasurecode
END
```

This stored procedure uses dynamic SQL to provide us complete control over the WHERE clause. Instead of there always being six checks on all columns, we now only include a check when the relevant parameter is supplied. Consider our first example from earlier:

```
EXEC dbo.search_products @product_number = 'BK-M18', @product_model =
'Mountain', @product_subcategory = 'Mountain Bikes';
```

Earlier, the search used all six WHERE clause sections, one per parameter, even when the parameter was NULL. With the new dynamic SQL version, the resulting command string will only include WHERE clause sections for parameters that are not NULL, as seen in Listing 3-3.

Listing 3-3. Output from the Stored Procedure in Listing 3-2

```
SELECT
        Product.Name AS product_name,
        Product.ProductNumber AS product_number,
        ProductModel.Name AS product_model_name,
        ProductSubcategory.Name AS product_subcategory_name,
        SizeUnitMeasureCode.Name AS size_unit_measure_code,
        WeightUnitMeasureCode.Name AS weight_unit_measure_code
FROM Production.Product
LEFT JOIN Production.ProductModel
ON Product.ProductModelID = ProductModel.ProductModelID
LEFT JOIN Production.ProductSubcategory
ON Product.ProductSubcategoryID = ProductSubcategory.ProductSubcategoryID
LEFT JOIN Production.UnitMeasure SizeUnitMeasureCode
ON Product.SizeUnitMeasureCode = SizeUnitMeasureCode.UnitMeasureCode
LEFT JOIN Production.UnitMeasure WeightUnitMeasureCode
ON Product.WeightUnitMeasureCode = SizeUnitMeasureCode.UnitMeasureCode
WHERE 1 = 1
        AND Product.ProductNumber LIKE @product_number
        AND ProductModel.Name LIKE @product_model
        AND ProductSubcategory.Name = @product_subcategory
```

Note that only the necessary WHERE clause segments are included. WHERE 1 = 1 is always present, regardless of the input parameters. While it's possible to add some additional logic to remove the need for the default WHERE clause, its inclusion comes at no significant cost and avoids adding any further complex logic to our growing stored procedure.

Custom Search Grids

At the moment, it may seem as though all this trouble to shrink the WHERE clause isn't worth it, but this is only the beginning! The next logical step is to examine another common use case for large-scale searching: custom search grids. In this slightly different search, the output columns are controlled by the user as well. Previously, we returned the same six columns for every search, but this is an unlikely scenario for any large application that wishes to incorporate any level of flexibility into its search functionality.

For this search, there are two fundamental ways in which to approach it. The first is to include all columns and joins in every query. The application can then pick and choose which are needed, and which ones to discard. For this option, instead of selecting six output columns, we would add every possible one that could be requested by the end user in their custom results grid. For very small tables, this would be functional and relatively maintainable, but consider scenarios where there are immense numbers of possible columns to choose from, such as in a File Explorer window shown in Figure 3-1.

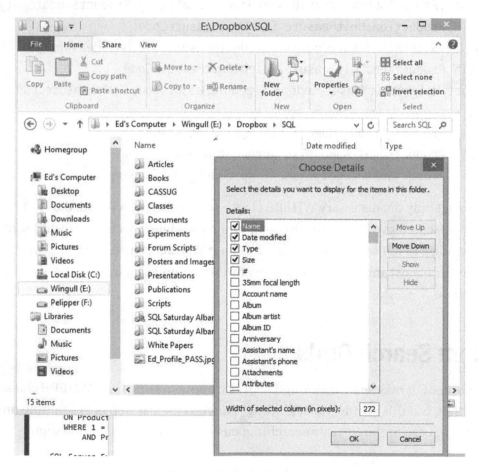

Figure 3-1. *Windows File Explorer column chooser*

In this column chooser, there are hundreds of columns to choose from, and the idea of always collecting all of this data, regardless of the user's needs, is quite scary. There are many file types for which only a small number of these choices would make sense to include, and collecting all of this data for every folder accessed would be inefficient and difficult to effective maintain.

If we were to apply this logic to our preceding stored procedure and include all possible columns from each of the six tables we queried, we would have to list 38 columns to ensure that the end user had everything they could potentially need from these entities. If every table relating to products in Adventureworks was added to our search query, the end result would contain hundreds of columns and be quite the challenge to ensure good performance. The downside of selecting everything extends to network IO, disk IO, memory, and server CPU, in addition to the performance of SQL Server in processing the query. All of this extra data would need to be moved from the database to the application before it could finally be sorted out, and the extra columns removed from the data set.

The second and more versatile solution for implementing a search grid is to make each part of the query dynamic. In addition to the WHERE clause, make the joins and the columns selected dynamic. This ensures that the command string that we ultimately execute is relatively small, only reads from the tables we need, and only returns the columns we want. To keep this example easy to read, we will assume that the product name and product number will always be returned. We will also assume that there will be an additional set of bits that can be passed in that will determine what other columns are chosen, which include some of the filter columns, as seen in Listing 3-4.

Listing 3-4. Search Grid Stored Procedure, Using Dynamic SQL

```
IF EXISTS (SELECT * FROM sys.procedures WHERE procedures.name = 'search_
products')
BEGIN
        DROP PROCEDURE dbo.search_products;
END
GO

CREATE PROCEDURE dbo.search_products
        @product_name NVARCHAR(50) = NULL, @product_number NVARCHAR(25) =
        NULL, @product_model NVARCHAR(50) = NULL,
        @product_subcategory NVARCHAR(50) = NULL, @product_sizemeasurecode
        NVARCHAR(50) = NULL,
```

```
    @product_weightunitmeasurecode NVARCHAR(50) = NULL,
    @show_color BIT = 0, @show_safetystocklevel BIT = 0, @show_
    reorderpoint BIT = 0, @show_standard_cost BIT = 0,
    @show_catalog_description BIT = 0, @show_subcategory_modified_date
    BIT = 0, @show_product_model BIT = 0,
    @show_product_subcategory BIT = 0, @show_product_sizemeasurecode
    BIT = 0, @show_product_weightunitmeasurecode BIT = 0
AS
BEGIN
    SET NOCOUNT ON;
    -- Add "%" delimiters to parameters that will be searched as
        wildcards.
    SET @product_name = '%' + @product_name + '%';
    SET @product_number = '%' + @product_number + '%';
    SET @product_model = '%' + @product_model + '%';

    DECLARE @sql_command NVARCHAR(MAX);
    -- Define the parameter list for filter criteria.
    DECLARE @parameter_list NVARCHAR(MAX) = '@product_name NVARCHAR(50),
    @product_number NVARCHAR(25),
    @product_model NVARCHAR(50), @product_subcategory NVARCHAR(50),
    @product_sizemeasurecode NVARCHAR(50),
    @product_weightunitmeasurecode NVARCHAR(50)';

    -- Generate the command string section for the SELECT columns.
    SELECT @sql_command = '
    SELECT
        Product.Name AS product_name,
        Product.ProductNumber AS product_number,';
        IF @show_product_model = 1 SELECT @sql_command = @sql_command + '
            ProductModel.Name AS product_model_name,';
        IF @show_product_subcategory = 1 SELECT @sql_command = @sql_
        command + '
            ProductSubcategory.Name AS product_subcategory_name,';
        IF @show_product_sizemeasurecode = 1 SELECT @sql_command =
        @sql_command + '
            SizeUnitMeasureCode.Name AS size_unit_measure_code,';
```

```
    IF @show_product_weightunitmeasurecode = 1 SELECT @sql_command
    = @sql_command + '
        WeightUnitMeasureCode.Name AS weight_unit_measure_code,';
    IF @show_color = 1 SELECT @sql_command = @sql_command + '
        Product.Color AS product_color,';
    IF @show_safetystocklevel = 1 SELECT @sql_command = @sql_
    command + '
        Product.SafetyStockLevel AS product_safety_stock_level,';
    IF @show_reorderpoint = 1 SELECT @sql_command = @sql_command + '
        Product.ReorderPoint AS product_reorderpoint,';
    IF @show_standard_cost = 1 SELECT @sql_command = @sql_command + '
        Product.StandardCost AS product_standard_cost,';
    IF @show_catalog_description = 1 SELECT @sql_command = @sql_
    command + '
        ProductModel.CatalogDescription AS productmodel_catalog_
        description,';
    IF @show_subcategory_modified_date = 1 SELECT @sql_command =
    @sql_command + '
        ProductSubcategory.ModifiedDate AS product_subcategory_
        modified_date';
-- In the event that there is a comma at the end of our command
   string, remove it before continuing.
IF (SELECT SUBSTRING(@sql_command, LEN(@sql_command), 1)) = ','
    SELECT @sql_command = LEFT(@sql_command, LEN(@sql_command) - 1);
SELECT @sql_command = @sql_command + '
FROM Production.Product'
-- Put together the JOINs based on what tables are required by the
   search.
IF (@product_model IS NOT NULL OR @show_product_model = 1 OR @show_
catalog_description = 1)
    SELECT @sql_command = @sql_command + '
LEFT JOIN Production.ProductModel
ON Product.ProductModelID = ProductModel.ProductModelID';
```

```
IF (@product_subcategory IS NOT NULL OR @show_subcategory_modified_
date = 1 OR @show_product_subcategory = 1)
    SELECT @sql_command = @sql_command + '
LEFT JOIN Production.ProductSubcategory
ON Product.ProductSubcategoryID = ProductSubcategory.
ProductSubcategoryID';
IF (@product_sizemeasurecode IS NOT NULL OR @show_product_
sizemeasurecode = 1)
    SELECT @sql_command = @sql_command + '
LEFT JOIN Production.UnitMeasure SizeUnitMeasureCode
ON Product.SizeUnitMeasureCode = SizeUnitMeasureCode.
UnitMeasureCode';
IF (@product_weightunitmeasurecode IS NOT NULL OR @show_product_
weightunitmeasurecode = 1)
    SELECT @sql_command = @sql_command + '
LEFT JOIN Production.UnitMeasure WeightUnitMeasureCode
ON Product.WeightUnitMeasureCode = SizeUnitMeasureCode.
UnitMeasureCode'

SELECT @sql_command = @sql_command + '
WHERE 1 = 1'
-- Build the WHERE clause based on which tables are referenced and
   required by the search.
IF @product_name IS NOT NULL
    SELECT @sql_command = @sql_command + '
    AND Product.Name LIKE @product_name'
IF @product_number IS NOT NULL
    SELECT @sql_command = @sql_command + '
    AND Product.ProductNumber LIKE @product_number'
IF @product_model IS NOT NULL
    SELECT @sql_command = @sql_command + '
    AND ProductModel.Name LIKE @product_model'
IF @product_subcategory IS NOT NULL
    SELECT @sql_command = @sql_command + '
    AND ProductSubcategory.Name = @product_subcategory'
```

```
      IF @product_sizemeasurecode IS NOT NULL
            SELECT @sql_command = @sql_command + '
            AND SizeUnitMeasureCode.Name = @product_sizemeasurecode'
      IF @product_weightunitmeasurecode IS NOT NULL
            SELECT @sql_command = @sql_command + '
            AND WeightUnitMeasureCode.Name = @product_weightunitmeasurecode'

      PRINT @sql_command;
      EXEC sp_executesql @sql_command, @parameter_list, @product_name,
      @product_number,
      @product_model, @product_subcategory, @product_sizemeasurecode,
      @product_weightunitmeasurecode
END
GO

EXEC dbo.search_products @product_number = 'BK-M18', @product_model =
'Mountain', @product_subcategory = 'Mountain Bikes';
EXEC dbo.search_products @product_name = 'Mountain-500 Black, 48';
EXEC dbo.search_products;
EXEC dbo.search_products @product_name = 'Mountain-500 Black, 48', @show_
safetystocklevel = 1, @show_reorderpoint = 1, @show_standard_cost = 1 ;
GO
```

The first change here is that there are ten new parameters that correspond to each
column that can be added to the search results grid. This looks a bit haphazard, though
an explicit parameter list is convenient for easy troubleshooting. Each is explicitly named
and easy to understand and document. One alternative to the use of individual bits
would be to implement a bitmap and adjust individual bits within a single parameter.
This reduces the parameter list from one parameter for each optional column to just
one for all optional columns. It will also reduce readability and maintainability, as the
parameter will now be a hexadecimal number instead of a set of bits. For example, if
bit 1, bit 6, and bit 7 were selected, the resulting VARBINARY representation of that
bitmap would be 0x00000061. In order to make this usable and maintainable, each bit
would need to be documented so that anyone who modifies or works with this stored
procedure would know exactly how it works.

While this stored procedure has many parameters, most will not be needed at any one time, unless the end user truly wants to filter on and display everything. Note that the additional bit parameters are not included in the parameters for sp_executesql. These bit columns are used in building our command string only, but are not required within the dynamic SQL. As a result, adding additional bits does not cause the sp_executesql statement to grow, although it will add more parameters to the search_products stored procedure. As a result, the sp_executesql statement is the same in this example as it was in the previous one.

The column list has been broken down into a series of parameter checks as well. Any optional column is only included if its respective bit parameter is set. For example, if @show_product_model is set to 1, then the ProductModel.Name column will be included in the SELECT statement. The following EXEC statement illustrates a single filter on ProductModel.Name and the inclusion of that name, as well as the product color:

```
EXEC dbo.search_products @product_model = 'Mountain', @show_product_model = 1,
@show_color = 1
```

The resulting command string for this search is as follows in Listing 3-5.

Listing 3-5. Command String Generated from Stored Procedure in Listing 3-4

```
SELECT
      Product.Name AS product_name,
      Product.ProductNumber AS product_number,
      ProductModel.Name AS product_model_name,
      Product.Color AS product_color
FROM Production.Product
LEFT JOIN Production.ProductModel
ON Product.ProductModelID = ProductModel.ProductModelID
WHERE 1 = 1
      AND ProductModel.Name LIKE @product_model
```

Note that the actual T-SQL executed is only what is needed to service the user's request, and nothing more. All sections of the query were customized to meet the exact search that was requested.

The example here only returns columns that are explicitly called out by the user. If desired, the T-SQL can be written such that we return all columns in a table if any one of them is selected, or just the columns that could be selected by the end user. Using this methodology, if `@show_product_model` = 1, then `ProductModel.Name` and `ProductModel.CatalogDescription` would be selected. The application could then remove any unneeded columns. This alternative would be easier to maintain and update over time but would sacrifice a small amount of performance, as more data would be returned than is needed, as seen in Listing 3-6.

Listing 3-6. Search Proc with a Simplified SELECT Statement, Using Fewer Conditionals

```
IF EXISTS (SELECT * FROM sys.procedures WHERE procedures.name = 'search_
products')
BEGIN
     DROP PROCEDURE dbo.search_products;
END
GO

-- Search with a check to avoid empty searches.
CREATE PROCEDURE dbo.search_products
     @product_name NVARCHAR(50) = NULL, @product_number NVARCHAR(25) =
     NULL, @product_model NVARCHAR(50) = NULL,
     @product_subcategory NVARCHAR(50) = NULL, @product_sizemeasurecode
     NVARCHAR(50) = NULL,
     @product_weightunitmeasurecode NVARCHAR(50) = NULL,
     @show_color BIT = 0, @show_safetystocklevel BIT = 0, @show_
     reorderpoint BIT = 0, @show_standard_cost BIT = 0,
     @show_catalog_description BIT = 0, @show_subcategory_modified_date
     BIT = 0, @show_product_model BIT = 0,
     @show_product_subcategory BIT = 0, @show_product_sizemeasurecode
     BIT = 0, @show_product_weightunitmeasurecode BIT = 0
AS
BEGIN
     SET NOCOUNT ON;

     IF COALESCE(@product_name, @product_number, @product_model, @product_
     subcategory,
                    @product_sizemeasurecode, @product_
                    weightunitmeasurecode) IS NULL
          RETURN;
```

75

```
    -- Add "%" delimiters to parameters that will be searched as
       wildcards.
    SET @product_name = '%' + @product_name + '%';
    SET @product_number = '%' + @product_number + '%';
    SET @product_model = '%' + @product_model + '%';

    DECLARE @sql_command NVARCHAR(MAX);
    -- Define the parameter list for filter criteria.
    DECLARE @parameter_list NVARCHAR(MAX) = '@product_name NVARCHAR(50),
    @product_number NVARCHAR(25),
    @product_model NVARCHAR(50), @product_subcategory NVARCHAR(50),
    @product_sizemeasurecode NVARCHAR(50),
    @product_weightunitmeasurecode NVARCHAR(50)';

-- Generate the simplified command string section for the SELECT columns.
SELECT @sql_command = '
    SELECT
            Product.Name AS product_name,
            Product.ProductNumber AS product_number,';
        IF @show_product_model = 1 OR @show_catalog_description = 1
        SELECT @sql_command = @sql_command + '
                ProductModel.Name AS product_model_name,
                ProductModel.CatalogDescription AS productmodel_catalog_
                description,';
        IF @show_product_subcategory = 1 OR @show_subcategory_modified_
        date = 1 SELECT @sql_command = @sql_command + '
                ProductSubcategory.Name AS product_subcategory_name,
                ProductSubcategory.ModifiedDate AS product_subcategory_
                modified_date,';
        IF @show_product_sizemeasurecode = 1 SELECT @sql_command =
        @sql_command + '
                SizeUnitMeasureCode.Name AS size_unit_measure_code,';
        IF @show_product_weightunitmeasurecode = 1 SELECT @sql_command =
        @sql_command + '
                WeightUnitMeasureCode.Name AS weight_unit_measure_code,';
```

```
    IF @show_color = 1 OR @show_safetystocklevel = 1 OR @show_
    reorderpoint = 1 OR @show_standard_cost = 1
    SELECT @sql_command = @sql_command + '
        Product.Color AS product_color,
        Product.SafetyStockLevel AS product_safety_stock_level,
        Product.ReorderPoint AS product_reorderpoint,
        Product.StandardCost AS product_standard_cost';
-- In the event that there is a comma at the end of our command
   string, remove it before continuing.
IF (SELECT SUBSTRING(@sql_command, LEN(@sql_command), 1)) = ','
        SELECT @sql_command = LEFT(@sql_command, LEN(@sql_command) - 1);
SELECT @sql_command = @sql_command + '
FROM Production.Product'
-- Put together the JOINs based on what tables are required by the
   search.
IF (@product_model IS NOT NULL OR @show_product_model = 1 OR @show_
catalog_description = 1)
        SELECT @sql_command = @sql_command + '
LEFT JOIN Production.ProductModel
ON Product.ProductModelID = ProductModel.ProductModelID';
IF (@product_subcategory IS NOT NULL OR @show_subcategory_modified_
date = 1 OR @show_product_subcategory = 1)
        SELECT @sql_command = @sql_command + '
LEFT JOIN Production.ProductSubcategory
ON Product.ProductSubcategoryID = ProductSubcategory.
ProductSubcategoryID';
IF (@product_sizemeasurecode IS NOT NULL OR @show_product_
sizemeasurecode = 1)
        SELECT @sql_command = @sql_command + '
LEFT JOIN Production.UnitMeasure SizeUnitMeasureCode
ON Product.SizeUnitMeasureCode = SizeUnitMeasureCode.
UnitMeasureCode';
```

```
        IF (@product_weightunitmeasurecode IS NOT NULL OR @show_product_
        weightunitmeasurecode = 1)
                SELECT @sql_command = @sql_command + '
        LEFT JOIN Production.UnitMeasure WeightUnitMeasureCode
        ON Product.WeightUnitMeasureCode = SizeUnitMeasureCode.UnitMeasureCode'

        SELECT @sql_command = @sql_command + '
        WHERE 1 = 1'
        -- Build the WHERE clause based on which tables are referenced and
            required by the search.
        IF @product_name IS NOT NULL
                SELECT @sql_command = @sql_command + '
                AND Product.Name LIKE @product_name'
        IF @product_number IS NOT NULL
                SELECT @sql_command = @sql_command + '
                AND Product.ProductNumber LIKE @product_number'
        IF @product_model IS NOT NULL
                SELECT @sql_command = @sql_command + '
                AND ProductModel.Name LIKE @product_model'
        IF @product_subcategory IS NOT NULL
                SELECT @sql_command = @sql_command + '
                AND ProductSubcategory.Name = @product_subcategory'
        IF @product_sizemeasurecode IS NOT NULL
                SELECT @sql_command = @sql_command + '
                AND SizeUnitMeasureCode.Name = @product_sizemeasurecode'
        IF @product_weightunitmeasurecode IS NOT NULL
                SELECT @sql_command = @sql_command + '
                AND WeightUnitMeasureCode.Name = @product_
                weightunitmeasurecode'

        PRINT @sql_command;
        EXEC sp_executesql @sql_command, @parameter_list, @product_name,
        @product_number,
        @product_model, @product_subcategory, @product_sizemeasurecode,
        @product_weightunitmeasurecode
END
GO
```

The preceding T-SQL shows the difference that using fewer conditionals makes. The resulting command string will potentially contain some extra columns, but the stored procedure has become simpler, with five conditionals instead of ten. Consider this an alternative for smaller searches, or those where the data sets are straightforward. If the number of columns required per table were to increase in the future, this might need to be redesigned to maintain efficient query execution. Alternatively, for very small tables, `SELECT TableName.*` could also be used to further reduce the size of the stored procedure. The following T-SQL shows this change for the `ProductModel` table:

```
IF @show_product_model = 1 OR @show_catalog_description = 1 SELECT
@sql_command = @sql_command + 'ProductModel.*,';
```

While simple, this would return an indeterminate number of columns, which could become a bottleneck in the future if tables continue to add new columns. In addition, with this syntax, we lose control over the column names, which could result in duplicates in a case where many tables use the same column names for different data elements. In *AdventureWorks*, we would have no way to differentiate between the product name and the product model name, as both columns are simply called "Name." Please use caution whenever returning all columns from a table using *. This can be a useful tool for a small table with a very predictable and unchanging structure. On the other hand, if the table changes, this stored procedure could easily break or return additional unexpected data.

The joins in our dynamic search only happen when a column is required from a table. This occurs if a column is explicitly requested via an input parameter bit, or if it is filtered on.

The combination of dynamic joins, dynamic SELECT statement, and dynamic WHERE ensures that we do not access any table that isn't required for the search grid. While our stored procedure has become larger, the command strings generated by it are shrinking, which is the primary goal of this exercise.

Search Grid Considerations

The stored procedure presented is a huge leap forward in terms of customization, but it is more complex than our previous searches. With any added complexity comes a variety of considerations that will help in making intelligent design decisions, as well as avoid pitfalls associated with this level of flexibility.

Disallow Blank Searches

A common theme throughout all of the searches so far has been to provide the end user with as much control as possible over what they see and can filter on. This can potentially be dangerous, though, if the data set is large and the user requests a huge amount of that data. It's generally a good practice to not allow a user to perform a blank search unless the data set is sufficiently small or paged in such a way that it won't be a strain on the database server—that is, if they go to the search page and click "Go" without providing any additional details, then we should either do nothing or return a meaningful error:

```
IF COALESCE(@product_name, @product_number, @product_model, @product_
subcategory, @product_sizemeasurecode, @product_weightunitmeasurecode) IS NULL
    RETURN;
```

This additional COALESCE statement at the start of the stored procedure will immediately exit if none of the filter criteria are populated. Consider these EXEC statements:

```
EXEC dbo.search_products @show_product_model = 1;
EXEC dbo.search_products;
```

For both of these search attempts, the stored procedure will exit as soon as it reaches the COALESCE check above. If preferred, RAISEERROR can be used to throw a specific error back to the application that the search originated from. Regardless, it's up the application as to how to handle scenarios where no data set is returned, or an error is thrown, to ensure that the end user receives a friendly and helpful message that explains why their search was invalid.

When a search returns too much data, it can pose a security threat, as a repeated operation that is excessively expensive could hog system resources and act as a denial of service attack, whether intentional or not.

Data Paging

It is rare that we would want to blindly return all rows in a result set. Consider your favorite Internet search engine: it's unlikely that any will return more than 25 results at a time by default. In a web search scenario, a single search could return millions of hits. For the sake of the search provider and your own computer, avoiding returning millions of rows is beneficial!

Paging can be accomplished in a number of ways, depending on the version of SQL Server that you are developing with. The simplest method is for the application to request a specific set of IDs, and then request additional sets of IDs whenever the user clicks "Next." Since users typically won't click through hundreds of pages of search results, querying the database each time they click isn't likely to be a significant drain on resources. If a data set is such that the end user will want to eventually view everything, then selecting all of the data and allowing the application to page through it as necessary will likely be more efficient than selecting 25 rows over and over again. The following T-SQL will return 25 products where the color is NULL:

```
SELECT
       Name,
       ProductNumber,
       Color,
       Size,
       DaysToManufacture
FROM Production.Product
WHERE Product.Color IS NULL
AND ProductID BETWEEN 316 AND 359
```

Alternatively, a common table expression (CTE) can be used so that row numbers can be compared, instead of directly pulling IDs for a set of products:

```
WITH CTE_PRODUCTS AS (
       SELECT
              ROW_NUMBER() OVER (ORDER BY ProductID ASC) AS rownum,
              Name,
              ProductNumber,
              Color,
              Size,
              DaysToManufacture
       FROM Production.Product
       WHERE Product.Color IS NULL)
SELECT
       Name,
       ProductNumber,
       Color,
       Size,
       DaysToManufacture
```

```
FROM CTE_PRODUCTS
WHERE rownum BETWEEN 5 AND 29;
```

The results returned by each of these queries are the same. While the second query is easier for the application to process (as it doesn't need to manage ProductIDs), it will be less efficient because it needs to reorder the data each time a search is performed. The ID search simply grabs 25 rows using a clustered index seek, rather than adding row numbers to the entire data set, prior to paging.

OFFSET allows for paging without the need for window functions or explicit ID references. The following statement will return 25 products, starting at the 51st product, based on the ProductID:

```
SELECT
      Name,
      ProductNumber,
      Color,
      Size,
      DaysToManufacture
FROM Production.Product
WHERE Product.Color IS NULL
ORDER BY ProductID ASC
OFFSET 50 ROWS
FETCH NEXT 25 ROWS ONLY
```

Using this syntax, an ORDER BY clause must be present, as it is necessary to determine the column to page off of. The OFFSET determines how many rows to skip before selecting the data we are interested in. Lastly, FETCH NEXT tells SQL Server how many rows to retrieve from that starting point. FETCH NEXT is optional and if omitted, all data after the offset will be returned. This syntax is the simplest and easiest to use from an application perspective, as the OFFSET and FETCH NEXT row counts can be provided by an application, T-SQL, or user input, in order to quickly return exactly the result set desired.

We will investigate performance in further detail in a later chapter, but for now it is worth mentioning that paging performance can vary greatly based on the T-SQL syntax used. Different use cases will lend themselves to different approaches, though each option mentioned is capable of effectively returning paged results based on whatever user input is provided.

Conditional Paging

If the size of a data set can vary greatly, then it may be beneficial to perform some initial intelligence on the data prior to gathering it. For example, if we know that a data set contains only 13 rows, then there is no need to page it. We can select all rows from our 13 row results in a single statement and have no further work to do. Similarly, if a result set is 30 rows, we know that it will fit on 1 to 2 pages, depending on how many results are displayed per page. For both of those scenarios, it is likely that the end user will view most, if not all, results most of the time. If a search returns a huge set of results, then we know that paging is necessary. In addition, we know that the user will almost certainly not view all results in the set. If results are returned based on a relevance score, such as with a web search engine, then it's very likely the user will only view the first 10 or 20 before either moving on or adjusting their search criteria.

The page size can also be dynamic, if desired, as an additional way to make the result set as useful as possible. For example, if 26 results are returned, having to click to a new page for a single result would be somewhat wasteful. Instead, simply returning all 26 at once would be easier, more efficient, and convenient for the user. If results are verbose and include additional details that consume a large amount of space, then returning fewer results automatically (based on how verbose) could be advantageous.

Knowing how an application works can help in determining the optimal method of paging. The following is an example of a search where we return line item details for orders based on a tracking number wildcard search. As a common search, it's likely that `CarrierTrackingNumber` will be indexed and that most searches will be for a single tracking number only, but the application may have different requirements with regard to how to execute the search, as seen in Listing 3-7.

Listing 3-7. Sales Order Detail Search, with a Variety of Input Parameters

```
CREATE PROCEDURE dbo.search_sales_order_detail
@tracking_number NVARCHAR(25), @offset_by_this_many_rows INT = 0, @row_
count_to_return INT = 25, @return_all_results BIT = 0
AS
BEGIN
    SET NOCOUNT ON;
    -- Add wildcard delimiters to the tracking number.
    SELECT @tracking_number = '%' + @tracking_number + '%';
```

```
-- If the result set is small, return all results to the application
   for display.
IF @return_all_results = 1
BEGIN
    SELECT
        SalesOrderHeader.OrderDate,
        SalesOrderHeader.ShipDate,
        SalesOrderHeader.Status,
        SalesOrderHeader.PurchaseOrderNumber,
        SalesOrderDetail.CarrierTrackingNumber,
        SalesOrderDetail.OrderQty,
        SalesOrderDetail.UnitPrice,
        SalesOrderDetail.UnitPriceDiscount,
        SalesOrderDetail.LineTotal,
        Product.Name,
        Product.ProductNumber
    FROM Sales.SalesOrderHeader
    INNER JOIN Sales.SalesOrderDetail
    ON SalesOrderHeader.SalesOrderID = SalesOrderDetail.
    SalesOrderID
    INNER JOIN Production.Product
    ON SalesOrderDetail.ProductID = Product.ProductID
    WHERE CarrierTrackingNumber LIKE @tracking_number
    ORDER BY SalesOrderDetail.SalesOrderDetailID;
END
ELSE
BEGIN
    SELECT
        SalesOrderHeader.OrderDate,
        SalesOrderHeader.ShipDate,
        SalesOrderHeader.Status,
        SalesOrderHeader.PurchaseOrderNumber,
        SalesOrderDetail.CarrierTrackingNumber,
        SalesOrderDetail.OrderQty,
```

```
                SalesOrderDetail.UnitPrice,
                SalesOrderDetail.UnitPriceDiscount,
                SalesOrderDetail.LineTotal,
                Product.Name,
                Product.ProductNumber
        FROM Sales.SalesOrderHeader
        INNER JOIN Sales.SalesOrderDetail
        ON SalesOrderHeader.SalesOrderID = SalesOrderDetail.SalesOrderID
        INNER JOIN Production.Product
        ON SalesOrderDetail.ProductID = Product.ProductID
        WHERE CarrierTrackingNumber LIKE @tracking_number
        ORDER BY SalesOrderDetail.SalesOrderDetailID
        OFFSET @offset_by_this_many_rows ROWS
        FETCH NEXT @row_count_to_return ROWS ONLY;
    END
END
GO
```

This search provides four options. The tracking number input, which can be all or part of a tracking number, is the only required option. @offset_by_this_many_rows determines if we are skipping ahead in the search and @row_count_to_return indicates the number of rows to select. The @return_all_results parameter can be set to 1 in order to bypass all paging logic and return everything. This can be useful if the input is a complete tracking number, where returning all parts of the shipment would make logical sense, and it's unlikely that the data returned would be unusually large. In this example, the application handles the check for the input format to verify this, but the stored procedure could do this as well if it were universally constant that a full tracking number results in all data being returned.

Defaults are placed on the input parameters to simplify assumptions, but could be left off if the application wished to always populate them. Let's consider some sample input to this new search:

```
EXEC dbo.search_sales_order_detail '4911-403C-98', NULL, NULL, 1;
```

This search is for a complete tracking number. As a result, the application indicated that all results should be returned, regardless of the data size. This is accomplished by setting @return_all_results to "1". This execution returns 12 rows, which constitute every sales order detail that has a carrier tracking number of "4911-403C-98".

```
EXEC dbo.search_sales_order_detail '491';
```

This search is much more generic, only searching for three characters of a tracking number. Without any additional input, the stored procedure defaults to selecting the first 25 rows only. If more are required, the application will need to provide additional parameter values to account for this:

```
EXEC dbo.search_sales_order_detail '491', 25, 50, 0;
```

By adding an offset of 25 rows, and a row count of 50, this stored procedure call will return the next 50 rows of this tracking number search. If the user continues to click "Next," then more results would be returned by increasing the offset. Alternatively, the user could refine their search, adding more characters to their tracking number input string in order to more effectively find what they are looking for.

This example did not involve any dynamic SQL, but the techniques used can be applied to any searching mechanism to include some level of pagination in the result set. Paging is a common and often necessary way to add control over a data set, increase customization by the end user, and maintain good performance by not returning too much data at one time.

Search Limitations

If you've ever tried searching a folder on your computer using very generic search terms, you've experienced the latency associated with running a very generic search. When building a search procedure for any application, it's important to disallow or limit any user input that could cause strain on their search experience, as well as on server performance. A common approach is to not allow blank searches. That is, if the user tries to click "Go" with no text in any search box, either do nothing or return a message requesting more information. Alternatively, the search could simply grab the first 50 results, display them, and wait for further user input as to the next steps to take. At no point in the process do we want to return excessive amounts of data from the database server, nor do we want to make the end user wait forever for that data to appear.

An additional way to limit data volume is to ensure that too many columns cannot be requested from a custom search grid. If a results grid could theoretically have 500 different columns, it would be in our best interest to limit them to a much smaller number. Depending on the application, 10 columns may be enough, or 25, or maybe even 50. That limit would be based on average application usage, as well as the size of the columns and the amount of resources needed to return the data. If the search begins to experience lag after the 30th column, then capping the number of columns in the results grid to 25 would be sensible.

Input-Based Search

In our previous example, we allowed parameters to be passed into a search stored procedure that allowed for quite a bit of customization. As an additional step, we can parse user input and determine from the format what sort of data is being searched for. This is useful for the corner search box found on many web pages. In these applications, there is sometimes an advanced search feature available, but the average user wants to enter text in a single place and receive immediate feedback. These searches can be a bit messy, as we may need to search many types of data, and running a blanket search on many different columns at once will likely perform poorly and return false positives. If the search instructions indicate that the text can be entered in one of many forms before defaulting to a single text description, then we can optimize our search to focus on a select few indexed columns rather than every possible search criteria all at once. Listing 3-8 illustrates a sales order search that allows a variety of inputs to be entered.

Listing 3-8. Sales Order Detail Search That Detects Input Type Based on String Form

```
IF EXISTS (SELECT * FROM sys.procedures WHERE procedures.name = 'search_
sales_order_detail')
BEGIN
        DROP PROCEDURE dbo.search_sales_order_detail;
END
GO

CREATE PROCEDURE dbo.search_sales_order_detail
        @input_search_data NVARCHAR(25), @offset_by_this_many_rows INT = 0,
        @row_count_to_return INT = 25, @return_all_results BIT = 0
```

```
AS
BEGIN
      SET NOCOUNT ON;
      -- For this search procedure, do not allow blank input.  If blank is
         entered, return immediately with no result set.
      -- Input parameter does not allow NULLs.
      IF LTRIM(RTRIM(@input_search_data)) = ''
            RETURN;

      -- Pad the input string with spaces, in case it isn't 25 characters
         long.  This will avoid string truncation below.
      SET @input_search_data = @input_search_data + REPLICATE(' ', 25 -
      LEN(@input_search_data));

      -- Parse the @input_search_data to determine the data it references.
      DECLARE @input_type NVARCHAR(25);

      -- Search by Sales Order Number: Starts with "SO" and at least 5
         numbers.
      IF (LEFT(@input_search_data, 2) = 'SO' AND ISNUMERIC(SUBSTRING
      (@input_search_data, 3, 5)) = 1)
            SET @input_type = 'SalesOrderNumber';
      ELSE
      -- Search by Purchase Order Number: Starts with "PO" and at least 10
         numbers.
      IF (LEFT(@input_search_data, 2) = 'PO' AND ISNUMERIC(SUBSTRING
      (@input_search_data, 3, 10)) = 1)
            SET @input_type = 'PurchaseOrderNumber';
      ELSE
      -- Search by Account Number: Starts with two number, a hyphen, 4
         numbers, a hyphen, and at least 6 additional numbers.
      IF (ISNUMERIC(LEFT(@input_search_data, 2)) = 1 AND SUBSTRING(@input_
      search_data, 3, 1) = '-' AND ISNUMERIC(SUBSTRING(@input_search_data,
      4, 4)) = 1
            AND SUBSTRING(@input_search_data, 8, 1) = '-' AND
            ISNUMERIC(SUBSTRING(@input_search_data, 9, 6)) = 1)
            SET @input_type = 'AccountNumber';
```

```
ELSE
-- Search by Carrier Tracking Number: 4 Alphanumeric, 1 hyphen, 4
   alphanumeric, one hyphen, and two alphanumeric.
IF (PATINDEX('%[^a-zA-Z0-9]%' , LEFT(@input_search_data, 4)) = 0
AND SUBSTRING(@input_search_data, 5, 1) = '-' AND PATINDEX('%[^a-
zA-Z0-9]%' , SUBSTRING(@input_search_data, 6, 4)) = 0
      AND SUBSTRING(@input_search_data, 10, 1) = '-' AND
      PATINDEX('%[^a-zA-Z0-9]%' , SUBSTRING(@input_search_data,
      11, 2)) = 0)
      SET @input_type = 'CarrierTrackingNumber';
ELSE
      -- Search by Product Number: Starts with two letters, a dash,
         and four alphanumeric characters: AA-12YZ.
IF (PATINDEX('%[^a-zA-Z]%' , LEFT(@input_search_data, 2)) = 0 AND
SUBSTRING(@input_search_data, 3, 1) = '-' AND PATINDEX('%[^a-
zA-Z0-9]%' , SUBSTRING(@input_search_data, 4, 4)) = 0)
      SET @input_type = 'ProductNumber';
ELSE
-- Default our input to carrier tracking number, if no other format
   is identified.
      SET @input_type = 'CarrierTrackingNumber';

-- Remove additional padding to prevent bad string matches.
-- Add a wildcard delimiter to the end of the input, to account for
   additional characters at the end.
SELECT @input_search_data = LTRIM(RTRIM(@input_search_data)) + '%';

DECLARE @sql_command NVARCHAR(MAX);
DECLARE @parameter_list NVARCHAR(MAX);

-- Create the parameter list and initial command string.
SET @parameter_list = '@input_search_data NVARCHAR(25), @offset_by_
this_many_rows INT, @row_count_to_return INT';
SET @sql_command = '
      SELECT
            SalesOrderHeader.OrderDate,
            SalesOrderHeader.ShipDate,
            SalesOrderHeader.Status,
```

```
                SalesOrderHeader.PurchaseOrderNumber,
                SalesOrderHeader.AccountNumber,
                SalesOrderHeader.SalesOrderNumber,
                SalesOrderDetail.CarrierTrackingNumber,
                SalesOrderDetail.OrderQty,
                SalesOrderDetail.UnitPrice,
                SalesOrderDetail.UnitPriceDiscount,
                SalesOrderDetail.LineTotal,
                Product.Name,
                Product.ProductNumber
        FROM Sales.SalesOrderHeader
        INNER JOIN Sales.SalesOrderDetail
        ON SalesOrderHeader.SalesOrderID = SalesOrderDetail.SalesOrderID
        INNER JOIN Production.Product
        ON SalesOrderDetail.ProductID = Product.ProductID';

-- Based on the value of @input_type, dynamically generate the WHERE
    clause.
IF @input_type = 'ProductNumber'
        SET @sql_command = @sql_command + '
        WHERE Product.ProductNumber LIKE @input_search_data';
ELSE IF @input_type = 'SalesOrderNumber'
        SET @sql_command = @sql_command + '
        WHERE SalesOrderHeader.SalesOrderNumber LIKE @input_search_
        data';
ELSE IF @input_type = 'PurchaseOrderNumber'
        SET @sql_command = @sql_command + '
        WHERE SalesOrderHeader.PurchaseOrderNumber LIKE @input_search_
        data';
ELSE IF @input_type = 'AccountNumber'
        SET @sql_command = @sql_command + '
        WHERE SalesOrderHeader.AccountNumber LIKE @input_search_data';
ELSE IF @input_type = 'CarrierTrackingNumber'
        SET @sql_command = @sql_command + '
        WHERE SalesOrderDetail.CarrierTrackingNumber LIKE @input_
        search_data';
```

```
SET @sql_command = @sql_command + '
    ORDER BY SalesOrderDetail.SalesOrderDetailID';

-- If there are any row limitations, append them here.
SET @sql_command = @sql_command + '
    OFFSET @offset_by_this_many_rows ROWS';
IF @return_all_results = 0
    SET @sql_command = @sql_command + '
    FETCH NEXT @row_count_to_return ROWS ONLY;';

PRINT @sql_command;
EXEC sp_executesql @sql_command, @parameter_list, @input_search_data,
@offset_by_this_many_rows, @row_count_to_return;
END
```

String comparisons early in the stored procedure check @input_search_data and determine the alphanumeric and symbol locations within the string. Based on parsing this parameter, the type of data stored in it is assessed, and the @input_type assigned. When we build our dynamic SQL statement, the WHERE clause is completely based on the type of input provided. PATINDEX is used to determine if any characters not in a specific range are present in a string. If we want to verify that a string of four characters are alphanumeric, then checking to see if any characters not in the ranges of a-z, A-Z, or 0-9 will accomplish that goal. The carat "^" is used to indicate a logical NOT, so the comparison string '%[^a-zA-Z0-9]%' will return a nonzero result if any non-alphanumeric characters are present in the input string.

Alternatively, a drop-down menu could appear along with the search box, indicating what the input type is. This is also effective, but the preceding example was focused on the idea of a one-click solution, which is advantageous when the number of potential inputs (and their structure) is limited. It's also a simpler and faster interface for the end user to learn and utilize. The input parsing could be managed in the application as well, if that was preferable.

The main downside to the implementation is flexibility, but if the application controls what types of input can be provided, then there will be no need to check for every possible combination of letters and numbers. While not demonstrated, it would also be possible to use more generic checks for different data types. For example, any string with PO in front is a purchase order number, or any that begins with SO is a sales order number. In this implementation, we defaulted to the carrier tracking number in the event that the input string did not match up with any of our type checks. This is arbitrary and could default to any format, or return with no results (if that were preferable).

The following are a handful of example executions of the aforementioned stored procedure:

```
EXEC dbo.search_sales_order_detail @input_search_data = 'BK-M82B-42';
```

This represents a search for a specific product, based on the product number. The resulting WHERE clause in the command string will appear as a check only against this column:

```
WHERE Product.ProductNumber LIKE @input_search_data
ORDER BY SalesOrderDetail.SalesOrderDetailID
OFFSET @offset_by_this_many_rows ROWS
FETCH NEXT @row_count_to_return ROWS ONLY;
```

The remainder of the statement is constant for any executions where we do not explicitly want to return all results (using the @return_all_results parameter).

```
EXEC dbo.search_sales_order_detail @input_search_data = 'PO125', @offset_
by_this_many_rows = 0, @row_count_to_return = 50, @return_all_results = 0;
```

This statement searches for a portion of a purchase order number while returning 50 rows at a time, instead of the default of 25:

```
WHERE SalesOrderHeader.PurchaseOrderNumber LIKE @input_search_data
ORDER BY SalesOrderDetail.SalesOrderDetailID
OFFSET @offset_by_this_many_rows ROWS
FETCH NEXT @row_count_to_return ROWS ONLY;
```

The only difference between this T-SQL segment and the last is the filtering on PurchaseOrderNumber rather than ProductNumber. The row offset and row count to return are specified by their respective parameters, regardless of the values passed in.

```
EXEC dbo.search_sales_order_detail @input_search_data = 'SO43662', @return_
all_results = 1;
```

This is a search based on a specific sales order number. By setting @return_all_results to 1, the FETCH NEXT section is omitted, resulting in the following command string:

```
WHERE SalesOrderHeader.SalesOrderNumber LIKE @input_search_data
ORDER BY SalesOrderDetail.SalesOrderDetailID
OFFSET @offset_by_this_many_rows ROWS
```

The offset is still specified, but will default to zero as no value was provided. Alternatively, we can remove this clause altogether when @offset_by_this_many_rows is zero.

Result Row Count

It can be advantageous to return the total row count of a query, even if we are only returning a paged set of 25 (or 10 or 50) rows. We may want to know that a result set contains 118 rows, and that only 25 are being displayed at the moment. Oftentimes the end user will need to know that, in addition to currently viewing rows 51-75, that they are viewing those rows out of a total set of 118. This provides immediate feedback on the effectiveness of their search terms, as well as some validation that the result set is what they expect. If the total row count were too high, the response would be to refine the search to be more specific. If the row count was too low, then we'd want to verify that we are entering valid data and that the data we are searching for is actually there.

This count can be calculated ahead of time as a separate operation, which would result in an additional query using the same filters as the data retrieval itself. Listing 3-9 is an example that uses a simple purchase order search.

Listing 3-9. Retrieving a Count of Rows for a Specific Result Set

```
SELECT
        COUNT(*)
FROM Sales.SalesOrderHeader
INNER JOIN Sales.SalesOrderDetail
ON SalesOrderHeader.SalesOrderID = SalesOrderDetail.SalesOrderID
INNER JOIN Production.Product
ON SalesOrderDetail.ProductID = Product.ProductID
WHERE SalesOrderHeader.PurchaseOrderNumber LIKE 'PO125%';
```

This count can be executed as a separate query and cached for later use, in the event that the user continues to page through their current result set. This allows us to only perform an expensive count once, rather than each time the same data set is accessed. The query in Listing 3-10 returns 290 as the count of rows matching the criteria specified.

Listing 3-10. Retrieving Current and Total Row Counts Alongside the Result Set

```
SELECT
        COUNT(SalesOrderDetailID) OVER (ORDER BY SalesOrderDetailID ROWS
        BETWEEN UNBOUNDED PRECEDING AND CURRENT ROW) AS row_count_current,
        COUNT(SalesOrderDetailID) OVER (ORDER BY SalesOrderDetailID ROWS BETWEEN
        UNBOUNDED PRECEDING AND UNBOUNDED FOLLOWING) AS row_count_total,
        SalesOrderHeader.OrderDate,
        SalesOrderHeader.ShipDate,
        SalesOrderHeader.Status,
        SalesOrderHeader.PurchaseOrderNumber,
        SalesOrderHeader.AccountNumber,
        SalesOrderHeader.SalesOrderNumber,
        SalesOrderDetail.CarrierTrackingNumber,
        SalesOrderDetail.OrderQty,
        SalesOrderDetail.UnitPrice,
        SalesOrderDetail.UnitPriceDiscount,
        SalesOrderDetail.LineTotal,
        Product.Name,
        Product.ProductNumber
FROM Sales.SalesOrderHeader
INNER JOIN Sales.SalesOrderDetail
ON SalesOrderHeader.SalesOrderID = SalesOrderDetail.SalesOrderID
INNER JOIN Production.Product
ON SalesOrderDetail.ProductID = Product.ProductID
WHERE SalesOrderHeader.PurchaseOrderNumber LIKE 'PO125%'
ORDER BY SalesOrderDetail.SalesOrderDetailID;
```

This query returns the same result set, but includes a few counts alongside that data. The first count, row_count_current, is the row number of the current sales order detail record as ordered by the SalesOrderDetailID. row_count_total, on the other hand, will return the total row count for the result set, regardless of the current row number (which is 290, as it was previously). The ROWS addition is syntax that allows us to determine the window over which the window function processes rows of data over more specifically. ROWS UNBOUNDED PRECEEDING AND CURRENT ROW will count from the start of the result set through the current row, hence returning an increasing row count based on the ORDER BY clause. ROWS UNBOUNDED PRECEEDING AND UNBOUNDED FOLLOWING, on the other hand, will return a count of all rows in the data set, regardless of the current row number. UNBOUNDED PRECEEDING references the start of the result set, whereas UNBOUNDED FOLLOWING references the end of the result set.

The last step is to combine our efforts above so that we can retrieve row counts while also paging the data set, as seen in Listing 3-11.

Listing 3-11. Retrieving Current and Total Row Counts Alongside the Result Set with Data Paging

```
WITH CTE_SEARCH_DATA AS (
    SELECT
        COUNT(SalesOrderDetailID) OVER (ORDER BY SalesOrderDetailID
        ROWS BETWEEN UNBOUNDED PRECEDING AND CURRENT ROW) AS row_count_
        current,
        COUNT(SalesOrderDetailID) OVER (ORDER BY SalesOrderDetailID
        ROWS BETWEEN UNBOUNDED PRECEDING AND UNBOUNDED FOLLOWING) AS
        row_count_total,
        SalesOrderHeader.OrderDate,
        SalesOrderHeader.ShipDate,
        SalesOrderHeader.Status,
        SalesOrderHeader.PurchaseOrderNumber,
        SalesOrderHeader.AccountNumber,
        SalesOrderHeader.SalesOrderNumber,
        SalesOrderDetail.CarrierTrackingNumber,
        SalesOrderDetail.OrderQty,
        SalesOrderDetail.UnitPrice,
        SalesOrderDetail.UnitPriceDiscount,
        SalesOrderDetail.LineTotal,
        Product.Name,
        Product.ProductNumber
```

```
        FROM Sales.SalesOrderHeader
        INNER JOIN Sales.SalesOrderDetail
        ON SalesOrderHeader.SalesOrderID = SalesOrderDetail.SalesOrderID
        INNER JOIN Production.Product
        ON SalesOrderDetail.ProductID = Product.ProductID
        WHERE SalesOrderHeader.PurchaseOrderNumber LIKE 'PO125%')
SELECT
        *
FROM CTE_SEARCH_DATA
ORDER BY CTE_SEARCH_DATA.row_count_current
OFFSET 25 ROWS
FETCH NEXT 50 ROWS ONLY;
```

In this last example, we put the previous query into a common table expression and perform the paging operation using row_count_current to determine where to offset the result set from. The convenience of collecting data, row counts, and paging all in a single statement can be very useful, but must be weighed against performance. We will dive into the performance of these statements in a later chapter, but in the meantime, as always, test all new T-SQL thoroughly prior to release in order to avoid any inadvertent performance problems.

Dynamic SQL can be used to determine whether counts need to be included in the result set or not, as well. This can help reduce the amount of work needed when the result set is small, or if we don't need the row count for any further operations. Listing 3-12 illustrates this usage.

Listing 3-12. Dynamic SQL is Used to Make Row Counts into Optional Components of the Result Set

```
DECLARE @include_row_counts BIT = 0;
DECLARE @sql_command NVARCHAR(MAX);

SELECT @sql_command = '
WITH CTE_SEARCH_DATA AS (
        SELECT';
IF @include_row_counts = 1
```

```
        SELECT @sql_command = @sql_command + '
                COUNT(SalesOrderDetailID) OVER (ORDER BY SalesOrderDetailID
                ROWS BETWEEN UNBOUNDED PRECEDING AND CURRENT ROW) AS row_count_
                current,
                COUNT(SalesOrderDetailID) OVER (ORDER BY SalesOrderDetailID
                ROWS BETWEEN UNBOUNDED PRECEDING AND UNBOUNDED FOLLOWING) AS
                row_count_total,';
SELECT @sql_command = @sql_command + '
                SalesOrderHeader.OrderDate,
                SalesOrderHeader.ShipDate,
                SalesOrderHeader.Status,
                SalesOrderHeader.PurchaseOrderNumber,
                SalesOrderHeader.AccountNumber,
                SalesOrderHeader.SalesOrderNumber,
                SalesOrderDetail.CarrierTrackingNumber,
                SalesOrderDetail.OrderQty,
                SalesOrderDetail.UnitPrice,
                SalesOrderDetail.UnitPriceDiscount,
                SalesOrderDetail.LineTotal,
                Product.Name,
                Product.ProductNumber
        FROM Sales.SalesOrderHeader
        INNER JOIN Sales.SalesOrderDetail
        ON SalesOrderHeader.SalesOrderID = SalesOrderDetail.SalesOrderID
        INNER JOIN Production.Product
        ON SalesOrderDetail.ProductID = Product.ProductID
        WHERE SalesOrderHeader.PurchaseOrderNumber LIKE "PO125%")
SELECT
        *
FROM CTE_SEARCH_DATA';
IF @include_row_counts = 1
        SELECT @sql_command = @sql_command + '
ORDER BY CTE_SEARCH_DATA.row_count_current';
```

```
ELSE
SELECT @sql_command = @sql_command + '
ORDER BY CTE_SEARCH_DATA.OrderDate';
SELECT @sql_command = @sql_command + '
OFFSET 25 ROWS
FETCH NEXT 50 ROWS ONLY;';

PRINT @sql_command;
EXEC sp_executesql @sql_command;
```

The parameter @include_row_counts determines if the window functions are included in the command string or not, and updates the ORDER BY accordingly. In this specific example, it is set to zero and the resulting command string is as follows in Listing 3-13.

Listing 3-13. The Command String Generated In Listing 3-12, which Omits Row Count

```
WITH CTE_SEARCH_DATA AS (
    SELECT
            SalesOrderHeader.OrderDate,
            SalesOrderHeader.ShipDate,
            SalesOrderHeader.Status,
            SalesOrderHeader.PurchaseOrderNumber,
            SalesOrderHeader.AccountNumber,
            SalesOrderHeader.SalesOrderNumber,
            SalesOrderDetail.CarrierTrackingNumber,
            SalesOrderDetail.OrderQty,
            SalesOrderDetail.UnitPrice,
            SalesOrderDetail.UnitPriceDiscount,
            SalesOrderDetail.LineTotal,
            Product.Name,
            Product.ProductNumber
    FROM Sales.SalesOrderHeader
```

```
        INNER JOIN Sales.SalesOrderDetail
        ON SalesOrderHeader.SalesOrderID = SalesOrderDetail.SalesOrderID
        INNER JOIN Production.Product
        ON SalesOrderDetail.ProductID = Product.ProductID
        WHERE SalesOrderHeader.PurchaseOrderNumber LIKE 'PO125%')
SELECT
        *
FROM CTE_SEARCH_DATA
ORDER BY CTE_SEARCH_DATA.OrderDate
OFFSET 25 ROWS
FETCH NEXT 50 ROWS ONLY;
```

For a deeper look at window functions and how they are used, check out "Expert T-SQL Window Functions in SQL Server," by Kathi Kellenberger, published by Apress.

Additional Filtering Considerations

There are an infinite number of modifications that can be applied to any of these searching methods to achieve a specific functionality. For example, dynamic SQL can be used to control the grouping used in reporting queries to quickly retrieve specific sums or counts, while omitting others. Listing 3-14 is a simple example of a T-SQL statement that will include one of two different summations (or both, or neither), depending on an input parameter.

Listing 3-14. Sums/Counts Returned Based on Input Parameters, Using Dynamic SQL

```
DECLARE @start_date DATE = '2014-06-01';
DECLARE @end_date DATE = '2014-06-30';
DECLARE @include_order_count BIT = 1;
DECLARE @include_order_total BIT = 1;
IF @include_order_count = 0 AND @include_order_total = 0
        RETURN;
DECLARE @parameter_list NVARCHAR(MAX);
DECLARE @sql_command NVARCHAR(MAX);
```

```
SELECT @parameter_list = '@start_date DATE, @end_date DATE'

SELECT @sql_command = '
      SELECT';
IF @include_order_count = 1
SELECT @sql_command = @sql_command + '
      COUNT(DISTINCT SalesOrderDetail.SalesOrderDetailID) AS sales_order_
      count,';
IF @include_order_total = 1
SELECT @sql_command = @sql_command + '
      SUM(SalesOrderDetail.LineTotal) AS total_revenue,';
SELECT @sql_command = @sql_command + '
      1 AS place_holder
      FROM Sales.SalesOrderHeader
      INNER JOIN Sales.SalesOrderDetail
      ON SalesOrderHeader.SalesOrderID = SalesOrderDetail.SalesOrderID
      WHERE OrderDate BETWEEN @start_date AND @end_date';

PRINT @sql_command;
EXEC sp_executesql @sql_command, @parameter_list, @start_date, @end_date;
```

In the preceding code, two input bits determine if we should include a count of all sales order detail lines, a sum of all line charges, both, or neither. This can be extended greatly to reduce the number of complex operations necessary in a stored procedure. Alternatively, IF...THEN statements could be used to separately check whether each metric should be evaluated or not. This would work well for a small number of variables, but for a complex data set where there could be many different queries against many tables, gathering them all in a single efficient step may be a far fast and more efficient alternative to grabbing each, one at a time.

Alternatives

A common method of implementing search functionality is to use an ORM (object-relational mapping) to automatically generate T-SQL for search queries on an ad hoc basis. ORMs can be powerful, easy to implement, and inexpensive to maintain. Their strength lies in being able to generate T-SQL based on a relational model, without the need to write each and every query. By designing a relational model and mapping database objects to objects in application code, the need to write search queries is eliminated.

As a database grows and its schema becomes more complex, though, the challenges of producing efficient T-SQL will grow. The downside of automated T-SQL is that we lose control over how it is written and cannot easily differentiate between different use-cases. We may know as experienced database professionals how to join 15 tables together in a way that is quick and efficient, but the ORM may not be able to do so.

To choose the best tool for the job, consider the following questions about a given data model:

- Are there many entities to be joined, or are only a handful needed?

- Do we need to pick and choose for large numbers of columns?

- Is performance important, or can queries tolerate some amount of latency?

- How much control do we want over the specifics of a search?

The advantages of dynamic SQL are control and performance. With complete control over the structure of T-SQL, we gain the ability to tune and optimize performance to be as fast as possible. By being able to control our code, we can always get whatever results we are looking for, even if those results include unusual mathematical functions, aggregate functions, or other constructs not typically available within a standard ORM framework.

The downside of dynamic SQL for searching is that it requires more development time to write stored procedures to manage those queries. The goal should be to balance these needs to ensure that we use dynamic SQL in areas where the greatest gains can be achieved in performance and customization. An ORM will provide maintainability, but at the cost of flexibility and performance.

Conclusion

Using dynamic SQL to create flexible, efficient search routines creates a limitless number of ways in which we can access data quickly while customizing the T-SQL solution to match whatever challenges an application may send our way. We could easily have filled hundreds of pages with examples of how different combinations of parameters and T-SQL techniques could create a new or innovative search methodology.

Needless to say, the flexibility is, in itself, the source of innovation. When you run into challenges and are unsure how to get every possible result set that you are looking for, experiment and try turning hard-coded conventions into parameters. While a dynamic SQL stored procedure may appear at first glance to be more complex, the added lines of control logic can easily be formatted and documented to ensure that the resulting code is easy both to read and maintain.

CHAPTER 4

Permissions and Security

In Chapter 2, we did a thorough look into SQL injection and the multitude of ways in which poorly written TSQL can become a target for malicious attacks. Now, we are going to step back and review best practices for SQL Server security, with a focus on dynamic SQL and its typical use cases. Security is an immense topic; one that could easily consume thousands of pages given the opportunity. It also evolves with each day that passes, as new products are released and vulnerabilities are found in older ones. Our goal is to cover the most important and common places where we need to take care while developing database solutions using dynamic SQL, without veering too far into one-offs or edge cases.

The Principle of Least Privilege

The most important consideration in security comes from the Principle of Least Privilege. This says that for any application, the permissions available to it are exactly what are needed to perform its functions, and nothing more. At the database level, this principle is critically important, as database security is the last barrier against data theft. Once a hacker has gained unfettered access to our data, there is little left for us to protect against. The most important considerations are to determine what users an application should run under, and what permissions that user should be assigned.

The most significant mistake that companies often make is to use a sysadmin user for their applications. This is convenient because it will always work, regardless of the TSQL that is executed. No matter what the application does, this user will provide total access to everything. While convenient, it poses a security nightmare in that the application using this account could perform actions that shouldn't be allowed. Worse, if the application was somehow compromised and a malicious user gained access to execute TSQL commands, they would now have access to everything.

© Edward Pollack 2019
E. Pollack, *Dynamic SQL*, https://doi.org/10.1007/978-1-4842-4318-3_4

Consider the following list of hypothetical applications and functions:

- Order processing system

- File transfer application

- Report generation

- Software installer

- Backup software

Each of these applications performs very different functions and will have to access a database server very differently. What types of permissions should the SQL Server login and user be given to satisfy these functions? Does the application need read access? Write access? Will it need to alter any server configurations or settings? Does the application only access a single database or a set of databases? Can the application be limited to permissions on a small set of objects? Obviously, creating a manual policy with granular access to everything may be more work than it is worth, and would constitute the most in-depth solution. Without going into that much detail, what would the preceding applications generally need to operate?

1. **Order processing system**: Read and write access to a specific database or set of databases (select, insert, update, delete) would provide the ability to create, update, delete, and report on order statuses. If data were read/written via stored procedures, then the ability to execute those routines would be necessary. It is unlikely that the application would have any reason to adjust server settings, alter database schema, access file data, or access unrelated data in other databases or servers.

2. **File transfer application**: Read and write access to tables that document file transfers. The user will likely also need direct access to read and write to a file system. If possible, do not perform file access using xp_cmdshell. This system-stored procedure, when enabled on a database server, provides a huge amount of access to the operating system. A database login with access to data and the operating system is very powerful, and makes for a very tempting target for any hacker looking to compromise an application and its hardware.

3. **Report generation**: Read-only access ideally to only a separate reporting database. Reports generally run best when separated from the transactional data that is their overall data source. The ability to limit reports to read-only access greatly reduces the ways in which these applications can be hacked or broken. If desired, read-access can be further broken down into the tables or stored procedures required for these reports. This ensures that protected or sensitive data is only accessed if needed.

4. **Software installer**: When installing software, the application will often request as much in the way of permissions as possible, often looking for a sysadmin user. It's important that if this level of permissions are given, that they are temporary. Typically, installing or upgrading software is an infrequent event, and one that does not happen with any level of regularity. As such, if a separate user with high levels of permissions is needed, that it is never used for other applications, users, or functions. Do not use sa, or piggy-back on other service accounts where different uses may get mixed up. A DBA installing under their own account is acceptable, so long as they have the permissions required for the installation. Each application should be configured to operate under its own login, separate from other applications.

5. **Backup software**: The primary permissions required will be to take backups of our databases. This software may also need to access some metadata in order to read data about the databases or write log data, but this access will likely be minimal. It's possible that this software could run solely under a backup operator account with no need for any further permissions.

These were some typical examples based on common software applications that we'll see in development or IT, but with each environment comes its own suite of applications and security needs. As long as permissions are reduced to the minimum level required by an application, we can be assured that any security holes that could be exposed via extra permissions will never be realized.

> Provide each application with its own distinct login. This improves security, granularity of permissions, and the ability to debug and identify the source of a query running against a given database

The Principle of Least Privilege does not only apply to a database server, though. Security is best organized in layers, with the database being the lowest layer, and the last one to be accessed by the end user. Ensure that any applications that ultimately can access the database server also run with only the permissions they need. Each layer of security provides an additional lock on the vault that is your data.

Granular Permissions vs. Role Permissions

The most common permissions mistakes involve the server-level role of sysadmin or the database-level role of db_owner. Sysadmin provides a login with complete access to all SQL Server functions and is the most all-encompassing permission available to any login. The db_owner user role provides access to all maintenance and configuration functionality for a single database, as well as access to all objects within it. Both of these roles will generally provide far more access than is required by an application. They often are used for convenience, but can leave gaping security holes if a system were ever compromised.

In general, avoid giving any application login the sysadmin role, especially for an application that is accessible to the Internet and/or the general public. Db_owner is often given to an application that accesses a database unique to its function, but rarely are the permissions provided by that role necessary for the application to work as intended. Does the application need to alter database configuration settings, access system views, or have the ability to drop the database? Odds are good that those functions are not needed (or wanted!), and discretion should be taken when configuring the application user.

While assigning more granular roles may take more time, effort, and planning, doing so ensures that we don't leave a gaping hole where malicious actions could be taken against our database server. If an application only requires read and write access to a set of 20 tables, then consider assigning db_reader and db_writer, instead of db_owner. If the database contains other sensitive data, consider assigning permissions exclusively to those 20 tables, and no others. While we tend to trust the applications we use, vulnerabilities are found every day in both our own software, as well as publically available software, regardless of whether it is open source or proprietary. If any vulnerability could be exploited in an application we rely on, then ensuring it has minimal access to the database server will greatly reduce the damage caused by an attack, and ensure our data is as safe as possible.

To review all server and database roles in this space would be a lengthy and somewhat off-topic digression. Microsoft provides extensive documentation on all built-in roles, as well as how to create your own, if they are inadequate. The following MSDN links provide the current documentation on server and database roles, as well as links to many useful, related topics:

Server Roles: https://msdn.microsoft.com/en-us/library/ms188659.aspx

Database Roles: https://msdn.microsoft.com/en-us/library/ms189121.aspx

Dynamic SQL and Ownership Chaining

When writing, testing, and executing dynamic SQL, permissions run differently than what you may typically experience. Any string that is executed with EXEC or EXECUTE will be run under its own scope, though security context will not be changed. This can be confusing at first, and lead to security errors while running dynamic SQL. Listing 4-1 shows an example that illustrates this behavior.

Listing 4-1. Simple Stored Procedure to Demonstrate Ownership Chaining

```
CREATE PROCEDURE dbo.ownership_chaining_example
AS
BEGIN
    SET NOCOUNT ON;
    -- Select the current security context, for reference.
    SELECT SUSER_SNAME();
    SELECT COUNT(*) FROM Person.Person;

    DECLARE @sql_command NVARCHAR(MAX);
    SELECT @sql_command = 'SELECT SUSER_SNAME();
```

```
    SELECT COUNT(*) FROM Person.Person';

    EXEC sp_executesql @sql_command;
END
GO
```

When we execute this stored procedure, the results are exactly what we expect:
the user (me) for the current security context is returned and then the count of rows in
Person.Person is returned using standard TSQL. After this, the same operations are
performed using dynamic SQL. The results appear in Figure 4-1.

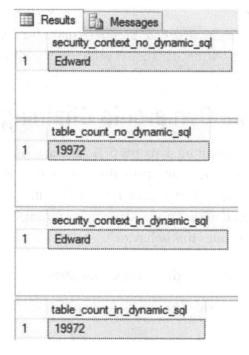

Figure 4-1. *Ownership chaining in inline TSQL vs. dynamic SQL*

The user Edward is a sysadmin, which provides it with complete access to everything
on this SQL Server. The results so far are no surprise: the security context and count
from Person.Person are returned, both outside of, and inside the dynamic SQL sections.
What happens if a different user executes the stored procedure, one with significantly
fewer permissions than my user possesses? To illustrate this, we will create a user called
VeryLimitedUser, with no permissions by default.

```
CREATE USER VeryLimitedUser WITHOUT LOGIN;
GO
CREATE ROLE VeryLimitedRole;
GO
ALTER ROLE VeryLimitedRole ADD MEMBER VeryLimitedUser;
GO
```

Next, we'll assign it execute permissions only on our preceding stored procedure:

```
GRANT EXECUTE ON dbo.ownership_chaining_xample TO VeryLimitedRole;
GO
```

With permissions assigned, we'll switch security contexts temporarily and execute the stored procedure using this new user:

```
EXECUTE AS USER = 'VeryLimitedUser';
GO
EXEC dbo.ownership_chaining_example;
GO
REVERT;
GO
```

The results from the execution are not the same as previously, as shown in Figure 4-2, and require some additional explanation to fully make sense of.

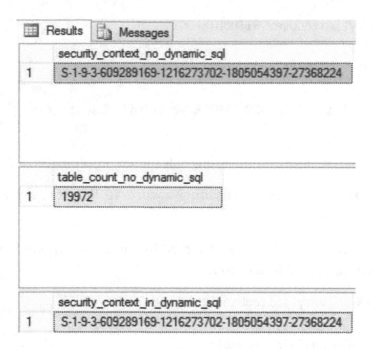

Figure 4-2. *Results prior to a permissions error resulting from a lack of ownership chaining*

Upon trying to select the count from `Person.Person` with the dynamic command, an error is returned by SQL Server:

```
Msg 229, Level 14, State 5, Line 40
The SELECT permission was denied on the object 'Person', database
'AdventureWorks2014', schema 'Person'.
```

Typically, when a user has execute permissions on a stored procedure, then any TSQL contained within the stored procedure will be run normally, regardless of what other objects the user has (or doesn't have) permissions to. In our example, `VeryLimitedUser` does not have read access to `Person.Person`. Despite this limitation, being granted execute permissions on the stored procedure allowed it to access the table. This was not the case for the select within the dynamic SQL statement. What happened here!?

The phenomenon demonstrated is ownership chaining. To facilitate efficient and meaningful security within a database with many objects, the permissions of the initial caller of TSQL are passed along through any additional TSQL within it. For example, when you execute a stored procedure (and have the permissions to do so), any additional TSQL called from within will also execute successfully. Similarly, a user with permissions to a view does not require permissions to all of the underlying objects as well. Once access to the view is granted, the subsequent permissions to tables, views, and functions beneath it are implicitly granted as well.

Ownership chaining greatly simplifies security within SQL Server and allows us to quickly & safely delegate permissions to a stored procedure or view without also having to grant access to every single object referenced within it. For a security administrator, this is a huge timesaver, and allows them to provide permissions based on logical or business need, without having to assign granular security for every referenced object.

There is one big exception to the rules of ownership chaining, though, and that is dynamic SQL. As soon as a dynamic SQL string is executed, the chain is broken, and execution resets to the permissions of the initial caller. In our preceding example, our `VeryLimitedUser` was able to access `Person.Person` without having explicit permissions to it, thanks to ownership chaining. The moment the dynamic SQL was executed, permissions were reverted back to `VeryLimitedUser`, outside of the context of the stored procedure itself. As a result, our user, with no explicit permissions to `Person.Person`, was unable to access it and an error was thrown.

Note that security contexts do not change when ownership chaining is broken. The same result was returned for the current user security context, regardless of the state of the ownership chain. Since the user has no login, the security context is returned as a system-generated numeric string instead.

Be aware of ownership chaining and ensure that the user that executes a stored procedure has adequate permissions for the proc itself, as well as any objects or dynamic SQL called from within.

Typically, this break of the ownership chain will not pose a problem, assuming the permissions that are assigned to the user itself are similar to those that are required for any TSQL (dynamic or otherwise) executed by it. Careful testing of stored procedures and TSQL statements that utilize dynamic SQL can ensure that the results are what are desired and that permission errors are not thrown unexpectedly. Always take the opportunity to test a newly written stored procedure using the login or user that will ultimately run it in production. Also test in an environment that is similar enough to production that we would catch any ownership chaining problems ahead of time. Oftentimes, developers work in sandbox environments with extensive permissions on their personal logins. As a result, everything runs successfully as a sysadmin or db_owner, but might not when the code is moved to production and permissions are more limited.

Changing Security Context On-the-Fly

Typically, the scenarios presented above with ownership chaining will not pose problems in database development. It is possible, though, that in an isolated scenario, we want to allow a specific TSQL statement or stored procedure to run under a different user's security context. One of two situations may arise in which the default permissions are not adequate. A user could have too few permissions and is triggering a variety of security errors due to the breaking of ownership chaining, or inadequate permissions for a specific object. Alternatively, we may have a user with far more permissions than are needed, and we wish to reduce them when executing a sensitive stored procedure.

There are a variety of ways to change security for a given object or execution, each of which we will demonstrate with examples below. Please note that these assignments should be the rare exception, not the rule. If you find that more and more stored procedures are being given special permissions on-the-fly, it may be a sign that your overall security methodology is flawed. Consider reassigning the application user to a better set of database roles, or if necessary, create a new role that provides everything needed. Manually adjusting permissions in TSQL is difficult to document and track, and as a result will greatly increase complexity over time. Minimizing these exceptions will greatly increase maintainability and make understanding your code easier, especially when troubleshooting bugs or unusual behavior.

One example of changing permissions was presented earlier, and that is to change the security context of a user by using EXECUTE AS. This requires that the user executing the context change has the permissions necessary to impersonate the user. This is important; otherwise a user with minimal permissions could try to impersonate a sysadmin or other account with extensive server access. Consider the following TSQL:

```
SELECT SUSER_SNAME() AS SUSER_SNAME, USER_NAME() AS USER_NAME, ORIGINAL_
LOGIN() AS ORIGINAL_LOGIN;
GO
```

```
EXECUTE AS USER = 'VeryLimitedUser';
SELECT SUSER_SNAME() AS SUSER_SNAME, USER_NAME() AS USER_NAME, ORIGINAL_
LOGIN() AS ORIGINAL_LOGIN;
GO
```

Here, we select some basic information about our current user, including the original login, which will return the initial login used for this connection regardless of what permissions have changed since then. Our initial permissions look like this:

```
Edward, dbo, Edward
```

After switching to our limited user, the current security info has changed to the following:

```
S-1-9-3-609289169-1216273702-1805054397-27368224, VeryLimitedUser, Edward
```

This shows that the login and user have changed to our limited access test user, but the original login is still Edward.

```
EXECUTE AS USER = 'Edward';
GO
```

Attempting to switch context back to Edward will fail though, returning the following error:

```
Msg 15517, Level 16, State 1, Line 48
Cannot execute as the database principal because the principal "Edward"
does not exist, this type of principal cannot be impersonated, or you do
not have permission.
```

Now that we are executing as VeryLimitedUser, switching to Edward fails because this user does not have the necessary permissions to impersonate a system administrator. The only way to return back to executing as Edward on this connection is using the REVERT command:

```
REVERT;
GO
SELECT SUSER_SNAME() AS SUSER_SNAME, USER_NAME() AS USER_NAME, ORIGINAL_
LOGIN() AS ORIGINAL_LOGIN;
GO
```

Now our security context is back where we started:

```
Edward, dbo, Edward
```

If we want to change security context and not be able to change again, the WITH NO REVERT option allows for this:

```
EXECUTE AS USER = 'VeryLimitedUser' WITH NO REVERT;
```

As soon as this additional option is added, permissions are locked into VeryLimitedUser for the remainder of this stored procedure or connection. Any attempt to EXECUTE AS another user or revert will fail:

```
REVERT;
GO
EXECUTE AS USER = 'Edward';
```

Running either of these statements will return the following errors:

```
Msg 15196, Level 16, State 1, Line 55
The current security context is non-revertible. The "Revert" statement
failed.
Msg 15517, Level 16, State 1, Line 56
Cannot execute as the database principal because the principal "Edward"
does not exist, this type of principal cannot be impersonated, or you do
not have permission.
```

The errors remind us that REVERT will not work, nor can we switch users. WITH NO REVERT is an excellent way to ensure that an entire stored procedure or connection is made with a single user and that there is no way for anyone to try and acquire more permissions than this. The only way to end an EXECUTE AS statement with this option is for the stored procedure to complete, or the connection to end or be terminated.

The next way to alter permissions is to assign a specific security context to a stored procedure. When this is done, that stored proc will always execute as this user when it executes, regardless of the user that calls it, as seen in Listing 4-2.

Listing 4-2. Stored Procedure Demonstrating EXECUTE AS OWNER

```
CREATE LOGIN Ed WITH PASSWORD = 'ThisIsATestofADBReaderLogin!';
GO
CREATE USER Ed FOR LOGIN Ed;
GO
ALTER ROLE db_datareader ADD MEMBER Ed;
GO

IF EXISTS (SELECT * FROM sys.procedures WHERE procedures.name = 'ownership_
chaining_example')
BEGIN
      DROP PROCEDURE dbo.ownership_chaining_example;
END
GO

CREATE PROCEDURE dbo.ownership_chaining_example
WITH EXECUTE AS 'Ed'
AS
BEGIN
      SET NOCOUNT ON;
      -- Select the current security context, for reference.
      SELECT SUSER_SNAME() AS security_context_no_dynamic_sql;
      SELECT COUNT(*) AS table_count_no_dynamic_sql FROM Person.Person;

      DECLARE @sql_command NVARCHAR(MAX);
      SELECT @sql_command = 'SELECT SUSER_SNAME() AS security_context_in_
      dynamic_sql;

      SELECT COUNT(*) AS table_count_in_dynamic_sql FROM Person.Person';

      EXEC sp_executesql @sql_command;
END
GO

GRANT EXECUTE ON dbo.ownership_chaining_example TO [VeryLimitedUser];
```

```
EXECUTE AS USER = 'VeryLimitedUser';
GO
SELECT SUSER_SNAME();
GO
EXEC dbo.ownership_chaining_example;
GO
```

The EXECUTE AS 'Ed' option will cause the stored procedure to always execute with the permissions of its owner, regardless of what user runs it. In this example, 'Ed' is a user with read-access to the database and execute access on this stored procedure.

This allows a user that normally would not have permissions to access the objects internal to the stored procedure to run it. Alternatively, a user with more permissions than the owner will still execute it with the owner's permissions. The owner of an object is typically its creator, unless changed at a future time.

A potentially more restrictive and useful permissions change is to force a stored procedure to execute within the context of its caller. This is similar to breaking the ownership chain, as was seen in dynamic SQL earlier. Typically, assigning execute permissions to a user will grant that user the ability to execute a stored procedure, even if they do not have access to all underlying objects. EXECUTE AS CALLER forces permissions to be checked in the scope of the user executing the proc, as well as the permissions on the proc itself. This does NOT apply to dynamic SQL, though. This behavior can be observed in Listing 4-3.

Listing 4-3. Stored Procedure Demonstrating EXECUTE AS CALLER

```
IF EXISTS (SELECT * FROM sys.procedures WHERE procedures.name = 'ownership_
chaining_example')
BEGIN
      DROP PROCEDURE dbo.ownership_chaining_example;
END
GO

CREATE PROCEDURE dbo.ownership_chaining_example
WITH EXECUTE AS CALLER
AS
```

```
BEGIN
    SET NOCOUNT ON;
    -- Select the current security context, for reference.
    SELECT SUSER_SNAME() AS security_context_no_dynamic_sql;
    SELECT COUNT(*) AS table_count_no_dynamic_sql FROM Person.Person;

    DECLARE @sql_command NVARCHAR(MAX);
    SELECT @sql_command = 'SELECT SUSER_SNAME() AS security_context_in_
    dynamic_sql;

    SELECT COUNT(*) AS table_count_in_dynamic_sql FROM Person.Person';

    EXEC sp_executesql @sql_command;
END
GO
```

When executed by a user with execute permissions, but not read permissions on
Person.Person, the stored procedure will run under the permissions of whichever user
calls it. As a result, all objects accessed within it will also check that user's permissions.
This ensures that the user that calls a stored procedure has permissions on all the objects
referenced from within. Dynamic SQL executes in its own scope and will result in the
execution failing if permissions on the underlying table are not provided to the user
executing it. If not in dynamic SQL, then it would behave normally.

It is important to remember that, regardless of any security adjustments mentioned,
dynamic SQL will still break the ownership chain. The only ways to ensure that dynamic
SQL executes successfully is to run the calling TSQL with a user that has adequate
permissions, add EXECUTE AS OWNER to the proc, or to grant more granular permissions
over the specific execution, which can be accomplished as seen in Listing 4-4.

Listing 4-4. Stored Procedure Embedding a Security Context Change in
Dynamic SQL

```
CREATE LOGIN EdwardJr WITH PASSWORD = 'AntiSemiJoin17', DEFAULT_DATABASE =
AdventureWorks2014;
GO
USE AdventureWorks2014
```

```
GO
CREATE USER EdwardJr FROM LOGIN EdwardJr;
EXEC sp_addrolemember 'db_owner', 'EdwardJr';
GO

IF EXISTS (SELECT * FROM sys.procedures WHERE procedures.name = 'ownership_
chaining_example')
BEGIN
    DROP PROCEDURE dbo.ownership_chaining_example;
END
GO

CREATE PROCEDURE dbo.ownership_chaining_example
AS
BEGIN
    SET NOCOUNT ON;
    -- Select the current security context, for reference.
    SELECT SUSER_SNAME() AS security_context_no_dynamic_sql;
    SELECT COUNT(*) AS table_count_no_dynamic_sql FROM Person.Person;

    DECLARE @sql_command NVARCHAR(MAX);
    SELECT @sql_command = 'EXECUTE AS LOGIN = "EdwardJr";
    SELECT SUSER_SNAME() AS security_context_in_dynamic_sql;

    SELECT COUNT(*) AS table_count_in_dynamic_sql FROM Person.Person';

    EXEC sp_executesql @sql_command;
END
GO
```

Here, we explicitly change the security context within the dynamic SQL. This is another way to ensure a specific set of permissions once the ownership chain has been broken. In this case, EdwardJr is a new user with read, write, and execute permissions on all objects within this AdventureWorks database. This user has no other server permissions. If we execute this stored procedure as the sysadmin Edward:

```
EXEC dbo.ownership_chaining_example;
```

The results are as follows in Figure 4-3.

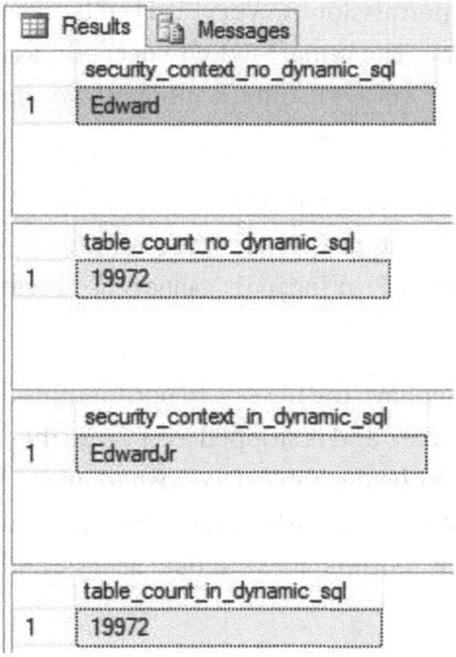

Figure 4-3. Changing security context when executing dynamic SQL

Note that the security context within the dynamic SQL is no longer the same as the stored procedure caller (Edward), but has been changed to our new user EdwardJr, which has far less permissions than a sysadmin. This is a great way to set a predictable level of permissions for dynamic SQL, when the breaking of the ownership chain is a frequent problem. If a user with limited permissions attempts to run this stored procedure, they will run into trouble.

```
GRANT EXECUTE ON dbo.ownership_chaining_example TO VeryLimitedRole;
EXECUTE AS USER = 'VeryLimitedUser';
EXEC dbo.ownership_chaining_example;
REVERT;
GO
```

Here, we grant execute permissions to `VeryLimitedUser`, switch security context, and run the stored procedure. The initial SELECT succeeds, as this user has adequate permissions via the GRANT EXECUTE, but the moment we attempt to switch to EdwardJr, an error is thrown:

```
Msg 15406, Level 16, State 1, Line 142
Cannot execute as the server principal because the principal "EdwardJr"
does not exist, this type of principal cannot be impersonated, or you do
not have permission.
```

The limited user does not have the necessary permissions to impersonate EdwardJr, or any other user for that matter, and is stopped as soon as the permissions change is attempted. This behavior may be desirable if we wish to limit who can execute a specific block of dynamic SQL. As always, let the business needs for your code dictate the minimal level of permissions required for your data access, and adjust as needed along the way, if necessary.

Where Do Security Disasters Come From?

There are many answers to this question, some obvious, others more unexpected. Let's consider one possible definition of a security disaster: any action that is taken, but not desired by the organization and its security personnel. This is intentionally generic, as we want to consider all ways in which "bad things" can happen. Everyone that has worked with databases for long enough has experienced one of these situations:

- A hacking attempt (or suspected hacking attempt) is made against your organization.

- A disgruntled (or malicious) employee alters data without the appropriate authority to do so.

- A developer forgets the WHERE clause in their ad hoc TSQL.

- A planned software release goes awry, resulting in lost data.

- Hardware or software failures result in infrastructure entering an undesirable state.

- Unwanted changes were made via a legitimate use of the application.

- A software or hardware upgrade have unintended consequences.

We could name many more disasters that would easily keep us awake at night, but the key to all of them can be boiled down to two basic categories: lack of planning and human error. How do we manage each risk in a way that is meaningful and nonobtrusive? With the intention of keeping this from straying too far from dynamic SQL, let's briefly review these risks and provide starting points for managing them.

Keep in mind from our discussions earlier that SQL injection, when exploited in the worst possible ways, can quickly hand complete control of a server over to the wrong person at the wrong time. We've already provided a solution to this specific security threat and stated that the best way to defend an application is to provide adequate security on multiple levels so that the sum of these efforts becomes extremely expensive to circumvent. There is no foolproof way to secure a system against all threats. In the same way that a sufficiently motivated robber could probably break into anyone's house, a hacker (or group) that is ambitious enough can find ways to make your life difficult. Discouraging an attack can be achieved by avoiding any glaring security holes that would make your application a tempting target. The robber that sees solid locks, strong windows, and distinct signs of a security system is less likely to risk their freedom over an endeavor that would likely land them in jail.

Lack of planning is rarely identified until it's too late. Companies often put off high availability and disaster recovery solutions until after their first disaster scare. The penetration test is performed for the first time after a high-profile hacking attempt is identified. More rigorous testing of upgrades is planned and conducted after an upgrade goes awry one day. Confirmations are added to the application after the first time a customer accidentally deletes a significant portion of their data. Proper planning can be achieved with a concerted effort by an employee who, as part of their job responsibilities, reviews application, software, and hardware features for common security threats. Ideally a team of individuals from different departments and backgrounds would be involved. While a database professional would likely catch bad TSQL within the server, a developer would find bad code in the application, and a customer service representative might know the top ways in which customers get in trouble with their data.

Do not assign database roles to users unless they absolutely need them. Avoid the sysadmin server role at all costs. Minimize use of the db_owner database role, unless truly required by an application or user.

As discussed earlier, providing applications and utilities with adequate permissions (but no more) is the key for a database administrator to avoid disasters. Consider that there are a plethora of functions in SQL Server that are included in sysadmin and db_owner by default. With each new version of SQL Server, new functionality is added, and those features are often included in those roles as well. As a result, if an application is assigned a user with one of these roles, then it may gain new permissions after an upgrade. Features, even those not currently used, such as replication, in-memory OLTP, Always On, and others may become configurable inadvertently under these roles. Always consider carefully when providing any application or employee with a login. Consider the access it has and the worst things they could possible do and decide if those scenarios are acceptable. It cannot be overstated that a user cannot cause trouble if their permissions don't allow it. This is especially true if permissions are implicitly granted via database or server roles.

Not all dangerous actions are technical in nature. Many, many terrible things result from human error, human nature, or some combination of the two. Consider a scenario that plays out daily at companies around the world: a support rep answers the phone. On the other end is a manager from another division. They sound knowledgeable and are requesting access to restricted data about one of your largest customers. The representative, fearful for their job, provides the data, hangs up, and forgets this ever happened. The trouble is, the person who called didn't work for the company at all, has gained access to important information, and only had to spend a few minutes to acquire it. This technique is known as social engineering and poses a great threat, as no amount of technology can stop us from using our software as it is meant to be used, especially if we are motivated to do so.

People with little technical knowledge can call, e-mail, text, and otherwise communicate with employees in an attempt to steal data. While we can laugh at the low-quality e-mails we receive and label them as being absurd, we ask, "Who would fall for them"? Depending on the targeted product, the click rate on e-mail scams is anywhere from 1% to 12%. In other words, if you work with 100 other people, at least a few of them are clicking on links within illegitimate e-mails. Only education and communication can prevent these threats from spreading. Limiting security helps by limiting the number of individuals with privileged access, but cannot stop a robbery when you unlock the door, open it, and invite a robber inside.

Some of our other examples earlier had a similar theme of accidental misfortune. The developer who forgets the WHERE clause or the user who misuses an application did not hack with the intent to cause trouble for your organization; they simply misused the tools they had at their disposal. There are two tactics to defend against these types of incidents. The first is utilizing the Principle of Least Privilege. It's worth overstating what has already been discussed: only provide users with the access they need to perform the daily functions of their job. An employee without production write-access cannot truncate or delete from a table. The brand new DBA cannot accidentally run a schema-altering script in production if they have no ability to make DDL changes. If an employee is to be fired, be sure to revoke their access immediately, to prevent any opportunity for retribution. Review security roles and user access annually (or more often if possible) to ensure that changes in your organization or software don't necessitate permissions changes.

The second defense against human nature is education. Make **ALL** employees aware of your company's data and security policies. If these policies don't exist, then work with the appropriate managers to create them. It is important to educate all employees, as anyone with access to data, whether via SQL Server Management Studio or terminal software at their desk, can potentially make mistakes that can cost a great deal in the long run. For developers, QA specialists, IT, and other technical folks, encourage accessing data safely. Many utilities exist that will highlight and color-code connection strings or warn against any TSQL statements that have no WHERE clause or affect an entire table. Knowing that you are connected to a production server can prevent the dreaded situation when a script was intended for the development database, but accidentally run in production.

Educating against nontechnical threats is equally important. Once employees understand how e-mail can be used to infect computers and steal information, they can be vigilant against those sorts of threats. This may mean making your own spam calls or intentionally sending spammy e-mails to catch those in need of an additional security lesson.

Writing well-structured, documented, and maintainable code is a critical first step toward maintaining data security. To take all of those efforts and have data compromised as a result of human error would be an example of the ultimate irony for any IT department. Take care to exercise diligence on all fronts so that any angle that your application could be attacked is well defended against. Whether a compromised database is due to a SQL injection hack, a fearful customer service representative, or a database administrator with a fat finger is irrelevant to an organization as a whole. The end results are similar and should provide the necessary motivation to secure an application environment as much as possible from the human factor.

Users, Passwords, and Inconvenience

We've discussed security roles, ownership chaining, and all of the ways in which human error can lead to disaster. What do all of these situations involve? Users. For any of these situations to come to fruition, a user's account must somehow be used against you. There are few actions that elicit more groans than having to change your password, but a strong and consistent password policy is a good defense against password hacking or old accounts that get resurrected for nefarious purposes.

When using Windows authentication, be sure to have all Windows users configured with an acceptable password policy. An ideal password policy is not complex, but enforces long passwords and ensures that users cannot cheat and use commonly hackable choices. Don't allow users to reuse passwords and do not force password resets too often. Frequent password resets result in us taking insecure shortcuts to try and remember passwords, such as post-it notes, password files, or other bad choices. Last, audit accounts for usage and purge any that are no longer needed. This is especially important for live user accounts in which a person could, in the future, try to log in when they no longer should have access. When it comes to logins, less is better!

Not only will this minimize the chances that an account could be compromised, it greatly reduces the chance that a lesser used (or forgotten) account could somehow be used without your knowing. Also ensure that Active Directory is kept up to date and that all employees' access is disabled when they leave the company. If a server allows mixed authentication, be sure to audit both SQL Server logins as well as Windows logins.

Microsoft is adamant that windows authentication is the recommended form of security in SQL Server, but to be certain that your server is as secure as possible, those Windows accounts must also be secure. When using Windows authentication, your SQL Server is only as safe as the Windows users that are provided access to it. Work with your network or systems administrator as necessary to ensure that all Windows accounts are secure, and then confirm that only necessary accounts have access to your SQL servers. If network access rules can be used to limit where a server can be accessed from, then use them! If an important SQL Server should only be accessed on a secure, internal network, then limit access to that network only. This greatly reduces access from other locations, offices, or the Internet at large.

If SQL Server authentication is used, then be sure to make the same smart decisions for each server, as seen in Figure 4-4.

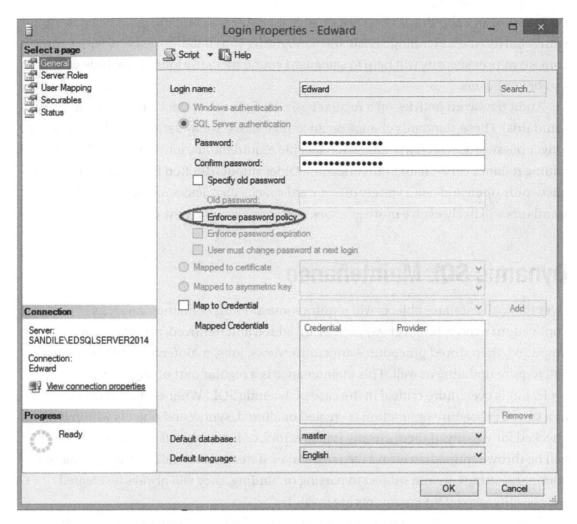

Figure 4-4. *Typical SQL Server user authentication options*

When any user is created, or by selecting the properties for a user, you can configure their security settings. Be sure to choose to enforce the password policy and expiration policy, as indicated by the check-box in Figure 4-4. These policies are inherited from Windows, either from a server policy or from an Active Directory/group policy. This policy can include additional security features, such as locking out users that fail too many login attempts.

Users, including IT professionals, will gripe about the inconvenience of account lockouts and dealing with policies. The benefits of these rules far outweigh the inconvenience. If employees are used to the password rules and have had a long history of them being applied fairly, their complaints will generally be minimized. It is often the breaking of habit that is most responsible for confusion and mistakes when dealing with security rules. Planning ahead and configuring your database servers with strong, consistent user security will help to safeguard your data in the long run at little cost to you or your users.

Audit password policies on a regular basis. How do yours stack up against industry standards? These standards change on an annual basis. Today's standards lend to using longer passwords with fewer character-specific requirements, fewer password resets, and adding reliance on 2-factor authentication. Older standards often forced users to change passwords often and use a variety of awkward special characters in doing so. In ten years, standards will likely evolve more as attack vectors evolve and new exploits are found.

Dynamic SQL Maintenance

Over time, all database objects will require some amount of maintenance. As applications evolve, tables grow, objects are added and removed, and software is upgraded, then stored procedures, functions, views, jobs, maintenance plans, and more will require updating as well. This maintenance is a regular part of any software life cycle, but is even more critical in the case of dynamic SQL. Whenever an object such as a stored procedure or function is created or altered, syntax and objects within it are checked for validity. If there are any syntax errors, or if any objects are incorrect, errors will be thrown immediately and the create/alter statement will fail. Since dynamic SQL command strings are not subject to parsing or binding, they will always be created successfully, even if their contents are invalid.

This poses a significant maintenance challenge for both developers and database administrators. How are objects maintained when their references are not enforced by any SQL Server restrictions? There are several solutions that can make our lives easier as application releases are being designed and planned. The first and most basic solution is to document stored procedures, jobs, functions, and other objects and their dependencies. There is no need to go into excessive detail, but this documentation should be easily searchable and allow anyone to quickly look up the basic functionality of an object and verify any major dependencies. Some organizations will implement this documentation in a database called a data dictionary. There are no codified rules for data dictionaries; they simply are a way to organize your database schema into a manageable reference guide. The details are left to each organization to manage as they see best for their own development and maintenance processes.

Whether implemented as a database, spreadsheet, Wiki, or text document, organizing your database objects in some fashion will provide an invaluable tool for the entire organization. They will easily be able to learn about database objects without having to track down a domain expert for help. In addition, when application changes are planned, determining the dependencies and areas that are affected by those changes will be significantly easier. The simplest data dictionary would simply be a list of tables, columns, indexes, stored procedures, and so on. Additional information can be added that describes the functionality of each object, the developers who worked most on them, and relationships to other objects or software modules.

At a higher level, if schema and source code are searchable, and we decide to modify a table, we can then quickly search schema and source code for that table name to verify if and how it is used.

If documentation is how we organize our application development environment, then cleanup is how we prevent an inevitable descent into an unmaintainable mess. Organizations greatly value the creation of new features in software and will generally show great interest in releasing new features rapidly, especially if those new features can earn money for the organization. A fine balance must be maintained between new features and technical debt. Technical debt is the accumulated to-do list that every developer knows all too well. The much-needed upgrade that no one has time for, cleaning up unused objects, performance optimization of old code, and so on are all examples of technical debt. No matter how good our documentation is, it becomes difficult to keep track of all of these exceptions and relics. Developers slowly forget about them as newer projects take the forefront, and older developers retire or move on. Cleaning up old database objects and references to deprecated TSQL is critical to keeping code maintainable.

The objects that we put out of sight and mind about today can easily become security holes in the future. The dynamic SQL that everyone forgot about quickly becomes the giant blob of string text that nobody wants to decipher. The application works and no one wants to mess with a poorly documented unknown object. Prevent this situation by making it a regular part of the release cycle to review all potential dependencies and take the appropriate actions to address them. Make sure that all objects that are no longer needed are removed. Those that require updating should be analyzed and the correct updates applied. These relics become security concerns as your software, security, and policies change. Old encryption algorithms that used to be considered solid and effective are eventually deprecated as modern technology renders them too weak to rely on anymore. The new coding standards that apply to all new stored procedures provide no defense against a poorly written proc from ten years ago. The TSQL written back when the company was a startup by developers putting in 16 hour days needs to be given the same treatment as the new objects that are created by a better equipped development team.

One way to track stored procedure execution is to create an execution log and add code to each stored procedure that inserts into the log the date and time it was executed. This is a fine tactic if we suspect an object is unused, but we are not certain of that fact. If enough time passes and there is no logged usage, then removal would be deemed safe. Remember to maintain the log table, though, removing old rows or those that are not relevant anymore.

While documentation is extremely helpful in determining how to utilize, reference, and manage new and existing objects, how do we perform those initial searches to find out what those many references are? SQL Server provides a number of system views that provide extensive details on database objects, how they relate to each other, and the TSQL text that their CREATE statements contain. By leveraging these views, we can build a multipurpose search stored procedure that uses a variety of system views and dynamic SQL to return a list of objects that contain a given search term, as seen in Listing 4-5.

Listing 4-5. Schema Search Stored Procedure

```
IF EXISTS (SELECT * FROM sys.procedures WHERE procedures.name = 'search_
all_schema')
BEGIN
    DROP PROCEDURE dbo.search_all_schema;
END
GO

CREATE PROCEDURE dbo.search_all_schema
    @searchString NVARCHAR(MAX)
AS
BEGIN
    SET NOCOUNT ON;

    -- This is the string you want to search databases and jobs
        for.  MSDB, model and any databases named like tempDB will be
        ignored.
```

```
SELECT @searchString = REPLACE @searchString, '[', '[[]');
    SELECT @searchString = '%' + @searchString + '%';
    DECLARE @sql NVARCHAR(MAX);
    DECLARE @database_name NVARCHAR(MAX);
    DECLARE @databases TABLE (database_name NVARCHAR(MAX));

    IF EXISTS (SELECT * FROM tempdb.sys.tables WHERE name = '#object_
    data')
    BEGIN
        DROP TABLE #object_data;
    END

    CREATE TABLE #object_data
    (    database_name NVARCHAR(MAX) NOT NULL,
        schemaname SYSNAME NULL,
        table_name SYSNAME NULL,
        objectname SYSNAME NOT NULL,
        object_type NVARCHAR(MAX) NOT NULL);

    IF EXISTS (SELECT * FROM tempdb.sys.tables WHERE name = '#index_
    data')
    BEGIN
        DROP TABLE #index_data;
    END

    CREATE TABLE #index_data
    (    database_name NVARCHAR(MAX) NOT NULL,
        schemaname SYSNAME NOT NULL,
        table_name SYSNAME NOT NULL,
        index_name SYSNAME NOT NULL,
        key_column_list NVARCHAR(MAX) NOT NULL,
        include_column_list NVARCHAR(MAX) NOT NULL);

    INSERT INTO @databases
        (database_name)
    SELECT
        name
```

```
FROM sys.databases
WHERE name NOT IN ('msdb', 'model', 'tempdb')
AND state_desc <> 'OFFLINE';

DECLARE DBCURSOR CURSOR FOR SELECT database_name FROM @databases;
OPEN DBCURSOR;
FETCH NEXT FROM DBCURSOR INTO @database_name;

WHILE @@FETCH_STATUS = 0
BEGIN
    SET @sql = '
    USE [' + @database_name + '];
    -- Tables
    INSERT INTO #object_data
        (database_name, schemaname, table_name, objectname,
        object_type)
    SELECT
        db_name() AS database_name,
        schemas.name AS schema_name,
        tables.name AS table_name,
        tables.name AS objectname,
        "Table" AS object_type
    FROM sys.tables
    INNER JOIN sys.schemas
    ON schemas.schema_id = tables.schema_id
    WHERE tables.name LIKE "' + @searchString + '";
    -- Columns
    INSERT INTO #object_data
        (database_name, schemaname, table_name, objectname,
        object_type)
    SELECT
        db_name() AS database_name,
        schemas.name AS schema_name,
        tables.name AS table_name,
        columns.name AS objectname,
        "Column" AS object_type
    FROM sys.tables
```

130

```
INNER JOIN sys.columns
ON tables.object_id = columns.object_id
INNER JOIN sys.schemas
ON schemas.schema_id = tables.schema_id
WHERE columns.name LIKE "' + @searchString + "';
-- Schemas
INSERT INTO #object_data
    (database_name, schemaname, table_name, objectname,
    object_type)
SELECT
    db_name() AS database_name,
    schemas.name AS schema_name,
    NULL AS table_name,
    schemas.name AS objectname,
    "Schema" AS object_type
FROM sys.schemas
WHERE schemas.name LIKE "' + @searchString + "';

-- Procedural TSQL
INSERT INTO #object_data
    (database_name, schemaname, table_name, objectname,
    object_type)
SELECT
    db_name() AS database_name,
    parent_schema.name AS schema_name,
    parent_object.name AS table_name,
    child_object.name AS objectname,
    CASE child_object.type
        WHEN "P" THEN "Stored Procedure"
        WHEN "RF" THEN "Replication Filter Procedure"
        WHEN "V" THEN "View"
        WHEN "TR" THEN "DML Trigger"
        WHEN "FN" THEN "Scalar Function"
        WHEN "IF" THEN "Inline Table Valued Function"
        WHEN "TF" THEN "SQL Table Valued Function"
        WHEN "R" THEN "Rule"
    END     AS object_type
```

```
FROM sys.sql_modules
INNER JOIN sys.objects child_object
ON sql_modules.object_id = child_object.object_id
LEFT JOIN sys.objects parent_object
ON parent_object.object_id = child_object.parent_object_id
LEFT JOIN sys.schemas parent_schema
ON parent_object.schema_id = parent_schema.schema_id
WHERE child_object.name LIKE "' + @searchString + "'
OR sql_modules.definition LIKE "' + @searchString + "';

-- Index Columns
WITH CTE_INDEX_COLUMNS AS (
      SELECT -- User indexes (with column name matching search
                  string).
            db_name() AS database_name,
            SCHEMA_DATA.name AS schemaname,
            TABLE_DATA.name AS table_name,
            INDEX_DATA.name AS index_name,
            STUFF(( SELECT   ", " + SC.name
                        FROM sys.tables AS ST
                        INNER JOIN sys.indexes SI
                        ON ST.object_id = SI.object_id
                        INNER JOIN sys.index_columns IC
                        ON SI.object_id = IC.object_id
                        AND SI.index_id = IC.index_id
                        INNER JOIN sys.all_columns SC
                        ON ST.object_id = SC.object_id
                        AND IC.column_id = SC.column_id
                        WHERE INDEX_DATA.object_id =
                        SI.object_id
                        AND INDEX_DATA.index_id = SI.index_id
                        AND IC.is_included_column = 0
                        ORDER BY IC.key_ordinal
                  FOR XML PATH("")), 1, 2, "") AS key_column_
                  list,
                  STUFF(( SELECT   ", " + SC.name
```

132

```
                    FROM sys.tables AS ST
                    INNER JOIN sys.indexes SI
                    ON ST.object_id = SI.object_id
                    INNER JOIN sys.index_columns IC
                    ON SI.object_id = IC.object_id
                    AND SI.index_id = IC.index_id
                    INNER JOIN sys.all_columns SC
                    ON ST.object_id = SC.object_id
                    AND IC.column_id = SC.column_id
                    WHERE INDEX_DATA.object_id = SI.object_id
                    AND INDEX_DATA.index_id = SI.index_id
                    AND IC.is_included_column = 1
                    ORDER BY IC.key_ordinal
                FOR XML PATH("")), 1, 2, "") AS include_
                column_list,
                "Index Column" AS object_type
        FROM sys.indexes INDEX_DATA
        INNER JOIN sys.tables TABLE_DATA
        ON TABLE_DATA.object_id = INDEX_DATA.object_id
        INNER JOIN sys.schemas SCHEMA_DATA
        ON SCHEMA_DATA.schema_id = TABLE_DATA.schema_id
        WHERE TABLE_DATA.is_ms_shipped = 0
        AND INDEX_DATA.type_desc IN ("CLUSTERED", "CLUSTERED"))
INSERT INTO #index_data
        (database_name, schemaname, table_name, index_name, key_
        column_list, include_column_list)
SELECT
        database_name, schemaname, table_name, index_name, key_
        column_list, ISNULL(include_column_list, "") AS include_
        column_list
FROM CTE_INDEX_COLUMNS
WHERE CTE_INDEX_COLUMNS.key_column_list LIKE "' +
@searchString + "'
```

```
            OR CTE_INDEX_COLUMNS.include_column_list LIKE "' +
        @searchString + "'
            OR CTE_INDEX_COLUMNS.index_name LIKE "' + @searchString + "';'
        EXEC sp_executesql @sql;

        FETCH NEXT FROM DBCURSOR INTO @database_name;
    END

    SELECT
            *
    FROM #object_data;

    SELECT
            *
    FROM #index_data

    -- Search to see if text exists in any job steps.
    SELECT
            j.job_id,
            s.srvname,
            j.name,
            js.step_id,
            js.command,
            j.enabled
    FROM msdb.dbo.sysjobs j
    INNER JOIN msdb.dbo.sysjobsteps js
    ON js.job_id = j.job_id
    INNER JOIN master.dbo.sysservers s
    ON s.srvid = j.originating_server_id
    WHERE js.command LIKE @searchString;

    DROP TABLE #object_data;
    DROP TABLE #index_data;
END
```

This stored procedure is somewhat extensive, but provides an excellent research tool that will search all databases on a server, as well as SQL Server Agent jobs, for any text provided as the @searchString. Since database level system views differ within each database, it is necessary to query these views on a database-by-database basis. Dynamic SQL is used to quickly iterate through all databases (except msdb, model, tempdb, and any offline databases). Three result sets are returned: database objects, indexes, and jobs. If desired, these output tables can be combined into a single output table using UNION ALL, but for the purposes of this demonstration, we'll keep them separate, which makes each more readable.

If we had a generic search to perform, perhaps to determine if the BusinessEntityContact table is referenced anywhere on the server, we could run the stored procedure as follows:

```
EXEC dbo.search_all_schema N'BusinessEntityContact';
```

The resulting data set in Figure 4-5 includes two views, one table-valued function, one table, and four indexes in a single database. No jobs were found with this name. If other databases existed with this text, then they would also be returned. If there was a desire to limit the database name so that we don't expend extra resources and return results from all databases, another parameter could easily be added to specify a database search term as well.

	database_name	schemaname	table_name	objectname	object_type
1	AdventureWorks2016CTP3	Person	BusinessEntityContact	BusinessEntityContact	Table
2	AdventureWorks2016CTP3	NULL	NULL	vStoreWithContacts	View
3	AdventureWorks2016CTP3	NULL	NULL	vVendorWithContacts	View
4	AdventureWorks2016CTP3	NULL	NULL	ufnGetContactInformation	SQL Table Valued Function

	database_name	schemaname	table_name	index_name	key_column_list	include_column_list
1	AdventureWorks2016CTP3	Person	BusinessEntityContact	PK_BusinessEntityContact_BusinessEntityID_PersonI...	BusinessEntityID, PersonID, ContactTypeID	
2	AdventureWorks2016CTP3	Person	BusinessEntityContact	AK_BusinessEntityContact_rowguid	rowguid	
3	AdventureWorks2016CTP3	Person	BusinessEntityContact	IX_BusinessEntityContact_PersonID	PersonID	
4	AdventureWorks2016CTP3	Person	BusinessEntityContact	IX_BusinessEntityContact_ContactTypeID	ContactTypeID	

job_id	srvname	name	step_id	command	enabled

Figure 4-5. *Example output from execution of a schema search, using a table name*

This search capability can be extremely useful when researching software changes, existing objects, and dependencies. Finding all instances of a table name requires seconds, rather than hours of research. This stored procedure can be used to search for more specific search terms, such as the name of a primary key:

```
EXEC dbo.search_all_schema N'PK_Sales';
```

The results in Figure 4-6 show a limited set of primary keys, all starting with the search term provided.

	database_name	table_name	objectname	object_type
6	AdventureWorks2012	SalesReason	PK_SalesReason_SalesReasonID	Index
7	AdventureWorks2012	SalesTaxRate	PK_SalesTaxRate_SalesTaxRateID	Index
8	AdventureWorks2012	SalesTerritory	PK_SalesTerritory_TerritoryID	Index
9	AdventureWorks2012	SalesTerritoryHistory	PK_SalesTerritoryHistory_BusinessEntityID_StartDate_Te...	Index
10	AdventureWorks2014	SalesOrderDetail	PK_SalesOrderDetail_SalesOrderID_SalesOrderDetailID	Index
11	AdventureWorks2014	SalesOrderHeader	PK_SalesOrderHeader_SalesOrderID	Index
12	AdventureWorks2014	SalesOrderHeaderSalesReason	PK_SalesOrderHeaderSalesReason_SalesOrderID_Sales...	Index
13	AdventureWorks2014	SalesPerson	PK_SalesPerson_BusinessEntityID	Index
14	AdventureWorks2014	SalesPersonQuotaHistory	PK_SalesPersonQuotaHistory_BusinessEntityID_QuotaD...	Index
15	AdventureWorks2014	SalesReason	PK_SalesReason_SalesReasonID	Index
16	AdventureWorks2014	SalesTaxRate	PK_SalesTaxRate_SalesTaxRateID	Index
17	AdventureWorks2014	SalesTerritory	PK_SalesTerritory_TerritoryID	Index
18	AdventureWorks2014	SalesTerritoryHistory	PK_SalesTerritoryHistory_BusinessEntityID_StartDate_Te...	Index
19	AdventureWorks2008	SalesOrderDetail	PK_SalesOrderDetail_SalesOrderID_SalesOrderDetailID	Index
20	AdventureWorks2008	SalesOrderHeader	PK_SalesOrderHeader_SalesOrderID	Index

Figure 4-6. *Example output from execution of a schema search, using a primary key name*

This illustrates some noise, as a number of primary keys happen to contain the specific name we were looking for. Removing the noise from the result set is a trivial task, though the additional results can be useful when looking for schema similar to our target search object. A final example in Figure 4-7 shows the results for a more specific search using the full schema and table name for an object.

```
EXEC dbo.search_all_schema N'Production.Product';
```

	database_name	table_name	objectname	object_type
1	AdventureWorks2014		search_products	Stored Procedure
2	AdventureWorks2014		search_sales_order_detail	Stored Procedure

	database_name	table_name	index_name	key_column_list	include_column_list

	job_id	srvname	name	step_id	command	enabled
1	BC7C6186-26B7-4A1E-9154-955D9C541B15	SANDILE\EDSQLSERVER2014	Product Test	1	SELECT COUNT(*) FROM Production.Product	1

Figure 4-7. *Example output from execution of a schema search, using a full table name*

This execution shows very specific results, as only two stored procedures and a lone job reference the full text of `Production.Product`.

Tools such as this can be invaluable ways in which to keep up with database schema maintenance effectively. If there are capabilities specific to your database environment that are not addressed by this stored procedure, consider modifying it to add further filters, search capabilities, or specific hard-coded needs for one application. There are many other objects in SQL Server that are not addressed here, but could be, such as:

- Replication publication names

- Linked server names

- Logins

- Users

- SSIS package details

- Synonyms

- Server-scoped DDL triggers

Adding any of these (or other metrics) would be a matter of adding code to either the database-specific dynamic SQL, or to the server-wide queries elsewhere in the proc. Results could be compressed into a single universal result set or broken out by type. Customization of code such as this can be easy to mold to the needs of a given organization, while allowing for nearly limitless functionality.

Use search capabilities to assist in removing deprecated features, updating dependencies, and ensuring that your team has the necessary knowledge to ensure that technical debt is addressed as effectively and efficiently as possible, before it becomes unmanageable. These regular searches can help ensure maximum security within your application, as potential security holes can be quickly found and patched. A search for "sp_executesql" and "EXEC" could help uncover all uses of dynamic SQL, which could be valuable in verifying that SQL injection is not possible from TSQL within the database server. Searching for a specific date, developer name, or project name could return stored procedures containing those words in their comments.

Cleaning House

A task that is often overlooked in favor of pushing forward with new features is the removal of old columns, tables, stored procedures, or other TSQL. A typical development cycle involves deprecating unused features, and essentially flagging them for future removal. What are often left out are the details as to how and when those objects are removed. Until such a time arrives, it is unlikely that they will be fully updated or maintained. For all intents and purposes, they are technical debt that will remain indefinitely unless special efforts are made to deal with them.

A key component to the creation of any object is the discussion of its maintenance. How do we maintain, archive, delete, or support a table or process once it is placed into a production environment?

Once we charge forward to work on upgrades, new features, and other research and development, cleanup becomes a distant memory. Even SQL Server itself is filled with a long list of deprecated features. A deprecated feature is one that is flagged for future removal, but remains in the interim for backwards compatibility purposes (or due to lack of motivation to remove it). To provide context, at the time of this writing, SQL Server 2017 contains a total of 352 deprecated features, keywords, and commands. In contrast, the number of discontinued features is a footnote in MSDN's documentation. Discontinued features are those that are removed from the product and no longer usable. Clearly it is much easier to end support for a feature and cease upgrading it than to go through the trouble of removing it altogether. If this is a slow transition for Microsoft, then clearly it is a challenge for anyone!

An excellent way to manage the deprecation and removal of software features is to build the discontinuation process into the standard development lifecycle. When a feature is flagged as no longer needed, include a timeline by which it will be removed. Beyond just creating a schedule, be sure to include enough details that the discontinuation can be acted upon. Consider these questions:

- What components need to be addressed in order for this feature to be completely removed?

- How much effort is required to remove each component?

- Who needs to be involved in each component's removal?

- Where in the development schedule for new features will this work fit in?

- What upkeep is required of these features in the interim, until they are removed?

As technical debt, this work will often fall lower in priority than new features. Asking and answering these questions can help ensure that important maintenance work is not forgotten. The last point is critically important when advocating for this work: what constant work and upkeep is required to properly maintain old components? This can incorporate software licensing costs, extra hardware usage, cloud storage and processing power, documentation, and anything else that could conceivably cost time and money.

In the same way that the tonsils or an appendix may act as liabilities to our health, old features slowly impede progress over time. Unlike tonsils, we can freely remove an old software feature whenever we decide to do so, with far lower risk than surgery.

More importantly, they provide areas that are more likely to suffer from security vulnerabilities, as they are no longer in the forefront of our development efforts. Oftentimes deprecated features are maintained quickly and with minimal QA, as they are no longer as critical to the application and may not even be used in the front end anymore. These are facts that must be wrestled with as part of the regular development of an application, but are of particular interest to DBAs when dynamic SQL is involved because it can provide additional access that may become undesirable over time.

If features are deprecated that use dynamic SQL, `xp_cmdshell`, or any other features of SQL Server that can potentially provide extra access to database objects, consider additional steps to secure them as part of the process. If the feature is no longer used by the application, consider removing the dynamic SQL portion and replacing it with a token placeholder. Similarly, security to that feature can be limited. This ensures that it cannot be abused in any way by any party, internal or external to your organization. This tactic can be employed for any TSQL that is no longer used but must be maintained so that software builds can complete successfully. If a feature is no longer used but cannot be dropped, consider reducing it to the smallest footprint allowed by your development process. Not only will this reduce security risks, but it will make the removal process easier when the time comes, as more of the functionality would already be gone.

The removal of unused code can be one of the most effective ways to prevent unexpected security breaches in the future.

A common error made when removing a feature is to accidentally leave it partially in use, or have some component of it still running in the application. Maybe a search procedure is still run when software is loaded, even if the results are not captured by the application. Another possibility is that there is a web page that is no longer linked by any active pages, but can still be accessed by entering a URL manually, or following a favorite to the same page. Removing core functionality as part of deprecation will highlight these missed opportunities and provide easy QA feedback so that these holes can be quickly closed. This can simplify the discontinuation process and remove the potential for future development errors or security breaches via unexpected/hidden code paths.

Login and User Usage

The Principle of Least Privilege tells us to provide logins and users with only what they need to serve their purpose, and nothing more. An additional implied step in order to be effective is to not share logins across multiple applications or users. Each individual SQL Server login, whether it uses Windows authentication or SQL Server authentication, should serve a distinct and singular purpose. This greatly improves security by

- making it easier to disable and later drop unused logins related to old applications or terminated employees.

- providing more granular control over permissions for each individual application.

- discouraging the sharing of users by different employees, especially if they are from different departments or in different roles.

- encouraging responsible development habits by maintaining a subtle focus on security.

- allowing for easier migration of applications to new servers or platforms.

- improving the response time to security threats, breaches, or attacks.

Consider a scenario when an application has db_owner privileges on three databases. A new employee starts and will be maintaining this application for your organization. They are provided with a standard login, access, and associated accounts. As a convenience, this user is also given the credentials for the login that is used by the application. This allows the new employee to immediately begin work on their application development without any additional security requests. A year later, the application expands and requires additional privileges to access some system views and manage some server settings.

Several years later, the employee leaves the company, and IT has forgotten that this user had access to an application login and fails to change passwords or consider the repercussions of these facts. The employee discovers that their access is still intact via the application login and decides to quietly steal some organizational data. From this point on, this organization is compromised and it is highly unlikely that the former employee's access will be caught until some action is taken that gets their attention. In addition to stealing data, they could also alter database settings, change data, or even drop the application databases.

The solution to this problem was to never let this employee share logins in the first place. This may have taken some additional time to either create a new login or alter their standard-issue credentials to incorporate these added permissions. Documentation would also be essential to ensuring that this user's additional access is available by anyone that may need to audit, alter, or disable their access. The longer a login is shared for, the easier it is to forget the nature of this duality and become complacent in its "just working."

An equally frustrating situation would be if an individual's login is used as the logins credentials for an application. This setup works for as long as the employee is working for the organization, but as soon as they leave, things get tricky. In the event that IT notices the shared user, they will be forced to quickly plan an ad hoc change of permissions. This may involve changing application passwords or creating a new application user. Either of these could require downtime in order to facilitate the change. If the shared user is not documented and is disabled as per standard procedures when this employee departs, then the application will immediately stop working. The result will be unplanned downtime and likely a late night for those in charge of the application. Similarly, database and job owners should never be a user's login, but instead a static login that will never change as the organization evolves.

Auditing Users and Logins

An additional safeguard against any undesired security situations is to schedule and implement regular audits of all SQL Server logins and users. Verify that permissions are adequate and relevant given current security policies and application needs. Ensure that all logins and users are required and that permissions that map logins to users are needed. This process may seem daunting, both from an organizational and technical standpoint, but can be made easier with the right scripts and effective communication with all stakeholders. Generally, managers and fellow employees will be happy to help you out to ensure that their data is secure and that compliance with any related standards is maintained.

In the realm of TSQL scripts, there are many possibilities that can be useful to us. We'll provide a few to get you started, but feel free to modify these or search the Web for more in-depth versions. Our goal is to identify all logins and users, customized securables, and mappings between logins and users. To begin, we'll take a brief look at all logins and roles on the server, using the script in Listing 4-6.

Listing 4-6. Script to Retrieve a List of Server Logins and Roles

```
SELECT
        server_principals.name AS Login_Name,
        server_principals.type_desc AS Account_Type
FROM sys.server_principals
WHERE server_principals.name NOT LIKE '%##%'
ORDER BY server_principals.name, server_principals.type_desc;
```

This query will return results that look similar to Figure 4-8.

	Login_Name	Account_Type
1	bulkadmin	SERVER_ROLE
2	dbcreator	SERVER_ROLE
3	diskadmin	SERVER_ROLE
4	EdPollack	SQL_LOGIN
5	Edward	SQL_LOGIN
6	EdwardJr	SQL_LOGIN
7	NT AUTHORITY\SYSTEM	WINDOWS_LOGIN
8	NT Service\MSSQL$EDSQLSERVER2014	WINDOWS_LOGIN
9	NT SERVICE\SQLAgent$EDSQLSERVER2014	WINDOWS_LOGIN
10	NT SERVICE\SQLWriter	WINDOWS_LOGIN
11	NT SERVICE\Winmgmt	WINDOWS_LOGIN
12	processadmin	SERVER_ROLE
13	public	SERVER_ROLE
14	sa	SQL_LOGIN
15	SANDILE\Edward	WINDOWS_LOGIN
16	securityadmin	SERVER_ROLE
17	serveradmin	SERVER_ROLE
18	setupadmin	SERVER_ROLE

Figure 4-8. *List of server logins and roles, from TSQL in Listing 4-6*

The results include all SQL logins, such as my own login, Edward, and my test logins, EdPollack and EdwardJr. The Windows authentication user SANDILE\Edward also exists on this server. In addition, included are a variety of system logins used by SQL Server services, and server level roles. Type can be filtered in order to limit the result set to nonsystem logins only. "U" indicates a Windows login, "S" indicates an SQL login, and "G" indicates a windows group. Filtering to these types only will reduce the result set to what we are likely most interested in auditing, as seen in Figure 4-9.

	Login_Name	Account_Type
1	EdPollack	SQL_LOGIN
2	Edward	SQL_LOGIN
3	EdwardJr	SQL_LOGIN
4	NT AUTHORITY\SYSTEM	WINDOWS_LOGIN
5	NT Service\MSSQL$EDSQLSERVER2014	WINDOWS_LOGIN
6	NT SERVICE\SQLAgent$EDSQLSERVER2014	WINDOWS_LOGIN
7	NT SERVICE\SQLWriter	WINDOWS_LOGIN
8	NT SERVICE\Winmgmt	WINDOWS_LOGIN
9	sa	SQL_LOGIN
10	SANDILE\Edward	WINDOWS_LOGIN

Figure 4-9. *Login list with server roles removed*

This query can easily be executed on all production servers and the results aggregated to provide a quick peek into which logins exist on which server, and can quickly provide insight into logins that shouldn't exist or that might be missing on a given server.

Our next research will involve exposing customized securables. If specific permissions were granted on an object, we definitely want to know what they are, who they have been given to, and verify that they are indeed necessary. This is an area that is particularly vulnerable to carelessness or oversight, as it can be slow and cumbersome to verify these details from the SQL Server Management Studio GUI.

Listing 4-7. Script That Lists Any User-Created Securables

```
SELECT
    OBJECT_NAME(database_permissions.major_id) AS object_name,
     USER_NAME(database_permissions.grantee_principal_id) AS role_name,
     database_permissions.permission_name
FROM sys.database_permissions
WHERE database_permissions.class = 1
AND OBJECTPROPERTY(database_permissions.major_id, 'IsMSSHipped') = 0
ORDER BY OBJECT_NAME(database_permissions.major_id);
```

The query in Listing 4-8 returns a list of any object-level permissions that were explicitly assigned, as seen in Figure 4-10. Any system securables were omitted to remove a large amount of noise from the list.

	object_name	role_name	permission_name
1	ownership_chaining_example	VeryLimitedRole	EXECUTE
2	ownership_chaining_example	EdwardJr	EXECUTE
3	search_all_schema	Edward	EXECUTE
4	search_products	EdwardJr	EXECUTE

Figure 4-10. *Object-level permissions with system securables removed*

On my local server, there are a handful of permissions granted to some stored procedures. It may seem odd that my sysadmin user, Edward, is included, but in the event that my user ever has its permissions reduced, knowledge of any additional securables I possess would be critical to completing that task in its entirety.

This query can be run across production servers to let you know what special permissions were assigned over time to different users and roles, and can ensure that any security changes that are implemented take into account any and all exceptions that may exist already.

One additional task that we will often want to complete is to collect the associations between server logins and users within each database. These relationships determine additional permissions a login may have within a given database. For example, a login may have no explicit permissions assigned at the server level, but could be given a variety of permissions at the database level that would coincide with job or application responsibilities.

Listing 4-8. TSQL to Return Relationships Between Server Logins and Database Users

```
CREATE TABLE #login_user_mapping (
    login_name NVARCHAR(MAX),
    database_name NVARCHAR(MAX),
    user_name NVARCHAR(MAX),
    alias_name NVARCHAR(MAX));

INSERT INTO #login_user_mapping
EXEC master.dbo.sp_msloginmappings;

SELECT
      *
FROM #login_user_mapping
ORDER BY database_name,
         user_name;

DROP TABLE #login_user_mapping;
```

The script in Listing 4-8 collects a list of login mappings using an SQL Server system-stored procedure, inserting the results directly into a temp table. The results are then returned from the temp table. The output of `sp_msloginmappings` is formatted as a single output set per login name, and as a result would be very difficult to use in reporting or analysis. By returning results directly into a temp table, we can get all of the mapping data into a single result set, which we can filter, sort, or read at our leisure. The result set on my local machine can be seen in Figure 4-11.

	login_name	database_name	user_name	alias_name
12	Edward	AdventureWorks2008	Edward	NULL
13	EdPollack	AdventureWorks2012	EdPollack	NULL
14	Edward	AdventureWorks2012	Edward	NULL
15	Edward	AdventureWorks2014	Edward	NULL
16	EdwardJr	AdventureWorks2014	EdwardJr	NULL
17	##MS_AgentSigningCertificate##	master	##MS_AgentSigningCertificate##	NULL
18	##MS_PolicyEventProcessingLogin##	master	##MS_PolicyEventProcessingLogin##	NULL
19	sa	master	dbo	NULL
20	EdPollack	master	EdPollack	NULL
21	sa	model	dbo	NULL
22	EdPollack	model	EdPollack	NULL
23	##MS_PolicyEventProcessingLogin##	msdb	##MS_PolicyEventProcessingLogin##	NULL
24	##MS_PolicyTsqlExecutionLogin##	msdb	##MS_PolicyTsqlExecutionLogin##	NULL
25	sa	msdb	dbo	NULL
26	EdPollack	msdb	EdPollack	NULL
27	sa	tempdb	dbo	NULL
28	EdPollack	tempdb	EdPollack	NULL

Figure 4-11. *Full list of all login/user mappings on this SQL Server*

Each login is associated to a database and user. If any aliases existed, they would also be returned. This lets us keep track of which databases a given login has any permissions to. Typically, when a login is deleted, any users associated with that login will remain in their respective databases until acted upon by an administrator. The results returned by the preceding query can ensure that we properly clean up all database users when we disable or drop a server login.

There are many other system views and stored procedures that can be used to analyze SQL Server security, but the handful shown should provide a solid starting point with which to take stock of your database environment and identify any significant security flaws that could be easily addressed once this information is known.

Memory Consumption

Earlier, we briefly discussed the effects of string truncation on dynamic SQL and how it can cause command strings to be executed incorrectly, or throw errors. Most of our dynamic SQL examples thus far have had relatively short command strings whose lengths were predetermined, based on the parameters that were passed in. In a scenario where the length of the command string is controlled by a specific number of objects, or amount of data, the resulting string can potentially be very large. Like other scalar parameters you define in SQL server, the command string is stored in memory. Consider the dynamic SQL in Listing 4-9.

Listing 4-9. Dynamic SQL to Check Database Integrity on All Databases on This Instance

```
DECLARE @databases TABLE
      (database_name NVARCHAR(MAX));

INSERT INTO @databases
      (database_name)
SELECT
      databases.name
FROM sys.databases;

DECLARE @sql_command NVARCHAR(MAX) = '';

SELECT @sql_command = @sql_command + '
DBCC CHECKDB (' + database_name + ');'
FROM @databases;

PRINT @sql_command;
EXEC sp_executesql @sql_command;
```

This dynamic SQL will create a command string that will run DBCC CHECKDB on all databases on this SQL Server instance. The command string will consist of one line per database, regardless of how many databases exist on the server. Since this particular command is short, the command string on my server will appear like this:

```
DBCC CHECKDB (master);
DBCC CHECKDB (tempdb);
DBCC CHECKDB (model);
DBCC CHECKDB (msdb);
DBCC CHECKDB (AdventureWorks2012);
DBCC CHECKDB (AdventureWorks2014);
DBCC CHECKDB (AdventureWorks2008);
```

While this example is short, consider what might happen if there were 500 databases on my server. In that scenario, the command string would be 500 lines long. This would still not be terribly large, but introduces a potential memory issue if the object count or text involved became too long. For example, what if we were to assemble a row count report for all tables in all databases on the server? In that scenario, on a server with 500 databases and 500 tables per database, we would have a command string that was 250,000 lines long. If the text of each command were similar to *"SELECT COUNT(*) FROM schema_name.table_name"*, then each line of text would be about 300 bytes. The total command string size would be approximately 75MB, which is well below the amount of memory that a server is likely to have, but illustrates a potential performance and security threat that unbounded statements can pose.

When writing dynamic SQL, be conscious of the length of a command string. If it can grow unbounded, consider adding a cutoff to prevent it from getting excessively large. Alternatively, batch the statements so that sets of rows are processed, rather than all of them at one time. While it is rare that a command string would grow to be gigabytes in size, it is not out of the realm of possibility, nor should it be ignored. Excessive growth could also occur due to developer error, if we forgot to increment a counter or advance a cursor. If we allow the string to grow indefinitely, server memory would eventually run out. The result would likely be some variety of SQL Server crash that could influence other applications whose databases are hosted on this server.

Listing 4-10. Dynamic SQL to Gather Row Counts of All Tables on This SQL Server Instance

```
SET NOCOUNT ON;

DECLARE @databases TABLE
     (database_name NVARCHAR(MAX));

CREATE TABLE #tables
     (database_name NVARCHAR(MAX),
      schema_name NVARCHAR(MAX),
      table_name NVARCHAR(MAX),
      row_count BIGINT);

DECLARE @sql_command NVARCHAR(MAX) = '';
```

```
INSERT INTO @databases
        (database_name)
SELECT
        databases.name
FROM sys.databases
WHERE databases.name <> 'tempdb';

DECLARE @current_database NVARCHAR(MAX);
WHILE EXISTS (SELECT * FROM @databases)
BEGIN
        SELECT TOP 1 @current_database = database_name FROM @databases;

        SELECT @sql_command = @sql_command + '
            USE [' + @current_database + ']
            INSERT INTO #tables
                    (database_name, schema_name, table_name, row_count)
            SELECT
                    "' + @current_database + '",
                    schemas.name,
                    tables.name,
                    0
            FROM sys.tables
            INNER JOIN sys.schemas
            ON tables.schema_id = schemas.schema_id';
        EXEC sp_executesql @sql_command;
        DELETE FROM @databases WHERE database_name = @current_database;
END

SELECT @sql_command = '';
SELECT @sql_command = @sql_command + '
    USE [' + database_name + '];
    UPDATE table_list
            SET row_count = (SELECT SUM(partitions.rows)
                                        FROM sys.partitions
                                        INNER JOIN sys.tables ON
                                        partitions.object_id = tables.
                                        object_id
```

```
                                        INNER JOIN sys.schemas ON
                                        schemas.schema_id = tables.
                                        schema_id
                                        WHERE table_list.table_name =
                                        tables.name
                                        AND table_list.schema_name =
                                        schemas.name
                                        AND index_id < 2) -- Ignore
                                        the partitions from the non-
                                        clustered indexes if any exist.
    FROM #tables table_list
    WHERE table_list.schema_name = "' + [schema_name] + "'
    AND table_list.table_name = "' + table_name + "'
    AND table_list.database_name = "' + database_name + "';'
FROM #tables;
--EXEC sp_executesql @sql_command;

SELECT
    *
FROM #tables;

DROP TABLE #tables;
GO
```

The TSQL in Listing 4-11 uses dynamic SQL to construct a long command string that will gather row counts for all tables in all databases on the server (with the exception of TempDB). The more databases and the more tables on the server, the larger the string will be. Before executing the command string, we return the length in bytes, which is calculated as two times the number of characters in the string. The characters are multiplied by two to account for the fact that the command string is the NVARCHAR data type, which consists of double-byte UNICODE characters. On my local server with six databases, the length of this command string is 3.04MB. On a server with many more databases and tables, the length could become prohibitively long. Following is an example of batching that limits the number of rows that are processed at one time, ensuring that the command string cannot grow too large. In this specific example, we process row counts for each database separately, which would generally be adequate in limiting the overall size of our command strings. The TSQL for this can be found in Listing 4-11.

Listing 4-11. Dynamic SQL to Gather Row Counts of All Tables on This SQL Server Instance Using Batched Command String Creation

```
SET NOCOUNT ON;

DECLARE @databases TABLE
      (database_name NVARCHAR(MAX));

CREATE TABLE #tables
      (database_name NVARCHAR(MAX),
       schema_name NVARCHAR(MAX),
       table_name NVARCHAR(MAX),
       row_count BIGINT);

DECLARE @sql_command NVARCHAR(MAX) = ";

INSERT INTO @databases
      (database_name)
SELECT
      databases.name
FROM sys.databases
WHERE databases.name <> 'tempdb';

DECLARE @current_database NVARCHAR(MAX);
WHILE EXISTS (SELECT * FROM @databases)
BEGIN
      SELECT TOP 1 @current_database = database_name FROM @databases;

      SELECT @sql_command = ";

      SELECT @sql_command = @sql_command + '
            USE [' + @current_database + ']
            INSERT INTO #tables
                  (database_name, schema_name, table_name, row_count)
            SELECT
                  "' + @current_database + "',
                  schemas.name,
                  tables.name,
                  0
```

```
        FROM sys.tables
        INNER JOIN sys.schemas
        ON tables.schema_id = schemas.schema_id';
    EXEC sp_executesql @sql_command;

    SELECT @sql_command = '';
    SELECT @sql_command = @sql_command + '
        USE [' + database_name + '];
        UPDATE table_list
            SET row_count = (SELECT SUM(partitions.rows)
                                    FROM sys.partitions
                                    INNER JOIN sys.tables ON
                                    partitions.object_id = tables.
                                    object_id
                                    INNER JOIN sys.schemas ON
                                    schemas.schema_id = tables.
                                    schema_id
                                    WHERE table_list.table_name =
                                    tables.name
                                    AND table_list.schema_name =
                                    schemas.name
                                    AND index_id < 2) -- Ignore
                                    the partitions from the non-
                                    clustered indexes if any exist.
        FROM #tables table_list
        WHERE table_list.schema_name = "' + [schema_name] + '"
        AND table_list.table_name = "' + table_name + '"
        AND table_list.database_name = "' + database_name + '";'
    FROM #tables
    WHERE database_name = @current_database;

    EXEC sp_executesql @sql_command;

    DELETE FROM @databases WHERE database_name = @current_database;
END
```

```
SELECT
      *
FROM #tables;

DROP TABLE #tables;
GO
```

The only difference in the rewrite of our row count TSQL is that the collection of row counts happens in the main loop, after each database's tables are enumerated. This breaks up our command string generation into one per database. Instead of creating a 3MB command string, we create and execute six different ones, none of which are more than 475KB. In a scenario where the length of a command string could become very long due to a large number of objects being analyzed, batching can ensure that memory pressure never becomes a security or stability concern, even when executed on extremely large data sets.

Row Level Security

Introduced in SQL Server 2016, this feature allows far more granular control over table data access. Using this feature, we can restrict access based on the criteria specified within a function that we write. Doing this, we can incorporate user names, logins, and other data into the function and cross it with data in a table.

To demonstrate the power of this feature, we'll introduce an employee login table, populate it with some test data, create a few test logins, and implement row level security on top of these structures, as seen in Listing 4-12.

Listing 4-12. Create an Employee Login Table, Insert Test Data, and Create Logins/Users for Testing Purposes

```
CREATE TABLE dbo.employee_login
(      employee_id INT NOT NULL IDENTITY(1,1) CONSTRAINT PK_employee
       PRIMARY KEY CLUSTERED,
      first_name VARCHAR(100) NOT NULL,
      last_name VARCHAR(100) NOT NULL,
      username VARCHAR(50) NOT NULL,
      login_owner_username VARCHAR(50) NOT NULL);
GO
```

```
INSERT INTO dbo.employee_login
        (first_name, last_name, username, login_owner_username)
VALUES
        ('Ed', 'Pollack', 'Ed', 'Ed'),
        ('Ed', 'Pollack', 'epollack', 'Ed'),
        ('Ed', 'Pollack', 'edwardjr', 'Ed'),
        ('Theresa', 'Pollack', 'Theresa', 'Theresa'),
        ('Nolan', 'Pollack', 'Nolan', 'Ed'),
        ('Donna', '', 'Donna', 'Donna'),
        ('Joe', '', 'Joe', 'Joe'),
        ('Giganotosaurus', '', 'GFunk', 'Troodon'),
        ('Tyrannosaurus', '', 'Trex', 'Troodon'),
        ('Pteranodon', '', 'Pteranodon', 'Troodon'),
        ('Troodon', '', 'Troodon', 'Ed');
GO

CREATE LOGIN [Ed] WITH PASSWORD = 'test_password', CHECK_POLICY = OFF,
CHECK_EXPIRATION = OFF;
CREATE USER [Ed] FROM LOGIN [Ed];
ALTER ROLE db_datareader ADD MEMBER [Ed];
GO

CREATE LOGIN [Troodon] WITH PASSWORD = 'test_password', CHECK_POLICY = OFF,
CHECK_EXPIRATION = OFF;
CREATE USER [Troodon] FROM LOGIN [Troodon];
ALTER ROLE db_datareader ADD MEMBER [Troodon];
GO

CREATE LOGIN [Nolan] WITH PASSWORD = 'test_password', CHECK_POLICY = OFF,
CHECK_EXPIRATION = OFF;
CREATE USER [Nolan] FROM LOGIN [Nolan];
ALTER ROLE db_datareader ADD MEMBER [Nolan];
GO
```

We now have a table called employee_login, as well as some test data to work with. The key column for this demonstration will be login_owner_username, which indicates the user name of the person who owns this account. Our goal will be to ensure that the only people that can view an account are those that own it. Other users should not have access, even if the account in question is theirs. We've also created three logins that will be used to validate this behavior. Each is granted full read access to Adventureworks (the current database we are using).

The next step is to create a security function that will be used to validate data against our security policy. Our example function, as seen in Listing 4-13, will be simple: check if the user name matches login_owner_username within employee_login. If so, return data; otherwise, do not.

Listing 4-13. Create a Table-Valued Function That Defines Our Security Criteria

```
CREATE FUNCTION dbo.fn_employee_login_security_function (@user_name AS
VARCHAR(50))
RETURNS TABLE
WITH SCHEMABINDING
AS
RETURN
    SELECT
            1 AS fn_security_predicate_result
        FROM dbo.employee_login
        WHERE @user_name = SUSER_NAME();
```

The function returns a 1 if security is successfully validated on a given row. Here, we are comparing the function's input against the currently logged in user name. Our last step is to create a security policy that will use the preceding function to actively filter data against it, as seen in Listing 4-14.

Listing 4-14. Create a Security Policy That Implements an Existing Security Function

```
CREATE SECURITY POLICY employee_login_security_policy
ADD FILTER PREDICATE dbo.fn_employee_login_security_function(login_owner_
username)
ON dbo.employee_login
WITH (STATE = ON);
GO
```

The filter predicate passes `login_owner_username` into the function we created above, without any additional WHERE clause or restrictions. As a result, this security policy will apply to the entire table.

I am currently logged in as a user called `epollack`. Given that, I'll try to select all data from our test table:

```
SELECT
     *
FROM dbo.employee_login;
```

Despite being a sysadmin, no data is returned, as seen in Figure 4-12.

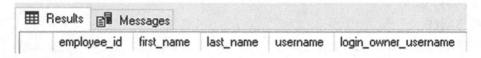

Figure 4-12. *Results of a SELECT against employee_login, as an unauthorized user*

Since epollack is not a value for any row in the table, zero results are returned, despite my being a sysadmin and having read access granted to the entire table. Row level security overrides this and ensures that I only see what I am supposed to see.

Now, let's impersonate the login Ed and try again:

```
EXECUTE AS LOGIN = 'Ed';
```

```
SELECT
     *
FROM dbo.employee_login;
```

```
REVERT
```

The results can be seen in Figure 4-13.

	employee_id	first_name	last_name	username	login_owner_username
1	1	Ed	Pollack	Ed	Ed
2	2	Ed	Pollack	epollack	Ed
3	3	Ed	Pollack	edwardjr	Ed
4	5	Nolan	Pollack	Nolan	Ed
5	11	Troodon		Troodon	Ed

Figure 4-13. *Results of a SELECT against employee_login, as a user with some row level access*

Only the rows that obey the security policy and had a login owner defined as Ed were returned. This functionality extends to other queries as well. For example, aggregate functions, such as MIN, MAX, and COUNT, will only include rows that are validated successfully by the security policy.

If I were to run a SELECT and COUNT vs. the table as the login Troodon, then I'll get back the list of dinosaurs the user has access to, as seen in Figure 4-14.

	employee_id	first_name	last_name	username	login_owner_username
1	8	Giganotosaurus		GFunk	Troodon
2	9	Tyrannosaurus		Trex	Troodon
3	10	Pteranodon		Pteranodon	Troodon

	(No column name)
1	3

Figure 4-14. *Results of a SELECT against employee_login, as a user with differing row level access*

The options for customizing row level security are limitless. We could create lists of specific users based on tabular metadata, and then apply that access to other objects. Logins with specific roles, securables, or text within the user name could be given granular permissions based on that metadata. Application logins could be used, instead, to regulate who has access to data. As a feature, row level security is a very flexible way to further restrict access to ensure that we can best follow the principal of least privilege.

Signing Stored Procedures

One additional way to control access to stored procedures is to use a certificate to sign it, allowing permissions to be granted without the need to explicitly assign them to a user. This allows a login and user to be created with no permissions assigned to them, and trust to be established to objects via use of the certificate.

More importantly to us, this security applies to access within the scope of a stored procedure or dynamic SQL within it! Let's jump in and configure a login, user, and certificate, as seen in Listing 4-15.

Listing 4-15. Create a Login, User, and Certificate for Testing a Signed Stored Procedure

```
CREATE LOGIN SecurityTestUser WITH PASSWORD = 'SecurityTest%UserForSigned
ProcsDemo!StrongPassword^12345!'
GO

CREATE USER SecurityTestUser FOR LOGIN SecurityTestUser;
GO

CREATE CERTIFICATE SecurityTestCertificate
    ENCRYPTION BY PASSWORD = 'Security&Test@Certificate135790Password!!!'
        WITH SUBJECT = 'Secure Stored Proc Access',
        EXPIRY_DATE = '1/1/2021';
GO
```

This sets us up with a certificate that we will use to sign a stored procedure, as well as a user and login that will be used to test it. In Listing 4-16, we'll create a stored procedure that validates current security credentials both in its scope and within the scope of a dynamic SQL statement. We'll also sign it using the certificate that we recently defined.

Listing 4-16. Create a Stored Procedure and Sign It Using a Certificate

```
IF EXISTS (SELECT * FROM sys.procedures WHERE procedures.name =
'GetPersonCount')
BEGIN
      DROP PROCEDURE dbo.GetPersonCount;
END
GO

CREATE PROCEDURE dbo.GetPersonCount
AS
BEGIN
      SELECT
            *
      FROM sys.user_token;

      DECLARE @sql_command NVARCHAR(MAX);
      SELECT @sql_command = '
            SELECT
                  *
            FROM sys.user_token;
            SELECT COUNT(*) FROM Person.Person';

      EXEC sp_executesql @sql_command;
END
GO

ADD SIGNATURE TO GetPersonCount
BY CERTIFICATE SecurityTestCertificate
WITH PASSWORD = 'Security&Test@Certificate135790Password!!!';
GO
```

Now that these structures are available, we can create a database user from the certificate. This user is special in that it will be associated with the ownership chain of any objects it has permissions to. Listing 4-17 shows the creation of this user, as well as the assigning of permission to it and our previous test user.

Listing 4-17. Create a Database User from the Certificate and Assign
Permissions to Our Test Objects

```
CREATE USER TestUserFromCertificate
FROM CERTIFICATE SecurityTestCertificate;
GO

GRANT SELECT
ON Person.Person
TO TestUserFromCertificate;
GO

GRANT EXECUTE
ON dbo.GetPersonCount
TO TestUserFromCertificate;
GO

GRANT EXECUTE
ON dbo.GetPersonCount
TO SecurityTestUser;
GO
```

With these structures created, we can test object access as the login
SecurityTestUser and see what happens. Listing 4-18 shows tests using my admin
login, and then executing as our test login.

Listing 4-18. Create a Database User from the Certificate and Assign
Permissions to Our Test Objects

```
EXEC dbo.GetPersonCount;
GO
SELECT
      *
FROM Person.Person;
GO
SELECT
      *
FROM Person.Password;
GO
```

```
EXECUTE AS LOGIN = 'SecurityTestUser';
GO
EXEC dbo.GetPersonCount;
GO
SELECT
      *
FROM Person.Person;
GO
SELECT
      *
FROM Person.Password;
GO

REVERT;
GO
```

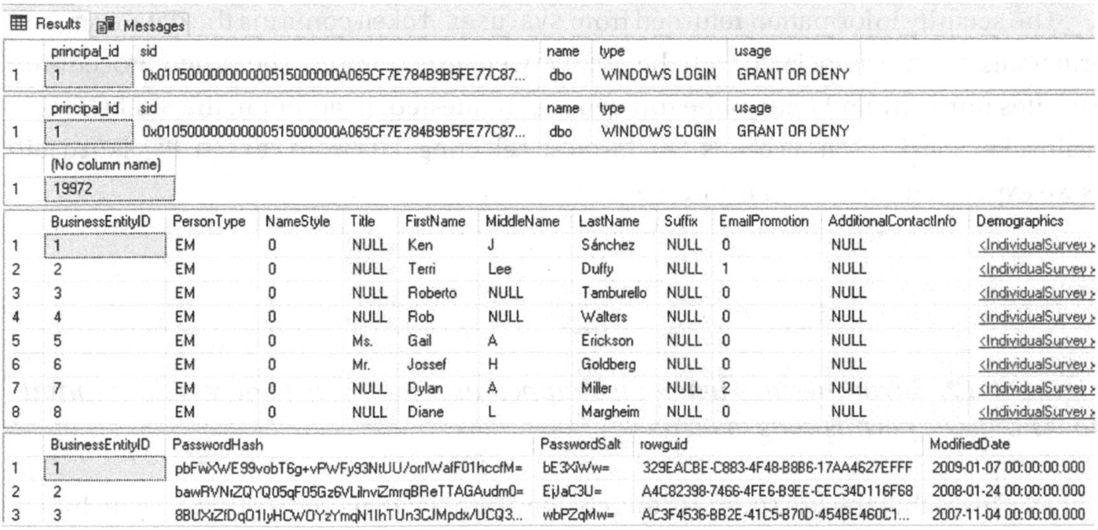

First, we'll test as me. As an admin login with permissions to do anything, the results are predictable and provide a good starting point. Figure 4-15 shows what happens when I execute the stored procedure, select from `Person.Person`, and select from `Person.Password`.

Figure 4-15. *Security info and results from test queries as a sysadmin login*

We can see the security info for my Windows user, both in the stored procedure and the dynamic SQL contained within.it. The row count within the dynamic SQL is returned correctly. In addition, the SELECT operations against `Person.Person` and `Person.Password` also execute correctly. With the more obvious test case out of the way, we can execute the same code, but as `SecurityTestUser`, as seen in Figure 4-16.

	principal_id	sid	name	type	usage
1	32	0x8F4FB5A4AD0E5C4C8ACC5A84819AB0AA	SecurityTestUser	SQL USER	GRANT OR DENY
2	0	0x010500000000000904000000083741B006749C04BA943C02...	public	ROLE	GRANT OR DENY
3	33	0x0106000000000009010000000DCDFD45510450F4DC6F49F...	TestUserFromCertificate	USER MAPPED TO CERTIFICATE	GRANT OR DENY

	principal_id	sid	name	type	usage
1	32	0x8F4FB5A4AD0E5C4C8ACC5A84819AB0AA	SecurityTestUser	SQL USER	GRANT OR DENY
2	0	0x010500000000000904000000083741B006749C04BA943C02...	public	ROLE	GRANT OR DENY
3	33	0x0106000000000009010000000DCDFD45510450F4DC6F49F...	TestUserFromCertificate	USER MAPPED TO CERTIFICATE	GRANT OR DENY

	(No column name)
1	19972

	BusinessEntityID	PersonType	NameStyle	Title	FirstName	MiddleName	LastName	Suffix	EmailPromotion	AdditionalContactInfo	Demographics
1	1	EM	0	NULL	Ken	J	Sánchez	NULL	0	NULL	<IndividualSurv
2	2	EM	0	NULL	Terri	Lee	Duffy	NULL	1	NULL	<IndividualSurv
3	3	EM	0	NULL	Roberto	NULL	Tamburello	NULL	0	NULL	<IndividualSurv
4	4	EM	0	NULL	Rob	NULL	Walters	NULL	0	NULL	<IndividualSurv
5	5	EM	0	Ms.	Gail	A	Erickson	NULL	0	NULL	<IndividualSurv
6	6	EM	0	Mr.	Jossef	H	Goldberg	NULL	0	NULL	<IndividualSurv
7	7	EM	0	NULL	Dylan	A	Miller	NULL	2	NULL	<IndividualSurv
8	8	EM	0	NULL	Diane	L	Margheim	NULL	0	NULL	<IndividualSurv

Figure 4-16. *Output when a user is mapped from a certificate and used to retrieve data*

The security information returned from `sys.user_token` confirms the database principals that are associated with the user we were executing as. The stored procedure executes normally and returns the row count as requested. In addition, the SELECT against `Person.Person` succeeds. Our last test, selecting data from `Person.Password` fails as we expect it to, as seen in Figure 4-17.

```
Results    Messages
Msg 229, Level 14, State 5, Line 839
The SELECT permission was denied on the object 'Password', database 'AdventureWorks2016CTP3', schema 'Person'.
```

Figure 4-17. *Error message when the mapped user attempts to access data that it does not have permissions to view*

The key is that the user permissions chained into the dynamic SQL that we included in the stored procedure and did not revert to the object owner or caller.

Signing a stored procedure using a certificate allows for more granular control over security without needing to explicitly redefine permissions against every underlying object in question. By granting permissions to the certificate, we no longer need to worry about granular table access details that would previously have been an issue when dealing with ownership chaining.

This also can simplify the granting and revoking of permissions, as there is no need to modify logins, but instead a certificate user. Unlike EXECUTE AS, this process does not change the execution context of the stored procedure, but permissions are managed as if they were.

Signing stored procedures is a simple and easy-to-use alternative for managing security across different scopes when the alternative is micromanaging permissions on many objects.

Conclusion

All of this security advice may seem distant to the topic of dynamic SQL, but it's important in ensuring that the development we do is both effective and secure. Taking any or all of these best practices and suggestions and implementing them greatly reduces the risk of SQL injection, as well as other exploits that could inadvertently create vulnerabilities in your system. If this topic interests you, there are many books and courses out there that will dive into security in much greater detail. This chapter is intended to provide an introduction and overview of SQL Server security, with a focus on dynamic SQL and the greatest security threats to it.

As we charge forward with further examples of how dynamic SQL can perform powerful searches, maintenance, or data transformations, keep in mind how security-related considerations can have lasting repercussions for the integrity of not only your queries, but your SQL Server as a whole. It is far easier to make the correct decisions now than to return at a later date and clean up the mistakes of previous development efforts.

CHAPTER 5

Managing Scope

Our discussions of security have alluded to the fact that dynamic SQL does not run in the same scope as the remainder of TSQL in the same stored procedure. In addition to breaking the ownership chain, variables declared locally and globally will not have easy access to each other. When writing application code or stored procedures, passing variables into and out requires a bit of planning, ensuring that the inputs and outputs are correct. Working with dynamic SQL is very similar, and luckily we have a variety of ways in which to manage variables effectively without any level of inconvenience.

What Is Scope?

To make understanding scope as easy as possible, some definitions of what we are talking about should be provided, as well as a few examples of why this is an important topic. Scope can be defined as where and how long a variable or object is available for within any SQL Server object. Consider the following simple TSQL statement:

```
DECLARE @FirstName NVARCHAR(50) = 'Edward';

SELECT
    *
FROM Person.Person
WHERE FirstName = @FirstName;
```

This is about as simple as TSQL gets, but what is the scope of the variable we just defined? Without any interruptions or changes in control within these statements, @FirstName is in scope throughout the example, and can be used (as we expect it could be) by the SELECT statement immediately after it. What happens if we end the batch prior to returning the results?

© Edward Pollack 2019

E. Pollack, *Dynamic SQL*, https://doi.org/10.1007/978-1-4842-4318-3_5

```
DECLARE @FirstName NVARCHAR(50) = 'Edward';
GO

SELECT
       *
FROM Person.Person
WHERE FirstName = @FirstName;
```

This simple change, a "GO" before the SELECT, will result in an error:

```
Msg 137, Level 15, State 2, Line 20
Must declare the scalar variable "@FirstName".
```

When the batch was ended, all locally defined variables were no longer available and in scope for the remainder of this TSQL. "GO", by definition, will end a batch and trigger this behavior whenever used. Any TSQL that is encapsulated within its own object, such as a trigger, function, or stored procedure, will also execute within their own scope. Any attempt to access variables defined within these objects from outside of them will result in errors similar to this.

```
CREATE PROCEDURE dbo.get_people
AS
BEGIN
    DECLARE @FirstName NVARCHAR(50) = 'Edward';

    SELECT
           *
    FROM Person.Person
    WHERE FirstName = @FirstName;
END
GO

EXEC dbo.get_people;
SELECT @FirstName;
```

The preceding stored procedure will perform the same search as previously. Attempting to execute it as shown yields the exact same results, with the previous error being returned because our TSQL cannot be bound. By default, variables declared within a stored procedure are not available from anywhere outside of it. In our example, SQL Server has no idea what @FirstName is, as it was defined within the stored procedure only. The same convention also applies to dynamic SQL, and is important to understand when determining where variables are to be declared, modified, and returned.

Parameters can be added to stored procedures to facilitate the easy movement of data in and out of them so that their values can remain in scope and be used elsewhere in your work. The following example in Listing 5-1 shows how variables can be passed into a stored procedure, and how values can be explicitly returned as well:

Listing 5-1. Stored Procedure Illustrating Input and Output Parameters

```
IF EXISTS (SELECT * FROM sys.procedures WHERE procedures.name = 'get_people')
BEGIN
      DROP PROCEDURE dbo.get_people;
END
GO
CREATE PROCEDURE dbo.get_people
      @first_name NVARCHAR(50), @person_with_most_entries NVARCHAR(50) OUTPUT
AS
BEGIN
      DECLARE @person_count INT;

      SELECT TOP 1
            @person_with_most_entries = Person.FirstName
      FROM Person.Person
      GROUP BY Person.FirstName
      ORDER BY COUNT(*) DESC;

      SELECT
            *
      FROM Person.Person
      WHERE FirstName = @first_name;

      RETURN @@ROWCOUNT;
END
GO
```

In this example, we pass in a first name that will be used in the search. We also pass in an additional string that will be overwritten with the most common first name in Person.Person. Within the stored procedure, all rows in Person.Person will be returned that have the first name passed in. Last, the count of rows with that first name will be used as the return value from the stored proc. An example execution would look like this:

```
DECLARE @person_with_most_entries NVARCHAR(50);
DECLARE @person_count INT;

EXEC @person_count = dbo.get_people 'Edward', @person_with_most_entries OUTPUT;

SELECT @person_with_most_entries AS person_with_most_entries;
SELECT @person_count AS person_count
```

Note the use of the OUTPUT keyword. This TSQL reserved word can be used in a number of ways, but when working with a stored procedure as seen in the preceding, it signifies that the parameter that is being passed in will retain changes to its value as the stored procedure executes. For this to work properly, OUTPUT must also be specified in the parameter list for the stored procedure as well.

When executed, a search will be performed and all people with the name "Edward" will be returned. In addition, the @person_with_most_entries variable will also be updated as an output variable. Last, the count of people with the first name provided will be returned from the stored procedure and stored in @person_count. When those variables are selected at the end, the expected values are returned, as seen in Figure 5-1.

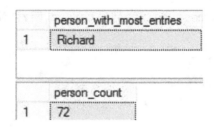

Figure 5-1. *Results from the dbo.get_people stored procedure*

Why Is Scope Important?

So far, scope appears to be an inconvenience that we are forced to deal with when working with variables and parameters. The nuisance is not without merit, though, as it provides an immense level of security that would otherwise be unavailable in SQL Server.

Scope exists to isolate unrelated objects from each other. By Microsoft's definition, scope is a stored procedure, trigger, function, or batch. Two statements are in the same scope if they are within the same stored procedure, trigger, function, or batch. It is similar behavior in practice to how local and global variables behave in application code.

If variables, parameters, and temporary objects were available everywhere, regardless of where they were called from, then what would stop someone from accessing data that they are not authorized to access? How would two variables named @username interact when declared separately but at the same time?

As a result, scope is an important aspect of SQL Server security, and one that we rely on to write predictable, maintainable, and easy-to-debug code. While understanding scope improves our ability to write quality dynamic SQL, it also improves the rest of the TSQL we write, as scope is a feature that affects all database code, regardless of its location.

Managing Scope in Dynamic SQL

Dealing with scope in Dynamic SQL isn't terribly different than when working with a stored procedure. Imagine everything within the dynamic SQL statement as being separate from the remainder of your TSQL and act accordingly. To illustrate the similarities, consider the following TSQL, which is similar to our previous search examples:

```
DECLARE @sql_command NVARCHAR(MAX);

SELECT @sql_command = '
DECLARE @FirstName NVARCHAR(50) = "Edward";
SELECT
      *
FROM Person.Person
WHERE FirstName = @FirstName;'
EXEC sp_executesql @sql_command;
SELECT @FirstName
```

In this case, the variable @FirstName is declared within the command string, and as such is not available outside of the scope of the dynamic SQL statement. The SELECT at the end will fail as @FirstName no longer exists:

```
Msg 137, Level 15, State 2, Line 84
Must declare the scalar variable "@FirstName".
```

Similarly, a variable declared outside of a command string will be unavailable for use on the inside. Last, multiple command strings each execute in their own scope. A variable declared in one command string will not be available in another dynamic SQL statement.

169

To manage our code correctly, we need to treat variables in a given scope as isolated and unrelated to those in a different scope. In this chapter we will discuss a variety of ways in which data can be shared between different scopes. This will allow us to share data when needed, or intentionally not share data when we would prefer more privacy or security within a given scope. SQL Server provides many ways to isolate or share data, allowing us to choose which method is best for a given situation.

Using OUTPUT in Dynamic SQL

By default, any variables that are passed into sp_executesql are read-only. That is, they can be used within the scope of the dynamic SQL whenever needed, but when the dynamic SQL is complete, and execution returns to the calling TSQL, any changes to parameters are not saved. Consider the TSQL in Listing 5-2, focusing on the UPDATE of the @FirstName parameter.

Listing 5-2. Dynamic SQL: Updating Parameters Within the Command String

```
DECLARE @sql_command NVARCHAR(MAX);
DECLARE @parameter_list NVARCHAR(MAX);
DECLARE @first_name NVARCHAR(50) = 'Edward';

SELECT @sql_command = '
SELECT
     *
FROM Person.Person
WHERE FirstName = @first_name;
SELECT @first_name = "Xavier";
SELECT @first_name;
'

SELECT @parameter_list = '@first_name NVARCHAR(50)'
EXEC sp_executesql @sql_command, @parameter_list, @first_name;

SELECT @first_name;
GO
```

In the preceding example, the last action taken within the command string is to reassign the name "Xavier" to the parameter @first_name. Even though the parameter is read-only, we are allowed to change the value of it within the dynamic SQL. The new value will remain relevant and in-scope until the end of the dynamic SQL. It is important to note that, despite the fact that we used the same variable name for the first name both within and outside of our dynamic SQL, they are still treated as completely separate variables. Depending on your applications, there may be value in using different variable names, which would help differentiate between separate variables, or in using the same variable names, which would make it more obvious when a distinct value is being used across TSQL statements, each with a different scope. The output from the preceding code is shown in Figure 5-2.

	BusinessEntityID	PersonType	NameStyle	Tit
1	3731	IN	0	NI
2	13658	IN	0	NI
3	4241	IN	0	NI
4	3732	IN	0	NI
5	13631	IN	0	NI
6	4229	IN	0	NI
7	13657	IN	0	NI
8	567	SC	0	Mi
9	13651	IN	0	NI
10	3746	IN	0	NI

	(No column name)
1	Xavier

	(No column name)
1	Edward

Figure 5-2. *Reassigning a variable within dynamic SQL without the OUTPUT operator*

The results of the search are retuned, as we expected them to be. The SELECT of the first name from within the dynamic SQL shows that our reassignment of the parameter is allowed, and succeeded. When we check the variable again, after the dynamic SQL execution is complete, though, we can see that @first_name is set to "Edward" instead of "Xavier." As a slight adjustment, we can go ahead and change the variable names, as shown in Listing 5-3, which helps emphasize that they are distinct and separate from each other.

Listing 5-3. Rewrite of TSQL from Listing 5-2, which Returns the Same Results

```
DECLARE @sql_command NVARCHAR(MAX);
DECLARE @parameter_list NVARCHAR(MAX);
DECLARE @first_name_calling_sql NVARCHAR(50) = 'Edward';

SELECT @sql_command = '
SELECT
     *
FROM Person.Person
WHERE FirstName = @first_name_within_dynamic_sql;
SELECT @first_name_within_dynamic_sql = "Xavier";
SELECT @first_name_within_dynamic_sql;
'

SELECT @parameter_list = '@first_name_within_dynamic_sql NVARCHAR(50)'
EXEC sp_executesql @sql_command, @parameter_list, @first_name_calling_sql;

SELECT @first_name_calling_sql;
```

The results from this slightly different version are exactly the same as before. The only difference was that we changed the name of the variable in our calling TSQL to @first_name_calling_sql and the parameter for the dynamic SQL statement to @first_name_within_dynamic_sql.

What if we intentionally want any changes to our parameters made within the dynamic SQL to be saved and passed back out to the parameters that were passed in initially? The solution is nearly the same as with a stored procedure. Simply add OUTPUT to any parameter that is to pass its value back to the calling TSQL and it will work very similarly to our examples earlier, as seen in Listing 5-4.

Listing 5-4. Using OUTPUT to Permanently Modify a Parameter

```
DECLARE @sql_command NVARCHAR(MAX);
DECLARE @parameter_list NVARCHAR(MAX);
DECLARE @first_name_calling_sql NVARCHAR(50) = 'Edward';

SELECT @sql_command = '
SELECT
     *
FROM Person.Person
```

```
WHERE FirstName = @first_name_within_dynamic_sql;
SELECT @first_name_within_dynamic_sql = "Xavier";
SELECT @first_name_within_dynamic_sql;
'

SELECT @parameter_list = '@first_name_within_dynamic_sql NVARCHAR(50) OUTPUT'
EXEC sp_executesql @sql_command, @parameter_list, @first_name_calling_sql
OUTPUT;

SELECT @first_name_calling_sql;
```

In this example, we explicitly flag the first name parameter as an OUTPUT parameter. This indicates that, if the value is changed within the dynamic SQL, that change will be persisted after the command string has been executed and we switch back to the scope of the calling TSQL. The output is seen in Figure 5-3.

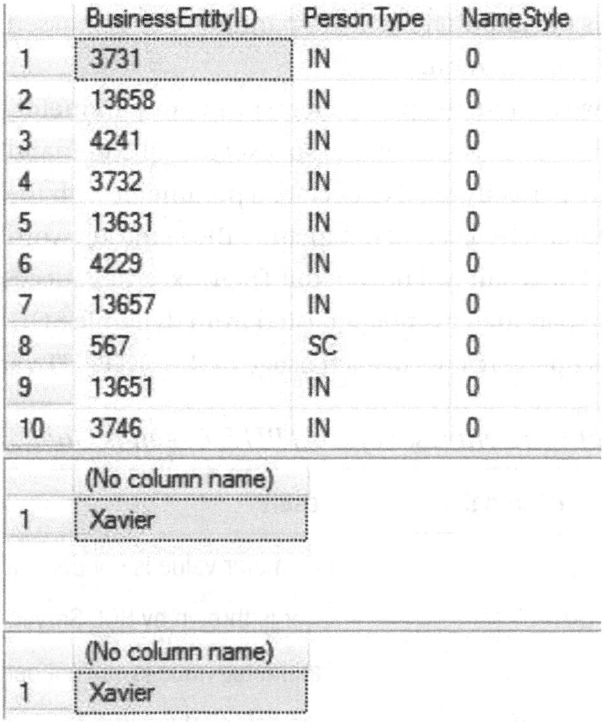

	BusinessEntityID	PersonType	NameStyle
1	3731	IN	0
2	13658	IN	0
3	4241	IN	0
4	3732	IN	0
5	13631	IN	0
6	4229	IN	0
7	13657	IN	0
8	567	SC	0
9	13651	IN	0
10	3746	IN	0

	(No column name)
1	Xavier

	(No column name)
1	Xavier

Figure 5-3. *Results when OUTPUT was used to persist @first_name_within_dynamic_sql*

This time, when we change the value of `@first_name_within_dynamic_sql` to "Xavier," that value is passed from the dynamic SQL back to sp_executesql and remains until we act on it again. This is immensely useful when we want a parameter to change within dynamic SQL or we would like to pass variables in and out seamlessly.

Note that in this TSQL, the OUTPUT keyword is appended to both the parameter list and the parameter name in the sp_executesql statement. The keyword must be applied in both places or the parameter value will not be updated as expected. If OUTPUT is omitted from the parameter list, then SQL Server does not know that it is intended to be persisted from our dynamic SQL statement. The result is an explicit error message calling this out:

```
Msg 8162, Level 16, State 2, Line 152
The formal parameter "@first_name_within_dynamic_sql" was not declared as
an OUTPUT parameter, but the actual parameter passed in requested output.
```

Luckily the message is very easy to understand, and makes it clear how to fix the error. SQL Server does not allow an OUTPUT parameter to be passed into a variable that is not declared in the same fashion.

What happens if we declare the parameter within our parameter list as an OUTPUT variable, but do not declare it as such in the sp_executesql command? In this scenario, no error is thrown. It is perfectly legal to declare a parameter with the OUTPUT keyword within the parameter list and not include the same keyword when executing the command string. The result will be that the TSQL executes successfully, and the value of the first name parameter is not persisted from dynamic SQL back to the calling TSQL. Table 5-1 sums up the results of each usage of the OUTPUT variable.

Table 5-1. *Results of Different Uses of OUTPUT. Green Is Good, Red Is Bad*

Parameter List	Input Variable	Result
		Parameter value is not persisted.
	OUTPUT	Error is thrown by SQL Server.
OUTPUT		Parameter value is still not persisted.
OUTPUT	OUTPUT	Parameter value persisted from dynamic SQL.

The only way to successfully alter the value of a parameter and return it to the calling TSQL is to use OUTPUT on both the parameter list and the variable being passed in.

To avoid confusion when writing dynamic SQL, avoid the mixed scenarios where one variable is declared as OUTPUT but not the other. The results in one case will be an error message, which is certainly not desirable. The other ambiguous case will make for a difficult-to-understand piece of code whose purpose will not be clear to any other developer, and could lead to coding mistakes in the future.

Any parameter may be passed into dynamic SQL that is allowed to be passed into a stored procedure, including tables and even cursors. Table variables, discussed in the next section, are read-only, though, and may not be set as OUTPUT parameters.

Table Variables and Temporary Tables

An additional way of persisting data in SQL Server is to create table variables or temporary tables and store data in them. The behavior of each of these is somewhat unique, and offers an alternate way to manage data within dynamic SQL. Let's discuss each in a bit more detail and illustrate each behavior and how it could impact your TSQL.

Table Variables

Consider the TSQL in Listing 5-5.

Listing 5-5. Results of Using a Table Variable Within Dynamic SQL that Is Declared Outside of It

```
DECLARE @sql_command NVARCHAR(MAX);
DECLARE @parameter_list NVARCHAR(MAX);

DECLARE @last_names TABLE (
    last_name NVARCHAR(50));

SELECT @sql_command = '
SELECT DISTINCT
    FirstName
FROM Person.Person
WHERE LastName IN (SELECT last_name FROM @last_names)'

EXEC sp_executesql @sql_command;
```

Running this TSQL results immediately in an error:

```
Msg 1087, Level 15, State 2, Line 197
Must declare the table variable "@last_names".
```

The @last_names table variable may be created at the start of our example, but does not exist within the scope of the dynamic SQL. We try to return a set of first names using that data, but it cannot be found. As a result, any attempt to access it will fail. We can pass a table variable into dynamic SQL, but it requires the additional step of declaring a custom type and using it as the data type, as seen in Listing 5-6.

Listing 5-6. Passing a Table Variable into Dynamic SQL

```
CREATE TYPE last_name_table AS TABLE
      (last_name NVARCHAR(50));
GO

DECLARE @sql_command NVARCHAR(MAX);
DECLARE @parameter_list NVARCHAR(MAX);
DECLARE @first_name_calling_sql NVARCHAR(50) = 'Edward';

DECLARE @last_names AS last_name_table;

INSERT INTO @last_names
      (last_name)
SELECT
      LastName
FROM Person.Person WHERE FirstName = @first_name_calling_sql;

SELECT @sql_command = '
SELECT DISTINCT
      FirstName
FROM Person.Person
WHERE LastName IN (SELECT last_name FROM @last_name_table)
'

SELECT @parameter_list = '@first_name_within_dynamic_sql NVARCHAR(50),
@last_name_table last_name_table READONLY'
EXEC sp_executesql @sql_command, @parameter_list, @first_name_calling_sql,
@last_names;
```

The first step is to create a table type once that will be used for the remainder of this example. It's passed as a parameter into sp_executesql just like any other parameter, but must be declared as READONLY within the parameter list. Table variables are always read-only and cannot be modified within the dynamic SQL that they are passed into. If we were to try and delete from the table variable, or make any change to it at all, we would then receive an error:

```
Msg 10700, Level 16, State 1, Line 255
The table-valued parameter "@last_name_table" is READONLY and cannot be
modified.
```

SQL Server provides a very direct error message, reminding you that attempting to alter the read-only table variable will fail.

Temporary Tables

Temporary tables behave similarly to table variables, but are declared, persisted, and disposed of differently. Unlike a table variable, a temporary table will persist until dropped, or until its calling session ends. Let's retry our initial example, but using a temporary table instead of a table variable, as seen in Listing 5-7.

Listing 5-7. Results of Using a Temp Table Within Dynamic SQL that is Declared Outside of It

```
DECLARE @sql_command NVARCHAR(MAX);
DECLARE @parameter_list NVARCHAR(MAX);

CREATE TABLE #last_names (
     last_name NVARCHAR(50));

SELECT @sql_command = '
SELECT DISTINCT
     FirstName
FROM Person.Person
WHERE LastName IN (SELECT last_name FROM #last_names)'

EXEC sp_executesql @sql_command;

DROP TABLE #last_names
```

This time, we do not receive an error message, but instead a result set (albeit an empty one). What if we modify the temporary table within the dynamic SQL? Listing 5-8 shows the resulting TSQL.

Listing 5-8. Results of Modifying a Temp Table Within Dynamic SQL

```
DECLARE @sql_command NVARCHAR(MAX);
DECLARE @parameter_list NVARCHAR(MAX);

CREATE TABLE #last_names (
     last_name NVARCHAR(50));

INSERT INTO #last_names
     (last_name)
SELECT 'Thomas'

SELECT @sql_command = '
SELECT DISTINCT
     FirstName
FROM Person.Person
WHERE LastName IN (SELECT last_name FROM #last_names);

INSERT INTO #last_names
     (last_name)
SELECT "Smith";
'

EXEC sp_executesql @sql_command;

SELECT * FROM #last_names;

DROP TABLE #last_names;
```

The results indicate that the temp table was not only accessible within the dynamic SQL, but was written successfully, as seen in Figure 5-4.

Figure 5-4. Temporary tables created outside of dynamic SQL are also accessible within

The first result set shows that the temporary table is accessible within dynamic SQL. The second result set shows that it can be modified within the dynamic SQL and those results persisted later on in our example. This is very useful, and provides a simple way to manage data that needs to pass between dynamic SQL and other TSQL seamlessly. Since we are on a roll, what happens when we declare a temporary table within dynamic SQL and attempt to access it later in our code? Listing 5-9 shows the TSQL to accomplish this.

Listing 5-9. Results of Creating a Temp Table Within Dynamic SQL and Accessing It Later

```
DECLARE @sql_command NVARCHAR(MAX);
DECLARE @parameter_list NVARCHAR(MAX);

SELECT @sql_command = '
CREATE TABLE #last_names (
      last_name NVARCHAR(50));
```

```
INSERT INTO #last_names
      (last_name)
SELECT "Thomas";
'

EXEC sp_executesql @sql_command;

SELECT DISTINCT
      FirstName
FROM Person.Person
WHERE LastName IN (SELECT last_name FROM #last_names);
```

Our luck has run out, and the preceding example resulted in an error:

```
Msg 208, Level 16, State 0, Line 316
Invalid object name '#last_names'.
```

While a temporary table declared in our calling TSQL is accessible within dynamic SQL, the reverse is not true. The table #last_names exists only within the scope of our dynamic SQL and will not be available elsewhere. Similarly, referencing the temp table in another block of dynamic SQL later in our code will result in the same error. In other words, the following example will also fail with the same error message, as shown in Listing 5-10.

Listing 5-10. Reusing a Temp Table in Subsequent Dynamic SQL Is Also Not Valid

```
DECLARE @sql_command NVARCHAR(MAX);
DECLARE @parameter_list NVARCHAR(MAX);

SELECT @sql_command = '
CREATE TABLE #last_names (
      last_name NVARCHAR(50));

INSERT INTO #last_names
      (last_name)
SELECT "Thomas";
'

EXEC sp_executesql @sql_command;
```

```
SELECT @sql_command = '
SELECT DISTINCT
      FirstName
FROM Person.Person
WHERE LastName IN (SELECT last_name FROM #last_names);'

EXEC sp_executesql @sql_command;
```

Each section of dynamic SQL exists within its own isolated scope, and will not share locally defined objects.

Be mindful when creating and accessing temporary tables, to ensure that they are available where needed and not out of scope when required later in your code. Also, keep in mind that these temp tables are only available within your current SQL Server connection. If you attempt to access a temp table created in this connection from a separate application or connection, it will also be unavailable.

Last, a temporary table will be automatically dropped when its connection is ended. It is a good practice to drop temp tables when your work with them is complete, but if you don't, SQL Server will remove them for you. This automatic removal only occurs when the connection under which the temp table was created is ended. If that connection is maintained indefinitely, then the temp table will also remain indefinitely. If a table with the same name were later declared within the same session, an error would result because the table already exists.

One additional note on temporary tables: if you are operating repeatedly on them to retrieve a small subset of rows, consider indexing. A temp table may have a clustered index defined on it, as well as nonclustered indexes. Primary keys may also be added to enforce uniqueness when necessary. Indexing a commonly queried column or set of columns can greatly improve performance by reducing reads and producing higher quality execution plans.

Global Temporary Tables

One final option that is available for us are global temporary tables. These tables are declared just like standard temp tables, but with a prefix of "##" instead of "#." Global temp tables are available server-wide for any TSQL accessing the same SQL Server instance they are created on. This access is not restricted based on connection or by database access.

Once created, a global temp table will persist until all connections to it are ended. The table may be created within the scope of dynamic SQL or the calling TSQL and will still be available within any other scope on the server.

Consider the example in Listing 5-11, similar to our preceding code.

Listing 5-11. Example of Global Temporary Table Usage

```
DECLARE @sql_command NVARCHAR(MAX);
DECLARE @parameter_list NVARCHAR(MAX);

SELECT @sql_command = '
CREATE TABLE ##last_names (
      last_name NVARCHAR(50));

INSERT INTO ##last_names
      (last_name)
SELECT "Thomas";'

EXEC sp_executesql @sql_command;

SELECT @sql_command = '
SELECT DISTINCT
      FirstName
FROM Person.Person
WHERE LastName IN (SELECT last_name FROM ##last_names);'

EXEC sp_executesql @sql_command;

SELECT * FROM ##last_names;
-- DROP TABLE ##last_names;
```

In this TSQL, we declare a global temp table within dynamic SQL. We then select some first names from `Person.Person`, using the global temp table, and later access it again in our calling TSQL. Everything works exactly as intended (this does happen sometimes)! Note that at the end of the example, we did not drop the global temp table. As a result, it will remain available until either all connections using it are ended, or we explicitly drop it. This can be beneficial if we want to access it again here, or from another location. It can also be problematic if we forget about it and try to declare a temp table with the same name in the future:

```
CREATE TABLE ##last_names (
    last_name NVARCHAR(50));
```

When we run this table creation, an error is generated:

```
Msg 2714, Level 16, State 6, Line 351
There is already an object named '##last_names' in the database.
```

It is critically important to manage global temp tables within any code that creates or uses them. Forgetting to drop a temp table may turn out OK if you happen to end the connection and it is automatically removed by SQL Server. If another connection is made to the table, though, then it will not be dropped by SQL Server, as it will still be in use. The best practice for dealing with any temporary tables is to drop them when they no longer are needed. This removes any possibility of the table persisting and being accessed inadvertently later on, or being created when it already exists.

Always drop a temporary table when it is no longer needed. This ensures that it does not interfere with future table creation and is not somehow accessed when no longer needed.

Since we have our table ##last_names available, we may as well demonstrate another feature of global temporary tables: their availability anywhere on the server:

```
CREATE DATABASE temp_table_test;
GO
USE temp_table_test;
GO
SELECT
    *
FROM ##last_names;
```

Even within our new database, the global temporary table was still available. Since we've yet to drop this SQL Server connection, it will remain available indefinitely to any other connection on the server. This leads into a discussion of global temp table security, for which there happens to be none. Once created, a global temporary table is not only available everywhere, but to any login or user in any database, without restrictions.

In the last chapter, we created a user called "VeryLimitedUser", which only had access to a single stored procedure and no explicit access to any other database, tables, or SQL Server functionality. What happens when this user tries to access our global temp table?

```
EXECUTE AS USER = 'VeryLimitedUser';
GO
SELECT
        *
FROM ##last_names;
REVERT;
GO
DROP TABLE ##last_names;
GO
```

Despite having nearly no permissions on our server, this user was able to select data from the global temp table without issue. This raises a potential security concern with global temporary tables in that they are by design, accessible by anyone else on the server, regardless of their specific permissions. In addition, it is not possible to place permissions on a global temp table to restrict this behavior. Be mindful of any global temp tables that you create and be sure that, in the event another user was to somehow access it, that this access would not be problematic. If your global temp table contains any sensitive data, consider storing it in another format, such as a table variable, standard temporary table, or in a permanent table that is used for staging or temporary data. Hashing or encrypting the data can also be a good way to limit its access elsewhere, if security is a concern, as it will reduce usability from other connections.

Even if a user does not know the exact name of a global temp table, they could query TempDB.sys.tables to determine its name and then query it freely. This backdoor would require read access to TempDB, but from there a sneaky person could learn about objects that they have not been granted direct access to, and read data from them once identified.

Another issue that can occur is if two global temp tables are created from two different connections that are given the same name. Since these tables are global and in scope for the entire SQL Server instance, no two may share the same name. If this occurs, an error will be thrown, and the second person to attempt to declare the new table will be unable to continue without renaming it to a name that is not in use.

Avoid using global temporary tables whenever possible. Their lack of access controls and scope make them obvious security and maintainability hazards.

I would propose as a best practice to never use global temporary tables. Their functionality can be mirrored using other more secure (and more reliable) methods. If you need to maintain legacy code with global temp tables, do everything you can to minimize access and sensitive data in them. Ultimately, replacing those tables with temporary tables, table variables, or permanent tables would be preferable. Global temp tables are an excellent example of why scope is important and how access that is too easy and convenient can result in insecure and unpredictable code.

Using Permanent Tables for Temporary Storage

For a scenario where temporary data is stored very often for a specific functionality, creating a permanent table can be an efficient and secure way to manage this data. For our previous example, we could alternatively manage the list of last names in the manner shown in Listing 5-12.

Listing 5-12. Using a Permanent Table for Temporary Storage

```
CREATE TABLE dbo.last_names_staging (
     last_name NVARCHAR(50) NOT NULL CONSTRAINT PK_last_names_staging
     PRIMARY KEY CLUSTERED);
DECLARE @sql_command NVARCHAR(MAX);
DECLARE @parameter_list NVARCHAR(MAX);

SELECT @sql_command = '

INSERT INTO dbo.last_names_staging
     (last_name)
SELECT "Thomas";'

EXEC sp_executesql @sql_command;
```

```
SELECT @sql_command = '
SELECT DISTINCT
       FirstName
FROM Person.Person
WHERE LastName IN (SELECT last_name FROM dbo.last_names_staging);'

EXEC sp_executesql @sql_command;

SELECT * FROM dbo.last_names_staging;
```

In this example, everything works as it did in our previous examples, except that our "temporary storage" is rather permanent. It may seem counterintuitive to create a permanent object to store temporary data, but there are many benefits in doing so:

- Data is persisted permanently, regardless of connection.

- Table can be accessed from anywhere on the server, regardless of database.

- Security can be applied to the table, ensuring only authorized access.

- Indexes, statistics, and constraints may be added to the table and will persist indefinitely.

- No need to access TempDB.

The drawbacks of using a permanent table are few, but significant:

- It becomes a permanent object that requires maintenance and documentation.

- Usage must be managed so that data is always relevant.

To summarize all of the preceding points: use permanent tables when data needs to be stored on a more long-term basis, or when optimization becomes important. While indexes can be placed on temporary tables and table variables (with limitations), having a permanent place to stage temporary data can be extremely convenient and removes the need to constantly manage temporary objects.

Permanent tables also provide us with the ability to recover more fully from a disaster. If a SQL Server were to failover, crash, or restart, then any data in the permanent table would be there when the server became available again as it was prior to the crash. Temporary objects, on the other hand, would not be recovered. If the staging of temporary data is critical and we want to ensure that intermediary states are tracked and maintained, then a permanent table is an excellent way to provide this level of support and availability.

Equally importantly, limit the use of tables for this purpose to only when it is sensible and efficient. Creating permanent tables for all temporary data creation/access could quickly result in a plethora of objects that require care and maintenance. One option to assist with organization would be to create the table in its own schema, thus separating it from the rest of the objects in the database. Alternatively, for smaller use cases, appending a prefix to these tables may suffice, in order to organize and find them easily.

One final consideration for temporary data is to use a Memory-Optimized table. If we want the flexibility and durability of a permanent table, but also want speed, then a Memory-Optimized table will provide all the benefits of a standard table without using TempDB. Instead, data will be stored in memory, providing significantly faster speeds. Creating the table with durability of SCHEMA_AND_DATA will ensure that it is recovered properly from an outage situation. If data permanence is not important, then a Memory-Optimized table with durability of SCHEMA_ONLY will perform extremely fast, while not persisting data in the event of a restart. The cost to use Memory-Optimized tables is memory, while saving disk resources and IO against TempDB. If the volume of temporary data is very large, consider your memory resources carefully before implementing.

When a "permanent temporary table" is no longer needed, it can easily be dropped. This cleanup step is important, as we don't want to clutter a server with unneeded, temporary, or unused objects. This is true for traditional tables or Memory-Optimized tables. Creating any permanent database object carries with it the implicit responsibility to document and manage it effectively. When the day comes that it is no longer needed, take the added time to deprecate and ultimately remove it.

Output Data Directly to a Table from Dynamic SQL

One final way to collect data from any stored procedure, including dynamic SQL, is to insert it directly into a table as a part of the EXEC statement. This example, as seen in Listing 5-13, is a new twist on our temporary storage seen previously, eliminating the need to explicitly manage it within dynamic SQL.

Listing 5-13. Inserting Dynamic SQL Output Directly into Another Table

```
DECLARE @sql_command NVARCHAR(MAX);
DECLARE @parameter_list NVARCHAR(MAX);

CREATE TABLE #last_names (
      last_name NVARCHAR(50));

SELECT @sql_command = '
SELECT
      LastName
FROM Person.Person
WHERE FirstName = "Edward";
'

INSERT INTO #last_names
  (last_name)
EXEC sp_executesql @sql_command;

SELECT
      *
FROM #last_names

DROP TABLE #last_names;
```

In this example, we declare the temporary table #last_names at the start of the TSQL. Note that when we execute our command string, the output is directly placed into the temp table, without the need for passing parameters or managing additional objects. This is a very convenient way to save the output from dynamic SQL or any other stored procedure, and to do so quickly and efficiently. This is also an excellent way to save the output from a system stored procedure, as seen in Listing 5-14.

Listing 5-14. Using the INSERT...EXEC Syntax to Collect Output from sp_who

```
CREATE TABLE #sp_who_data
(
      spid SMALLINT,
      ecid SMALLINT,
      status NCHAR(30),
      loginame NCHAR(128),
```

```
    hostname NCHAR(128),
    blk CHAR(5),
    dbname NCHAR(128),
    cmd NCHAR(16),
    request_id INT
)

INSERT INTO #sp_who_data
(spid, ecid, status, loginame, hostname, blk, dbname, cmd, request_id)
EXEC sp_who;

SELECT * FROM #sp_who_data
WHERE dbname = 'AdventureWorks2016CTP3'; -- Optional filter criteria.  Feel
free to remove if not needed.

DROP TABLE #sp_who_data;
```

A very common administrative need is to view the current SQL Server connections and gather details about who is connected to what database, and what they are up to. While executing sp_who gathers that data, it only outputs it to the results window. On a busy server with many connections, we will want to filter that data by database, user, or some other criteria. We may also want to log that data permanently, for auditing or other security purposes. The ability to insert that data directly into a table allows us to efficiently filter it down to a single database and get only the connections there, rather than on the entire server. Note that the data types in the #sp_who_data table were taken from MSDN and are not a byproduct of my active imagination: https://msdn. microsoft.com/en-us/library/ms174313.aspx

This same syntax can be applied to any stored procedure, system stored procedure, or dynamic SQL output. While it is convenient, it is also somewhat inflexible. The table that the data is to be inserted into must be defined ahead of time, and be exactly the same structure as the output data. While it would be convenient to execute our command string while also creating a temporary table, SQL Server does not allow that syntax:

```
SELECT
    EXEC sp_who
INTO #sp_who_data;
```

```
SELECT INTO #sp_who_data
EXEC sp_who;
```

```
SELECT INTO #sp_who_data
(EXEC sp_who);
```

No matter how creative we get, there is no way to force SQL Server to create the temporary table on-the-fly for you. SELECT INTO is not allowed in conjunction with stored procedure execution, and no rearrangement of the preceding TSQL will make this magically work. As a result, we must always define the target table for our output ahead of time.

Conclusion

While scope prevents us from effortlessly moving data in between dynamic SQL, our other TSQL, and additional stored procedure executions, a number of tools exist that provide many ways in which to accomplish this anyway. As with any toolbox, always choose the correct tool for each job. Typically, the more temporary the data, the less need there is for creating elaborate structures or methodologies to manage it.

If data is needed once, or only for the duration of a specific stored procedure, consider using the INSERT...EXEC syntax or a temporary table. If data should be persisted, then a permanent table may be a great way to manage that temporary data. Global temporary tables, regardless of use case, should generally be avoided, as they afford no security and will pose maintainability issues when multiple sessions create or access the same table.

Cleanup

The following TSQL will clean up any objects created in this chapter, if they exist:

```
IF EXISTS (SELECT * FROM sys.procedures WHERE procedures.name = 'get_people')
BEGIN
    DROP PROCEDURE dbo.get_people;
END
GO
IF EXISTS (SELECT * FROM sys.databases WHERE databases.name = 'temp_table_test')
BEGIN
    DROP DATABASE temp_table_test;
END
GO
```

CHAPTER 6

Performance Optimization

No discussion of dynamic SQL would be complete without a dive into its performance. Dynamic SQL can greatly improve performance, but can also increase complexity if not used effectively. As was the case with security, optimization is a topic that could easily occupy significantly larger books than this one. As such, we will try to maintain a focus on dynamic SQL and any performance concerns that relate to it.

Query Execution

Before jumping into the performance of dynamic SQL and a variety of ways to monitor and tune it, it is necessary to quickly review the process of query execution. What happens when you execute a TSQL statement through the moment that the results are returned and it is complete? Query execution is typically broken into four steps:

Parsing

A query is checked for syntax and if there are any unidentified or invalid TSQL commands, an error will be thrown. In addition, the query is broken into a list of very high-level steps that will be followed by SQL Server throughout the remainder of this process. These steps are simple operations, such as selecting data from a table, joining another table, or executing some dynamic SQL or stored procedure.

Binding

This step is primarily concerned with validating objects and ensuring that they are both valid and used in the correct context. Tables, columns, functions, stored procedures, and any other named objects are checked against SQL Server's system catalogs to verify that the names are correct and that they are being referenced correctly. At this point, if no error has been received, then we know that syntax and object names are all correct.

© Edward Pollack 2019
E. Pollack, *Dynamic SQL*, https://doi.org/10.1007/978-1-4842-4318-3_6

The list generated in the parsing step is used with this new information to generate what is known as an algebrized tree. This tree is a listing of steps that must be performed in order for the query to execute correctly.

Optimization

This is the most complex part of the execution process and involves SQL Server needing to take the tree from the binding step and find a good execution plan for it very, very quickly. This work proceeds similarly to the way a chess program attempts to find the best move at any point in the game. Basically, the query optimizer comes up with a possible execution plan and assigns a cost to it, then evaluates more execution plans until it decides that it has found the best plan, or one that is good enough. SQL Server can evaluate thousands of execution plans before deciding which to use.

Query optimization is a race against time, as the query itself will take time to process, but the optimization process also takes time. The optimizer needs to weigh this in order to not waste too much time optimizing a simple query, but also take enough time that it finds a plan that performs well. For example, if we had a query that took 2 seconds to execute, and the optimizer could spend 1 more second to save a ½ second during execution, then it would have wasted that time in doing so. If it could save 1.5 seconds using only 0.1 seconds of effort, then it would be a great deal. In addition to time, server resources such as CPU are considered. This process happens very quickly and is one of the most complex components of SQL Server.

The result of optimization is a list of detailed steps that SQL Server can execute, in order, to return the results desired in the original query.

Execution

The steps from the optimization process are executed, and any actions required are taken to complete them.

Optimization Tools

To review performance and make intelligent decisions based on it, we need to define a set of tools that we will use going forward that will assist in this process. It is impossible to make consistently good decisions regarding performance without multiple metrics that we are comfortable using. If a query is slow, we need to know which part of it is the bottleneck and identify why this is the case.

Query Execution Plan

Query execution plans are the first, and most visual of the tools available to us. Execution plans are the steps that the optimizer came up with during the optimization step and are then executed by SQL Server.

The actual execution plan from a query can be viewed in SQL Server by clicking on the "Include Actual Execution Plan" icon in SQL Server Management Studio, or using the keyboard shortcut Ctrl-M, as seen in Figure 6-1.

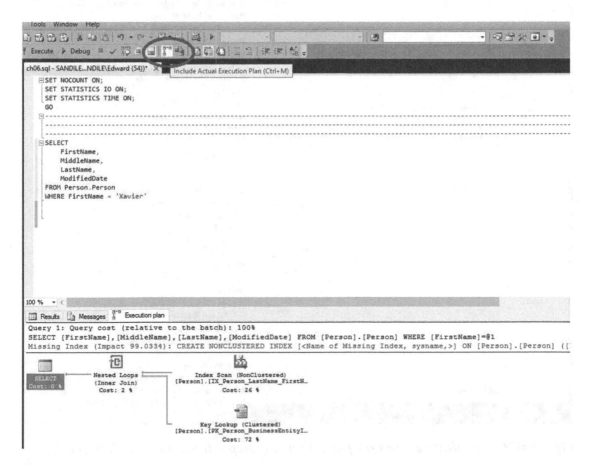

Figure 6-1. *Turning on and using query execution plans in SQL Server Management Studio*

The icon to turn on the actual execution plan is circled in the figure. What you get in return for turning this on is an additional tab in the results window, labeled "Execution Plan." Included in this tab is a section for every query executed, including the query text. The graphical portion is read from right-to-left and is made of icons that represent operations performed by SQL Server, such as reading a table, joining data sets, sorting, and so on. If SQL Server thinks that a new index could help query performance, it will suggest it in green between the query text and the graphical plan. Hovering over an icon will produce details on the step, including rows processed, estimated IO, CPU, and subtree cost, as shown in Figure 6-2.

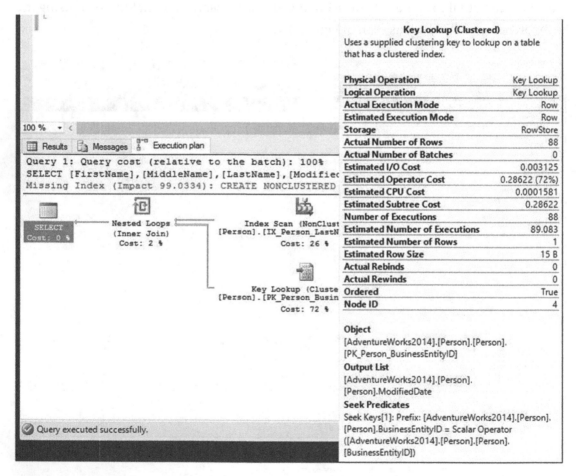

Figure 6-2. *Viewing detailed properties for any step within an execution plan*

Subtree cost is an indication of the cost determined during the optimization step and provides an idea of which parts of the query are most expensive to execute, as well as how the optimizer believed a query would perform prior to execution.

The width of the lines in between steps will indicate the relative number of rows processed by that step. Hovering over one of these lines will provide some basic information about the data transfer represented by the line. Figure 6-3 shows an example of these details.

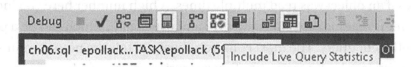

e to the batch): 100%
me], [LastName], [ModifiedDat
4): CREATE NONCLUSTERED INE

	Index Scan (NonClustered
	[Person].[IX Person LastName
Actual Number of Rows	88
Estimated Number of Rows	89.083
Estimated Row Size	130 B
Estimated Data Size	11 KB

[Person].[PK_Person_BusinessE

Figure 6-3. *Viewing details of the output from one step of the execution plan*

Execution plans may also include warnings, errors, or other issues that SQL Server ran into while executing a query. When in doubt, take a closer look at any troublesome steps, which could reveal useful information about why a query is performing poorly. Hovering over any part of an execution plan will provide additional details on the step. Opening the properties for a step will return an additional array of information regarding how the step performed.

Starting in SQL Server 2016, live query statistics were introduced, allowing you to view execution progress as a query moves through the process from parsing and binding to optimization and execution. This may be turned on by clicking on the icon directly next to the "Include Actual Execution Plan" button shown in Figure 6-4.

Debug   ✓   ...   ch06.sql - epollack...TASK\epollack (59   Include Live Query Statistics   OT

Figure 6-4. *Viewing live query statistics*

Live query statistics will update details of execution plan progress as steps complete. This can be a big timesaver when debugging large, complex, or slow queries, as you can get feedback on performance without having to wait until an entire process completes.

STATISTICS IO

SQL Server can provide information about which tables were read, and how many reads occurred against them. This can be turned on with the following TSQL:

```
SET STATISTICS IO ON;
```

This is very important information, as it indicates overall IO use. If a query is running slow, it could be the result of excessive reads against a table. The execution plan may not always convey the enormity of an IO bottleneck, but the knowledge that a query that returns two rows is taking a million reads to do so is an indication of a possible problem. Often, the two will correlate with each other, providing a solid foundation on which to understand why a query is slow. Once enabled, STATISTICS IO will add additional details to the text output screen, as shown in Figure 6-5.

```
100 %   ▾  <
  Results    Messages   Execution plan
   Table 'Person'. Scan count 1, logical reads 387, physical reads 0, read-ahead reads 0, lob logical reads 0,
```

Figure 6-5. *Example output from STATISTICS IO*

While there are a number of operations detailed in Figure 6-5, we will limit our discussion to the first four:

Object

This is the name of the table or view that is being accessed.

Scan Count

This indicates if an object was read multiple times. A high number here can indicate that SQL Server is reading the same data over and over again, which can be a potential sign of an inefficient query. The most common causes of this are nested common-table expressions, correlated subqueries, or other scenarios where a table is accessed more than once within a single statement.

Logical Reads

This is the number of reads made on the object indicated, regardless of whether the data is cached in memory or not. This will be the metric we refer to throughout this chapter whenever we are concerned with IO read activity, as it will remain static for a given query, even if the physical reads change.

Physical Reads

This is the number of reads where the data was not yet in the buffer cache. Whenever data is read for a query, it is placed into memory and remains there until it ages out or is replaced at a later time. The initial read of data into memory from your storage system can be very expensive. If queries are constantly making physical reads, that could be a sign that queries are reading too much data, or that there is memory pressure on the server.

When you execute a query and access data for the first time, this number typically will be the same as the logical reads, but all subsequent executions will show zero for this metric because the data will now be in memory from the first execution.

STATISTICS TIME

What is likely the most important metric to any consumer of data is the time it took for the server to return the data we are looking for. As database professionals, the most common complaint we will ever hear is, "It's slow!" This metric breaks out the execution time for each step, which can be useful in determining which query in a stored procedure took the most time to execute. The following is the output for STATISTICS TIME for the same query used in the preceding execution plan:

```
SQL Server parse and compile time:
  CPU time = 0 ms, elapsed time = 0 ms.
SQL Server Execution Times:
  CPU time = 0 ms, elapsed time = 64 ms.
```

Parse and compile time is the time spent by SQL Server to perform the parsing, binding, and optimization steps that we discussed earlier. Execution time is the actual time spent on running the query itself.

These times are very useful, but must be taken with a grain of salt. Execution times are affected by many different variables. If an execution plan is cached and reused, then the parse and compile time will be zero. If data is cached in memory, then the execution time will be much faster. External factors, such as network latency, IO latency, or contention from other processes can all affect execution time. As a result, it's important to base your optimization decisions on many trial executions of the query, to ensure that we are not making decisions based on exceptions or edge cases. Similarly, if your test system's hardware and query load differs from production, then take that into account as well as execution times being higher or lower as a result. A development server with no other processes running will outperform a similar system with a heavy SQL Server load running.

As a rule of thumb, when timing a query's execution, I will try to run it at least 10 to 20 times to get a good idea of how it would perform in a production environment where it may be run over and over. How often you personally test a query will be based on its importance, complexity, and your organization's QA policies. When in doubt, take the time to run enough trials such that you are comfortable with the results and confident in using those results when justifying your decisions to others, if necessary.

Use All of These Tools!

It is important to use as many performance metrics as possible when analyzing a query's performance. An execution plan by itself may not tell the entire story, nor would execution times give you all the information needed to tune a query. While more tools exist, the preceding three (execution plan, statistics IO, and statistics time) when used in concert provide a very solid understanding of how a query performs, where a bottleneck exists, and some hints as to where to begin tuning to improve performance.

Dynamic SQL vs. Standard SQL

While the TSQL that executes within a command string will be handled by SQL Server like any other standard SQL statement, there are some potential differences that are important to point out regarding performance:

Query Parsing and Binding

A big piece of the first two stages of query execution are checking syntax, object names, and verifying that you didn't make any mistakes when writing your query that would prevent it from being executed. The contents of strings are evaluated at runtime, and are not subject to these processes when you initially write and test a query. Since a dynamic SQL command string is a string, it will not be checked for the validity of its contents until you've executed it. You can parse a query, verifying syntax by clicking this icon, as seen in Figure 6-6.

Figure 6-6. *Manually parsing a query in SQL Server Management Studio*

This can allow you to verify syntax and check for any obvious mistakes before trying to execute your TSQL. The following query will generate a syntax error when parsing:

```
SELECT & FROM Person.Person;
```

My typo replaced the asterisk (*) with an ampersand (&). When I clicked the parse icon to validate my syntax, the result was an error:

```
Msg 102, Level 15, State 1, Line 18
Incorrect syntax near '&'.
```

Alternatively, if this were written as dynamic SQL, no such error would be thrown:

```
DECLARE @sql_command NVARCHAR(MAX);
SELECT @sql_command = 'SELECT & FROM Person.Person;';
EXEC (@sql_command);
```

The parser doesn't check the contents of @sql_command until it is executed and is then treated as a brand new query that needs to be parsed, bound, optimized, and executed. It parses without an error, but will throw a similar error when executed:

```
Msg 102, Level 15, State 1, Line 19
Incorrect syntax near '&'.
```

As a result, it is important to carefully print and test command strings prior to executing them.

Execution Plan Caching

A query execution plan is generated for every unique query that executes in SQL Server. What makes a query unique? This is determined by its exact text. Optimizing a query to generate an execution plan takes time and server resources and is a relatively expensive process, especially for more complex queries. Consider the query in Listing 6-1, which hypothetically runs frequently on a server, 500 times per minute.

Listing 6-1. Example TSQL that Will Generate a New Execution Plan for Each First Name

```
DECLARE @FirstName NVARCHAR(MAX) = 'Edward';
DECLARE @sql_command NVARCHAR(MAX);
SELECT @sql_command = '
     SELECT
          *
     FROM Person.Person
     WHERE FirstName = "' + @FirstName + "';
';
PRINT @sql_command;
EXEC sp_executesql @sql_command;
```

When this is executed for the first time, an execution plan is created for its exact text, which will print out as follows:

```
     SELECT
          *
     FROM Person.Person
     WHERE FirstName = 'Edward';
```

Note that the name "Edward" is included in the SQL text. Let's say that the query runs again, but for a different name:

```
DECLARE @FirstName NVARCHAR(MAX) = 'Xavier';
DECLARE @sql_command NVARCHAR(MAX);
SELECT @sql_command = '
     SELECT
          *
```

```
FROM Person.Person
WHERE FirstName = "' + @FirstName + "';
'

PRINT @sql_command;
EXEC sp_executesql @sql_command;
```

The resulting SQL text will be different than the previous run of the query:

```
SELECT
      *
FROM Person.Person
WHERE FirstName = 'Xavier';
```

As a result, each will receive a different execution plan. Checking the data from our time statistics, we can see that some finite amount of time was spent on handling the query prior to execution:

```
SQL Server parse and compile time:
  CPU time = 0 ms, elapsed time = 1 ms.
```

One ms may not seem like much, but if executed 500 times per minute, we would end up with 720,000ms of extra execution time every day! For a more complex query, this could add up to a huge amount of latency. When an execution plan is reused, the time indicated for the parse and compile time will be zero, which is much more desirable for a query that is executed often.

The fix for this dilemma is the same as the fix for many of our security and SQL injection concerns in earlier chapters: parameterize the query! This rewrite of the preceding query changes FirstName into a parameter that can be used over and over with the same execution plan:

```
DECLARE @FirstName NVARCHAR(MAX) = 'Edward';
DECLARE @sql_command NVARCHAR(MAX);
DECLARE @parameter_list NVARCHAR(MAX) = '@first_name NVARCHAR(MAX)';
SELECT @sql_command = '
      SELECT
            *
      FROM Person.Person
      WHERE FirstName = @first_name;'
```

```
PRINT @sql_command;
EXEC sp_executesql @sql_command, @parameter_list, @FirstName;
```

When @sql_command is printed out for this version of our simple query, the resulting text is as follows:

```
SELECT
        *
FROM Person.Person
WHERE FirstName = @first_name;
```

The query text will be the same, no matter what value of @FirstName is passed in to the dynamic SQL command string. As a result, we will only pay the price of optimizing the query once, and then the execution plan will be reused over and over from that point on. That's 12 minutes of latency shaved off of this query per day. If it were a more complex query that required 20ms to parse and compile, then the savings would be 4 hours of latency!

Let's quickly prove this out and show that the behavior I am describing is true, not just theoretical. First, we'll clear out the procedure cache, which will provide us with a clean slate to work on, with no distractions:

```
DBCC FREEPROCCACHE;
```

Executing this DBCC command will clear all execution plan data out of cache. This is an excellent way to create a clean environment to test in, but should only be used in isolated environments where important workloads cannot be affected! For our test purposes on local test servers here, this is a fine way to aid our work.

Never clear out the procedure cache in production unless you absolutely mean it! This removes all query execution plan data from cache, and on a busy server could cause immense latency because queries will need to be reoptimized!

Now, let's run our previous queries on Person.Person a few times, each one with a variety of different names. This is solely to add execution data to the cache for the upcoming demo, and therefore any queries run on this table will end up in cache and visible below. Once done, we can build a TSQL statement that will read query data from the cache for us, as shown in Listing 6-2.

Listing 6-2. TSQL that Can Retrieve SQL Text from the Query Plan Cache

```
SELECT
        cached_plans.objtype AS ObjectType,
        OBJECT_NAME(sql_text.objectid, sql_text.dbid) AS ObjectName,
        cached_plans.usecounts AS ExecutionCount,
        sql_text.TEXT AS QueryText
FROM sys.dm_exec_cached_plans AS cached_plans
CROSS APPLY sys.dm_exec_sql_text(cached_plans.plan_handle) AS sql_text
WHERE sql_text.TEXT LIKE '%Person.Person%';
```

This returns only a handful of relevant columns from the plan cache for our viewing pleasure, but could be altered to return quite a bit more data, if we wanted. The results of this query are as shown in Figure 6-7.

	Object Type	Object Name	Execution Count	Query Text
1	Adhoc	NULL	1	SELECT cached_plans.objtype AS ObjectType, OBJECT_NAME(sql_text.objectid, sql_text.dbid) AS Obje...
2	Prepared	NULL	7	(@first_name NVARCHAR(MAX)) SELECT * FROM Person.Person WHERE FirstName = @first_name;
3	Adhoc	NULL	1	SELECT * FROM Person.Person WHERE FirstName = 'T-Rex!!!';
4	Adhoc	NULL	1	SELECT * FROM Person.Person WHERE FirstName = 'Jesse';
5	Adhoc	NULL	1	SELECT * FROM Person.Person WHERE FirstName = 'James';
6	Adhoc	NULL	1	SELECT * FROM Person.Person WHERE FirstName = 'Thomas';
7	Adhoc	NULL	1	SELECT * FROM Person.Person WHERE FirstName = 'Xavier';
8	Adhoc	NULL	1	SELECT * FROM Person.Person WHERE FirstName = 'Edward';

Figure 6-7. *Sample data from the query plan cache*

The results are every query that is currently in the plan cache with TSQL text that includes the string "Person.Person." The first query is the one we just ran to collect this data. The second is our parameterized query, which I ran for a variety of different first names. Notice that the execution count indicates that it has been reused a number of times. The remaining six queries are the nonparameterized queries from earlier, executed for the names "Edward" "Xavier," "Thomas," "Jesse," "James," and "T-Rex!!!". Regardless, of the results (or lack thereof) returned, a separate entry is in the plan cache for all of these, even though the queries are essentially the same.

Note that under the object type, the parameterized query is listed as "Prepared," rather than "Adhoc," which indicates that the TSQL that was executed had no variables that could alter the TSQL text within it. By being completely parameterized, the query plan also becomes deterministic. Changing the first name we are searching for doesn't alter the SQL text, and therefore does not alter the execution plan. In the event that this query was executed very often for a large variety of first names, the nonparameterized query would quickly fill up the plan cache with a pile of entries for the same search. This would be very wasteful over time, not only consuming resources in constantly compiling query execution plans, but eventually bumping other, more important queries out of cache. As a result, whenever working with any query that is to be executed often, make sure that it can execute over and over but only need a single execution plan.

Simplifying Queries

In our earlier discussion of dynamic searches, we were able to use dynamic SQL as a way to remove excessive joins or WHERE clauses from TSQL statements. While the dynamic SQL was more complex, the resulting TSQL that was executed was simpler. Now that we have some performance evaluation tools at our disposal, we can put that claim to the test! See Listing 6-3 for this stored procedure.

The following is a dynamic search that we wrote in Chapter 4. This stored procedure may seem long, but its length ensures that no table is queried and no column returned unless needed for the search that is being performed.

Listing 6-3. Dynamic Search Procedure that Selectively Queries Objects When Needed

```
IF EXISTS (SELECT * FROM sys.procedures WHERE procedures.name = 'search_
products')
BEGIN
     DROP PROCEDURE dbo.search_products;
END
GO
-- Search with a check to avoid empty searches.
CREATE PROCEDURE dbo.search_products
     @product_name NVARCHAR(50) = NULL, @product_number NVARCHAR(25) =
     NULL, @product_model NVARCHAR(50) = NULL,
     @product_subcategory NVARCHAR(50) = NULL, @product_sizemeasurecode
     NVARCHAR(50) = NULL,
     @product_weightunitmeasurecode NVARCHAR(50) = NULL,
     @show_color BIT = 0, @show_safetystocklevel BIT = 0,
     @show_reorderpoint BIT = 0, @show_standard_cost BIT = 0,
```

```
      @show_catalog_description BIT = 0, @show_subcategory_modified_date
      BIT = 0, @show_product_model BIT = 0,
      @show_product_subcategory BIT = 0, @show_product_sizemeasurecode
      BIT = 0, @show_product_weightunitmeasurecode BIT = 0
AS
BEGIN
      SET NOCOUNT ON;

      IF COALESCE(@product_name, @product_number, @product_model,
      @product_subcategory,
                    @product_sizemeasurecode, @product_weightunitmeasurecode)
                    IS NULL
          RETURN;

      -- Add "%" delimiters to parameters that will be searched as wildcards.
      SET @product_name = '%' + @product_name + '%';
      SET @product_number = '%' + @product_number + '%';
      SET @product_model = '%' + @product_model + '%';

      DECLARE @sql_command NVARCHAR(MAX);
      -- Define the parameter list for filter criteria.
      DECLARE @parameter_list NVARCHAR(MAX) = '@product_name NVARCHAR(50),
      @product_number NVARCHAR(25),
      @product_model NVARCHAR(50), @product_subcategory NVARCHAR(50),
      @product_sizemeasurecode NVARCHAR(50),
      @product_weightunitmeasurecode NVARCHAR(50)';

-- Generate the simplified command string section for the SELECT columns.
SELECT @sql_command = '
      SELECT
            Product.Name AS product_name,
            Product.ProductNumber AS product_number,';
            IF @show_product_model = 1 OR @show_catalog_description = 1
            SELECT @sql_command = @sql_command + '
                  ProductModel.Name AS product_model_name,
                  ProductModel.CatalogDescription AS productmodel_catalog_
                  description,';
```

207

```
        IF @show_product_subcategory = 1 OR @show_subcategory_modified_
        date = 1 SELECT @sql_command = @sql_command + '
                ProductSubcategory.Name AS product_subcategory_name,
                ProductSubcategory.ModifiedDate AS product_subcategory_
                modified_date,';
        IF @show_product_sizemeasurecode = 1 SELECT @sql_command =
        @sql_command + '
                SizeUnitMeasureCode.Name AS size_unit_measure_code,';
        IF @show_product_weightunitmeasurecode = 1 SELECT @sql_command =
        @sql_command + '
                WeightUnitMeasureCode.Name AS weight_unit_measure_code,';
        IF @show_color = 1 OR @show_safetystocklevel = 1 OR @show_
        reorderpoint = 1 OR @show_standard_cost = 1
        SELECT @sql_command = @sql_command + '
                Product.Color AS product_color,
                Product.SafetyStockLevel AS product_safety_stock_level,
                Product.ReorderPoint AS product_reorderpoint,
                Product.StandardCost AS product_standard_cost';
-- In the event that there is a comma at the end of our command
   string, remove it before continuing.
IF (SELECT SUBSTRING(@sql_command, LEN(@sql_command), 1)) = ','
        SELECT @sql_command = LEFT(@sql_command, LEN(@sql_command) - 1);
SELECT @sql_command = @sql_command + '
FROM Production.Product'
-- Put together the JOINs based on what tables are required by the
   search.
IF (@product_model IS NOT NULL OR @show_product_model = 1 OR
@show_catalog_description = 1)
        SELECT @sql_command = @sql_command + '
LEFT JOIN Production.ProductModel
ON Product.ProductModelID = ProductModel.ProductModelID';
IF (@product_subcategory IS NOT NULL OR @show_subcategory_modified_
date = 1 OR @show_product_subcategory = 1)
        SELECT @sql_command = @sql_command + '
LEFT JOIN Production.ProductSubcategory
```

```
ON Product.ProductSubcategoryID = ProductSubcategory.
ProductSubcategoryID';
IF (@product_sizemeasurecode IS NOT NULL OR @show_product_
sizemeasurecode = 1)
      SELECT @sql_command = @sql_command + '
LEFT JOIN Production.UnitMeasure SizeUnitMeasureCode
ON Product.SizeUnitMeasureCode = SizeUnitMeasureCode.UnitMeasureCode';
IF (@product_weightunitmeasurecode IS NOT NULL OR @show_product_
weightunitmeasurecode = 1)
      SELECT @sql_command = @sql_command + '
LEFT JOIN Production.UnitMeasure WeightUnitMeasureCode
ON Product.WeightUnitMeasureCode = SizeUnitMeasureCode.UnitMeasureCode';

SELECT @sql_command = @sql_command + '
WHERE 1 = 1';
-- Build the WHERE clause based on which tables are referenced and
   required by the search.
IF @product_name IS NOT NULL
      SELECT @sql_command = @sql_command + '
      AND Product.Name LIKE @product_name';
IF @product_number IS NOT NULL
      SELECT @sql_command = @sql_command + '
      AND Product.ProductNumber LIKE @product_number';
IF @product_model IS NOT NULL
      SELECT @sql_command = @sql_command + '
      AND ProductModel.Name LIKE @product_model';
IF @product_subcategory IS NOT NULL
      SELECT @sql_command = @sql_command + '
      AND ProductSubcategory.Name = @product_subcategory';
IF @product_sizemeasurecode IS NOT NULL
      SELECT @sql_command = @sql_command + '
      AND SizeUnitMeasureCode.Name = @product_sizemeasurecode';
IF @product_weightunitmeasurecode IS NOT NULL
      SELECT @sql_command = @sql_command + '
      AND WeightUnitMeasureCode.Name = @product_weightunitmeasurecode';
```

```
    PRINT @sql_command;
    EXEC sp_executesql @sql_command, @parameter_list, @product_name,
    @product_number,
    @product_model, @product_subcategory, @product_sizemeasurecode,
    @product_weightunitmeasurecode;
END
```

This stored procedure is written such that a table is only queried if data from it is needed for a WHERE clause or join. In addition, columns are only returned by the query if they are required by the calling application. Now that this is created, let's run it for a possible user search, as seen in Listing 6-4.

Listing 6-4. Execution Example for the Stored Procedure in Listing 6-3

```
EXEC dbo.search_products @product_name = 'Mountain Frame', @product_number =
'FR-M21B', @product_model = 'LL Mountain Frame',
@product_subcategory = 'Mountain Frames', @show_color = 0,
@show_safetystocklevel = 0,
@show_reorderpoint = 0, @show_standard_cost = 1, @show_catalog_description = 1,
@show_subcategory_modified_date = 0,
@show_product_model = 1, @show_product_subcategory = 1
```

This search has a variety of parameters passed in, as well as a few that were omitted. The user has no interest in the measurements of the bike frames, and therefore left out parameters for those variables. The result set is for five mountain bike frames shown in Figure 6-8.

	product_name	product_number	product_model_name	productmodel_catalog_description	product_subcategory_name	product_subcategory_modified_date	product_color
1	LL Mountain Frame - Black, 40	FR-M21B-40	LL Mountain Frame	NULL	Mountain Frames	2008-04-30 00:00:00.000	Black
2	LL Mountain Frame - Black, 42	FR-M21B-42	LL Mountain Frame	NULL	Mountain Frames	2008-04-30 00:00:00.000	Black
3	LL Mountain Frame - Black, 44	FR-M21B-44	LL Mountain Frame	NULL	Mountain Frames	2008-04-30 00:00:00.000	Black
4	LL Mountain Frame - Black, 48	FR-M21B-48	LL Mountain Frame	NULL	Mountain Frames	2008-04-30 00:00:00.000	Black
5	LL Mountain Frame - Black, 52	FR-M21B-52	LL Mountain Frame	NULL	Mountain Frames	2008-04-30 00:00:00.000	Black

Figure 6-8. *Results from the Search Proc, as Executed from the TSQL in Listing 6-4*

The command string that was executed is shown in Listing 6-5.

Listing 6-5. The Command String Generated by the Execution of Our Search
Proc in Listing 6-4

```
SELECT
    Product.Name AS product_name,
    Product.ProductNumber AS product_number,
        ProductModel.Name AS product_model_name,
        ProductModel.CatalogDescription AS productmodel_catalog_
        description,
        ProductSubcategory.Name AS product_subcategory_name,
        ProductSubcategory.ModifiedDate AS product_subcategory_
        modified_date,
        Product.Color AS product_color,
        Product.SafetyStockLevel AS product_safety_stock_level,
        Product.ReorderPoint AS product_reorderpoint,
        Product.StandardCost AS product_standard_cost
FROM Production.Product
LEFT JOIN Production.ProductModel
ON Product.ProductModelID = ProductModel.ProductModelID
LEFT JOIN Production.ProductSubcategory
ON Product.ProductSubcategoryID = ProductSubcategory.ProductSubcategoryID
WHERE 1 = 1
    AND Product.Name LIKE @product_name
    AND Product.ProductNumber LIKE @product_number
    AND ProductModel.Name LIKE @product_model
    AND ProductSubcategory.Name = @product_subcategory
```

Some joins and WHERE clauses were omitted from this TSQL, as they were not
required by the parameters passed in. How did this affect performance? Here are the IO
statistics for this execution.

```
Table 'ProductModel'. Scan count 0, logical reads 10, physical reads 0,
read-ahead reads 0, lob logical reads 0, lob physical reads 0, lob read-
ahead reads 0.
Table 'ProductSubcategory'. Scan count 0, logical reads 10, physical reads 0,
read-ahead reads 0, lob logical reads 0, lob physical reads 0, lob read-ahead
reads 0.
```

Table 'Product'. Scan count 1, logical reads 14, physical reads 0, read-ahead reads 0, lob logical reads 0, lob physical reads 0, lob read-ahead reads 0.

The overall IO was 34 reads: ten on ProductModel, ten on ProductSubcategory, and fourteen on Product. The execution plan for the same execution is shown in Figure 6-9.

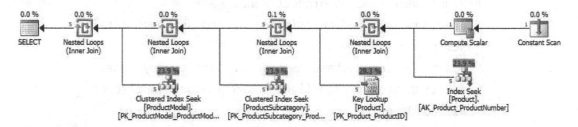

Figure 6-9. *Execution Plan for the Stored Procedure in Listing 6-4*

The plan shows access to the three tables referenced in the IO stats and the various steps required to put that data together for us. For comparison, the estimated subtree cost for the entire query is 0.014.

The alternative to a dynamic search would be a static search, where all tables are automatically joined and all columns returned, in case we need them. This is shown in the stored procedure in Listing 6-6.

Listing 6-6. Search Procedure that Checks and Returns All Data, Regardless of Parameters

```
IF EXISTS (SELECT * FROM sys.procedures WHERE procedures.name = 'search_
products')
BEGIN
     DROP PROCEDURE dbo.search_products;
END
GO

CREATE PROCEDURE dbo.search_products
     @product_name NVARCHAR(50) = NULL, @product_number NVARCHAR(25) = NULL,
     @product_model NVARCHAR(50) = NULL,
     @product_subcategory NVARCHAR(50) = NULL, @product_sizemeasurecode
     NVARCHAR(50) = NULL,
```

```
        @product_weightunitmeasurecode NVARCHAR(50) = NULL
AS
BEGIN
        SELECT @product_name = '%' + @product_name + '%';
        SELECT @product_number = '%' + @product_number + '%';
        SELECT @product_model = '%' + @product_model + '%';

        SELECT
                Product.Name AS product_name,
                Product.ProductNumber AS product_number,
                ProductModel.Name AS product_model_name,
                ProductModel.CatalogDescription AS productmodel_catalog_
                description,
                ProductSubcategory.Name AS product_subcategory_name,
                ProductSubcategory.ModifiedDate AS product_subcategory_
                modified_date,
                SizeUnitMeasureCode.Name AS size_unit_measure_code,
                WeightUnitMeasureCode.Name AS weight_unit_measure_code,
                Product.Color AS product_color,
                Product.SafetyStockLevel AS product_safety_stock_level,
                Product.ReorderPoint AS product_reorderpoint,
                Product.StandardCost AS product_standard_cost
        FROM Production.Product
        LEFT JOIN Production.ProductModel
        ON Product.ProductModelID = ProductModel.ProductModelID
        LEFT JOIN Production.ProductSubcategory
        ON Product.ProductSubcategoryID = ProductSubcategory.ProductSubcategoryID
        LEFT JOIN Production.UnitMeasure SizeUnitMeasureCode
        ON Product.SizeUnitMeasureCode = SizeUnitMeasureCode.UnitMeasureCode
        LEFT JOIN Production.UnitMeasure WeightUnitMeasureCode
        ON Product.WeightUnitMeasureCode = SizeUnitMeasureCode.UnitMeasureCode
        WHERE (Product.Name LIKE @product_name OR @product_name IS NULL)
        AND (Product.ProductNumber LIKE @product_number OR @product_number IS NULL)
        AND (ProductModel.Name LIKE @product_model OR @product_model IS NULL)
        AND (ProductSubcategory.Name = @product_subcategory OR @product_
        subcategory IS NULL)
```

```
    AND (SizeUnitMeasureCode.Name = @product_sizemeasurecode OR
    @product_sizemeasurecode IS NULL)
    AND (WeightUnitMeasureCode.Name = @product_weightunitmeasurecode OR
    @product_weightunitmeasurecode IS NULL);
END
```

This TSQL is much easier to read and understand. The search is straightforward, returning all possible columns that we may want, joining all tables, and checking all search parameters in the WHERE clause, even if they are not specified in the stored procedure parameters. The only differences in output are any extra columns that we had explicitly left out in our previous version. We can run the exact same execution statement as before in order to evaluate performance:

```
EXEC dbo.search_products @product_name = 'Mountain Frame', @product_number
= 'FR-M21B', @product_model = 'LL Mountain Frame',
@product_subcategory = 'Mountain Frames'
```

The execution plan and IO statistics for this new version are as follows in Figure 6-10.

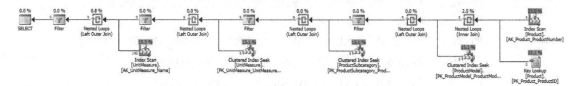

Figure 6-10. *Execution plan for the more inclusive search proc*

```
Table 'UnitMeasure'. Scan count 1, logical reads 21, physical reads 0,
read-ahead reads 0, lob logical reads 0, lob physical reads 0, lob read-
ahead reads 0.
Table 'ProductSubcategory'. Scan count 0, logical reads 10, physical reads 0,
read-ahead reads 0, lob logical reads 0, lob physical reads 0, lob read-ahead
reads 0.
Table 'ProductModel'. Scan count 0, logical reads 10, physical reads 0,
read-ahead reads 0, lob logical reads 0, lob physical reads 0, lob read-
ahead reads 0.
Table 'Product'. Scan count 1, logical reads 14, physical reads 0, read-
ahead reads 0, lob logical reads 0, lob physical reads 0, lob read-ahead
reads 0.
```

The primary difference in performance was that we had to access the `UnitMeasure` table twice to gather data on both size and weight measurements for the product. While we did not require those columns for the search that was run, the simplified TSQL does not discern between what we need and don't need. It trades simplicity in design for complexity in performance.

The result is that our same search as before required an additional 21 reads, and the subtree cost was 0.022. How did execution time compare? On my local server, in a trial of 20 executions, the dynamic SQL approach took 40ms to run, on average. The "simplified" version took 50ms. These decreases in performance may not seem immense, as they are querying tables that are relatively small. If the `UnitMeasure` table had been larger, then the extra work would have also become more significant. Additionally, what if instead of 4 tables, we had to query 100? What if the possible columns that were options for the user to select from numbered in the thousands? If we were forced to read from 100 tables frequently when not needed, the results would be very noticeable on a production server.

Also keep in mind that each search that accesses different tables will result in a unique execution plan. In this case, that behavior is encouraged, as we would prefer a smaller and leaner execution when less objects need to be queried. Extra plans will not be created for different parameter values, though, but only in scenarios where the text of the query itself is changed. This would happen whenever joins are added, the WHERE clause is given additional parameters, or columns are added to

When a very large number of tables, columns, filters, or other variables are involved, the resulting search needs to be intelligent enough to not query objects that are unneeded. The necessary logic to accomplish this can be executed in application code or in SQL Server, but must be dealt with in some manner that eliminates the extra resource overhead needed for querying those unneeded objects. Dynamic SQL is an excellent tool to accomplish this, though thorough documentation and clean coding are required so that the increased performance is not gained at the expense of maintainability.

Paging Performance

Paging can be an expensive process, especially when used frequently. Interactive searches often require additional aggregate data that may not exist at the row level, such as:

- Total row count

- Current row number

- Sum, average, min, or max values for a column

- Page size

- Related or correlated results

Returning this data in-line with a result set presents many questions, such as whether to calculate the aggregates separately, or with window functions? This is an area where there are no singular answers. The size, distribution, and indexing of the overall data sources matter. In addition, knowing what percentage of the result set is returned can influence our decision making process as well. To begin this analysis, let's review a handful of different ways in which we can page data, and dig into the performance of each method.

In the following query in Listing 6-7, we return 25 search results as the user is paging through.

Listing 6-7. Basic Data Paging, Using Row Numbers Based on Order Date

```
WITH CTE_PRODUCTS AS (
     SELECT
          ROW_NUMBER() OVER (ORDER BY OrderDate ASC) AS rownum,
          SalesOrderHeader.SalesOrderID,
          SalesOrderHeader.Status,
          SalesOrderHeader.OrderDate,
          SalesOrderHeader.ShipDate,
          SalesOrderDetail.UnitPrice,
          SalesOrderDetail.LineTotal
     FROM Sales.SalesOrderHeader
     INNER JOIN Sales.SalesOrderDetail
     ON SalesOrderHeader.SalesOrderID = SalesOrderDetail.SalesOrderID
     WHERE SalesOrderHeader.SalesPersonID = 277
     )
SELECT
     *
FROM CTE_PRODUCTS
WHERE rownum BETWEEN 51 AND 75
```

The performance of this query is relatively straightforward, as seen in Figure 6-11.

Table 'SalesOrderDetail'. Scan count 9, logical reads 42, physical reads 0, read-ahead reads 0, lob logical reads 0, lob physical reads 0, lob read-ahead reads 0.
Table 'SalesOrderHeader'. Scan count 1, logical reads 689, physical reads 0, read-ahead reads 0, lob logical reads 0, lob physical reads 0, lob read-ahead reads 0.

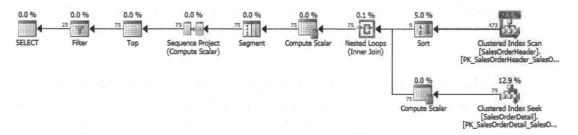

Figure 6-11. *Execution Plan for the Basic Paging TSQL in Listing 6-7*

The resulting execution plan is composed of a seek on SalesOrderDetail and a scan on SalesOrderHeader as we collect data on a specific sales person's orders. Note that the reads on SalesOrderDetail are relatively low. Paging can improve read performance on your storage system, as we ultimately return much less data than the total amount at one time.

This leads to an important consideration: do we return all data at once, saving it for when the user clicks "Next," or do we only return 25 rows and wait for the user to ask for more before returning it? This question can be addressed by adjusting the number of rows returned in our outermost SELECT statement. The following is the STATISTICS IO output for scenarios where we return rows 51-200, 51-500, and 51-1000, respectively:

Table 'SalesOrderDetail'. Scan count 19, logical reads 79, physical reads 0, read-ahead reads 0, lob logical reads 0, lob physical reads 0, lob read-ahead reads 0.
Table 'SalesOrderHeader'. Scan count 1, logical reads 689, physical reads 0, read-ahead reads 0, lob logical reads 0, lob physical reads 0, lob read-ahead reads 0.

Table 'SalesOrderDetail'. Scan count 41, logical reads 157, physical reads 0, read-ahead reads 0, lob logical reads 0, lob physical reads 0, lob read-ahead reads 0.

Table 'SalesOrderHeader'. Scan count 1, logical reads 689, physical reads 0, read-ahead reads 0, lob logical reads 0, lob physical reads 0, lob read-ahead reads 0.

Table 'SalesOrderDetail'. Scan count 77, logical reads 277, physical reads 0, read-ahead reads 0, lob logical reads 0, lob physical reads 0, lob read-ahead reads 0.
Table 'SalesOrderHeader'. Scan count 1, logical reads 689, physical reads 0, read-ahead reads 0, lob logical reads 0, lob physical reads 0, lob read-ahead reads 0.

Our reads increase as we commit to returning more data from SalesOrderDetail. To make a smart decision about performance, we must decide, on average, how many times a user will click "Next." If they typically only view a page or two and move on to other work, then returning a small data set each time is optimal. If the user will eventually page through most, or the entire data set, then simply returning everything to a temporary table or to the application would make more sense.

Let's add some complexity to the query above. What if we want to include the total result count along with the search results? There are many ways we could accomplish it. In Listing 6-8 are a few examples along with performance metrics and notes.

Listing 6-8. Data Paging, Including Total Result Count as a Subquery in the Outermost SELECT

```
WITH CTE_PRODUCTS AS (
    SELECT
        ROW_NUMBER() OVER (ORDER BY OrderDate ASC) AS rownum,
        SalesOrderHeader.SalesOrderID,
        SalesOrderHeader.Status,
        SalesOrderHeader.OrderDate,
        SalesOrderHeader.ShipDate,
        SalesOrderDetail.UnitPrice,
        SalesOrderDetail.LineTotal
    FROM Sales.SalesOrderHeader
    INNER JOIN Sales.SalesOrderDetail
    ON SalesOrderHeader.SalesOrderID = SalesOrderDetail.SalesOrderID
```

```
    WHERE SalesOrderHeader.SalesPersonID = 277
    )
SELECT
    *,
    (SELECT COUNT(*) FROM CTE_PRODUCTS) AS total_result_count
    FROM CTE_PRODUCTS
WHERE rownum BETWEEN 51 AND 75;
```

In this first example, we create a subquery in our final SELECT that returns the total count of rows within the common table expression. In this case, we will return the entire result set and recalculate the row count every time the user requests more results. The performance for this method is seen in Figure 6-12.

```
Table 'SalesOrderDetail'. Scan count 10, logical reads 318, physical reads
0, read-ahead reads 0, lob logical reads 0, lob physical reads 0, lob read-
ahead reads 0.
Table 'SalesOrderHeader'. Scan count 2, logical reads 692, physical reads
0, read-ahead reads 0, lob logical reads 0, lob physical reads 0, lob read-
ahead reads 0.
Table 'Workfile'. Scan count 0, logical reads 0, physical reads 0, read-
ahead reads 0, lob logical reads 0, lob physical reads 0, lob read-ahead
reads 0.
Table 'Worktable'. Scan count 0, logical reads 0, physical reads 0, read-
ahead reads 0, lob logical reads 0, lob physical reads 0, lob read-ahead
reads 0.
```

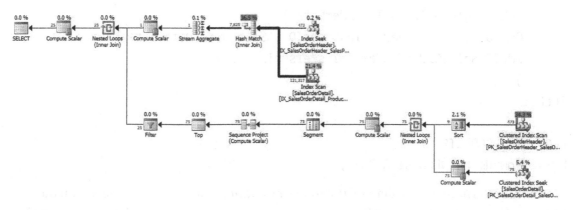

Figure 6-12. *Search query performance when the row count is returned with each execution*

To calculate the count, additional access to each table was required, and now we scan each table once and seek each table once. Our overall reads increased by 279, or 38%. This isn't a very efficient method, but it is convenient, and could be controlled easily with dynamic SQL. Once the count has been acquired once, it could be stored and reused by the application, with dynamic SQL filtering out the additional subselect from our final query. This leads us to ask if we shouldn't just calculate the row count separately and reuse it for as long as necessary, as shown in Listing 6-9.

Listing 6-9. Data Paging, Calculating the Row Count as a Separate Operation

```
SELECT COUNT(*) AS total_result_count
FROM Sales.SalesOrderHeader
INNER JOIN Sales.SalesOrderDetail
ON SalesOrderHeader.SalesOrderID = SalesOrderDetail.SalesOrderID
WHERE SalesOrderHeader.SalesPersonID = 277;

WITH CTE_PRODUCTS AS (
      SELECT
            ROW_NUMBER() OVER (ORDER BY OrderDate ASC) AS rownum,
            SalesOrderHeader.SalesOrderID,
            SalesOrderHeader.Status,
            SalesOrderHeader.OrderDate,
            SalesOrderHeader.ShipDate,
            SalesOrderDetail.UnitPrice,
            SalesOrderDetail.LineTotal
      FROM Sales.SalesOrderHeader
      INNER JOIN Sales.SalesOrderDetail
      ON SalesOrderHeader.SalesOrderID = SalesOrderDetail.SalesOrderID
      WHERE SalesOrderHeader.SalesPersonID = 277
      )
SELECT
      *
FROM CTE_PRODUCTS
WHERE rownum BETWEEN 51 AND 75;
```

In this alternative, we calculate the total row count prior to fetching the actual data. This can be returned to the application once and used repeatedly, until the user discards this particular search. This could be done via a RETURN value in a stored procedure, as a result set to a waiting application, saving it into a temporary table for repeated use later, or other, similar methods. This behavior is illustrated in Figure 6-13.

```
Table 'Workfile'. Scan count 0, logical reads 0, physical reads 0, read-
ahead reads 0, lob logical reads 0, lob physical reads 0, lob read-ahead
reads 0.
Table 'Worktable'. Scan count 0, logical reads 0, physical reads 0, read-
ahead reads 0, lob logical reads 0, lob physical reads 0, lob read-ahead
reads 0.
Table 'SalesOrderDetail'. Scan count 1, logical reads 276, physical reads 0,
read-ahead reads 0, lob logical reads 0, lob physical reads 0, lob read-
ahead reads 0.
Table 'SalesOrderHeader'. Scan count 1, logical reads 3, physical reads 0,
read-ahead reads 0, lob logical reads 0, lob physical reads 0, lob read-
ahead reads 0.

Table 'SalesOrderDetail'. Scan count 9, logical reads 42, physical reads 0,
read-ahead reads 0, lob logical reads 0, lob physical reads 0, lob read-
ahead reads 0.
Table 'SalesOrderHeader'. Scan count 1, logical reads 689, physical reads 0,
read-ahead reads 0, lob logical reads 0, lob physical reads 0, lob read-
ahead reads 0.
```

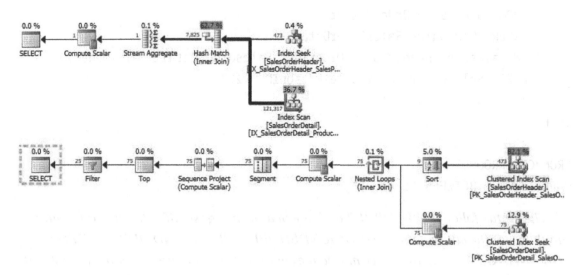

Figure 6-13. *Performance of the search when we cache the row count prior to execution*

The IO data shows that the cost to calculate the row count this way is identical to the previous example. The two execution plans shown cover the count (the first plan) and the data select (the second plan). Overall, the effort is similar to before in terms of operations required and the resources consumed by each.

In the next example, we move the count in with the common table expression, as seen in Listing 6-10.

Listing 6-10. Data Paging, Using a Window Function to Calculate the Total Row Count

```
WITH CTE_PRODUCTS AS (
    SELECT
        ROW_NUMBER() OVER (ORDER BY OrderDate ASC) AS rownum,
        COUNT(SalesOrderDetail.SalesOrderDetailID) OVER (ORDER BY
        SalesOrderDetail.SalesOrderDetailID ROWS BETWEEN UNBOUNDED
        PRECEDING AND UNBOUNDED FOLLOWING) AS total_result_count,
        SalesOrderHeader.SalesOrderID,
        SalesOrderHeader.Status,
        SalesOrderHeader.OrderDate,
        SalesOrderHeader.ShipDate,
        SalesOrderDetail.UnitPrice,
        SalesOrderDetail.LineTotal
    FROM Sales.SalesOrderHeader
    INNER JOIN Sales.SalesOrderDetail
    ON SalesOrderHeader.SalesOrderID = SalesOrderDetail.SalesOrderID
    WHERE SalesOrderHeader.SalesPersonID = 277
    )
SELECT
    *
FROM CTE_PRODUCTS
WHERE rownum BETWEEN 51 AND 75;
```

The syntax following the ORDER BY (known as framing) signifies that the row count should be for the entire data set (UNBOUNDED PRECEEDING AND UNBOUNDED FOLLOWING). Once again, we've moved the count calculation into the data retrieval, but how does it perform?

Table 'Worktable'. Scan count 3, logical reads 16130, physical reads 0, read-ahead reads 0, lob logical reads 0, lob physical reads 0, lob read-ahead reads 0.
Table 'SalesOrderDetail'. Scan count 473, logical reads 1626, physical reads 0, read-ahead reads 0, lob logical reads 0, lob physical reads 0, lob read-ahead reads 0.
Table 'SalesOrderHeader'. Scan count 1, logical reads 689, physical reads 0, read-ahead reads 0, lob logical reads 0, lob physical reads 0, lob read-ahead reads 0.

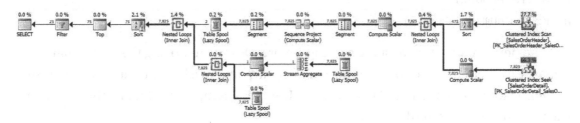

Figure 6-14. *Performance when determining row counts using a window function*

What happened!? We can see in Figure 6-14 that the execution plan seems simple enough, with each of the two tables being accessed once. The IO statistics, though, tell a very different story! In order to calculate the count within the CTE, SQL Server recalculates it for every single row that is processed in the result set! The reads are many orders of magnitude higher than all of the previous examples and show that syntax that looks good doesn't always perform well! We can simplify the TSQL in an attempt to improve performance, as seen in Listing 6-11.

Listing 6-11. Data Paging, with a Simplified Window Function

```
WITH CTE_PRODUCTS AS (
    SELECT
        ROW_NUMBER() OVER (ORDER BY OrderDate ASC) AS rownum,
        COUNT(*) OVER () AS total_result_count,
        SalesOrderHeader.SalesOrderID,
        SalesOrderHeader.Status,
        SalesOrderHeader.OrderDate,
        SalesOrderHeader.ShipDate,
```

```
            SalesOrderDetail.UnitPrice,
            SalesOrderDetail.LineTotal
    FROM Sales.SalesOrderHeader
    INNER JOIN Sales.SalesOrderDetail
    ON SalesOrderHeader.SalesOrderID = SalesOrderDetail.SalesOrderID
    WHERE SalesOrderHeader.SalesPersonID = 277
    )
SELECT
    *
FROM CTE_PRODUCTS
WHERE rownum BETWEEN 51 AND 75;
```

The performance is almost the same as before. Despite removing the additional syntax, this method preforms extremely inefficiently, and in a larger data set would result in significantly more reads and latency as SQL Server attempts to calculate the count on each row throughout the data.

One final option is to persist the entire data set from the start. If the search results are not excessively large, or if we can limit them to a relatively compact segment, then we can optimize for this specific scenario, as seen in Listing 6-12.

Listing 6-12. Data Paging, Using a Row Count Calculation after the Data Is Selected

```
SELECT
    ROW_NUMBER() OVER (ORDER BY OrderDate ASC) AS rownum,
    SalesOrderHeader.SalesOrderID,
    SalesOrderHeader.Status,
    SalesOrderHeader.OrderDate,
    SalesOrderHeader.ShipDate,
    SalesOrderDetail.UnitPrice,
    SalesOrderDetail.LineTotal
INTO #orders
FROM Sales.SalesOrderHeader
INNER JOIN Sales.SalesOrderDetail
ON SalesOrderHeader.SalesOrderID = SalesOrderDetail.SalesOrderID
WHERE SalesOrderHeader.SalesPersonID = 277;
```

```
SELECT @@ROWCOUNT AS total_result_count;

CREATE CLUSTERED INDEX IX_temp_orders_rownum ON #orders (rownum);

SELECT * FROM #orders WHERE rownum BETWEEN 1 AND 25;
SELECT * FROM #orders WHERE rownum BETWEEN 26 AND 50;
SELECT * FROM #orders WHERE rownum BETWEEN 51 AND 75;
SELECT * FROM #orders WHERE rownum BETWEEN 76 AND 100;

DROP TABLE #orders;
```

Here, we select the entire data set into a temp table. We then grab the total row count using @@ROWCOUNT, which does not require any data access to be returned. Since we are assuming a need to access much of the data returned, the next action is to create a clustered index on the temp table on rownum. This ensures that every query that filters on rownum will be very efficient. Here are the IO statistics for this version of the search.

```
Table 'SalesOrderDetail'. Scan count 473, logical reads 1626, physical
reads 0, read-ahead reads 0, lob logical reads 0, lob physical reads 0, lob
read-ahead reads 0.
Table 'SalesOrderHeader'. Scan count 1, logical reads 689, physical reads 0,
read-ahead reads 0, lob logical reads 0, lob physical reads 0, lob read-
ahead reads 0.

Table '#orders'. Scan count 1, logical reads 62, physical reads 0, read-
ahead reads 0, lob logical reads 0, lob physical reads 0, lob read-ahead
reads 0.
Table '#orders'. Scan count 1, logical reads 2, physical reads 0, read-
ahead reads 0, lob logical reads 0, lob physical reads 0, lob read-ahead
reads 0.

Table '#orders'. Scan count 1, logical reads 2, physical reads 0, read-
ahead reads 0, lob logical reads 0, lob physical reads 0, lob read-ahead
reads 0.

Table '#orders'. Scan count 1, logical reads 2, physical reads 0, read-
ahead reads 0, lob logical reads 0, lob physical reads 0, lob read-ahead
reads 0.
```

Table '#orders'. Scan count 1, logical reads 2, physical reads 0, read-ahead reads 0, lob logical reads 0, lob physical reads 0, lob read-ahead reads 0.

We pay a hefty price up front for gathering the data in our search, racking up 2,315 reads! Adding the index costs another 62 reads on our temp table, but from this point on, all of the paged results come very inexpensively because we can use that index effectively. Based on IO, is all of this effort worth it? Our original search required 731 reads. Based on that number, we would come out ahead with this new approach after our 4th time paging through the result set. As stated previously, retrieving all of the data at once is effective when the data set is not prohibitively large and we know that we will want to page through a number of times, on average.

The query execution plans in Figure 6-15 tell a similar story.

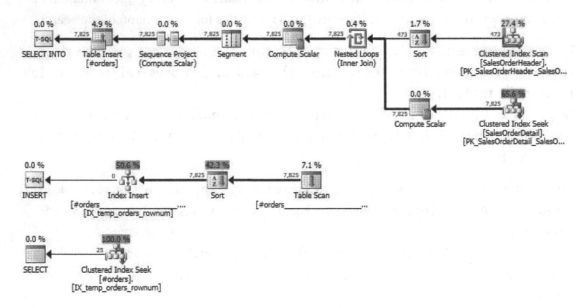

Figure 6-15. *Performance when we gather all data up-front, for repeated querying later*

The 3rd execution plan is repeated for each subsequent paging search result executed against the existing data set. The subtree cost is 1.99 for the data collection query, 0.8 for the index creation, and 0.003 to return paged search results. The results correlate well with the IO statistics: quite a bit of effort is expended up front to retrieve the 7,825 rows in the entire result set, but from that point on, access is comparatively inexpensive.

Note that by saving and reusing the count, it won't update if the underlying data changes. This can be tolerated in some search scenarios, where the result set must stay the same until the search is run again, but may not be acceptable in all use cases. If a data set needs to be refreshed with each click through the results, then storing results and counts for later may not be good enough to meet that business need. In scenarios such as this, consider the structure of the data, and if new data is appended to the end of the data set, and therefore could be retrieved as an additional operation on top of the existing search. For instance, in the prceding example we could check the maximum `SalesOrderDetailID` in the temp table and then add to the data set any additional new data in `SalesOrderHeader` and `SalesOrderDetail` that is newer. Alternatively, if the data has a last modified date and/or last create date, we could use those dates to quickly gather data that changed since the initial search was completed.

One final paging option that we've not yet assessed is the OFFSET functionality, which allows you to order a result set, offset to any row number in that ordering, and select any number of rows starting at that point. This TSQL is shown in Listing 6-13.

Listing 6-13. Data Paging, Using OFFSET

```
SELECT
      SalesOrderHeader.SalesOrderID,
      SalesOrderHeader.Status,
      SalesOrderHeader.OrderDate,
      SalesOrderHeader.ShipDate,
      SalesOrderDetail.UnitPrice,
      SalesOrderDetail.LineTotal
FROM Sales.SalesOrderHeader
INNER JOIN Sales.SalesOrderDetail
ON SalesOrderHeader.SalesOrderID = SalesOrderDetail.SalesOrderID
WHERE SalesOrderHeader.SalesPersonID = 277
ORDER BY SalesOrderDetailID ASC
OFFSET 50 ROWS
FETCH NEXT 25 ROWS ONLY
```

The syntax for OFFSET is straightforward and allows you to page a data set without calculating row numbers yourself. The IO statistics and execution plan for this example are shown in Figure 6-16.

Table 'SalesOrderDetail'. Scan count 9, logical reads 45, physical reads 0, read-ahead reads 0, lob logical reads 0, lob physical reads 0, lob read-ahead reads 0.

Table 'SalesOrderHeader'. Scan count 1, logical reads 689, physical reads 0, read-ahead reads 0, lob logical reads 0, lob physical reads 0, lob read-ahead reads 0.

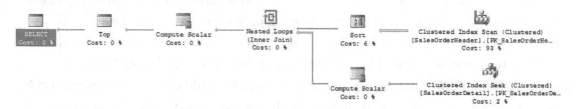

Figure 6-16. *Performance of paging using the OFFSET operator*

The execution plan is similar to what we have seen already, and the reads are similar to what we got in the first example using ROW_NUMBER. The key to using OFFSET is to make sure that the ORDER BY is on the column that you would like to page by. In these preceding examples, OrderDate was used to determine the order of the result set, but others could have been used, depending on business needs.

Keep in mind that the best columns to use for paging are those that are ever increasing. If a new row can be inserted into an older data set, then the potential exists for missing or duplicate rows. For example, if I created a new sales order, but populated the order date with a date in the past, then there is a chance that a paged data set in-flight could be disrupted. If this is not a tolerable possibility, then use an identity or increasing ID column for paging purposes.

Filtered Indexes

By default, an index will apply to all rows in a given table. On large tables, indexes can become expensive to read as well as time-consuming resource-intensive to maintain. If we have a common query or set of queries that all rely on the same filters, we can create an index that only applies to those filter conditions. This filtered index will only apply when those exact filters are used, so it is important to get it right the first time!

A common use of filtered indexes is when we have a table for which a particular status or flag signifies data that we are interested in, whereas the remainder of the data will consistently be ignored. Consider the stored procedure in Listing 6-14, which executes a search of purchase orders.

Listing 6-14. Simple Dynamic Search, with a Common Status Filter

```
IF EXISTS (SELECT * FROM sys.procedures WHERE procedures.name = 'get_in_
process_purchasing_data')
BEGIN
     DROP PROCEDURE dbo.get_in_process_purchasing_data;
END
GO

CREATE PROCEDURE dbo.get_in_process_purchasing_data
     @return_detail_data BIT
AS
BEGIN
     SET NOCOUNT ON;
     DECLARE @sql_command NVARCHAR(MAX);

     SELECT @sql_command = '
     SELECT
          PurchaseOrderHeader.PurchaseOrderID,
          PurchaseOrderHeader.OrderDate,
          PurchaseOrderHeader.ShipDate,
          PurchaseOrderHeader.SubTotal,
          PurchaseOrderHeader.Freight';
     IF @return_detail_data = 1
          SELECT @sql_command = @sql_command + ',
          PurchaseOrderDetail.PurchaseOrderDetailID,
          PurchaseOrderDetail.OrderQTY,
          PurchaseOrderDetail.UnitPrice,
          Product.Name,
          Product.ProductNumber';
     SELECT @sql_command = @sql_command + '
     FROM purchasing.PurchaseOrderHeader
```

```
    INNER JOIN purchasing.PurchaseOrderDetail
    ON PurchaseOrderHeader.PurchaseOrderID = PurchaseOrderDetail.
    PurchaseOrderID';
    IF @return_detail_data = 1
        SELECT @sql_command = @sql_command + '
        INNER JOIN Production.Product
        ON Product.ProductID = PurchaseOrderDetail.ProductID';
    SELECT @sql_command = @sql_command + '
    WHERE PurchaseOrderHeader.Status = 2';

    EXEC sp_executesql @sql_command;
END
GO
```

This stored procedure performs a search using a parameter that determines if detailed data can be returned or not. More importantly, a common filter exists in all executions:

```
WHERE PurchaseOrderHeader.Status = 2
```

To illustrate a baseline for performance, let's add a standard covering index that will help reduce reads on PurchaseOrderHeader:

```
CREATE NONCLUSTERED INDEX IX_PurchaseOrderHeader_status_INC
ON Purchasing.PurchaseOrderHeader (OrderDate, status)
INCLUDE (PurchaseOrderID, ShipDate, SubTotal, Freight);
GO
```

Now, we can execute this for a detailed run:

```
EXEC dbo.get_in_process_purchasing_data @return_detail_data = 1;
```

The result set is comprised of 57 rows, containing all columns that could be returned by the dynamic SQL within the stored procedure. The performance for this execution is as follows:

```
Table 'Product'. Scan count 0, logical reads 114, physical reads 0, read-
ahead reads 0, lob logical reads 0, lob physical reads 0, lob read-ahead
reads 0.
```

Table 'PurchaseOrderDetail'. Scan count 12, logical reads 24, physical reads 0, read-ahead reads 0, lob logical reads 0, lob physical reads 0, lob read-ahead reads 0.

Table 'PurchaseOrderHeader'. Scan count 1, logical reads 24, physical reads 0, read-ahead reads 0, lob logical reads 0, lob physical reads 0, lob read-ahead reads 0.

Note that even with the covering index, there are still 24 reads on PurchaseOrderHeader. The execution plan is as follows in Figure 6-17.

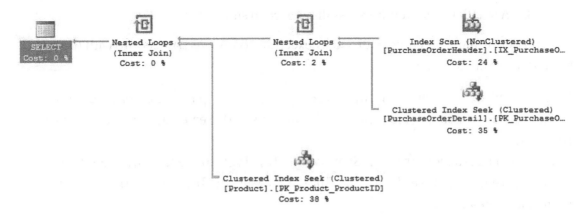

Figure 6-17. *Execution plan when a covering index is used for the search query*

The subtree cost for the entire query is 0.095894. Since there is an automatic filter on status = 2 for this stored procedure, we can improve our index by adding the filter to the index itself:

```
IF EXISTS (SELECT * FROM sys.indexes WHERE indexes.name = 'IX_
PurchaseOrderHeader_status_INC')
BEGIN
    DROP INDEX IX_PurchaseOrderHeader_status_INC ON Purchasing.
    PurchaseOrderHeader
END
GO

CREATE NONCLUSTERED INDEX IX_PurchaseOrderHeader_status_INC
ON Purchasing.PurchaseOrderHeader (OrderDate, status)
INCLUDE (PurchaseOrderID, ShipDate, SubTotal, Freight)
WHERE status = 2;
```

Note the filter underneath the INCLUDE portion of the index. Adding a filter to the index will alter its structure to only include data pertaining to rows that match the filter. In a table where we are interested in consistently querying a very small portion of it, a filtered index can greatly improve performance:

1. Since the index is smaller, it is faster for SQL Server to read it, therefore returning data faster with fewer logical reads.

2. A smaller index reduces the time it takes to perform index maintenance on it.

3. A smaller index requires less disk space to store.

The performance metrics returned by executing our stored procedure with the new filtered index are as follows:

```
Table 'Product'. Scan count 0, logical reads 114, physical reads 0, read-
ahead reads 0, lob logical reads 0, lob physical reads 0, lob read-ahead
reads 0.
Table 'PurchaseOrderDetail'. Scan count 12, logical reads 24, physical
reads 0, read-ahead reads 0, lob logical reads 0, lob physical reads 0, lob
read-ahead reads 0.
Table 'PurchaseOrderHeader'. Scan count 1, logical reads 2, physical reads 0,
read-ahead reads 0, lob logical reads 0, lob physical reads 0, lob read-
ahead reads 0.
```

There are only two logical reads on PurchaseOrderHeader, a fraction of what we saw before! This improved execution plan can be seen in Figure 6-18.

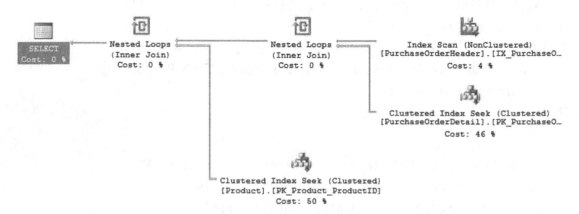

Figure 6-18. *Performance when a filtered covering index is utilized*

Note that even though the execution plan looks similar to before, the cost of the index scan on `PurchaseOrderHeader` has decreased, and the overall subtree cost has decreased by 25%.

Filtered indexes are excellent ways to manage queries on tables where only a small subset is needed regularly. On very large tables, the performance difference can be dramatic! Use caution though, as filtered indexes come with two caveats:

1. WHERE clauses must be precise. While the query optimizer will try its best to use a filtered index, it can only make use of it when the query's WHERE clause overlaps that of the index. If the query changes enough so that the filters don't match, then SQL Server will ignore the filtered index and try to use another instead.

2. When data is written to a table with a filtered index, SQL Server must check to see whether the changed data matches the filter. This means that small numbers of extra reads may be required when altering data to properly maintain the filtered index. While this cost is generally low, it is important to recognize it when working on large data sets. For the preceding example, any UPDATE that modifies status will need to verify if those changes will result in data being added or removed from the filtered index. In filtered indexes with a compound WHERE clause, modifications to any column of it will result in similar checks.

The benefits will typically outweigh the costs when considering a filter on an index. If a table contains 100 million rows, of which 10,000 contain current or relevant data, then we could expect reads on the index as well as storage to be reduced to about 0.01% of the original amount, which is an immense improvement!

Cardinality

When considering performance concerns, it is important to discuss cardinality and what it means for the queries we execute. Cardinality refers to the number of rows affected by an operation. When optimizing a query, SQL Server must determine how many rows will be affected by each part of the execution plan. This is extremely important, as that count will determine important decisions, such as whether to scan or seek a table, or whether to use a merge or hash join. An explanation of cardinality would be incomplete without a brief overview of statistics.

Statistics

By default, statistics are created on all indexes and columns in any given table. Statistics provide a simple, yet powerful list of values within a table. For example, we can view the statistics on a given index with the following statement:

```
DBCC SHOW_STATISTICS ("Sales.SalesOrderheader", IX_SalesOrderHeader_
CustomerID);
```

The output of this execution is comprised of three sets of data, as seen in Figure 6-19.

	Name	Updated	Rows	Rows Sampled	Steps	Density	Average key length	String index	Filter Expression	Unfiltered Rows
1	IX_SalesOrderHeader_CustomerID	Jul 17 2014 4:11PM	31465	31465	153	0.6162394	8	NO	NULL	31465

	All density	Average Length	Columns
1	5.230399E-05	4	CustomerID
2	3.178134E-05	8	CustomerID, SalesOrderID

	RANGE_HI_KEY	RANGE_ROWS	EQ_ROWS	DISTINCT_RANGE_ROWS	AVG_RANGE_ROWS
1	11000	0	3	0	1
2	11019	47	17	18	2.611111
3	11091	186	28	71	2.619718
4	11142	132	17	50	2.64
5	11185	109	27	42	2.595238
6	11223	160	27	37	4.324324
7	11262	125	27	38	3.289474
8	11300	149	27	37	4.027027
9	11331	84	27	30	2.8
10	11417	173	7	85	2.035294

Figure 6-19. *Sample output of DBCC SHOW_STATISTICS*

The first row returned is an overview of the statistics, including the name, last update time, total rows in the table, and sampled rows. The rows sampled will equal the row count for smaller tables, but in larger tables will be smaller. Updating statistics isn't free, and scanning millions of rows to update may not be worth the effort if data is relatively uniform in nature. The Steps are the number of ranges that the data was broken into, where 200 is the maximum SQL Server will use. For the preceding example, a total of 31,465 rows were sampled (the entire table) and broken into 153 ranges in which values of CustomerID were counted.

The second result set shows the density for each column involved in the index, including the clustered index column(s), which this index refers back to. Density is equal to 1 / (# of distinct values). For the preceding values:

```
SELECT DISTINCT CustomerID FROM Sales.SalesOrderheader;
```

This returns 19,119 distinct values for CustomerID. 1 / 19119 = 5.230399E-05, which is the value provided above. The combination of CustomerID and SalesOrderID (the clustered primary key column) is as unique as the primary key in this case:

```
SELECT DISTINCT CustomerID, SalesOrderID FROM Sales.SalesOrderheader;
```

The results of this query are 31,465 values: 1 / 31465 = 3.178134E-05, the second value above.

Density is an important metric for the query optimizer, as it provides quick insight into how unique a column is, and therefore how many potential values there will be on average for each individual value. To determine further details on this, and to expand upon density, we can review the last data set, which is the statistics histogram. The histogram shows ranges of values for CustomerID, and the number of rows for which their values fall into that range.

For example, let's take a look at a single row of the histogram.

RANGE_HI_KEY,	RANGE_ROWS,	EQ_ROWS,	DISTINCT_RANGE_ROWS,	AVG_RANGE_ROWS
11331	84	27	30	2.8
11417	173	7	85	2.035294
11439	68	6	21	3.238095

One hundred seventy-three values are found within the range 11,331 < X < 11,417. In addition to that range, there are seven values that are equal to the maximum value of the range (11,417). There are 85 possible values within this range (11,417 – 11,331 - 1), and the average range rows per value is 2.035294.

This is all well and good, but what does it mean for us? This data is somewhat esoteric, but it provides immense value to the query optimizer. It can cross-check filters, groupings, and joins with this data very quickly and determine how to process a query. If a filter is very inclusive and it turns out that it will return most rows in a table, then a table scan will likely be used. In scenarios like this, it's faster to return everything than it is to selectively pick and choose a large volume of rows separately. If a filter is very exclusive, the optimizer will quickly realize that an index seek is the fastest way to return the results.

The query optimizer is only as good as the data that is provided to it by statistics. If this data becomes inaccurate for any reason, then the result can be suboptimal execution plans, poor performance, and users calling you at absurdly late hours of the night looking for help.

There are three settings in SQL Server that guide how statistics are handled within a database. All are included in system views and can be reviewed for a given database like this:

```
SELECT
     is_auto_update_stats_on,
     is_auto_create_stats_on,
     is_auto_update_stats_async_on
FROM sys.databases WHERE name = 'AdventureWorks2014';
```

Removing the filter will return info on all databases on this SQL Server. The results of the this query are as follows:

is_auto_update_stats_on	is_auto_create_stats_on	is_auto_update_stats_async_on
1	1	0

What do these values mean?

Auto_update_stats_on tells us if SQL Server will automatically update stale statistics, which by default is on. This does not guarantee statistics that will give you accurate execution plans, but handles a few scenarios when statistics are deemed stale. More on this in the following!

Auto_create_stats_on indicates if statistics will be automatically created on columns and indexes as needed, which is on by default. This is useful and should only be turned off if you are very confident about maintaining statistics manually. This setting does not apply to views, for which you will need to manually create statistics where needed.

Auto_update_stats_async_on determines if statistics should be updated before or after a query's execution and is off by default. Turning this on speeds up query execution, but can lead to inaccurate execution plans, and therefore is recommended to be kept off.

For these settings, the defaults are generally best, unless you have a very compelling reason to make changes. What does auto-updating statistics entail, and when does it happen?

By default, a database is set with AUTO_UPDATE_STATISTICS on. This will cause statistics to update based on rules that depend upon the version of SQL Server.

Up through SQL Server 2014, statistics would auto-update whenever

1. an empty table has rows inserted into it.

2. rhe row count in a table increases from less than 500 rows to more than 500 rows by a count of at least 500.

3. the row count in a table increases from greater than 500 rows by 500 rows + 20%.

Starting in SQL Server 2016, #3 on the list is replaced with the square root of (1,000 plus the table's row count). That number is the threshold of row count change needed to trigger a statistics update. This change accommodates larger tables where 20% change simply never occurs.

These scenarios update statistics when row counts change significantly, but are not necessarily comprehensive enough for a complex production environment. To ensure that statistics are completely up to date, even if the prceding criteria are not met, we can consider updating statistics manually or on a maintenance schedule. All statistics can be updated on a database in one fell swoop as follows:

```
EXEC sys.sp_updatestats;
```

This will recalculate all statistics on every table in your database. This is generally unadvised, as the volume of data that needs to be scanned can be quite large, take a long time, and cause contention for important production loads. If we cannot update everything all at once, then what alternatives are there?

Updating statistics can be a very IO-intensive operation. Only perform this maintenance when necessary, and only on objects where it is needed.

Statistics can be updated on any single object with the following syntax:

```
UPDATE STATISTICS Production.Product;
```

This will update all statistics on the table `Production.Product`. Additionally, a single statistics can be updated as well:

```
UPDATE STATISTICS Production.Product PK_Product_ProductID;
```

In this statement, we update only the statistics on the primary key for `Production.Product`.

The next logical question to ask is, "How do we know when we should update statistics manually?" Generally, this is a process that should not be worried about unless there is a reason. SQL Server's default settings tend to be reliable for most common database designs. If we don't need to perform expensive maintenance, then we certainly shouldn't! What happens when statistics do become stale, though? To help facilitate this, we'll turn off the automatic updating of statistics. This should never be done in a production environment! For testing purposes, though, this is an excellent way to watch the effect of stale statistics on query optimization and execution:

```
ALTER DATABASE AdventureWorks2014
SET AUTO_UPDATE_STATISTICS OFF;
```

After executing this, we can verify the statistics settings on our database using our query from earlier:

```
SELECT
    is_auto_update_stats_on,
    is_auto_create_stats_on,
    is_auto_update_stats_async_on
FROM sys.databases WHERE name = 'AdventureWorks2014';
```

is_auto_update_stats_on	is_auto_create_stats_on	is_auto_update_stats_async_on
0	1	0

Note that is_auto_update_stats_on is now disabled, and as a result, statistics will only update if we do it ourselves manually. For this example, we'll create a new index on Production.Product on the Weight column:

```
CREATE NONCLUSTERED INDEX IX_Product_Weight ON Production.Product (Weight);
Consider the following query:
SELECT
    ProductID,
    Weight,
    Name
FROM Production.Product
WHERE Weight = 170
```

This returns a single row (out of 504) from the table. The performance metrics are seen in Figure 6-20.

```
Table 'Product'. Scan count 1, logical reads 4, physical reads 0, read-
ahead reads 0, lob logical reads 0, lob physical reads 0, lob read-ahead
reads 0.
```

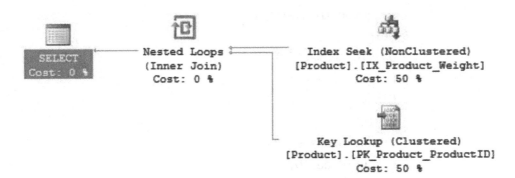

Figure 6-20. *Performance of a simple index seek operation*

This is a relatively straightforward example! Four reads on Production.Product and an execution plan that performs a seek on the new index, as well as a key lookup to retrieve the Name column, which is not in the index we created previously. Let's now insert a large number of new data into the table, as seen in Listing 6-15.

Listing 6-15. TSQL to Populate the Product Table with 1,999 New Products

```
-- Turn off execution plan here.
SET STATISTICS IO OFF
SET STATISTICS TIME OFF

DECLARE @count INT = 1
WHILE @count < 2000
BEGIN
    INSERT INTO Production.Product
            ( Name,
              ProductNumber,
              MakeFlag,
              FinishedGoodsFlag,
              Color,
```

```
                    SafetyStockLevel,
                    ReorderPoint,
                    StandardCost,
                    ListPrice,
                    Size,
                    SizeUnitMeasureCode,
                    WeightUnitMeasureCode,
                    Weight,
                    DaysToManufacture,
                    ProductLine,
                    Class,
                    Style,
                    ProductSubcategoryID,
                    ProductModelID,
                    SellStartDate,
                    SellEndDate,
                    DiscontinuedDate,
                    rowguid,
                    ModifiedDate
                    )
    SELECT
            'Hoverboard' + CAST(@count AS VARCHAR(25)),
            'HOV-' + CAST(@count AS VARCHAR(25)),
            1 AS MakeFlag,
            1 AS FinishedGoodsFlag,
            NULL AS Color,
            500 AS SafetyStockLevel,
            375 AS ReorderPoint,
            55 AS StandardCost,
            100 AS ListPrice,
            NULL AS Size,
            NULL AS SizeUnitMeasureCode,
            'G' AS WeightUnitMeasureCode,
            170 AS Weight,
            5 AS DaysToManufacture,
```

```
        NULL AS ProductLine,
        'H' AS Class,
        NULL AS Style,
        5 AS ProductSubcategoryID,
        97 AS ProductModelID,
        '1/1/2015' AS SellStartDate,
        NULL AS SellEndDate,
        NULL AS DiscontinuedDate,
        NEWID() AS rowguid,
        CURRENT_TIMESTAMP AS ModifiedDate

    SET @count = @count + 1
END
```

This query will insert 1,999 rows into `Production.Product`, all with the same weight (170). Turning off the execution plan as well as statistics metrics will greatly speed up the insert, since we are using a quick and dirty loop to complete the task. Once complete, let's rerun the same query from before that previously ran very efficiently:

```
SET STATISTICS IO ON;
SET STATISTICS TIME ON;
SET NOCOUNT ON;
SELECT
    ProductID,
    Weight,
    Name
FROM Production.Product
WHERE Weight = 170;
```

Execution completes quickly enough, but looking under the covers at performance reveals another story altogether. This can be seen in Figure 6-21.

```
Table 'Product'. Scan count 1, logical reads 4008, physical reads 0, read-
ahead reads 0, lob logical reads 0, lob physical reads 0, lob read-ahead
reads 0.
```

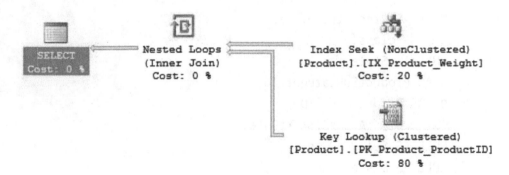

Figure 6-21. *Performance of the search query against a larger result set*

The execution plan is identical to what we got previously, but the reads on
`Production.Product` are significantly higher! 4,004 reads on a table with about 2,500
rows seems very high for a query that only returns three columns. By turning off statistics
auto-update, we removed the query optimizer's most important tool to find good
execution plans: accurate statistics. Let's review the statistics for the index we used in
Figure 6-22.

```
DBCC SHOW_STATISTICS ("Production.Product", IX_Product_Weight);
```

	RANGE_HI_KEY	RANGE_ROWS	EQ_ROWS	DISTINCT_RANGE_ROWS	AVG_RANGE_ROWS
89	29.90	1	1	1	1
90	30.00	0	2	0	1
91	149.00	1	1	1	1
92	168.00	0	2	0	1
93	170.00	0	1	0	1
94	185.00	0	1	0	1
95	189.00	0	1	0	1
96	215.00	0	2	0	1
97	218.00	0	1	0	1
98	222.00	0	1	0	1

Figure 6-22. *Stale statistics for the IX_Product_Weight index on Production.
Product*

Note that for the range including 170 there is only a single equality row, even though
we added 1,999 additional rows. The query optimizer cannot make a smart decision
with data that is this inaccurate. To illustrate this, we'll update the statistics on this index
manually:

```
UPDATE STATISTICS Production.Product IX_Product_Weight;
```

Running the prceding DBCC command to recheck the statistics on the IX_Product_Weight index reveals the changes we expect to see, as shown in Figure 6-23.

	RANGE_HI_KEY	RANGE_ROWS	EQ_ROWS	DISTINCT_RANGE_ROWS	AVG_RANGE_ROWS
89	29.90	1	1	1	1
90	30.00	0	2	0	1
91	149.00	1	1	1	1
92	168.00	0	2	0	1
93	170.00	0	2000	0	1
94	185.00	0	1	0	1
95	189.00	0	1	0	1
96	215.00	0	2	0	1
97	218.00	0	1	0	1

Figure 6-23. *Updated statistics for the IX_Product_Weight index on Production. Product*

Now there are 2,000 rows reported with a weight equal to 170, which matches our expectations after the inserts we executed. With statistics updated, let's run the test query one last time:

```
SELECT
    ProductID,
    Weight,
    Name
FROM Production.Product
WHERE Weight = 170
```

This time, performance metrics look much less concerning, as shown in Figure 6-24.

```
Table 'Product'. Scan count 1, logical reads 58, physical reads 0, read-
ahead reads 0, lob logical reads 0, lob physical reads 0, lob read-ahead
reads 0.
```

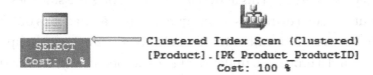

Figure 6-24. *Performance of the previous search query with updated statistics*

Only 58 reads were needed, instead of 4,004, and a clustered index scan was chosen as the most efficient data retrieval method. It turns out that, when we are looking to return a very large portion of a table, it's faster to simply return everything and discard what we don't need rather than traverse an index to find all of the necessary rows. As soon as the query optimizer had accurate data on the contents of the index, it was able to opt for a scan instead, knowing that this was the best course of action.

Sys.dm_db_stats_properties

The system dynamic management view sys.dm_db_stats_properties provides direct insight into the metrics and usage of a statistics object. This is valuable, as it allows us to more carefully pick and choose which statistics to update or not update on any given day. Consider the following query in Listing 6-16.

Listing 6-16. Returning Additional Metrics on Statistics Usage and Contents

```
SELECT
      schemas.name AS SchemaName,
      tables.name AS TableName,
      stats.name AS StatsName,
      dm_db_stats_properties.*
FROM sys.stats
INNER JOIN sys.tables
ON tables.object_id = stats.object_id
INNER JOIN sys.schemas
ON schemas.schema_id = tables.schema_id
CROSS APPLY sys.dm_db_stats_properties(tables.object_id, stats.stats_id)
WHERE dm_db_stats_properties.modification_counter > 0
ORDER BY dm_db_stats_properties.modification_counter DESC;
```

The column modification_counter is a count of updates to the underlying data of the statistics object in question. This allows us to cherry-pick the statistics that are likely to be the most out of date. The results of this query return all statistics objects in which at least one update has occurred, and orders them by those with the most updates first.

If we were to build a process to update statistics automatically, or were interested in learning about the statistics that are updated most frequently, the results would tell us everything we need to know, as seen in Figure 6-25.

	SchemaName	TableName	StatsName	object_id	stats_id	last_updated	rows	rows_sampled	steps	unfiltered_rows	modification_counter
1	dbo	employee_login	_WA_Sys_00000005_3414ACBA	873770170	2	2018-08-10 10:45:02.9566667	11	11	4	11	44
2	dbo	AWBuildVersion	_WA_Sys_00000004_2F10007B	789577851	3	2015-10-23 13:23:41.8900000	1	1	1	1	2
3	dbo	AWBuildVersion	_WA_Sys_00000002_2F10007B	789577851	4	2015-10-23 13:23:41.8933333	1	1	1	1	1
4	dbo	AWBuildVersion	_WA_Sys_00000003_2F10007B	789577851	2	2015-10-23 13:23:41.8900000	1	1	1	1	1

Figure 6-25. *Detailed metrics on statistics that have changed data since the last update*

We quickly learn that there are four statistics that may require updating, of which one has comparatively experienced significant change. We also learn a bit about the table sizes involved, the rows sampled, and the number of steps in the histogram. If we wanted to know if a statistics object was out of date, how it is used, or if we should update it, then this would be the perfect way to find out.

The amount of change that necessitates a statistics update will vary from system to system, but by taking some time to understand application usage of commonly accessed tables, we can get an idea for the correct filter to use on the modification_counter column. By ordering results by that change count, we can ensure that the stalest statistics are updated first. As time goes on, we may determine exceptional columns that should never be updated because they are write-only or change so much that maintaining accurate stats is not worth the effort. Alternatively, we may find statistics that are critically important and should always be updated. These rules can be combined with our query results earlier to paint a very clear picture of statistics maintenance and the best ways to maintain data for a given application.

Trace Flag 2371

Starting with SQL Server 2008R2 and prior to SQL Server 2016, there was an additional way to manage auto-updating statistics in SQL Server, and that is trace flag 2371. This trace flag is intended to address the needs of very large tables, in which the metrics used to auto-update statistics normally simply don't fit well. Wait for changes to 20% of a table with millions of rows, and you may be forced to wait for a very long time.

When you turn on this trace flag, the formula for when to update statistics is made somewhat dynamic. When a table exceeds 25,000 rows, the percentage of rows that need to be modified to trigger the update of statistics decreases. This addresses the needs of large tables while also not changing the functionality on smaller tables.

If you are responsible for a database that contains tables with millions or billions of rows, then this trace flag can be a significant boom to performance and a way to avoid having to manually manage statistics. This trace flag can be enabled as follows:

```
DBCC TRACEON (2371);
```

As always, do not make changes to SQL Server trace flags until you have performed a thorough assessment of your database environment and tested to ensure that this change is beneficial. While we get very excited when new performance features or options are available, performing adequate QA on these changes is critical to ensuring that they are both necessary and helpful.

More documentation on this trace flag can be found on MSDN in a very well-written article: `http://blogs.msdn.com/b/saponsqlserver/archive/2011/09/07/changes-to-automatic-update-statistics-in-sql-server-traceflag-2371.aspx`.

Back to Dynamic SQL

We've discussed statistics, how they are used, and how inaccurate statistics can affect performance. How does this relate to dynamic SQL and our day-to-day tasks? Cardinality is a measure of quantity used in every step of query optimization. In each step, the query optimizer must use statistics to determine how many rows it expects to be returned in that step, whether it be a seek, join, or filter. If statistics are inaccurate, even in a single step, it could result in a suboptimal execution plan in which performance is worse than it need be, or (worst case) unacceptably slow.

Cardinality can be checked by hovering over any step in an execution plan, as seen in Figure 6-26.

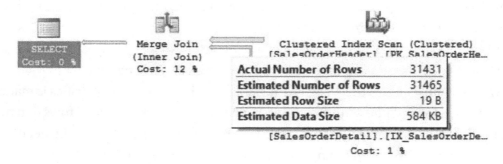

Figure 6-26. *Viewing row counts in SQL Server Management Studio*

Hovering over the arrow between the clustered index scan and merge join reveals that the optimizer estimated 31,465 rows to be output to the join. When executed, though, the actual number of rows was 31,431. A difference this small will rarely present a performance concern, but if you are reviewing a query execution plan and notice that the actual and estimated number of rows differ greatly, then definitely take a closer look at statistics and ensure they are accurate.

Dynamic SQL introduces scenarios where there can be queries that change all the time, or that shift between a handful of common use cases. The potential for statistics to be wrong, or for execution plans to get used or reused in suboptimal ways becomes higher. In Chapter 8 we'll discuss parameter sniffing and dive deeper into cardinality and the ways in which bad estimates can lead to performance headaches. Understanding these issues can greatly reduce the head scratching when they arise.

Query Hints

There are many ways in which we can provide the query optimizer with a nudge in order to get it to do exactly what we want. Consider one of the most common hints used in SQL Server, the NOLOCK hint, as used in Listing 6-17.

Listing 6-17. Example Usage of the NOLOCK Query Hint

```
SELECT
      SalesOrderDetail.SalesOrderDetailID,
      SalesOrderDetail.SalesOrderID,
      SalesOrderDetail.ProductID
FROM Sales.SalesOrderDetail WITH (NOLOCK)
WHERE ProductID = 713;
```

NOLOCK is a commonly used hint that can be used on SELECT statements that will avoid contention by reading existing data (dirty pages) from memory, even if other transactions are operating on the data involved. At first glance, this sounds spectacular—no contention! It's a double-edged sword, though, as it is very possible for us to run a SELECT while an UPDATE is in progress and never return data that was changed or not committed in that UPDATE statement.

NOLOCK is an example of a query hint, which is a somewhat poorly named feature because it is more of a command than a hint. Hints are often used as ways to fix performance problems when they arise. For example, a DBA that sees frequent locking or deadlocking may use NOLOCK to stop that contention from occurring. This hint can be useful in a reporting-style environment where the timeliness of data is not critical, and we simply need an idea of what data looked like at a given time. Even then, we would want to ask ourselves why we are running reporting queries in a highly transactional environment, and only when that question is answered, be comfortable in making this change.

The downside to using query hints is that we are telling the query optimizer exactly what to do, as though we are smarter than it. While there are times we may know better, things can change in any busy production environment. The hint that works perfectly today may be useless tomorrow, or hinder performance.

Liberal use of join hints will often be a potential mistake, as shown in Listing 6-18.

Listing 6-18. Using Join Hints to Force a Particular Join by the Optimizer

```
DECLARE @ProductID INT = 713;
SELECT
     SalesOrderDetail.SalesOrderDetailID,
     SalesOrderDetail.SalesOrderID,
     SalesOrderDetail.ProductID,
     SalesOrderHeader.OrderDate
FROM Sales.SalesOrderDetail
INNER LOOP JOIN Sales.SalesOrderHeader
ON SalesOrderDetail.SalesOrderID = SalesOrderHeader.SalesOrderID
WHERE ProductID = @ProductID;

SELECT
     SalesOrderDetail.SalesOrderDetailID,
     SalesOrderDetail.SalesOrderID,
     SalesOrderDetail.ProductID,
     SalesOrderHeader.OrderDate
FROM Sales.SalesOrderDetail
```

```
INNER MERGE JOIN Sales.SalesOrderHeader
ON SalesOrderDetail.SalesOrderID = SalesOrderHeader.SalesOrderID
WHERE ProductID = @ProductID;

SELECT
     SalesOrderDetail.SalesOrderDetailID,
     SalesOrderDetail.SalesOrderID,
     SalesOrderDetail.ProductID,
     SalesOrderHeader.OrderDate
FROM Sales.SalesOrderDetail
INNER HASH JOIN Sales.SalesOrderHeader
ON SalesOrderDetail.SalesOrderID = SalesOrderHeader.SalesOrderID
WHERE ProductID = @ProductID;
```

The query optimizer will choose what it considers the best join type when we join two tables together in a query. Sometimes we may find that if we override the default and force a particular join, we can get better performance. This may not always work, though, and if we review the prceding performance, we see a variety of results:

```
Warning: The join order has been enforced because a local join hint is used.
Table 'SalesOrderHeader'. Scan count 0, logical reads 1322, physical reads 0,
read-ahead reads 19, lob logical reads 0, lob physical reads 0, lob read-
ahead reads 0.
Table 'SalesOrderDetail'. Scan count 1, logical reads 3, physical reads 0,
read-ahead reads 0, lob logical reads 0, lob physical reads 0, lob read-
ahead reads 0.

Warning: The join order has been enforced because a local join hint is used.
Table 'Worktable'. Scan count 0, logical reads 0, physical reads 0, read-
ahead reads 0, lob logical reads 0, lob physical reads 0, lob read-ahead
reads 0.
Table 'SalesOrderHeader'. Scan count 1, logical reads 688, physical reads 0,
read-ahead reads 0, lob logical reads 0, lob physical reads 0, lob read-
ahead reads 0.
```

Table 'SalesOrderDetail'. Scan count 1, logical reads 3, physical reads 0, read-ahead reads 0, lob logical reads 0, lob physical reads 0, lob read-ahead reads 0.

Warning: The join order has been enforced because a local join hint is used. Table 'Workfile'. Scan count 0, logical reads 0, physical reads 0, read-ahead reads 0, lob logical reads 0, lob physical reads 0, lob read-ahead reads 0.
Table 'Worktable'. Scan count 0, logical reads 0, physical reads 0, read-ahead reads 0, lob logical reads 0, lob physical reads 0, lob read-ahead reads 0.
Table 'SalesOrderHeader'. Scan count 1, logical reads 689, physical reads 0, read-ahead reads 0, lob logical reads 0, lob physical reads 0, lob read-ahead reads 0.
Table 'SalesOrderDetail'. Scan count 1, logical reads 3, physical reads 0, read-ahead reads 0, lob logical reads 0, lob physical reads 0, lob read-ahead reads 0.

When we review the IO statistics, we see that forcing a loop join resulted in much higher reads than a hash or merge join. Different values of @ProductID may result in different joins producing better or worse performance results. Note that SQL Server reminds us that the join order has been enforced by our query hint. This is its way of gently telling us that whatever happens next is our fault and we cannot call up Microsoft and complain if the results aren't what we expected.

Similarly, the execution plans for the prceding queries look different, and each reflects different subtree costs. This can be seen by reviewing the three execution plans in Figure 6-27.

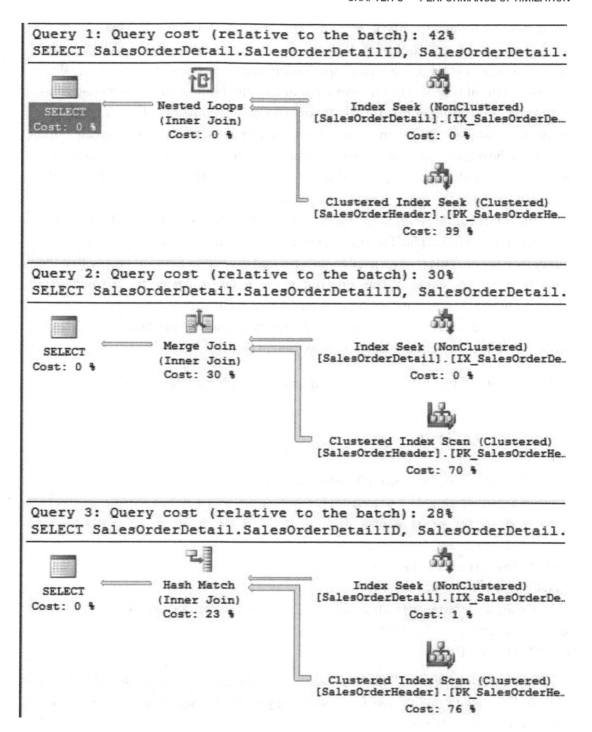

Figure 6-27. *Execution plans when different joins are forced with query hints*

In general, forcing specific joins is going to eventually backfire. Perhaps a hash join seems like the best choice right now, as we see a large table joining a small table, but data can change, as well as application usage. When our tweaks eventually become irrelevant, we will not remember or notice the problem until it is too late, and performance degrades as the use case for our changes no longer applies. Change is a constant in database design and management and we must write scripts that are nimble enough to be relevant in months, or even years from now. Query hints put constraints on our design, reducing the options that the optimizer can choose from. If those options would be useful in the future, then our hints will prevent their usage.

Another frequently used query hint is RECOMPILE, which will force SQL Server to create a new execution plan for a query, even if an adequate one already exists in the query plan cache. This is often used to sidestep bad execution plans or ensure that the best plan is found each time. The optimization process is expensive, though, and on a busy production server the costs associated with frequently recompiling large volumes of queries could result in unusually high CPU utilization and query latency. Let's take our last test query and add this hint to it, as seen in Listing 6-19.

Listing 6-19. Using a RECOMPILE Hint to Force a New Execution Plan to be Created and Used

```
DECLARE @ProductID INT = 713;
SELECT
      SalesOrderDetail.SalesOrderDetailID,
      SalesOrderDetail.SalesOrderID,
      SalesOrderDetail.ProductID,
      SalesOrderHeader.OrderDate
FROM Sales.SalesOrderDetail
INNER JOIN Sales.SalesOrderHeader
ON SalesOrderDetail.SalesOrderID = SalesOrderHeader.SalesOrderID
WHERE ProductID = @ProductID
OPTION (RECOMPILE);
```

Running this query, we'll find that nearly everything appears normal in the execution plan and IO statistics. Where we find a seemingly minor, yet significant difference is in the STATISTICS TIME results:

```
SQL Server parse and compile time:
  CPU time = 0 ms, elapsed time = 1 ms.
```

Within the output, we notice that no matter how many times we run the query, the parse and compile time is always non-zero. This is the price for forcing the execution plan to recompile. A millisecond may seem small, but for more complex queries with many tables and joins, the time can be much higher. Combine increased times with frequent execution and performance will be significantly impacted by the time and effort required to continuously create new execution plans.

Query hints should be used sparingly, only when necessary, and when all alternatives have been exhausted. Change over time can render hints destructive to database performance, rather than helpful.

We could easily review dozens of query hints, highlighting common usage, as well as potential pitfalls, but generally it is important to recognize that query hints are often ways to cheat our way past bigger problems. Very often, hints are used to cover up poorly designed tables, inefficiently written queries, bad indexing, or other mistakes that could be resolved to fix the performance problem.

There are legitimate uses for query hints, but it is important to view them as last resorts, rather than tools that should be implemented frequently. Only implement them after extremely thorough testing and assurances that the likelihood of breaking changes will be very low. A list of available query and table hints can be found on MSDN: `https://msdn.microsoft.com/en-us/library/ms181714.aspx`

Note the warning provided near the top of the article:

```
If one or more query hints cause the query optimizer not to generate a
valid plan, error 8622 is raised.
```

Some hints can remove the only valid transforms available from the query optimizer. If this happens, then a query can fail to execute, generate an error, and likely wake you up at an uncomfortably late hour. Knowledge of these options is important, but please use caution when implementing them. Use hints when deemed necessary and safe and utilize all alternatives first. If a query can be rewritten, an index added, or a view altered, consider those and similar changes first before bossing around the query optimizer.

Conclusion

Performance optimization is a huge topic, and this blast through many important topics only serves to scratch the surface. There is no shortage of ways in which we can dig deeper into query tuning, indexing, statistics, or other ways to improve performance.

Approach each problem with a plan in mind, and research it thoroughly. SQL Server provides many tools that allow us to easily assess performance, resource consumption, and ways to get our most important queries to execute faster. Always test and confirm the expected results of any change and be certain that your predictions match the test results. While it can be humbling to have one's performance hypothesis struck down by other metrics that were not considered, this result is still greatly preferred over releasing suboptimal changes into a production environment.

For the duration of this book, we will dig further into performance in many of our examples. This will allow us to apply what we have discussed and provide a variety of ways in which to test some of the conclusions we have drawn thus far. Look forward to many more examples of execution plans, statistics, and query comparisons that will aid in our exploration of dynamic SQL.

Cleanup

The TSQL in Listing 6-20 will clean up any objects created in this chapter, if they exist.

Listing 6-20. Script to Clean Up Any Objects Created in This Chapter, if Needed

```
IF EXISTS (SELECT * FROM sys.procedures WHERE procedures.name = 'search_
products')
BEGIN
     DROP PROCEDURE dbo.search_products;
END
GO
IF EXISTS (SELECT * FROM sys.indexes WHERE indexes.name = 'IX_
PurchaseOrderHeader_status_INC')
BEGIN
     DROP INDEX IX_PurchaseOrderHeader_status_INC ON Purchasing.
     PurchaseOrderHeader
END
```

```
GO
IF EXISTS (SELECT * FROM sys.procedures WHERE procedures.name = 'get_in_
process_purchasing_data')
BEGIN
      DROP PROCEDURE dbo.get_in_process_purchasing_data;
END
GO
DELETE
FROM Production.Product
WHERE Product.Name LIKE 'Hoverboard%';
```

CHAPTER 7

Scalable Dynamic Lists

Generating lists of data is a common task with a wide variety of use cases. Perhaps we want to output data to an application or file with a specific formatting or syntax. Maybe the best format to read a list of data is in a single line, rather than a tabular format. Maybe you want to store data in a table using a particular string format that needs to be quickly built prior to storing it.

While this is not an often advertised feature of SQL Server, it is one that can be implemented in ways that perform quite well. Alternatively, it is very easy to concoct list generation in ways that are unbelievably inefficient. This chapter will serve as a discussion of many different ways in which lists can be generated. In addition to syntax, we will review performance and maintainability to ensure that there is no question as to which method is the best for the job.

Performance tuning will be referenced frequently in this chapter. Please refer to Chapter 6 for details on reading execution plans, reviewing IO statistics, and other considerations with regard to dynamic SQL and query tuning and optimization.

What Is a Dynamic List?

The easiest way to introduce this topic is with an example. Let's consider a scenario where we want to output a comma separated list of IDs for a list of people. A common method that is to build this string piece by piece using a CURSOR, as seen in Listing 7-1.

© Edward Pollack 2019
E. Pollack, *Dynamic SQL*, https://doi.org/10.1007/978-1-4842-4318-3_7

Listing 7-1. Example of a Cursor-Based Approach to Building a Comma-Delimited List of IDs

```
DECLARE @nextid INT;
DECLARE @myIDs NVARCHAR(MAX) = '';

DECLARE idcursor CURSOR FOR
SELECT TOP 100
      BusinessEntityID
FROM Person.Person
ORDER BY LastName;
OPEN idcursor;
FETCH NEXT FROM idcursor INTO @nextid;

WHILE @@FETCH_STATUS = 0
BEGIN
      SET @myIDs = @myIDs + CAST(@nextid AS NVARCHAR) + ',';
      FETCH NEXT FROM idcursor INTO @nextid;
END
SET @myIDs = LEFT(@myIDs, LEN(@myIDs) - 1);
CLOSE idcursor;
DEALLOCATE idcursor;

SELECT @myIDs AS comma_separated_output;
```

In this TSQL, a CURSOR is declared for 100 IDs and is looped through, one by one, as the string @myIDs is slowly built up with IDs and commas. The last string modification uses the LEFT function to remove the trailing comma that is left over from the loop. The result will be 100 BusinessEntityIDs, each separated by commas. The text output will appear like this:

```
285,293,295,2170,38,211,2357,297,291,299,121,16867,16901,16724,10263,10312,...
```

We'll cut off the list here after 16 IDs, as there's no need to waste space with that ☺

In general, iteration should be avoided when writing TSQL in any scenario where a set-based approach could be applied. SQL Server is built to efficiently process sets of data, and when we try to pull data a row at a time, we will often see poor performance as the common result. This is an example of where TSQL that involves loops can be extremely inefficient. Let's first look at the execution plan.

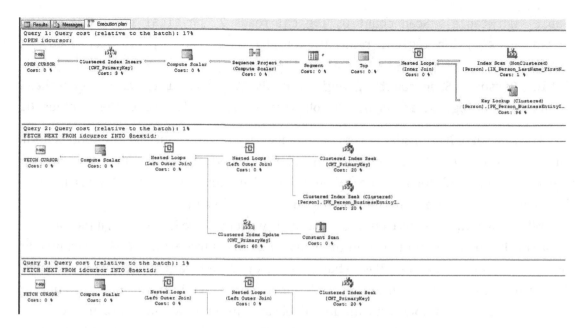

Figure 7-1. Execution plan for a simple SELECT query that iterates through a loop

The execution plan is cut off after the first two queries, as the next 99 are exactly the same as the 2nd. It's immediately clear that we must consider 101 execution plans in order to determine the overall effort expended by SQL Server when generating our list. As a result, it is necessary to read from `Person.Person` over 100 times, in addition to reading from the cursor itself, which is not a free operation. On my SQL Server, this took a total of 10 seconds to run. For a TSQL application whose purpose it is to read 100 IDs, this is quite slow! While much of this execution time results from generating 100 extra execution plans, it illustrates how any seemingly simple task performed often enough can become cumulatively painful.

To gain more insight into the inefficiency introduced here, we can review the IO statistics as well:

```
Table 'Worktable'. Scan count 0, logical reads 201, physical reads 0, read-
ahead reads 0, lob logical reads 0, lob physical reads 0, lob read-ahead
reads 0.
Table 'Person'. Scan count 1, logical reads 318, physical reads 0, read-
ahead reads 0, lob logical reads 0, lob physical reads 0, lob read-ahead
reads 0.
```

```
Table 'Worktable'. Scan count 0, logical reads 2, physical reads 0, read-
ahead reads 0, lob logical reads 0, lob physical reads 0, lob read-ahead
reads 0.
Table 'Person'. Scan count 0, logical reads 3, physical reads 0, read-ahead
reads 0, lob logical reads 0, lob physical reads 0, lob read-ahead reads 0.
```

The first set of IO statistics covers the initial cursor declaration. The 2nd represents a single iteration of the WHILE loop, which will be repeated another 99 times. If we add up the total logical reads for all of the queries involved, we get 1,019 reads, which is quite a lot given that we are only intending to return 100 integer values.

While the output of this example was exactly what we were looking for, it took a relatively immense amount of computing resources to get there. Imagine if we wanted a list of a thousand or a million IDs. What if instead of IDs, we wanted a list of large strings? The result could easily be millions of reads and a query that grinds our server to a halt! Correct output is desirable, but with unscalable and unmaintainable performance, code like this will come back to haunt us in the future as software changes and our assumptions about data size or acceptable performance metrics become invalidated.

Using XML to Create a Dynamic List

It's clear that generating a string using any form of loop is going to be inefficient for all but the tiniest data sets. An alternative that is widely used is to select the desired data from the underlying table and format it using XML. Consider the following example of this syntax, as seen in Listing 7-2, which generates the same list as the loop that was introduced earlier.

Listing 7-2. Generating a List of IDs Using XML

```
DECLARE @myIDs NVARCHAR(MAX) = '';

SET @myIDs = STUFF((SELECT TOP 100 ',' + CAST(BusinessEntityID AS NVARCHAR)
FROM Person.Person
ORDER BY LastName
FOR XML PATH("), TYPE
).value('.', 'NVARCHAR(MAX)'), 1, 1, '');

SELECT @myIDs;
GO
```

The first thing we notice is that the syntax is more complicated and somewhat less readable. The result set is the same, which is what we intended:

285,293,295,2170,38,211,2357,297,291,299,121,16867,16901,16724,10263,10312,...

To understand how XML generates this list, we can break the query up, starting with the innermost TSQL and then building upon it as we move forward:

```
SELECT TOP 100 ',' + CAST(BusinessEntityID AS NVARCHAR) AS ID_CSV
FROM Person.Person
ORDER BY LastName;
```

This SELECT statement returns a list of IDs, with a comma preceding each, as seen in Figure 7-2.

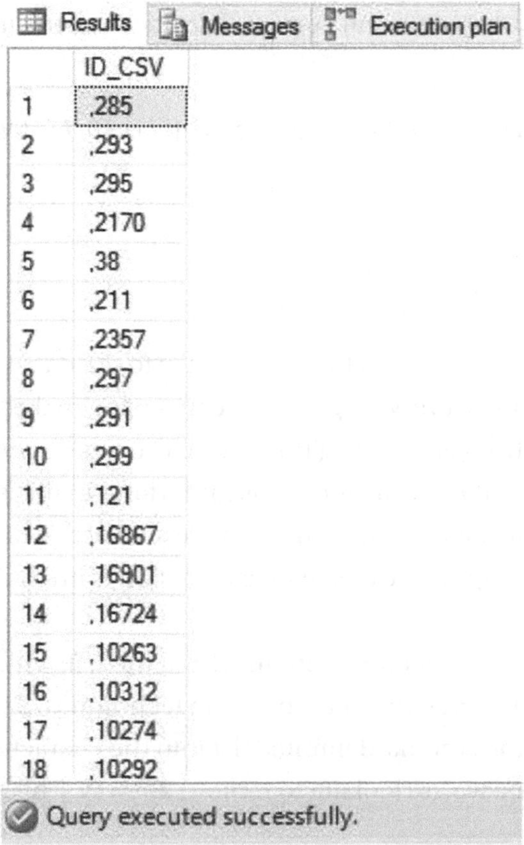

Figure 7-2. *ID list that will be used in an XML-generated list*

There is nothing out of the ordinary here. The next step will concatenate all of the rows of data above into an XML format, which in SQL Server will display as a comma-delimited list:

```
SELECT (SELECT TOP 100 ',' + CAST(BusinessEntityID AS NVARCHAR)
FROM Person.Person
ORDER BY LastName
FOR XML PATH(''));
```

The result of this SELECT will show a result that is on its way to being the finished product:

```
285,293,295,2170,38,211,2357,297,291,299,121,16867,16901,16724,10263,10312,...
```

There are two pieces of unfinished business that we need to deal with before we can consider this query fully dissected and correct. The first is to ensure that the XML output is the correct data type:

```
SELECT (SELECT TOP 100 ',' + CAST(BusinessEntityID AS NVARCHAR)
FROM Person.Person
ORDER BY LastName
FOR XML PATH(''), TYPE
).value('.', 'NVARCHAR(MAX)');
```

The XML value method converts the XML results to the data type provided prior to returning it. If this is a very long list, the conversion makes sure that we don't suffer from string truncation along the way. It also lets us choose between VARCHAR and NVARCHAR if the distinction is important. In this example, we choose NVARCHAR(MAX) as the data type to return. The results of this query are identical to the output from the last step, as the data type conversion is invisible to the SQL Server output we are viewing.

The last step is to remove that pesky comma from the left, which can be accomplished via a number of string manipulation techniques. STUFF was used earlier to cram the contents of the comma-delimited list into the character at position 1, which happens to be the comma we are looking to remove anyway. This method is convenient, as it can be accomplished in a single step without having to store the results in a variable if we don't need to. An alternative would be to use RIGHT or SUBSTRING to remove the leading comma:

```
DECLARE @myIDs NVARCHAR(MAX) = '';

SET @myIDs = (SELECT TOP 100 ',' + CAST(BusinessEntityID AS NVARCHAR)
FROM Person.Person
ORDER BY LastName
FOR XML PATH(''), TYPE
).value('.', 'NVARCHAR(MAX)');

SELECT RIGHT(@myIDs, LEN(@myIDs) - 1);
SELECT SUBSTRING(@myIDs, 2, LEN(@myIDs) - 1);
```

The results of each SELECT are identical, and match what we were looking for in the output:

```
285,293,295,2170,38,211,2357,297,291,299,121,16867,16901,16724,10263,10312,...
```

Now that we have established that XML can be used to generate a comma-delimited list, we should take the additional steps to performance test it and determine its level of efficiency. First, let's examine the IO statistics for the query:

```
Table 'Person'. Scan count 1, logical reads 3, physical reads 0, read-ahead reads 0, lob logical reads 0, lob physical reads 0, lob read-ahead reads 0.
```

This looks great! The reads are the equivalent of what we would expect if we were to simply run the SELECT statement from Person.Person with no additional formatting applied to it. Using XML reduced our reads from 1,019 to 3, which I consider an excellent deal any day of the week! Next, let's see how the execution plan looks in Figure 7-3.

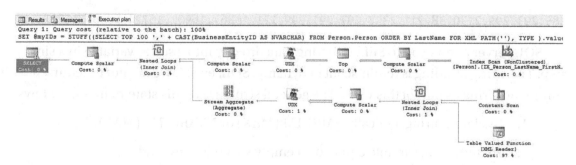

Figure 7-3. *Performance of list-generation using XML*

For a query that is grabbing a list of IDs, this is a bit complex. The magic that is performed behind the scenes by the XML reader isn't free, and that becomes clear here as it consumes 97% of the resources of the query. Examining the subtree cost of the execution plan, we find that it is about 1.09, which is similar to the query cost of the WHILE loop method. In other words, the XML cost is equal to about 100 queries in the loop from earlier. While we've reduced disk IO greatly, we risk consuming more CPU if we rely heavily on XML.

Set-Based String Building

While the XML solution was better, it was not perfect. The execution plan was somewhat confusing and illustrated that CPU consumption by XML can be high. Let's consider an additional option, as shown in Listing 7-3.

Listing 7-3. Generating a List of IDs by Building a String Directly into a Variable

```
DECLARE @myIDs NVARCHAR(MAX) = '';

SELECT TOP 100 @myIDs = @myIDs + CAST(BusinessEntityID AS NVARCHAR) + ','
FROM Person.Person
ORDER BY LastName;

SET @myIDs = LEFT(@myIDs, LEN(@myIDs) - 1);

SELECT @myIDs;
```

This TSQL is much more aesthetically pleasing. It is so simple that it begs us to scratch our heads and ask, "How does it work?" When we execute it, the results are the same as our examples thus far:

```
285,293,295,2170,38,211,2357,297,291,299,121,16867,16901,16724,10263,10312,...
```

SQL Server allows you to SELECT string data directly into a scalar variable in a single step. The string building is reminiscent of dynamic SQL, even if we are not executing a command string as part of this work. The general structure of this statement is as follows:

1. Declare a string, typically VARCHAR(MAX) or NVARCHAR(MAX).

2. Set the string variable equal to an empty string (or any leading characters that you'd like).

3. SELECT @variable = @variable + combination of columns and string data.

4. Remove the trailing comma from the end of the string.

5. Proceed with our comma-separated list as needed.

First, let's take a look at the IO statistics to determine how much data was read in order to generate this list:

Table 'Person'. Scan count 1, logical reads 3, physical reads 0, read-ahead reads 0, lob logical reads 0, lob physical reads 0, lob read-ahead reads 0.

As with the XML solution, the reads are the same as the SELECT query on its own would have required. Three reads to generate that list is excellent, and given that, we move on to examine the execution plan in Figure 7-4.

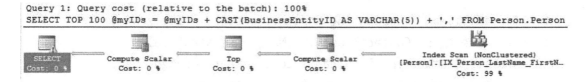

Figure 7-4. *Performance of list-generation using a string-based SELECT*

Our execution plan is about as simple as it gets: a single scan of the target table and some inexpensive operations to assemble the string. The subtree cost for this is 0.004, which is significantly lower than all other string-building techniques that we've discussed so far. Removing the element of XML greatly reduces the overhead that the XML reader requires to crunch data into the desired output format. Additionally, SQL Server can build the string in a completely set-based operation with no need for iteration, temporary tables, or any other expensive mediums.

This method is exceptionally fast, efficient, and easy to code and maintain. The lack of loops or XML makes the resulting TSQL easy enough for a beginner to experiment with and understand. Only minimal documentation would be required to explain what this does and why the method was chosen.

The dynamically built list is not limited to a single column or scalar string value. We are free to build the string out of as many data elements as we wish, whether they are column data, scalar variables, string literals, or strings converted from other data types. Listing 7-4 shows how to generate a list like with multiple variables.

Listing 7-4. Building a List with Multiple Columns and String Literals

```
DECLARE @myData NVARCHAR(MAX) = ";

SELECT @myData =
        @myData + 'ContactTypeID: ' + CAST(ContactTypeID AS NVARCHAR) +
        ',Name: ' + Name + ','
FROM person.ContactType
SET @myData = LEFT(@myData, LEN(@myData) - 1);

SELECT @myData;
```

This example is similar to the previous one, but we've thrown in the Name column, as well as the column names preceding the values themselves. The syntax for this TSQL is identical to the previous example, with the only difference being the columns and literals that are concatenated in the SELECT statement. The value of @myData ends up being

```
ContactTypeID: 1,Name: Accounting Manager,ContactTypeID: 2,Name:
Assistant Sales Agent,ContactTypeID: 3,Name: Assistant Sales
Representative,ContactTypeID: 4,Name: Coordinator Foreign
Markets,ContactTypeID: 5,Name: Export Administrator,...
```

If you wanted headers for your data, additional columns, labels, or any other useful information embedded into the string, getting them there is relatively straightforward. There's no limit to what you can include in the string, though it is worth examining the length of the output to ensure that whatever application, report, or file is accepting the data can handle whatever the maximum expected size could be.

One final simplification that we can make is to eliminate the need to remove the trailing comma at the end with a clever use of ISNULL. Listing 7-5 shows this short example.

Listing 7-5. Using ISNULL to Eliminate the Leading Comma Within the SELECT Statement

```
DECLARE @myData NVARCHAR(MAX);

SELECT @myData =
        ISNULL(@myData + ',',") + 'ContactTypeID: ' + CAST(ContactTypeID AS
        NVARCHAR) + ',Name: ' + Name
FROM person.ContactType;

SELECT @myData;
```

266

ISNULL can accomplish this by checking the value of @myData to see if it is NULL:

1. Do not assign an initial empty string value to @myData.

2. If @myData is NULL, which occurs on the first value only, then insert a blank.

3. If @myData is not NULL, then insert a comma.

This logic will implicitly eliminate the leading comma that would have been introduced, thereby reducing the number of SQL statements we need by one. The results of this query are identical to the previous example. The performance of the TSQL is also the same as previously. COALESCE can also be used instead of ISNULL with the exact same effect:

```
DECLARE @myData NVARCHAR(MAX);

SELECT @myData =
    COALESCE(@myData + ',',"") + 'ContactTypeID: ' + CAST(ContactTypeID AS
    NVARCHAR) + ',Name: ' + Name
FROM person.ContactType;

SELECT @myData;
```

Whether you use an ISNULL, LEFT, or COALESCE statement is a matter of personal preference, but suffice it to say that these options are significantly better than a loop or XML, each of which carries additional complexity and performance concerns.

Revisiting Security

While the various string building methods just presented are not dynamic SQL in the traditional sense, they share many of the strengths and weaknesses found when creating command strings for use in dynamic SQL. The lengthy list of security concerns presented in previous chapters is as relevant here as they were before.

In any scenario where we are building strings using at least one parameter that is entered from an outside source, the threat of SQL injection becomes as real as it was when we performed an open-ended web search. The example in Listing 7-6 illustrates string building using a stored procedure that accepts parameters from an external source:

Listing 7-6. A Reminder of SQL Injection when Building a List with Dynamic SQL

```
CREATE PROCEDURE dbo.return_person_data
     @last_name NVARCHAR(MAX) = NULL, @first_name NVARCHAR(MAX) = NULL
AS
BEGIN
     SET NOCOUNT ON;
     DECLARE @return_data NVARCHAR(MAX) = '';
     DECLARE @sql_command NVARCHAR(MAX);
     DECLARE @parameter_list NVARCHAR(MAX);

     SELECT @parameter_list = '@output_data NVARCHAR(MAX) OUTPUT';

     SELECT @sql_command = '
     SELECT
          @output_data = @output_data + "ID: " + CAST(BusinessEntityID AS
          NVARCHAR) + ", Name: " + FirstName + " " + LastName + ","
     FROM Person.Person
     WHERE 1 = 1'
     IF @last_name IS NOT NULL
          SELECT @sql_command = @sql_command + '
          AND LastName LIKE "%' + @last_name + '%"';
     IF @first_name IS NOT NULL
          SELECT @sql_command = @sql_command + '
          AND FirstName LIKE "%' + @first_name + '%"';

     PRINT @sql_command;
     EXEC sp_executesql @sql_command, @parameter_list, @return_data OUTPUT;

     SELECT @return_data = LEFT(@return_data, LEN(@return_data) - 1);

     SELECT @return_data;
END
```

The preceding stored procedure combines dynamic SQL and list building to generate a comma separated list of IDs and names. It also manages to create several glaring security risks. Let's consider some executions of this proc:

```
EXEC dbo.return_person_data @first_name = 'Edward';
```

268

The results of this execution are what we expect:

```
ID: 3731, Name: Edward Adams,ID: 13658, Name: Edward Alexander,ID: 4241,
Name: Edward Anderson,ID: 3732, Name: Edward Baker,ID: 13631, Name: Edward
Barnes,ID: 4229, Name: Edward Brown,ID: 13657, Name: Edward Bryant...
```

The list is truncated after the 7th value, as there's no need to list the extensive list of people from AdventureWorks with the first name of "Edward." The generated string contains an ID, and a name, which is the combination of each person's first name, last name, and a space inserted in between. Commas separate each field, with the trailing comma removed by the final LEFT statement.

What happens when the user passes in a blank?

```
EXEC dbo.return_person_data @first_name = '';
```

In this scenario, my server churns for almost 3 minutes before returning results. With 19,972 rows in `Person.Person`, it turns out that it takes a significant amount of time to render all of those IDs and names. While we often get used to memory being significantly faster than disk, it is not infinitely so. SQL Server needs to temporarily cache data to disk while the query completes. The results are the following IO statistics:

```
Table 'Person'. Scan count 1, logical reads 109, physical reads 0, read-
ahead reads 0, lob logical reads 0, lob physical reads 0, lob read-ahead
reads 0.
Table 'Worktable'. Scan count 0, logical reads 758369, physical reads 0,
read-ahead reads 0, lob logical reads 244941773, lob physical reads 0, lob
read-ahead reads 3909272.
```

Where did 244,941,773 reads come from? That unbelievable number comes from the volume of data being returned in conjunction with the blank search string. SQL Server cannot manage this operation on-the-fly in memory and is forced to use TempDB instead, which is significantly slower. Reads on Person.Person are not significant, but Worktable reads are very, very impressive!

This is an important call-out to quality assurance that testing is critically important in any application. If a search can theoretically return tens of thousands of rows, be sure to implement some method of paging or limiting of the data set so that a lazy or careless user doesn't bring your server down with an empty search.

Let's return to the malicious example that caused us to lose sleep in an earlier chapter:

```
EXEC dbo.return_person_data @first_name = 'whatever"; SELECT * FROM Person.
Password; SELECT "';
```

Here, we intentionally close the search string with arbitrary text ("whatever") and begin a new SQL statement with a SELECT from `Person.Password`. This situation is as dangerous as it was earlier, as the intended query returns an empty set of people, and instead the `Person.Password` table is returned. The resulting command string for this parameter value is as unfortunate as it appears to be:

```
SELECT
     @output_data = @output_data + 'ID: ' + CAST(BusinessEntityID AS
     NVARCHAR) + ', Name: ' + FirstName + ' ' + LastName + ','
FROM Person.Person
WHERE 1 = 1
AND FirstName LIKE '%whatever'; SELECT * FROM Person.Password; SELECT '%'
```

This TSQL throws an error as well, on top of this already messy result set:

```
Msg 537, Level 16, State 3, Procedure return_person_data, Line 204
Invalid length parameter passed to the LEFT or SUBSTRING function.
```

Since `@output_data` is NULL, its length is NULL, which is not a valid input for the LEFT function. Despite this, the password list was returned prior to the error message generating. Depending on application and error handling settings, the hacker that entered this TSQL may have gotten the data they wanted.

Whenever inputs are provided by an outside source, be sure to parameterize your `sp_executesql` statement to ensure that there is no way for dangerous TSQL to be inserted into your command string. This is shown in Listing 7-7.

Listing 7-7. Dynamic SQL List Generation Using Parameters for Inputs

```
IF EXISTS (SELECT * FROM sys.procedures WHERE procedures.name = 'return_
person_data')
BEGIN
     DROP PROCEDURE dbo.return_person_data;
END
GO
```

```
CREATE PROCEDURE dbo.return_person_data
     @last_name NVARCHAR(MAX) = NULL, @first_name NVARCHAR(MAX) = NULL
AS
BEGIN
     SET NOCOUNT ON;
     SELECT @last_name = '%' + @last_name + '%';
     SELECT @first_name = '%' + @first_name + '%';

     DECLARE @return_data NVARCHAR(MAX) = '';
     DECLARE @sql_command NVARCHAR(MAX);
     DECLARE @parameter_list NVARCHAR(MAX);

     SELECT @parameter_list = '@output_data NVARCHAR(MAX) OUTPUT,
     @first_name NVARCHAR(MAX), @last_name NVARCHAR(MAX)';

     SELECT @sql_command = '
     SELECT
          @output_data = @output_data + "ID: " + CAST(BusinessEntityID AS
          NVARCHAR) + ", Name: " + FirstName + " " + LastName + ","
     FROM Person.Person
     WHERE 1 = 1'
     IF @last_name IS NOT NULL
          SELECT @sql_command = @sql_command + '
          AND LastName LIKE @last_name';
     IF @first_name IS NOT NULL
          SELECT @sql_command = @sql_command + '
          AND FirstName LIKE @first_name';

     PRINT @sql_command;
     EXEC sp_executesql @sql_command, @parameter_list, @return_data OUTPUT,
     @first_name, @last_name;

     SELECT @return_data = LEFT(@return_data, LEN(@return_data) - 1);

     SELECT @return_data;
END
```

This updated stored procedure contains parameters for @first_name and @last_
name. When we execute our examples again, what happens?

```
EXEC dbo.return_person_data @first_name = 'Edward';
```

The results from this execution are the same as earlier. All data for people with the first name of "Edward" are returned as expected.

```
EXEC dbo.return_person_data @first_name = '';
```

The blank search still takes 3 minutes to run, but at least it does so securely!

```
EXEC dbo.return_person_data @first_name = 'Edward"; SELECT * FROM Person.
Password; SELECT "';
```

The attempt to use SQL injection to retrieve passwords still generates an error, with the zero being passed to the LEFT function as the input length. Luckily, parameterization removes the ability for the end user to inject their own TSQL into any of the parameters, so they do not gain access to `Person.Password` as they did previously.

We should be diligent and fix the looming errors in the above example. Letting SQL server grind away for minutes on a big query could be as destructive to our server as error messages or SQL injection attempts could be. Similarly, allowing an error to creep through to the UI is also a bad practice. We should prevent errors from being generated, regardless of the user input. Let's patch the holes in Listing 7-8 and hope that QA doesn't find any more.

Listing 7-8. List Generation Stored Procedure, with Fixes for Long Waits and Error Messages

```
IF EXISTS (SELECT * FROM sys.procedures WHERE procedures.name = 'return_
person_data')
BEGIN
        DROP PROCEDURE dbo.return_person_data;
END
GO

CREATE PROCEDURE dbo.return_person_data
        @last_name NVARCHAR(MAX) = NULL, @first_name NVARCHAR(MAX) = NULL
AS
BEGIN
        SET NOCOUNT ON;
        SELECT @last_name = '%' + @last_name + '%';
        SELECT @first_name = '%' + @first_name + '%';
```

```
DECLARE @return_data NVARCHAR(MAX) = '';
DECLARE @sql_command NVARCHAR(MAX);
DECLARE @parameter_list NVARCHAR(MAX);

SELECT @parameter_list = '@output_data NVARCHAR(MAX) OUTPUT,
@first_name NVARCHAR(MAX), @last_name NVARCHAR(MAX)';

SELECT @sql_command = '
SELECT TOP 25
    @output_data = @output_data + "ID: " + CAST(BusinessEntityID AS
    NVARCHAR) + ", Name: " + FirstName + " " + LastName + ","
FROM Person.Person
WHERE 1 = 1'
IF @last_name IS NOT NULL
    SELECT @sql_command = @sql_command + '
    AND LastName LIKE @last_name';
IF @first_name IS NOT NULL
    SELECT @sql_command = @sql_command + '
    AND FirstName LIKE @first_name';

PRINT @sql_command;
EXEC sp_executesql @sql_command, @parameter_list, @return_data OUTPUT,
@first_name, @last_name;

IF LEN(@return_data) > 0 AND @return_data IS NOT NULL
    SELECT @return_data = LEFT(@return_data, LEN(@return_data) - 1);

SELECT @return_data;
END
```

In this variation on our stored procedure, we introduce a TOP 25 to the list-building
SELECT statement. This limits the result set to 25 people only, preventing a runaway
query that could consume immense server resources. In addition, a check was placed
on the LEFT function near the end of the stored procedure that checks if the length of
@return_data is NULL or 0. This ensures that, if there is no result set, we don't throw
errors when trying to manipulate it. These options could be added as parameters as well,
if we wanted to configure rows returned or other behavior.

The steps that we walked through are an important reminder that security is an ever-present concern and that the situations that could bring a server to its knees may not always be the obvious ones. Quality assurance is extremely important! Ensure that any software that you are writing is thoroughly tested for all possible values, regardless of whether they are normal use cases or oddball edge cases. Empty searches, empty result sets, and SQL injection attempts are all situations that can be easily dealt with, but we must identify these threats to effectively respond to them. Even for internal processes where inputs are well understood, caution is still worth the effort.

STRING_AGG

Introduced in SQL Server 2017, this new string function allows columnar data in a table to be transformed into a customized data set. This provides an alternative to dynamic SQL for scenarios in which there is only a single field and separator to parse, or when grouping is desired.

Let's start with a simple example in Listing 7-9 where we generate a string of order numbers.

Listing 7-9. Generating a List of Order Numbers Using a String-Building Method

```
DECLARE @myData NVARCHAR(MAX);

SELECT @myData =
       ISNULL(@myData + ',',") + SalesOrderHeader.SalesOrderNumber
       FROM Sales.SalesOrderHeader
WHERE SalesOrderHeader.OrderDate = '5/31/2011';

SELECT @myData;
```

The results are what we expect: a list of order numbers, as seen in Figure 7-5.

Figure 7-5. *List of order numbers, generated by a list-building query*

We can rewrite the query as seen in Listing 7-10, using the function STRING_AGG to get the same results.

Listing 7-10. Generating a List of Order Numbers Using the STRING_AGG Function

```
SELECT
     STRING_AGG(SalesOrderHeader.SalesOrderNumber, ',')
     FROM Sales.SalesOrderHeader
WHERE SalesOrderHeader.OrderDate = '5/31/2011';
```

This function only allows a single separator at one time, so more complex lists with multiple delimiters would require either more string manipulation or multiple uses of STRING_AGG to accomplish. The syntax is simple, though, and performance is identical to our previous list-building approach, both for IO and query cost.

A feature of STRING_AGG that is unique and can be leveraged to generate data sets that would otherwise be challenging is the WITHIN GROUP clause. This allows multiple lists to be generated based on a grouping clause. Consider the following query in Listing 7-11.

Listing 7-11. Generating Multiple Lists for Given Order Dates

```
SELECT
     SalesOrderHeader.OrderDate, STRING_AGG(SalesOrderHeader.
     SalesOrderNumber, ',') WITHIN GROUP (ORDER BY SalesOrderHeader.
     SalesOrderID ASC) AS OrderList
FROM Sales.SalesOrderHeader
WHERE SalesOrderHeader.OrderDate BETWEEN '5/31/2011' AND '6/30/2011'
GROUP BY SalesOrderHeader.OrderDate;
```

The results of this query are shown in Figure 7-6 and illustrate a new functionality: generating multiple lists simultaneously.

	OrderDate	OrderList
1	2011-05-31 00:00:00.000	SO43659,SO43660,SO43661,SO43662,SO43663,SO43664,S...
2	2011-06-01 00:00:00.000	SO43702,SO43703,SO43704,SO43705
3	2011-06-02 00:00:00.000	SO43706,SO43707,SO43708,SO43709,SO43710
4	2011-06-03 00:00:00.000	SO43711,SO43712
5	2011-06-04 00:00:00.000	SO43713,SO43714,SO43715,SO43716,SO43717
6	2011-06-05 00:00:00.000	SO43718,SO43719,SO43720,SO43721
7	2011-06-06 00:00:00.000	SO43722,SO43723,SO43724
8	2011-06-07 00:00:00.000	SO43725,SO43726,SO43727
9	2011-06-08 00:00:00.000	SO43728,SO43729,SO43730,SO43731,SO43732,SO43733
10	2011-06-09 00:00:00.000	SO43734,SO43735,SO43736

Figure 7-6. *Multiple order lists, grouped by the order date*

Without the need to loop through the table, we were able to apply grouping and string building to SalesOrderHeader to generate a list of order IDs per order date within the date range specified. The cost to do this is only marginally higher than the order list we generated for a single date. As a bonus, we applied sorting to the orders within the list, allowing us to take control over the ordering of order numbers within each individual list. If we leave out the WITHIN GROUP clause, we can still generate grouped lists, but would not apply any ordering to the result set.

STRING_AGG is an aggregate function, just like MIN, MAX, or SUM. As a result, it can be used alongside a GROUP BY clause and combined with other aggregate metrics. Consider the expanded example in Listing 7-12.

Listing 7-12. Adding Order Count and Aggregate Sorting into the Result Set

```
SELECT
    SalesOrderHeader.OrderDate, STRING_AGG(SalesOrderHeader.
SalesOrderNumber, ',') AS OrderList, COUNT(*) AS OrderCount
FROM Sales.SalesOrderHeader
WHERE SalesOrderHeader.OrderDate BETWEEN '5/31/2011' AND '6/30/2011'
GROUP BY SalesOrderHeader.OrderDate
ORDER BY COUNT(*) DESC;
```

Figure 7-7 shows a result set that has been manipulated on the aggregate and list level.

	OrderDate	OrderList	OrderCount
1	2011-05-31 00:00:00.000	SO43659,SO43660,SO43661,SO43662,SO43663,SO43664,S...	43
2	2011-06-21 00:00:00.000	SO43784,SO43785,SO43786,SO43787,SO43788,SO43789,S...	11
3	2011-06-18 00:00:00.000	SO43768,SO43769,SO43770,SO43771,SO43772,SO43773,S...	8
4	2011-06-26 00:00:00.000	SO43812,SO43813,SO43814,SO43815,SO43816,SO43817,S...	8
5	2011-06-27 00:00:00.000	SO43820,SO43821,SO43822,SO43823,SO43824,SO43825,S...	8
6	2011-06-13 00:00:00.000	SO43747,SO43748,SO43749,SO43750,SO43751,SO43752,S...	7
7	2011-06-08 00:00:00.000	SO43728,SO43729,SO43730,SO43731,SO43732,SO43733	6
8	2011-06-02 00:00:00.000	SO43706,SO43707,SO43708,SO43709,SO43710	5
9	2011-06-04 00:00:00.000	SO43713,SO43714,SO43715,SO43716,SO43717	5
10	2011-06-28 00:00:00.000	SO43828,SO43829,SO43830,SO43831,SO43832	5

Figure 7-7. Multiple order lists with order count and aggregate sorting added

This query structure allows for multiple levels of customization. We may filter, order, and manipulate the contents of the order list to structure it exactly as we would like for our text output. We can also add or manipulate additional aggregate fields, such as COUNT. Last, we can order the entire result set, allowing the most significant lists to be returned at the top of our list.

If you want to build a string from an aggregated data set prior to SQL Server 2017, the simplest approach would be the following:

- Build an aggregate query that returns the necessary columns for the resulting string.

- Place those aggregated results into a temporary table.

- Build a string using our previous methods with the data in the temp table.

This allows us to reuse fast, reliable methods of string building over a grouped data set. The additional overhead of using a temp table is small compared with the IO or CPU costs associated with using iteration or XML.

STRING_AGG provides list-generating functionality that otherwise would require iteration or some other expensive trickery to accomplish. Its usage is limited to only a single separator, but this still provides an immense amount of usability that previously was not available in a built-in SQL Server function. As a bonus, its syntax is simple and easy to use, making it a perfect tool when multiple lists need to be efficiently generated in a single TSQL statement.

Conclusion

The list building presented here is not the same sort of dynamic SQL that we have discussed thus far in this book. While it is generally simpler and does not require a separate execution to get our result set, many commonalities exist between it and the command strings that we built earlier.

In any scenario where we are accepting user input to build a string, parallels can immediately be drawn between the SQL injection threats that we tackled earlier and the ones that can be similarly identified when we want to list names or ID numbers.

In addition to SQL injection, dynamic lists share similarities in syntax, string manipulation, formatting, security, and the ability to combine them with additional dynamic SQL to create even greater flexibility. With added complexity is an added need for careful testing, both for unexpected input as well as SQL injection attempts. While dynamically generated lists may not always carry the threats associated with external user input, being consistently aware of best practices regarding parameterization and QA can ensure that our TSQL is the highest quality and most secure possible.

CHAPTER 8

Parameter Sniffing

In Chapter 6 we introduced a number of tools, methods, and tips for performance optimization. A critical component that was briefly discussed was the query plan cache. Whenever a query is executed for the first time, an execution plan is generated by the query optimizer. This process is expensive, and therefore it is beneficial to minimize the work that is performed by it. Execution plans are placed into the query plan cache when optimization is complete, where they will remain until sufficient changes occur in execution, available memory, or the underlying data to push that plan out of cache.

This process by which execution plans are saved is critical to optimal SQL Server performance. Whenever a query is executed that matches a query in cache, the existing plan will be used. This allows SQL Server to bypass the optimizer and jump directly to execution, saving us time and resources along the way! Without this feature, we would be forced to add significant resources to busy servers to account for the resources needed to constantly optimize every query that is executed.

What Is Parameter Sniffing?

Execution plans are placed in cache based on a query hash that is assigned to it when the plan is generated. This hash is based on the exact text of the query itself and will be different if any part of a query is different. As a result, parameterizing queries allows us to reuse the same plan over and over, regardless of the value of the parameter. The execution plan will be created based on the parameter value that is passed into the query during its first execution. Each subsequent execution will reuse the same plan, regardless of the value.

This leads us to a question of accuracy: will the plan that was chosen during the first execution of a query be the best plan for all possible values going forward? If parameters that are passed into a stored procedure are somewhat consistent, then odds are very good that the initially created plan will be good enough for all future executions. In this

© Edward Pollack 2019
E. Pollack, *Dynamic SQL*, https://doi.org/10.1007/978-1-4842-4318-3_8

scenario, query plan caching is working perfectly for us, and we will have no reason to consider performance concerns. What if parameter values are sporadic, and lead to a wide variety of possible results? Given enough time, an execution plan will be generated that will not be the best plan for other parameter values.

Execution plan reuse for different parameters is the definition of parameter sniffing and is an inadvertent side effect of SQL Server's usage of the query plan cache. Suboptimal plan reuse is a potential way in which this behavior can cause us performance troubles. Before getting started, let's introduce a stored procedure that will read some data from the query plan cache based on a string search of the query text itself. This will save us time later on when researching the contents of the plan cache and how they relate to the performance of example queries to follow. Listing 8-1 shows this stored procedure, which we will be using throughout the rest of this chapter.

Listing 8-1. Stored Procedure to Read Optimization and Execution Data from the Query Plan Cache

```
IF EXISTS (SELECT * FROM sys.procedures WHERE procedures.name = 'read_
query_plan_cache')
BEGIN
    DROP PROCEDURE dbo.read_query_plan_cache;
END
GO

CREATE PROCEDURE dbo.read_query_plan_cache
    @text_string NVARCHAR(MAX) = NULL
AS
BEGIN
    SELECT @text_string = '%' + @text_string + '%';
    DECLARE @sql_command NVARCHAR(MAX);
    DECLARE @parameter_list NVARCHAR(MAX) = '@text_string NVARCHAR(MAX)';

    IF @text_string IS NULL
        SELECT @sql_command = '
            SELECT TOP 25
                DB_NAME(execution_plan.dbid) AS database_name,
                cached_plans.objtype AS ObjectType,
```

```
                        OBJECT_NAME(sql_text.objectid, sql_text.dbid) AS
                        ObjectName,
                        query_stats.creation_time,
                        query_stats.last_execution_time,
                        query_stats.last_worker_time AS cpu_last_execution,
                        query_stats.last_logical_reads AS reads_last_
                        execution,
                        query_stats.last_elapsed_time AS duration_last_
                        execution,
                        query_stats.last_rows AS rows_last_execution,
                        cached_plans.size_in_bytes,
                        cached_plans.usecounts AS ExecutionCount,
                        sql_text.TEXT AS QueryText,
                        execution_plan.query_plan,
                        cached_plans.plan_handle
                FROM sys.dm_exec_cached_plans cached_plans
                INNER JOIN sys.dm_exec_query_stats query_stats
                ON cached_plans.plan_handle = query_stats.plan_handle
                CROSS APPLY sys.dm_exec_sql_text(cached_plans.plan_
                handle) AS sql_text
                CROSS APPLY sys.dm_exec_query_plan(cached_plans.plan_
                handle) AS execution_plan';
    ELSE
        SELECT @sql_command = '
                SELECT TOP 25
                        DB_NAME(execution_plan.dbid) AS database_name,
                        cached_plans.objtype AS ObjectType,
                        OBJECT_NAME(sql_text.objectid, sql_text.dbid) AS
                        ObjectName,
                        query_stats.creation_time,
                        query_stats.last_execution_time,
                        query_stats.last_worker_time AS cpu_last_execution,
                        query_stats.last_logical_reads AS reads_last_
                        execution,
```

```
                          query_stats.last_elapsed_time AS duration_last_
                          execution,
                          query_stats.last_rows AS rows_last_execution,
                          cached_plans.size_in_bytes,
                          cached_plans.usecounts AS ExecutionCount,
                          sql_text.TEXT AS QueryText,
                          execution_plan.query_plan,
                          cached_plans.plan_handle
                  FROM sys.dm_exec_cached_plans cached_plans
                  INNER JOIN sys.dm_exec_query_stats query_stats
                  ON cached_plans.plan_handle = query_stats.plan_handle
                  CROSS APPLY sys.dm_exec_sql_text(cached_plans.plan_
                  handle) AS sql_text
                  CROSS APPLY sys.dm_exec_query_plan(cached_plans.plan_
                  handle) AS execution_plan
            WHERE sql_text.TEXT LIKE @text_string';

            EXEC sp_executesql @sql_command, @parameter_list, @text_string
END
GO
```

This stored procedure will greatly simplify our research, as we can pass it any query text and it will return a variety of data about queries in cache, their execution plans, and performance metrics on the last execution. It is also a great example of using dynamic SQL to perform a common SQL Server research task. We will use this to collect information on queries as we test them here, but it can be reused in any circumstance where you would like to search the plan cache for specific information. TOP 25 is used on the SELECT statements to limit the result set. On a busy server this could otherwise return a very large amount of data, which could adversely affect server or client performance.

Parameter Sniffing Examples

In order to be sure we are getting clean test results, we will clear the query plan cache. As advised earlier in this book, do not run this in a production environment or any place where consistent performance is expected. Clearing the query plan cache is an excellent way to debug queries by forcing them to create fresh new plans with each execution, but as the optimizer takes significant resources to do its job, we should only ever do this in isolated environments:

```
DBCC FREEPROCCACHE;
```

You may also provide a specific plan handle as a parameter to this DBCC command. This would allow you to clear only a single plan of choice from cache, rather than everything. For simplicity, we will clear the entire cache here, but the syntax to clear a single query would look like this:

```
DBCC FREEPROCCACHE (0x06000700E8C6530730F36E6B030000000010000000000000000000
000000000000000000000000000000000000000);
```

The plan handle is included in the query plan cache search query, in case it's needed for further research. Now, to illustrate parameter sniffing, we'll create a simple stored procedure that searches `Production.Product` based on the `ProductModelID`, as seen in Listing 8-2.

Listing 8-2. Example Stored Procedure to be Used to Test Parameter Sniffing

```
IF EXISTS (SELECT * FROM sys.procedures WHERE procedures.name = 'get_
products_by_model')
BEGIN
    DROP PROCEDURE dbo.get_products_by_model;
END
GO

CREATE PROCEDURE dbo.get_products_by_model (@firstProductModelID INT,
@lastProductModelID INT)
AS
BEGIN
    SELECT
        PRODUCT.Name,
        PRODUCT.ProductID,
        PRODUCT.ProductModelID,
        PRODUCT.ProductNumber,
        MODEL.Name
    FROM Production.Product PRODUCT
```

```
    INNER JOIN Production.ProductModel MODEL
    ON MODEL.ProductModelID = PRODUCT.ProductModelID
    WHERE PRODUCT.ProductModelID BETWEEN @firstProductModelID AND
    @lastProductModelID;
END
```

Note that there are two parameters that are being passed into the stored procedure: @firstProductModelID and @lastProductModelID. Let's execute this for a small range of product IDs:

```
EXEC get_products_by_model 120, 125;
```

This returns six rows of data, as seen in Figure 8-1.

	Name	ProductID	ProductModelID	ProductNumber	Name
1	LL Mountain Rear Wheel	823	123	RW-M423	LL Mountain Rear Wheel
2	ML Mountain Rear Wheel	824	124	RW-M762	ML Mountain Rear Wheel
3	HL Mountain Rear Wheel	825	125	RW-M928	HL Mountain Rear Wheel
4	Touring-Panniers, Large	842	120	PA-T100	Touring-Panniers
5	Fender Set - Mountain	878	121	FE-6654	Fender Set - Mountain
6	All-Purpose Bike Stand	879	122	ST-1401	All-Purpose Bike Stand

Figure 8-1. *Result set for a restrictive product search that only returns six rows*

The performance metrics for this execution are as follows:

```
Table 'ProductModel'. Scan count 0, logical reads 12, physical reads 0,
read-ahead reads 0, lob logical reads 0, lob physical reads 0, lob read-
ahead reads 0.
Table 'Product'. Scan count 1, logical reads 15, physical reads 0, read-
ahead reads 0, lob logical reads 0, lob physical reads 0, lob read-ahead
reads 0.
```

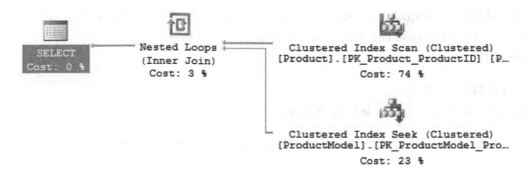

Figure 8-2. *Performance of a product search returning a small amount of data*

There were a total of 27 logical reads for this execution, and SQL Server utilized a scan and seek to get the necessary data from `Product` and `ProductModel` in order to return our results. To confirm what we see, and add some additional metrics, we can use our query plan cache stored procedure from earlier to learn more about this execution:

```
EXEC dbo.read_query_plan_cache 'get_products_by_model';
```

This returns a variety of useful information about this single execution of the stored procedure, as seen in Figure 8-3.

database_name	ObjectType	ObjectName	creation_time	last_execution_time
AdventureWorks2016CTP3	Proc	get_products_by_model	2018-09-21 07:25:13.493	2018-09-21 07:25:13.510

cpu_last_execution	reads_last_execution	duration_last_execution	rows_last_execution	size_in_bytes	ExecutionCount
1531	27	4050	6	65536	1

QueryText	query_plan
CREATE PROCEDURE dbo.get_products_by_model (@...	<ShowPlanXML xmlns="http://schemas.microsoft.com...

Figure 8-3. *Metrics returned by dbo.read_query_plan_cache for a restrictive search query*

In an effort to keep Figure 8-3 easy to read, I've wrapped the image of the query results to multiple lines, rather than trying to squeeze it into a single query result row. The following information can be gleaned from these results:

CPU: 936 microseconds

Reads: 29

Duration: 26ms (26,329 microseconds)

Rows Returned: 6

In addition, the query text and execution plan are also available here, if needed. Now, let's clear the plan cache and execute the same stored procedure, but for a different range of IDs:

```
DBCC FREEPROCCACHE;
EXEC get_products_by_model 0, 10000;
```

This execution returns 295 results, rather than 6, as seen in Figure 8-4.

	Name	ProductID	ProductModelID	Product Number	Name
1	HL Road Frame - Black, 58	680	6	FR-R92B-58	HL Road Frame
2	HL Road Frame - Red, 58	706	6	FR-R92R-58	HL Road Frame
3	Sport-100 Helmet, Red	707	33	HL-U509-R	Sport-100
4	Sport-100 Helmet, Black	708	33	HL-U509	Sport-100
5	Mountain Bike Socks, M	709	18	SO-B909-M	Mountain Bike Socks
6	Mountain Bike Socks, L	710	18	SO-B909-L	Mountain Bike Socks
7	Sport-100 Helmet, Blue	711	33	HL-U509-B	Sport-100
8	AWC Logo Cap	712	2	CA-1098	Cycling Cap
9	Long-Sleeve Logo Jersey, S	713	11	LJ-0192-S	Long-Sleeve Logo Jersey
10	Long-Sleeve Logo Jersey, M	714	11	LJ-0192-M	Long-Sleeve Logo Jersey
11	Long-Sleeve Logo Jersey, L	715	11	LJ-0192-L	Long-Sleeve Logo Jersey
12	Long-Sleeve Logo Jersey, XL	716	11	LJ-0192-X	Long-Sleeve Logo Jersey
13	HL Road Frame - Red, 62	717	6	FR-R92R-62	HL Road Frame
14	HL Road Frame - Red, 44	718	6	FR-R92R-44	HL Road Frame
15	HL Road Frame - Red, 48	719	6	FR-R92R-48	HL Road Frame
16	HL Road Frame - Red, 52	720	6	FR-R92R-52	HL Road Frame
17	HL Road Frame - Red, 56	721	6	FR-R92R-56	HL Road Frame
18	LL Road Frame - Black, 58	722	9	FR-R38B-58	LL Road Frame

Query executed successfully.   SANDILE\EDSQLSERVER14 (12.0...   SANDILE\Edward (54)   AdventureWorks2012   00:00:00   295 rows

Figure 8-4. *Product results for a less restrictive search returning 295 rows*

The performance is not significantly different, but a different execution plan was chosen, as seen in Figure 8-5.

```
Table 'Workfile'. Scan count 0, logical reads 0, physical reads 0, read-
ahead reads 0, lob logical reads 0, lob physical reads 0, lob read-ahead
reads 0.
Table 'Worktable'. Scan count 0, logical reads 0, physical reads 0, read-
ahead reads 0, lob logical reads 0, lob physical reads 0, lob read-ahead
reads 0.
Table 'Product'. Scan count 1, logical reads 15, physical reads 0, read-
ahead reads 0, lob logical reads 0, lob physical reads 0, lob read-ahead
reads 0.
Table 'ProductModel'. Scan count 1, logical reads 2, physical reads 1,
read-ahead reads 0, lob logical reads 0, lob physical reads 0, lob read-
ahead reads 0.
```

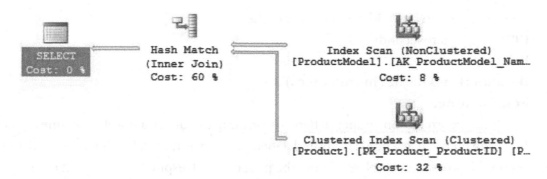

Figure 8-5. *Performance when a less restrictive search query is executed*

Since we were selecting such a large number of rows from the table, the query optimizer decided that an index scan on `ProductModel` would be more efficient. This is often a good decision as it becomes expensive to seek through an index when the number of rows being returned approaches a large portion of the table. The exact turning point will typically depend on the data size, but this is an excellent example of a situation where an index scan offers superior performance to an index seek.

Before reading the plan cache, we'll run `get_products_by_model` five more times, which will add additional data into the cache that will be useful to review below:

```
EXEC get_products_by_model 0, 10000;
EXEC get_products_by_model 0, 10000;
EXEC get_products_by_model 0, 10000;
EXEC get_products_by_model 0, 10000;
EXEC get_products_by_model 0, 10000;
```

As we did before, let's run our stored procedure to read information from the plan cache for this new execution of the search proc. The resulting metrics can be found in Figure 8-6.

```
EXEC dbo.read_query_plan_cache 'get_products_by_model';
```

	database_name	ObjectType	ObjectName	creation_time	last_execution_time	cpu_last_execution	reads_last_execution	duration_last_execution
1	AdventureWorks2012	Proc	get_products_by_model	2015-11-14 14:41:00.997	2015-11-14 14:41:01.813	1858	19	80324

rows_last_execution	size_in_bytes	ExecutionCount	QueryText		query_plan
295	65536	6	CREATE PROCEDURE dbo.get_products_by_model (@fir...		<ShowPlanXML xmlns="http://schemas.microsoft.com...

plan_handle
0x05000700F2182B44B049B87C03000000010000000000000.

Figure 8-6. *Metrics returned by dbo.read_query_plan_cache for a less restrictive search query*

The results are in line with what we saw earlier:

CPU: 1858 microseconds

Reads: 19

Duration: 80ms (80,324 microseconds)

Rows Returned: 295

Note that the execution count is 6 here. By running the query a number of times, we can illustrate plan reuse when it is desired. Once a plan was found, it will be retained and reused until it is eventually released from the plan cache. Despite the execution count, the results are almost identical for each execution.

So far there have been no surprises, each execution has returned the data we expected, and the optimizer did a great job of choosing the correct plan in order to minimize resource utilization. Let's clear the cache one last time and run our search proc twice in a row, first for a small range of product models and then with the large range:

```
DBCC FREEPROCCACHE;
EXEC get_products_by_model 120, 125;
EXEC get_products_by_model 0, 10000;
```

When we run this T-SQL, the first execution performs exactly as it did earlier. A plan is chosen with an index scan on `Product` and an index seek on `ProductModel`. The resulting execution plan and IO statistics are also exactly the same. When we run the second execution of our stored procedure, something unusual happens: it performs very poorly! The performance metrics for the second product search are in Figure 8-7 for the scenario where a wide range of IDs was passed in:

```
Table 'ProductModel'. Scan count 0, logical reads 590, physical reads 0,
read-ahead reads 0, lob logical reads 0, lob physical reads 0, lob read-
ahead reads 0.
Table 'Product'. Scan count 1, logical reads 15, physical reads 0, read-
ahead reads 0, lob logical reads 0, lob physical reads 0, lob read-ahead
reads 0.
```

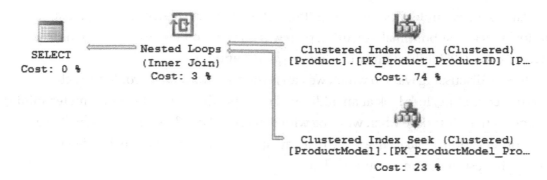

Figure 8-7. *Search performance when a suboptimal plan is reused*

This time, reads were significantly higher than what we'd expect for this stored procedure. The execution plan chosen was reused from the previous one for the narrow range of IDs (index seek on `ProductModel`), rather than one that is optimal for a large result set (index scan on `ProductModel`). Reading the plan cache helps us understand what happened:

```
EXEC dbo.read_query_plan_cache 'get_products_by_model';
```

The results in Figure 8-8 show that the execution plan that was created for the narrow range of IDs was reused for the second run, despite providing parameters that resulted in a very different cardinality.

	database_name	ObjectType	ObjectName	creation_time	last_execution_time	cpu_last_execution	reads_last_execution	duration_last_execution
1	AdventureWorks2012	Proc	get_products_by_model	2015-11-14 14:48:10.650	2015-11-14 14:48:10.677	2474	607	90353

rows_last_execution	size_in_bytes	ExecutionCount	QueryText	query_plan
295	49152	2	CREATE PROCEDURE dbo.get_products_by_model (@fir...	<ShowPlanXML xmlns="http://schemas.microsoft.com...

plan_handle
0x05000700F2182B44B049B87C030000000100000000000000...

Figure 8-8. *Metrics returned by dbo.read_query_plan_cache, illustrating parameter sniffing*

Note that `ExecutionCount` is 2. This is proof that the initial execution plan was reused for the second execution of the search proc. The rest of the metrics returned confirm the poor performance we viewed:

CPU: 2474 microseconds

Reads: 607

Duration: 90ms (90,353 microseconds)

Rows Returned: 295

This is an example of parameter sniffing when it directly harms query execution performance. A suboptimal execution plan was chosen and the result was significantly higher reads, CPU utilization, and a longer query runtime.

Before discussing ways in which we can resolve performance problems with parameter sniffing, let's look at an additional example that shows how parameter sniffing can potentially interfere when working with dynamic SQL. These examples will use sales orders and will take advantage of a new sales person to illustrate the effects of poor cardinality estimates on execution plans:

```
INSERT INTO Sales.SalesPerson
      (BusinessEntityID, TerritoryID, SalesQuota, Bonus, CommissionPct,
      SalesYTD, SalesLastYear, rowguid, ModifiedDate)
VALUES
      (1, 1, 1000000, 289, 0.17, 0, 0, NEWID(), CURRENT_TIMESTAMP);

UPDATE Sales.SalesOrderHeader
      SET SalesPersonID = 1
WHERE SalesPersonID IS NULL;

UPDATE STATISTICS Sales.SalesOrderHeader;
GO
```

These statements will create a new sales person and assign them to all sales orders that currently have no one assigned to them. In addition, we've updated statistics on the table to ensure that the optimizer is aware of the new data when making optimization decisions. This will provide us with a sales person with 27,659 sales orders assigned to them. Now we'll introduce a new stored procedure that will search sales orders based on a SalesPersonID that is provided as a parameter. In addition, the number of rows returned and offset can be provided, if we wish to page the results, as shown in Listing 8-3.

Listing 8-3. Search Procedure to be Used for Demonstrating Parameter Sniffing

```
IF EXISTS (SELECT * FROM sys.procedures WHERE procedures.name = 'get_sales_
orders_by_sales_person')
BEGIN
      DROP PROCEDURE dbo.get_sales_orders_by_sales_person;
END
GO
```

```
CREATE PROCEDURE dbo.get_sales_orders_by_sales_person
      @SalesPersonID INT, @RowCount INT, @Offset INT
AS
BEGIN
      DECLARE @sql_command NVARCHAR(MAX);
      DECLARE @parameter_list NVARCHAR(MAX) = '@SalesPersonID INT,
      @RowCount INT, @Offset INT';
      -- Add one to the offset to get the correct starting row.
      SELECT @Offset = @Offset + 1;

      SELECT @sql_command = '
      WITH CTE_PRODUCTS AS (
            SELECT
                  ROW_NUMBER() OVER (ORDER BY OrderDate ASC) AS rownum,
                  SalesOrderHeader.SalesOrderID,
                  SalesOrderHeader.Status,
                  SalesOrderHeader.OrderDate,
                  SalesOrderHeader.ShipDate,
                  SalesOrderDetail.UnitPrice,
                  SalesOrderDetail.LineTotal
            FROM Sales.SalesOrderHeader
            INNER JOIN Sales.SalesOrderDetail
            ON SalesOrderHeader.SalesOrderID = SalesOrderDetail.SalesOrderID
            WHERE SalesOrderHeader.SalesPersonID = @SalesPersonID
            )
      SELECT
            *
      FROM CTE_PRODUCTS
      WHERE rownum BETWEEN @Offset AND @Offset + @RowCount;';

      EXEC sp_executesql @sql_command, @parameter_list, @SalesPersonID,
      @RowCount, @Offset;
END
```

This stored procedure is completely parameterized, allowing us to change the inputs at execution time, without the need for any of the dynamic SQL to be adjusted. Let's start out by looking at the performance of a search involving our new sales person that we created:

```
DBCC FREEPROCCACHE;
EXEC dbo.get_sales_orders_by_sales_person 1, 1000, 0;
```

The query plan cache is cleared first, to ensure that the results are unaffected by any other queries executed on this server. The additional parameters are set to return 1,000 rows from the result set (which contains 27,659 rows), starting from row 1. The performance metrics for this execution are found in Figure 8-9.

```
Table 'SalesOrderDetail'. Scan count 1000, logical reads 3231, physical
reads 0, read-ahead reads 0, lob logical reads 0, lob physical reads 0, lob
read-ahead reads 0.
Table 'SalesOrderHeader'. Scan count 1, logical reads 689, physical reads 0,
read-ahead reads 0, lob logical reads 0, lob physical reads 0, lob read-
ahead reads 0.
```

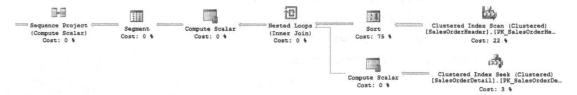

Figure 8-9. *Execution plan for a search that uses parameterized paging*

In addition, the execution metrics returned by our plan cache reading stored procedure can be seen in Figure 8-10:

```
EXEC dbo.read_query_plan_cache 'CTE_PRODUCTS';
```

	database_name	ObjectType	ObjectName	creation_time	last_execution_time	cpu_last_execution	reads_last_execution	duration_last_execution
1	AdventureWorks2012	Prepared	NULL	2015-11-16 16:20:08.147	2015-11-16 16:20:08.150	13726	4062	115309

rows_last_execution	size_in_bytes	ExecutionCount	QueryText		query_plan
1000	65536	1	(@SalesPersonID INT, @RowCount INT, @Offset IN...		<ShowPlanXML xmlns="http://schemas.microsoft.com...

plan_handle
0x060007009CB74F1D90C9B87C0300000001000000000000.

Figure 8-10. *Metrics returned by dbo.read_query_plan_cache for a parameterized search with paging*

Note that since some parameters were defined locally for the dynamic SQL, the stored procedure itself was not entered into the plan cache, and instead only the dynamic SQL statement. The contents of QueryText are as follows in Listing 8-4.

Listing 8-4. Resulting Query Text as Executed in the Dynamic Search with Paging

```
(@SalesPersonID INT, @RowCount INT, @Offset INT)
    WITH CTE_PRODUCTS AS (
        SELECT
            ROW_NUMBER() OVER (ORDER BY OrderDate ASC) AS rownum,
            SalesOrderHeader.SalesOrderID,
            SalesOrderHeader.Status,
            SalesOrderHeader.OrderDate,
            SalesOrderHeader.ShipDate,
            SalesOrderDetail.UnitPrice,
            SalesOrderDetail.LineTotal
        FROM Sales.SalesOrderHeader
        INNER JOIN Sales.SalesOrderDetail
        ON SalesOrderHeader.SalesOrderID = SalesOrderDetail.SalesOrderID
        WHERE SalesOrderHeader.SalesPersonID = @SalesPersonID
        )
    SELECT
        *
    FROM CTE_PRODUCTS
    WHERE rownum BETWEEN @Offset AND @Offset + @RowCount;
```

The desired effect is still achieved in that the query that we intend to run is fully parameterized and an execution plan will be reused whenever the stored procedure is executed. Searching for it in cache, though, required entering some text from the SELECT query, rather than the stored procedure name.

All of the above results show that the optimizer chose a clustered index scan on SalesOrderHeader and a clustered index seek on SalesOrderDetail. 3,926 reads were needed in order to query this large data set and the results from the query metrics are as follows:

CPU: 14ms (13,726 microseconds)
Reads: 4062

Duration: 115ms (115,309 microseconds)

Rows Returned: 1000

Let's clear the cache and repeat this exercise for a sales person with far fewer sales records:

```
DBCC FREEPROCCACHE;
EXEC dbo.get_sales_orders_by_sales_person 285, 1000, 0;
```

The result set for this execution is 245 rows, instead of 27,659. As such, limiting the result set to 1,000 rows will have no effect on what is returned by SQL Server. The performance metrics for this execution are as follows in Figure 8-11.

```
Table 'SalesOrderDetail'. Scan count 16, logical reads 53, physical reads 0,
read-ahead reads 0, lob logical reads 0, lob physical reads 0, lob read-
ahead reads 0.
Table 'SalesOrderHeader'. Scan count 1, logical reads 50, physical reads 0,
read-ahead reads 0, lob logical reads 0, lob physical reads 0, lob read-
ahead reads 0.
```

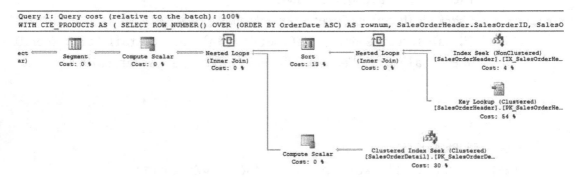

Figure 8-11. *Execution plan for a parameterized paged search with a small result set*

Only 103 reads were required to return this smaller data set, and the optimizer chose to use an index seek on `SalesOrderHeader` and a clustered index seek on `SalesOrderDetail`. Even though a key lookup is an expensive random IO operation, the optimizer still chose that over the alternative of scanning the entire table. Let's review the additional query stats for this execution, as seen in Figure 8-12.

```
EXEC dbo.read_query_plan_cache 'CTE_PRODUCTS';
```

	database_name	ObjectType	ObjectName	creation_time	last_execution_time	cpu_last_execution	reads_last_execution	duration_last_execution
1	AdventureWorks2012	Prepared	NULL	2015-11-16 16:25:31.670	2015-11-16 16:25:31.673	2127	103	94877

rows_last_execution	size_in_bytes	ExecutionCount	QueryText	query_plan
245	73728	1	(@SalesPersonID INT, @RowCount INT, @Offset IN...	\<ShowPlanXML xmlns="http://schemas.microsoft.com...

plan_handle
0x060007009CB74F1D90C9B87C030000000100000000000000.

Figure 8-12. *Metrics returned by dbo.read_query_plan_cache for a parameterized search with paging and a small result set*

The data above agrees with everything we've reviewed so far. This execution requires significantly less reads to return fewer rows and does so a bit faster than before.

CPU: 2127 microseconds

Reads: 103

Duration: 95ms (94,877 microseconds)

Rows Returned: 245

Now that we have established a baseline for the performance of our stored procedure with regards to large vs. small result sets, we can demonstrate parameter sniffing for a scenario that is the opposite of the one we reviewed earlier. Let's clear the query plan cache one last time and run the sales order search for our sales person with the very large number of orders assigned to them:

```
DBCC FREEPROCCACHE;
EXEC dbo.get_sales_orders_by_sales_person 1, 1000, 0;
```

A quick review of the performance metrics for this execution confirms that it behaves exactly the way it did earlier, as seen in Figure 8-13.

```
Table 'SalesOrderDetail'. Scan count 1000, logical reads 3231, physical
reads 0, read-ahead reads 0, lob logical reads 0, lob physical reads 0, lob
read-ahead reads 0.
Table 'SalesOrderHeader'. Scan count 1, logical reads 689, physical reads 0,
read-ahead reads 0, lob logical reads 0, lob physical reads 0, lob read-
ahead reads 0.
```

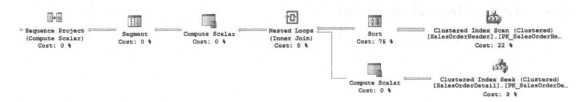

Figure 8-13. *Performance of the search from earlier, with a large result set*

Both the IO statistics and execution plan match our first execution from earlier. Now, let's execute the same stored procedure for the second use case that we presented, where the sales person has far fewer sales orders (without clearing the plan cache):

```
EXEC dbo.get_sales_orders_by_sales_person 285, 1000, 0;
```

While the results returned are the same as when we ran this same query earlier, the performance is significantly different. Figure 8-14 illustrates this with the IO statistics, as well as the execution plan.

```
Table 'SalesOrderDetail'. Scan count 16, logical reads 74, physical reads 0,
read-ahead reads 0, lob logical reads 0, lob physical reads 0, lob read-
ahead reads 0.
Table 'SalesOrderHeader'. Scan count 1, logical reads 689, physical reads 0,
read-ahead reads 0, lob logical reads 0, lob physical reads 0, lob read-
ahead reads 0.
```

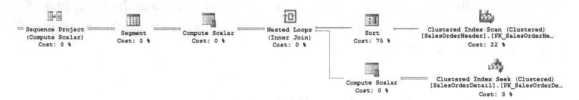

Figure 8-14. *Performance when the execution plan for a large result set is reused with a significantly smaller one*

Since we did not clear the query plan cache, the execution plan from above was reused for this execution of our stored procedure. The execution plan is the same as the previous execution: the optimizer uses a clustered index scan on SalesOrderHeader, even though this is not the optimal way to retrieve data from the table for the smaller cardinality illustrated in this example. As a result, the reads on SalesOrderHeader are significantly higher, and the reads on SalesOrderDetail about 50% higher. To show that plan reuse occurred, we'll run our read_query_plan_cache stored procedure one last time and review the results in Figure 8-15.

```
EXEC dbo.read_query_plan_cache 'CTE_PRODUCTS';
```

	database_name	ObjectType	ObjectName	creation_time	last_execution_time	cpu_last_execution	reads_last_execution	duration_last_execution
1	AdventureWorks2012	Prepared	NULL	2015-11-16 16:40:45.213	2015-11-16 16:43:54.407	3402	777	97993

rows_last_execution	size_in_bytes	ExecutionCount	QueryText		query_plan
245	65536	2	(@SalesPersonID INT, @RowCount INT, @Offset IN…		<ShowPlanXML xmlns="http://schemas.microsoft.com…

plan_handle
0x060007009CB74F1D90C9B87C030000000010000000000000.

Figure 8-15. *Metrics returned by dbo.read_query_plan_cache for a parameterized search with paging when parameter sniffing results in undesired plan reuse*

Summarizing the data above, we can pull out the most relevant details for review:

Executions: 2

CPU: 3402 microseconds

Reads: 777

Duration: 98ms (97,993 microseconds)

Rows Returned: 245

The execution count is the proof that our execution plan was indeed reused. In this scenario, reuse was not beneficial, and caused our query to take significantly greater resources to execute. On a larger, busier production database, performance could have been seriously degraded by this sort of parameter sniffing.

Identifying Parameter Sniffing

Undesired plan reuse will not always be apparent. Sometimes performance problems will be identified in a production environment, but not be immediately connected to a parameterization issue. Once we know that a query is being assigned a suboptimal execution plan, we can begin looking for symptoms that may be indicative of parameter sniffing:

- A stored procedure performs well sometimes and poorly at other times.

- A query begins performing poorly with no changes to any of the underlying schema.

- Tweaks, hacks, and T-SQL adjustments can temporarily resolve the problem.

- A stored procedure is excessively large.

- A stored procedure contains many different code paths and branching logic.

- A stored procedure has many parameters available.

- A query is known to return vastly different result sets based on parameter values.

The next logical question would be to ask how we deal with this phenomenon, and how to correctly compensate for parameter sniffing? To provide the best answer possible, we'll discuss a few additional considerations, before diving into a variety of solutions.

Design Considerations

Rule one for managing a phenomenon like parameter sniffing is to know your data! Since this is a SQL Server feature and not a bug, we need to carefully assess any scenario when it becomes problematic, before trying to implement a solution.

Let's take both of our examples above: what was the precise cause of undesired plan reuse? Ultimately it was the fact that multiple executions of the stored procedure resulted in wildly different cardinality estimates for the result set. One parameter value returned 245 rows whereas the other returned over a hundred times as much data.

When addressing parameter sniffing, we should ask a variety of questions to accurately gauge its severity, frequency, and effects of change:

1. How often is the query executed?

2. What is the most common order of magnitude for cardinality that will be returned by an execution? Was parameter sniffing helpful most of the time, or did it lead to poor execution plans more often than we would want?

3. How will increasing data sizes over time affect these cardinality estimates?

4. Are there other culprits involved, such as stale statistics, poorly written T-SQL, missing or fragmented indexes?

5. What are the most frequent parameter values that are likely to be passed to the stored procedure?

6. Do you already know the cardinality of the result set, regardless of inputs? That is, does a stored procedure always return a set number of rows?

7. Can a complex query be broken up into multiple simpler queries?

Often, queries that satisfy a business need will fit a regular pattern of usage. Determining that pattern and then finding situations that fall well outside of the norm can help in figuring out if our T-SQL is accommodating common use cases, or if we are inadvertently setting ourselves up for poor performance by writing for the exceptions rather than common occurrences.

Of the many ways in which queries can perform suboptimally, none are as poorly handled as parameter sniffing. The desire to fix a problem quickly and with few resources lends itself to a scenario in which we seek shortcuts and hacks. In addition, many sources of information about parameter sniffing are inaccurate or just plain wrong. Query hints, trace flags, local variables, and tinkering with the plan cache will rarely solve parameter sniffing challenges completely and correctly. We should use extreme caution when applying a bandage to parameter sniffing, as we will often inadvertently create a ticking time bomb that will result in bigger performance problems in the future.

Query Execution Details

How often does a query execute overall and how often does it execute in such a way that parameter sniffing is a discernable problem? If it is run constantly, then we need to ensure that it is efficient, as something that executes thousands of times a minute cannot afford to be slow or consume excessive resources. We would need to determine the most common use case and write T-SQL to accommodate it. If there are multiple common scenarios that run constantly, we could consider separate stored procedures for each one, multiple code paths within a single proc, or other ways to make the most out of each situation.

If a query executes infrequently, though, such as for a daily report or infrequent search, then recompiling the query plan each time would be a reasonable solution as it would ensure the best possible plan and not reuse an old plan. Since it is uncommonly run, the cost of recompilation would not be significant enough to cause our server any resource pressure due to the extra work the optimizer needs to perform each time. In these cases, you are at liberty to take a wider variety of actions to resolve the undesired plan reuse. Verify, though, that the query that is rarely executed today does not become more frequently used in the future. If the once-a-day query becomes popular and starts to be executed every 5 seconds throughout the day, then recompilation will become an expensive operation to perform so frequently.

A query hint may be used to force a recompile every time it executes by using OPTION (RECOMPILE). The syntax is as follows in Listing 8-5.

Listing 8-5. Example Usage of the RECOMPILE Query Hint

```
IF EXISTS (SELECT * FROM sys.procedures WHERE procedures.name = 'get_sales_
orders_by_sales_person')
BEGIN
      DROP PROCEDURE dbo.get_sales_orders_by_sales_person;
END
GO

CREATE PROCEDURE dbo.get_sales_orders_by_sales_person
      @SalesPersonID INT, @RowCount INT, @Offset INT
AS
BEGIN
      DECLARE @sql_command NVARCHAR(MAX);
      DECLARE @parameter_list NVARCHAR(MAX) = '@SalesPersonID INT,
      @RowCount INT, @Offset INT';

      SELECT @sql_command = '
      WITH CTE_PRODUCTS AS (
            SELECT
                  ROW_NUMBER() OVER (ORDER BY OrderDate ASC) AS rownum,
                  SalesOrderHeader.SalesOrderID,
                  SalesOrderHeader.Status,
                  SalesOrderHeader.OrderDate,
                  SalesOrderHeader.ShipDate,
                  SalesOrderDetail.UnitPrice,
                  SalesOrderDetail.LineTotal
            FROM Sales.SalesOrderHeader
            INNER JOIN Sales.SalesOrderDetail
            ON SalesOrderHeader.SalesOrderID = SalesOrderDetail.SalesOrderID
            WHERE SalesOrderHeader.SalesPersonID = @SalesPersonID
            )
      SELECT
            *
      FROM CTE_PRODUCTS
      WHERE rownum BETWEEN @Offset AND @Offset + @RowCount
      OPTION (RECOMPILE) ;';
```

```
      EXEC sp_executesql @sql_command, @parameter_list, @SalesPersonID,
      @RowCount, @Offset;
END
```

The only difference between this stored procedure and the one we worked with earlier was the addition of the RECOMPILE hint at the end of the SELECT query. With this in place, let's run our last parameter sniffing example:

```
DBCC FREEPROCCACHE;
EXEC dbo.get_sales_orders_by_sales_person 1, 1000, 0;

EXEC dbo.get_sales_orders_by_sales_person 285, 1000, 0;

EXEC dbo.read_query_plan_cache 'CTE_PRODUCTS';
```

Last time we executed the stored procedure in this manner, the query execution plan was reused, resulting in poor performance. Let's review the performance for the second execution in Figure 8-16, which was for the small result set:

```
Table 'SalesOrderDetail'. Scan count 16, logical reads 53, physical reads 0,
read-ahead reads 0, lob logical reads 0, lob physical reads 0, lob read-
ahead reads 0.
Table 'SalesOrderHeader'. Scan count 1, logical reads 50, physical reads 0,
read-ahead reads 0, lob logical reads 0, lob physical reads 0, lob read-
ahead reads 0.
```

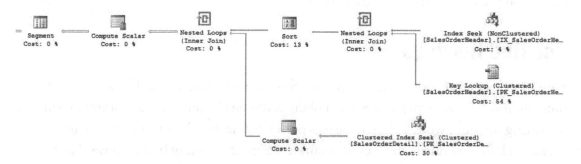

Figure 8-16. *Performance when the execution plan is recompiled at runtime, preventing reuse of a suboptimal plan*

This time around, SQL Server executed the query and recompiled the query plan at runtime to obtain the optimal plan for each set of parameters, rather than reuse the one for the large result set that preceded it.

As always, query hints should be used cautiously, and only when deemed necessary. The resources required by the optimizer to generate an execution plan are not trivial, and recompiling plans too frequently can result in additional CPU consumption and increased query latency. This tool is best used when you are certain that a query executes infrequently, or its cardinality is so sporadic that plan reuse often results in poor performance.

An additional consideration is to determine if poor performance resulting from plan reuse is the rule or the exception? Adding recompilation to a query because of an occasional anomaly would not be beneficial. It may be best to tolerate undesired plan reuse if a query executes optimally for a majority of the time. An alternative would be to trap and handle the rare and specific cases where it is a problem, if possible. Also worth investigating is if the anomaly is indicative of a bigger problem, such as a data validation error or illegitimate data being passed into your stored procedure. Sometimes parameter sniffing is the result of bad data or an application problem that requires further research to diagnose and resolve.

The tradeoff for recompiling an execution plan is to improve query execution performance at the cost of optimization performance. When determining if this tradeoff is worth it, consider the future: will this query execute similarly in the future? Could the application or query source change, resulting in new, unexpected behavior that could turn this good decision into a bad one? In addition, has your research been exhaustive enough to ensure that all use cases have been covered? If you can confidently answer these questions, then making the correct decision with regards to recompiling query execution plans should be straightforward.

The Red Herrings

Sometimes, bad execution plans may arise from other sources. If statistics are out of date, then suboptimal query execution plans could be chosen prior to parameter sniffing occurring. In other words, plan reuse was perfectly fine, but the optimizer initially created a bad plan due to the lack of accurate statistics, and that bad plan was later reused. In this scenario, a bad plan would have likely been generated even if plan reuse had not occurred. Verifying the estimated vs. actual row counts in an execution plan is a good way to spot potential statistics inaccuracies. See Chapter 6 for details on viewing, using, and updating statistics.

Realistically, any way in which T-SQL can be poorly written could lead us to accidentally blame parameter sniffing for undesired plan reuse. For example, let's look at a simple example in Listing 8-6 where a query was written in such a way that suboptimal performance was essentially guaranteed:

Listing 8-6. An AdventureWorks Query Guaranteed to Perform Poorly

```
SELECT DISTINCT
       PRODUCT.ProductID,
       PRODUCT.Name
FROM Production.Product PRODUCT
INNER JOIN Sales.SalesOrderDetail DETAIL
ON PRODUCT.ProductID = DETAIL.ProductID
OR PRODUCT.rowguid = DETAIL.rowguid
```

This query, which returns 266 rows, yields the performance metrics seen in Figure 8-17.

```
Table 'Product'. Scan count 5, logical reads 40, physical reads 0, read-ahead reads 0, lob logical reads 0, lob physical reads 0, lob read-ahead reads 0.
Table 'SalesOrderDetail'. Scan count 4, logical reads 4984, physical reads 0, read-ahead reads 0, lob logical reads 0, lob physical reads 0, lob read-ahead reads 0.
Table 'Worktable'. Scan count 4, logical reads 1209220, physical reads 0, read-ahead reads 0, lob logical reads 0, lob physical reads 0, lob read-ahead reads 0.
Table 'Worktable'. Scan count 0, logical reads 0, physical reads 0, read-ahead reads 0, lob logical reads 0, lob physical reads 0, lob read-ahead reads 0.
```

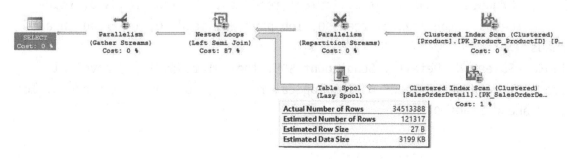

Figure 8-17. *Performance of an (intentionally) poorly written query*

Check out that row count heading into the nested loops! That's 34.5 million rows! Since `SalesOrderDetail` contains only 121,317 rows, we clearly have a problem that needs to be resolved here. It turns out that using an OR operator in a join can cause catastrophically bad performance, as the query optimizer has a very difficult time determining the best way to intersect the data sets efficiently.

If this query plan were reused in the future, it would perform poorly, not because of parameter sniffing, but because the query itself is poorly designed. If we rewrote the query itself to remove the OR, such as by using two statements separated by a UNION, we can realize significantly better performance. Listing 8-7 shows this improved T-SQL.

Listing 8-7. The Optimized Version of the Slow Query from Listing 8-6

```
SELECT
      PRODUCT.ProductID,
      PRODUCT.Name
FROM Production.Product PRODUCT
INNER JOIN Sales.SalesOrderDetail DETAIL
ON PRODUCT.ProductID = DETAIL.ProductID
UNION
SELECT
      PRODUCT.ProductID,
      PRODUCT.Name
FROM Production.Product PRODUCT
INNER JOIN Sales.SalesOrderDetail DETAIL
ON PRODUCT.rowguid = DETAIL.rowguid
```

While this T-SQL may seem longer and more complex than before, the query optimizer will have a significantly easier time finding a good plan for it:

```
Table 'Product'. Scan count 2, logical reads 30, physical reads 0, read-
ahead reads 0, lob logical reads 0, lob physical reads 0, lob read-ahead
reads 0.
Table 'SalesOrderDetail'. Scan count 505, logical reads 1554, physical
reads 0, read-ahead reads 0, lob logical reads 0, lob physical reads 0, lob
read-ahead reads 0.
```

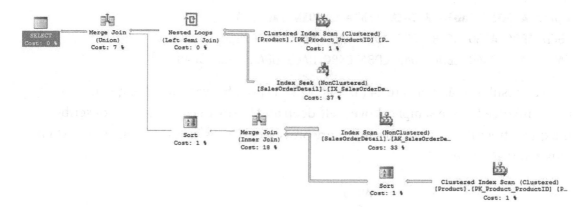

Figure 8-18. *Performance of the rewritten & optimized query in Listing 8-7*

The execution plan may also seem more complex, but this T-SQL syntax allowed the optimizer to break a complex problem into two simpler problems that could then be easily solved, combined, and the same result set returned. The reads were reduced by over 75 times and the runtime went from 10 seconds down to 100ms.

Dividing and conquering a complex query is often an excellent way to prevent the query optimizer from being unable to find the best possible plan. The preceding example was a scenario where a simple-looking query was a performance bomb for the optimizer to deal with. Separating it into two sections as shown was one solution, but using a temporary table or table variable to store the data in intermediary steps would also have been a valid solution to this performance problem.

Before assuming that parameter sniffing is the root cause of a performance problem, review the T-SQL involved and confirm that there are not more significant areas to address, such as poorly constructed T-SQL or bad database design.

If a query becomes large and unwieldy, consider breaking it into smaller, simpler queries. With each table that is joined into a query, the number of possible execution plans that the query optimizer must evaluate grows exponentially. Depending on the query style, the number of join orders that exist for n tables will either be n! (n factorial, for a query tree that is left-deep) or (2n-2)!/(n-1)! (an even larger number if the query tree is bushy). Consider for a moment the number of ways in which four tables in a left-deep join order can be ordered:

Table A JOIN Table B JOIN Table C JOIN Table D

ABCD ABDC ACBD ACDB ADBC ADCB BACD BADC BCAD BCDA BDAC BDCA
CABD CADB CBAD CBDA CDAB CDBA DABC DACB DBAC DBCA DCAB DCBA

The result is that there are 24 (4! = 4 * 3 * 2 * 1) possible ways to arrange the four tables involved in the sample above. Left-deep and bushy trees are ways to describe the query trees that are built by any query processor. This is how each type looks when illustrated as a tree.

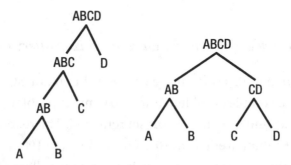

Figure 8-19. *Example of a left-deep query tree (left) and a bushy query tree (right)*

The left-deep tree consists of a sequence of tables that are joined one-at-a-time, while a bushy tree is composed of separately joined tables whose results are then joined together as each set of joins is completed. There are far more ways to express the ordering in a bushy tree, hence why the mathematical expression for the permutations of join orders is significantly larger than a left-deep tree.

Without entering an in-depth discussion of each type of query tree, it is safe to say that with each table added into a query, the number of ways the joins can be ordered will increase significantly. Removing even one table from a complex query and collecting the data from it separately can result in major performance gains.

Always test these changes and ensure that the refactored T-SQL truly performs better, and equally important, be certain that the data returned is the same as it was earlier. Highly transactional data may change in between an initial data collection and the final query, resulting in inconsistent data. As a result, be comfortable with the data that is being queried and don't blindly optimize without being certain that the output of the resulting query will be the same as the original.

Investigating indexing is also worthwhile. Verify that correct indexes are being used and that the operation against that index is the correct one. If a seek is expected, then check to see if a seek is being implemented by the optimizer. Should there be a key lookup? Could a covering index provide a significant performance improvement for a commonly executed query? If a filtered index should be used, does the index filter match the query filter exactly?

Before investigating parameter sniffing as the culprit to a performance problem, always verify that there are no other bigger problems that require tacking first. In addition to statistics, indexing, and T-SQL mistakes, it is possible that SQL Server configuration settings may also affect query performance. Parallelism, trace flags, and memory/CPU pressure could all lead to unexpected performance degradation.

Despite these possibilities, always start with the simplest solutions first, and then explore more complex ones when they are disproven. It is significantly more likely that a performance problem related to undesired plan reuse is simply the result of classic parameter sniffing, and not of some other mysterious origin. If not, then consider the impact of statistics, indexing, and query structure. Only when all else fails is it necessary to investigate the guts of your SQL Server installation for further clues. This will be a rare scenario if it ever happens, but being prepared and knowing where to look to solve performance problems can save immense time in the future.

Parameter Values

A good way to investigate parameter sniffing is to inspect the parameters themselves and the typical values that are being passed into them. Is a certain value or set of values very common? Are the values always different and indicative of a process that never repeats? Does a parameter typically receive a value that seems random, or do they follow a distinct pattern?

This knowledge can help determine the best course of action to take. If a small set of values are always passed into a stored procedure, then you may be able to make assumptions about them and design the T-SQL to take into account those artificial limits. Some useful observations include:

1. Is a parameter always NOT NULL?

2. Will a parameter always be set to the current date, or a current value for an important metric?

3. Is there a very limited set of values for a parameter?

4. Are parameter values seemingly random?

5. Is a particular value extremely common, or is that value more important or relevant than other values?

As noted earlier, it's important to consider the possibility of change. If application changes could impact parameter values, then it is necessary to anticipate that change and not write T-SQL that will be harmed by those changes in the future. If this can be verified, then use simplifying assumptions to rewrite stored procedures to be shorter, simpler, and easier for the optimizer to make the correct decisions as often as possible.

Additionally, knowing the cardinality of a result set can greatly affect how we write a stored procedure. For example, if a single row is always returned from a given stored proc, we can ensure that each section of it is optimized for that small result set. Similarly, if we are paging data and will always return 25 rows, or 50, then that information can be used to make sure the stored proc is written to return that row count and no more or less.

As was illustrated in Chapter 3, paging data sets can be optimized for a small result set when it is unlikely that we will request more data. If we know that a user will request page after page, though, then we can write our queries to return more data, in anticipation of the next click. The application knowledge that allows us to draw these conclusions also provides the information we need to write T-SQL that aligns with the business logic we are trying to satisfy.

Local Variables

To prepare for this example, let's add an index to `Production.Product`, which will help support the queries that we are about to run:

```
CREATE NONCLUSTERED INDEX NCI_production_product_ProductModelID ON
Production.Product (ProductModelID) INCLUDE (Name);
```

While not meant to influence queries from earlier in this chapter, the index will allow for a more straightforward demonstration of parameter sniffing going forward.

A tactic that is sometimes used to try and eliminate parameter sniffing is to redeclare variables locally, rather than using the parameters passed into a stored procedure. The effect of this may seem similar to the use of the RECOMPILE hint, but it more accurately mimics the use of OPTIMIZE FOR UNKNOWN. Often, performance is harmed in the long run by this change. To demonstrate the effect that this has, we will create a new version of our stored procedure from the start of this chapter and redefine all stored procedure parameters as local variables within it, as seen in Listing 8-8.

Listing 8-8. Stored Procedure that Redeclares Parameters as Local Variables

```
IF EXISTS (SELECT * FROM sys.procedures WHERE procedures.name = 'get_
products_by_model_local')
BEGIN
      DROP PROCEDURE dbo.get_products_by_model_local;
END
GO
CREATE PROCEDURE dbo.get_products_by_model_local (@firstProductModelID INT,
@lastProductModelID INT)
AS
BEGIN
      DECLARE @ProductModelID1 INT = @firstProductModelID;
      DECLARE @ProductModelID2 INT = @lastProductModelID;

      SELECT
            PRODUCT.Name,
            PRODUCT.ProductID,
            PRODUCT.ProductModelID,
            PRODUCT.ProductNumber,
            MODEL.Name
      FROM Production.Product PRODUCT
      INNER JOIN Production.ProductModel MODEL
      ON MODEL.ProductModelID = PRODUCT.ProductModelID
      WHERE PRODUCT.ProductModelID BETWEEN @ProductModelID1 AND
      @ProductModelID2;
END
```

Note that @firstProductModelID and @secondProductModelID have been assigned to @ProductModelID1 and @ProductModelID2, respectively. These new variables are then used in the final SELECT statement at the end of the stored procedure. Using this new version of our proc, let's test out performance using the example from earlier in this chapter:

```
DBCC FREEPROCCACHE;
EXEC dbo.get_products_by_model_local 120, 125;
EXEC dbo.get_products_by_model_local 0, 10000;
```

Here, we will establish a baseline for what the optimizer believes to the best plan for the product search. For the first execution, which covers a small range of product models, and therefore carries with it a small result set (only six rows), we find that the performance is different from the original version of the stored proc. The new IO statistics and execution plans for both are found in Figure 8-20, with the new on top, and the old one below:

Table 'Product'. Scan count 6, logical reads 24, physical reads 0, read-ahead reads 0, lob logical reads 0, lob physical reads 0, lob read-ahead reads 0.
Table 'ProductModel'. Scan count 1, logical reads 2, physical reads 0, read-ahead reads 0, lob logical reads 0, lob physical reads 0, lob read-ahead reads 0.

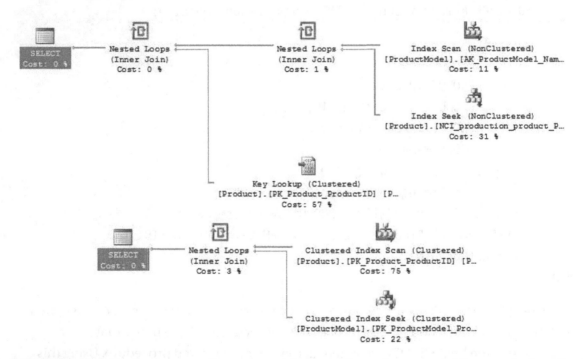

Figure 8-20. *Performance of a query with a small result set variables are declared and the stored proc parameters reassigned locally*

Declaring local variables and using them in the query resulted in a different execution plan, as well as different IO statistics. Now let's compare new vs. old for the second scenario above, where the result set is much larger. Figure 8-21 shows these performance metrics.

Table 'Product'. Scan count 128, logical reads 849, physical reads 0, read-ahead reads 0, lob logical reads 0, lob physical reads 0, lob read-ahead reads 0.
Table 'ProductModel'. Scan count 1, logical reads 2, physical reads 0, read-ahead reads 0, lob logical reads 0, lob physical reads 0, lob read-ahead reads 0.

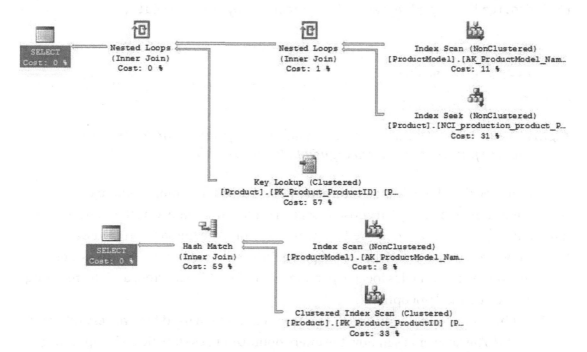

Figure 8-21. *Performance metrics for a large result set, when variables are declared and the stored proc parameters reassigned locally*

As seen, a different (and more complex) execution plan was chosen for the new version of our stored procedure. This version also required far more IO than previously to return the same data. In fact, the same execution plan was chosen by the query optimizer for both sets of parameters. This consistently leads to good performance when working with the small result set, but poor performance on the large result set. Parameter sniffing ***appears*** to no longer occur here, since the same plan is used for either set of parameter values, but if we execute our stored procedure a few times in a row, we can confirm that the plan is in fact being reused:

```
DBCC FREEPROCCACHE;
EXEC dbo.get_products_by_model_local 120, 125;
```

```
EXEC dbo.get_products_by_model_local 0, 10000;
EXEC dbo.get_products_by_model_local 120, 125;
EXEC dbo.get_products_by_model_local 0, 10000;
```

Now, let's review the data from the query plan cache for this stored procedure, as seen in Figure 8-22.

```
EXEC dbo.read_query_plan_cache 'get_products_by_model_local';
```

	database_name	ObjectType	ObjectName	creation_time	last_execution_time	cpu_last_execution	reads_last_execution	duration_last_execution
1	AdventureWorks	Proc	get_products_by_model_local	2015-11-17 08:24:08.727	2015-11-17 08:24:08.997	3751	853	162420

rows_last_execution	size_in_bytes	ExecutionCount	QueryText	query_plan
295	65536	4	CREATE PROCEDURE dbo.get_products_by_model_loca...	<ShowPlanXML xmlns="http://schemas.microsoft.com...

plan_handle
0x050005007BAB7C0BB0E937F9040000000010000000000000...

Figure 8-22. *Metrics returned by dbo.read_query_plan_cache for the product search where parameters are reassigned to local variables*

We can see that the only plan returned was executed four times, so there was plan reuse. Since the execution plan chosen for each set of parameters was the same, though, it did not matter that reuse occurred as the results would be the same, regardless of how many times we executed the stored procedure or the order of those executions. Despite redeclaring variables locally, parameter sniffing still occurred, and the resulting performance was still not optimal.

What happened here? Why was the same execution plan used for two very different sets of data? The answer lies in how the query optimizer uses statistics. The optimizer must make quick and intelligent decisions using whatever statistics are available to it when a query is executed. Any information that is unavailable until runtime will also be unavailable to the optimizer. The three pieces of information provided by statistics as introduced earlier were:

1. **Summary data**, which provides row count, average key length, and an overview of the statistics object.

2. **Density data**, which provides information on the uniqueness of each object bring tracked.

3. **Histogram data**, giving row counts for different values over the sample range of the statistics object.

For the query optimizer to make the most accurate decision possible, it requires all of this information. Unfortunately, some T-SQL techniques will force parameter data to become unavailable or unusable until runtime. This results in suboptimal execution plans as the optimizer is forced to make decisions without the benefit of the histogram data, density data, or both.

In the preceding example, where we declared local variables and reassigned the parameters to them, we took away the optimizer's ability to use the histogram. Previously we executed the stored procedure and the parameters were used to determine the execution plan the first time, and then the plan was reused each time thereafter. In this case, we executed the stored procedure for the first time and the summary and density data were all that was available for the optimizer to create an execution plan. Since local variables have unknown values until runtime, there is no way to check the histogram for cardinality data, and it is therefore omitted from the optimization process. As a result, the execution plan that was generated and reused had to be created based on assumptions. In addition, the execution plan chosen would be the same for any parameter values passed in, not just the two examples that we reviewed), since those values were unavailable until runtime.

In summary, this means that whenever we use local variables in a stored procedure, the query optimizer will need to make assumptions, and ultimately this can lead to poor cardinality estimates. Oftentimes in this situation, a DBA may find that the execution plan that is chosen happens to perform better than previously, but this is largely due to luck and the optimizer stumbling upon a plan that works well for the use cases that are being scrutinized. In other words, a mediocre execution plan performed adequately enough to trick us into believing that a parameter sniffing problem was solved.

To fully illustrate what is happening, let's take a closer look at the execution plans for a single execution of each version of the stored procedure, focusing on cardinality estimates versus the actual row counts from each IO step. First, the original stored procedure (running for the large result set) is shown in Figure 8-23.

```
DBCC FREEPROCCACHE;
EXEC dbo.get_products_by_model 0, 10000;
```

Index Scan (NonClustered)		**Clustered Index Scan (Clustered)**	
Scan a nonclustered index, entirely or only a range.		Scanning a clustered index, entirely or only a range.	
Physical Operation	Index Scan	**Physical Operation**	Clustered Index Scan
Logical Operation	Index Scan	**Logical Operation**	Clustered Index Scan
Actual Execution Mode	Row	**Actual Execution Mode**	Row
Estimated Execution Mode	Row	**Estimated Execution Mode**	Row
Storage	RowStore	**Storage**	RowStore
Actual Number of Rows	128	**Actual Number of Rows**	295
Actual Number of Batches	0	**Actual Number of Batches**	0
Estimated I/O Cost	0.003125	**Estimated I/O Cost**	0.0127546
Estimated Operator Cost	0.0034228 (8%)	**Estimated Operator Cost**	0.013466 (33%)
Estimated Subtree Cost	0.0034228	**Estimated Subtree Cost**	0.013466
Estimated CPU Cost	0.0002978	**Estimated CPU Cost**	0.0007114
Estimated Number of Executions	1	**Estimated Number of Executions**	1
Number of Executions	1	**Number of Executions**	1
Estimated Number of Rows	128	**Estimated Number of Rows**	295
Estimated Row Size	65 B	**Estimated Row Size**	96 B
Actual Rebinds	0	**Actual Rebinds**	0
Actual Rewinds	0	**Actual Rewinds**	0
Ordered	False	**Ordered**	False
Node ID	1	**Node ID**	2

Figure 8-23. *Execution plan details for the parameterized stored procedure*

Note that the actual and estimated number of rows is identical for both IO operations. This indicates that the optimizer had sufficient statistics data to correctly estimate the row counts for each step and choose a suitable execution plan. Once executed, the results confirmed the optimizer's work and we can give it a pat on the back for a job well done.

Here are the execution plan details for the IO steps when we declare local variables and use them instead of the stored procedure parameters, as seen in Figure 8-24.

```
DBCC FREEPROCCACHE;
EXEC dbo.get_products_by_model_local 0, 10000;
```

Index Scan (NonClustered)		Index Seek (NonClustered)	
Scan a nonclustered index, entirely or only a range.		Scan a particular range of rows from a nonclustered index.	
Physical Operation	Index Scan	**Physical Operation**	Index Seek
Logical Operation	Index Scan	**Logical Operation**	Index Seek
Actual Execution Mode	Row	**Actual Execution Mode**	Row
Estimated Execution Mode	Row	**Estimated Execution Mode**	Row
Storage	RowStore	**Storage**	RowStore
Actual Number of Rows	128	**Actual Number of Rows**	295
Actual Number of Batches	0	**Actual Number of Batches**	0
Estimated I/O Cost	0.003125	**Estimated I/O Cost**	0.003125
Estimated Operator Cost	0.0034228 (11%)	**Estimated Operator Cost**	0.0091354 (31%)
Estimated Subtree Cost	0.0034228	**Estimated CPU Cost**	0.0001597
Estimated CPU Cost	0.0002978	**Estimated Subtree Cost**	0.0091354
Estimated Number of Executions	1	**Number of Executions**	128
Number of Executions	1	**Estimated Number of Executions**	11.52
Estimated Number of Rows	11.52	**Estimated Number of Rows**	1
Estimated Row Size	65 B	**Estimated Row Size**	69 B
Actual Rebinds	0	**Actual Rebinds**	0
Actual Rewinds	0	**Actual Rewinds**	0
Ordered	False	Ordered	True
Node ID	2	Node ID	3

Figure 8-24. *Execution plan details for the stored procedure using local variables*

In this example, while the actual number of rows was the same as previously, the estimates are way off! 11.52 rows were estimated for the IO operation on `ProductModel` and 1 row estimated on `Product`. This is the source of the suboptimal execution plan that we reviewed previously.On the `ProductModel` table, the optimizer has no information to go on because the operation is an inequality with no parameters. For the `Product` table, the optimizer can use the density data to try and get a good estimate, but without the histogram it will fall short.

Do not redeclare parameters locally in a stored procedure. It is a trap!

There are many reasons why the query optimizer may make poor cardinality estimates when evaluating different parts of an execution plan. While some of those possibilities are normal and by-design, we certainly do not want to artificially limit the information available to it and cause even worse estimations to be made. Declaring local variables may appear to fix bad execution plans or eliminate parameter sniffing, but ultimately it will worsen the situation by limiting the optimizer's access to valuable information. Unless significant research has been done into the data and queries involved, localizing variables in a stored procedure will likely be a risky decision in the long run, even if it appears to solve a business need right now.

Forcing Cardinalities to the Optimizer

We have experimented with the query optimizer, recompiling plans or altering variable scope to try and improve query performance. An additional option is available when we have very complete knowledge of our data and wish to instruct the query optimizer on cardinality directly. In a query, we can use the OPTIMIZE FOR hint to directly instruct the optimizer on what value to accept as the cardinality for a parameter.

Let's reconsider the product model search from earlier in which we had declared local variables to try and manage cardinality. When we used local variables, we robbed the query optimizer of the ability to use the histogram data, thus forcing it to use less accurate estimates based on the remaining data. If we always returned a large data set and knew that as fact, we could consider telling the query optimizer to base cardinality on specific values, as shown in Listing 8-9.

Listing 8-9. Example of Using the OPTIMIZE FOR Query Hint

```
IF EXISTS (SELECT * FROM sys.procedures WHERE procedures.name = 'get_
products_by_model')
BEGIN
      DROP PROCEDURE dbo.get_products_by_model;
END
GO
CREATE PROCEDURE dbo.get_products_by_model (@firstProductModelID INT,
@lastProductModelID INT)
AS
BEGIN
      SELECT
            PRODUCT.Name,
            PRODUCT.ProductID,
            PRODUCT.ProductModelID,
            PRODUCT.ProductNumber,
            MODEL.Name
```

```
FROM Production.Product PRODUCT
INNER JOIN Production.ProductModel MODEL
ON MODEL.ProductModelID = PRODUCT.ProductModelID
WHERE PRODUCT.ProductModelID BETWEEN @firstProductModelID AND
@lastProductModelID
OPTION (OPTIMIZE FOR (@firstProductModelID = 0, @lastProductModelID =
10000));
END
```

In this example, we force the optimizer to base all analysis on the values that we provide only, rather than turning to statistics to determine the best way to proceed. When we do this, the performance returns to what we had seen earlier when it was using the optimal plan, as seen in Figure 8-25.

```
DBCC FREEPROCCACHE;
EXEC dbo.get_products_by_model 0, 10000;
```

```
Table 'Workfile'. Scan count 0, logical reads 0, physical reads 0, read-
ahead reads 0, lob logical reads 0, lob physical reads 0, lob read-ahead
reads 0.
Table 'Worktable'. Scan count 0, logical reads 0, physical reads 0, read-
ahead reads 0, lob logical reads 0, lob physical reads 0, lob read-ahead
reads 0.
Table 'Product'. Scan count 1, logical reads 16, physical reads 0, read-
ahead reads 0, lob logical reads 0, lob physical reads 0, lob read-ahead
reads 0.
Table 'ProductModel'. Scan count 1, logical reads 2, physical reads 0,
read-ahead reads 0, lob logical reads 0, lob physical reads 0, lob read-
ahead reads 0.
```

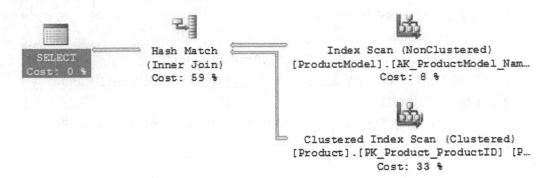

Figure 8-25. *Execution plan when we forced the cardinality for each parameter in the query*

The result is the optimal execution plan and only 18 reads. When we use this hint, it will choose this plan regardless of what values are passed in. OPTIMIZE FOR is intended for a use case in which you have extensive knowledge of the input parameters. This is an infrequent scenario, but one that can exist in stored procedures or code where the inputs and outputs are very predictable.

There is one additional way in which we can use the OPTIMIZE FOR hint, and that is to take away parameter values altogether and instruct the optimizer to make its decisions using only statistics, with no insight into parameter values. Let's try this out as well with the same stored procedure, as seen in Listing 8-10.

Listing 8-10. Example of Using the OPTIMIZE FOR UNKNOWN Query Hint

```
IF EXISTS (SELECT * FROM sys.procedures WHERE procedures.name = 'get_
products_by_model')
BEGIN
      DROP PROCEDURE dbo.get_products_by_model;
END
GO
CREATE PROCEDURE dbo.get_products_by_model (@firstProductModelID INT,
@lastProductModelID INT)
AS
BEGIN
      SELECT
            PRODUCT.Name,
            PRODUCT.ProductID,
            PRODUCT.ProductModelID,
```

```
        PRODUCT.ProductNumber,
        MODEL.Name
FROM Production.Product PRODUCT
INNER JOIN Production.ProductModel MODEL
ON MODEL.ProductModelID = PRODUCT.ProductModelID
WHERE PRODUCT.ProductModelID BETWEEN @firstProductModelID AND
@lastProductModelID
OPTION (OPTIMIZE FOR (@firstProductModelID UNKNOWN, @lastProductModelID
UNKNOWN));
END
```

In this example, instead of providing static values, we use UNKNOWN, which instructs the optimizer to not base its analysis on any particular parameter value but instead determine cardinality based solely on statistics. Let's check out the performance for this version of our stored procedure when we use this new hint, which can be found in Figure 8-26.

```
DBCC FREEPROCCACHE;
EXEC dbo.get_products_by_model 0, 10000;

Table 'Product'. Scan count 128, logical reads 849, physical reads 0, read-
ahead reads 0, lob logical reads 0, lob physical reads 0, lob read-ahead
reads 0.
Table 'ProductModel'. Scan count 1, logical reads 2, physical reads 0,
read-ahead reads 0, lob logical reads 0, lob physical reads 0, lob read-
ahead reads 0.
```

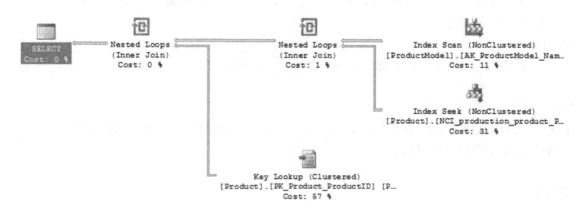

Figure 8-26. *Performance metrics when we use OPTIMIZE FOR UNKNOWN*

When we leave the optimizer to its own devices, it will resort to statistics to determine the best execution plan. In this case, the results are exactly what we got previously, when a poor plan was chosen. Typically, when the optimizer relies on statistics only, with no parameter guidance, it will create an execution plan that is geared towards the most common parameter values that could be passed in. In the preceding example, we are returning an unusually large amount of data, which the optimizer was not prepared for. The result was very similar to when we used local variables to bypass the optimizer's standard parameter analysis.

OPTIMIZE FOR, like all hints, can be very useful when applied to very specific or unusual circumstances. Use it with caution, as it may help performance for a select set of parameter values but could also greatly harm performance if other unexpected values are passed in. Query hints should always be applied conservatively, and only when you are certain that you have full knowledge of the queries involved, the parameter values, and a good handle on cardinality.

Dynamic SQL

An odd, but all-to-often recommended solution to parameter sniffing is to wrap the offending T-SQL in dynamic SQL and hard-code any parameters into the resulting command string. Consider a new version of our search stored proc from earlier, as seen in Listing 8-11.

Listing 8-11. Example of Using Dynamic SQL to Attempt to Control the Optimization Process of a Stored Procedure

```
IF EXISTS (SELECT * FROM sys.procedures WHERE procedures.name = 'get_
products_by_model')
BEGIN
      DROP PROCEDURE dbo.get_products_by_model;
END
GO
CREATE PROCEDURE dbo.get_products_by_model (@firstProductModelID INT,
@lastProductModelID INT)
AS
BEGIN
      DECLARE @sql_command NVARCHAR(MAX);
```

```
    SELECT @sql_command = '
            SELECT
                    PRODUCT.Name,
                    PRODUCT.ProductID,
                    PRODUCT.ProductModelID,
                    PRODUCT.ProductNumber,
                    MODEL.Name
            FROM Production.Product PRODUCT
            INNER JOIN Production.ProductModel MODEL
            ON MODEL.ProductModelID = PRODUCT.ProductModelID
            WHERE PRODUCT.ProductModelID BETWEEN ' +
CAST(@firstProductModelID AS NVARCHAR(MAX)) + ' AND ' +
CAST(@lastProductModelID AS NVARCHAR(MAX)) + ';';

    EXEC sp_executesql @sql_command;
END
GO
```

When we run through our examples from earlier, we find that the optimal plan is chosen each time. This is because we are hard-coding values for @firstProductModelID and @lastProductModelID into the query. Since execution plans are generated for each set of unique query text, we will get a different plan for each set of values.

Wrapping T-SQL in dynamic SQL mimics the behavior of OPTION (RECOMPILE) in that each set of parameters will receive its own execution plan. This will result in more accurate execution plans, but also the need to generate a new plan for each set of parameters. This can be more efficient than recompiling the stored procedure every time it executes, but comes with a few downsides:

- Like OPTION (RECOMPILE), we are forcing the query optimizer to consume more resources to generate execution plans more often.

- Extra execution plans can bloat the plan cache if too many are generated.

- The use of dynamic SQL should be well-documented as it will not be plainly obvious to a developer why we are doing this.

- Increased code complexity and the potential need to address SQL injection.

Dynamic SQL is an interesting and potentially efficient solution to parameter sniffing, but should be used carefully as the primary cost of its use is maintainability. Document its use completely and be confident that code will not change in the future in a way that would result in too many execution plans being generated for the single stored procedure. Since each set of parameters results in a new plan, we want to be certain that the variety of parameter values never becomes too high.

Trace Flag 4136

This trace flag disables plan reuse server-wide, removing the possibility that parameter sniffing can occur. While this may sound like a great idea, the result is similar to applying the OPTIMIZE FOR UNKNOWN query hint to all queries affected by it.

In general, this trace flag is a bad idea and its use will be relegated to highly specialized scenarios in which a server processes a unique workload that benefits from the removal of plan reuse. Trace flags, like query hints, should be used with extreme caution. Telling the query optimizer what to do requires in-depth knowledge of an application, how it works, its data, and the future of its behavior.

Starting in SQL Server 2016, parameter sniffing can be disabled at the database-level as well. While this provides a bit more control behavior related to parameterization, it still requires the same level of care that would be applied when considering using trace flag 4136.

Disabling parameter sniffing is ill-advised unless you have enough application and data knowledge to be able to confidently prove out that it will result in consistently adequate performance. If so, be sure to fully document its use as trace flags and database settings are well-hidden from the view of most developers and can easy be forgotten about as time passes.

Fix Bad Business Logic

We often blame parameter sniffing on SQL Server and seek ways to resolve it that involve tweaking queries or settings to improve performance and allow us to move onto other more important tasks. The most common cause of parameter sniffing is poor database design, suboptimal T-SQL, or bad architecture decisions. Despite seeming unrelated to parameter sniffing, we can single out a set of mistakes that are easy to identify and that can be used as red flags to identify the cause of parameter sniffing.

Too Many Possible Code Paths

When a stored procedure contains many possible branches that can be accessed based on parameter values, the ability to generate a good execution plan becomes challenging. If there are ten different blocks of code that can be executed, each will be assigned an execution plan. The results of these branches can be passed through to other sections of code that depend on them. Plans for those branches won't change, even if the data inputs do.

This is a common problem when there is a desire for a single stored procedure to solve many different problems. A stored procedure with too many code paths will be easily identifiable by the presence of lots of branching logic (IF, THEN, ELSE, GOTO, etc.) and the propensity for any one section of code to be executed while many others are not. This in itself can be tolerable, but when the outputs of a branched section are used as inputs to additional branches, then the potential for a bad plan to be generated is greatly increased.

The simplest solution is to break each code path into a separate stored procedure. The benefit is that each proc will better represent a single use case and will be far more likely to be assigned an execution plan that is relevant to all parameter values. Splitting a large problem into smaller, simpler problems is often a great way to improve performance, increase maintainability, and make code easier to read and understand.

Lots of Parameters

The more parameters a stored procedure has, the more ways in which combinations of them can result in unexpected performance. Similar to how a query with more tables becomes harder to optimize, a stored procedure with many parameters has far more combinations that can result in undesired plan reuse.

If parameter sniffing is identified on a stored procedure that has a large number of parameters, consider ways in which the parameter count can be reduced by:

- Splitting the stored procedure into smaller, simpler stored procs.

- Remove parameters that are not used or that have the same value all the time.

- Ensure that no parameters are redeclared locally.

- Combine parameters that are ultimately responsible for the same set of results.

- Remove parameters used solely for branching and separate those logical units into new stored procedures.

Reducing the parameter count in a stored procedure is an easy and straightforward way to address parameter sniffing, and is guaranteed to improve performance by simplifying the number of code paths available and allowing the optimizer to generate an execution plan using far fewer variables to do so.

Stored Procedure is Huge

A larger stored procedure contains more T-SQL statements that need to be optimized and therefore more decisions that need to be made to generate an execution plan. When a stored procedure is immense, it is often a sign of a desire to cram large amounts of business logic into a single place. This lends itself to there being too many code paths and too many different ways in which a single execution plan may not be capable of servicing all possible combinations of variables or data sets that are passed to and from each section of code.

The easiest fix is to break the stored procedure into smaller, more manageable pieces. This is a common theme in optimization, and while turning one object into three may seem complex, it will create code patterns that lend themselves to more efficient execution plans and more consistent performance. Similarly, try to move business logic and formatting into code. This simplifies queries and allows the database to do what it is best at: storing and retrieving data.

If a stored proc is immense, ask yourself: "why is it so huge"? What can we do to simplify it and make it more manageable? If a specific section consistently performs poorly, can we separate or address just that component of the stored procedure? Finding a single large, problematic query and breaking it into two or three smaller ones may improve stored procedure performance overall by eliminating a single hard-to-optimize expensive query. Are we spending immense resources to generate HTML output for a web page when application code might be better suited for that task? These are all useful considerations when determining how to break up a large problem and when diagnosing a poorly performing behemoth.

Conclusion

Query execution plan reuse is an important feature in SQL Server that conserves memory and CPU while allowing common queries to execute quickly and efficiently. When parameter sniffing leads to poor performance, it should be diagnosed carefully to ensure that it is indeed the cause, and not a symptom of another, bigger problem.

When suboptimal parameter sniffing is found, analyze the data to determine metrics that describe the parameters, data, and usage patterns. This research will greatly help in determining the best course of action (if any) that should be taken. Test potential solutions for all use cases and ensure as much as possible that application or query changes in the future will not invalidate your changes.

Query tuning and refactoring can be a more useful tool than query hints. Consider different ways that a query can be written to execute more efficiently. In addition, look for simplifying assumptions that may allow for a query to be reduced or rewritten into something simpler and easier for the optimizer to digest. Sometimes that effort will completely remove parameter sniffing as a problem, thus eliminating the need for further research or the need to resort to query hints or hacks to achieve success.

Cleanup

The T-SQL in Listing 8-12 will clean up any objects created in this chapter, if they exist, except for the stored procedure `read_query_plan_cache`, which may come in handy later on:

Listing 8-12. Script that Cleans Up Any Objects Created in This Chapter

```
IF EXISTS (SELECT * FROM sys.indexes WHERE indexes.name = 'NCI_production_
product_ProductModelID')
BEGIN
        DROP INDEX NCI_production_product_ProductModelID ON Production.Product;
END
GO
IF EXISTS (SELECT * FROM sys.procedures WHERE procedures.name = 'get_
products_by_model_local')
```

```
BEGIN
    DROP PROCEDURE dbo.get_products_by_model;
END
GO
IF EXISTS (SELECT * FROM sys.procedures WHERE procedures.name = 'get_sales_
orders_by_sales_person')
BEGIN
    DROP PROCEDURE dbo.get_sales_orders_by_sales_person;
END
GO
```

CHAPTER 9

Dynamic Pivot and Unpivot

PIVOT is an extremely efficient way to alter the structure of a result set, expanding a single column of values into a set of separate columns. UNPIVOT does the exact opposite, taking a set of columns and resolving them into a single output column. Both of these operators can be very useful in reporting, analytics, or when trying to format existing data into a specific structure as required by an application.

A significant limitation of both operators is that the column or name list for each must be defined prior to runtime in our TSQL. This can be acceptable if the name list is static or predictable enough that we will not need to modify our code frequently to allow it to work. If this list changes, though, we are forced to create many different stored procedures or functions to handle the many list values, or force limitations into our code to prevent having to do this.

There is a fun and effective alternative to either of these options, and that is to use dynamic SQL in order to generate our name lists on the fly. Once we introduce the dynamic aspect to this operator, we can write TSQL that incorporates all values in a column, a variable list, or those provided by user input. Without dynamic SQL, it is very difficult and inefficient to accomplish tasks such as this without writing significantly longer or more complex TSQL to generate a similar result set.

PIVOT

Pivot is common in analytics when we are looking to resolve transactional data into a columnar structure for use in reporting or metrics. The easiest way to introduce the challenge we just presented is with an example. Consider the TSQL in Listing 9-1, which returns some quantity data, as well as color for products that are in an inventory.

© Edward Pollack 2019
E. Pollack, *Dynamic SQL*, https://doi.org/10.1007/978-1-4842-4318-3_9

Listing 9-1. Query to Return Select Product Data from AdventureWorks

```
SELECT
        PRODUCT.Name AS product_name,
        PRODUCT.Color AS product_color,
        PRODUCT_INVENTORY.LocationID,
        PRODUCT.ReorderPoint,
        PRODUCT_INVENTORY.Quantity AS product_quantity
FROM Production.Product PRODUCT
LEFT JOIN Production.ProductInventory PRODUCT_INVENTORY
ON PRODUCT.ProductID = PRODUCT_INVENTORY.ProductID;
```

	product_name	product_color	LocationID	ReorderPoint	product_quantity
745	Road-250 Red, 44	Red	60	75	51
746	Road-250 Red, 48	Red	7	75	99
747	Road-250 Red, 48	Red	60	75	86
748	Road-250 Red, 52	Red	7	75	67
749	Road-250 Red, 52	Red	60	75	81
750	Road-250 Red, 58	Red	7	75	104
751	Road-250 Red, 58	Red	60	75	123
752	Road-250 Black, 44	Black	7	75	56
753	Road-250 Black, 44	Black	60	75	78
754	Road-250 Black, 48	Black	7	75	116
755	Road-250 Black, 48	Black	60	75	49
756	Road-250 Black, 52	Black	7	75	100
757	Road-250 Black, 52	Black	60	75	88
758	Road-250 Black, 58	Black	7	75	65
759	Road-250 Black, 58	Black	60	75	83
760	Road-550-W Yellow...	Yellow	7	75	67
761	Road-550-W Yellow...	Yellow	60	75	81
762	Road-550-W Yellow...	Yellow	7	75	73
763	Road-550-W Yellow	Yellow	60	75	60

Figure 9-1. *The query in Listing 9-1 is simple enough, and will return these results*

Note that a single product may have quantities in multiple locations. What if management was looking to correlate popularity and inventory with the color of a variety of products across all of those locations? They request a report where, instead of a row per product that includes color, there is a row per product name, and additional columns for each color specified. This would allow easy analysis to take place per product per color. PIVOT is the simplest way to accomplish the task, as seen in Listing 9-2.

Listing 9-2. Common Usage of PIVOT, to Report on Products by Color

```
SELECT
        *
FROM
(       SELECT
                PRODUCT.Name AS product_name,
                PRODUCT.Color AS product_color,
                PRODUCT.ReorderPoint,
                PRODUCT_INVENTORY.Quantity AS product_quantity
        FROM Production.Product PRODUCT
    LEFT JOIN Production.ProductInventory PRODUCT_INVENTORY
    ON PRODUCT.ProductID = PRODUCT_INVENTORY.ProductID
) PRODUCT_DATA
PIVOT
(       SUM(product_quantity)
        FOR product_color IN ([Black], [Blue], [Grey], [Multi], [Red],
        [Silver], [Silver/Black], [White], [Yellow])
) PIVOT_DATA;
```

In the preceding example, we move the previous query into a FROM clause that will be used for pivoting. The correct syntax for PIVOT requires two new components:

1. An aggregate function that will act on all values if multiple values exist. In the initial SELECT statement that returns product data, there were many duplicate rows. Here, we choose to use SUM whenever this occurs, which will add up product quantities if there are multiple rows with the same product name.

2. A value list for all values that will be changed from row data into column headers. In this case, the list is of colors from `Product. Color`.

The output of this statement in Figure 9-2 illustrates the creation of the new columns.

	product_name	ReorderPoint	Black	Blue	Grey	Multi	Red	Silver	Silver/Black	White	Yellow
89	Mountain-500 Silver, 44	75	NULL	NULL	NULL	NULL	NULL	153	NULL	NULL	NULL
90	Mountain-500 Silver, 48	75	NULL	NULL	NULL	NULL	NULL	155	NULL	NULL	NULL
91	Mountain-500 Silver, 52	75	NULL	NULL	NULL	NULL	NULL	194	NULL	NULL	NULL
92	Road-150 Red, 44	75	NULL	NULL	NULL	NULL	223	NULL	NULL	NULL	NULL
93	Road-150 Red, 48	75	NULL	NULL	NULL	NULL	140	NULL	NULL	NULL	NULL
94	Road-150 Red, 52	75	NULL	NULL	NULL	NULL	128	NULL	NULL	NULL	NULL
95	Road-150 Red, 56	75	NULL	NULL	NULL	NULL	163	NULL	NULL	NULL	NULL
96	Road-150 Red, 62	75	NULL	NULL	NULL	NULL	133	NULL	NULL	NULL	NULL
97	Road-250 Black, 44	75	134	NULL	NULL	NULL	NULL	NULL	NULL	NULL	NULL
98	Road-250 Black, 48	75	165	NULL	NULL	NULL	NULL	NULL	NULL	NULL	NULL
99	Road-250 Black, 52	75	188	NULL	NULL	NULL	NULL	NULL	NULL	NULL	NULL
100	Road-250 Black, 58	75	148	NULL	NULL	NULL	NULL	NULL	NULL	NULL	NULL
101	Road-250 Red, 44	75	NULL	NULL	NULL	NULL	163	NULL	NULL	NULL	NULL

Figure 9-2. *Output of the PIVOT query in Listing 9-2*

The results show nine new columns, which are the exact same that we defined in the query that we wrote earlier. In a scenario where multiple rows from our original query shared the same product name, the quantities were added. For example, for the product "Road-250 Black, 48" there were two rows returned by the original query, with quantities of 116 and 49, respectively, for the color black. In the output generated by the PIVOT output, we can see that the two rows were combined into one with a quantity of 165 for the same color. If multiple products existed with the same name, but in different colors, then multiple columns would be populated with quantity data for a single product after the PIVOT was applied.

There is a single weakness in this approach, and that is that the column list must be explicitly provided in the PIVOT statement prior to runtime. Any attempt to rewrite the PIVOT to use a dynamic list without dynamic SQL will fail, as shown in both Listings 9-3 and 9-4.

Listing 9-3. Attempt to Use a Subselect Within a PIVOT Statement (Unsuccessfully)

```
SELECT
        *
FROM
(       SELECT
            PRODUCT.Name AS product_name,
            PRODUCT.Color AS product_color,
            PRODUCT.ReorderPoint,
```

```
                PRODUCT_INVENTORY.Quantity AS product_quantity
        FROM Production.Product PRODUCT
    LEFT JOIN Production.ProductInventory PRODUCT_INVENTORY
    ON PRODUCT.ProductID = PRODUCT_INVENTORY.ProductID
) PRODUCT_DATA
PIVOT
(       SUM(product_quantity)
        FOR product_color IN (SELECT Color FROM Production.Product)
) PIVOT_DATA;
```

Listing 9-4. Attempt to Use a Table Variable Within a PIVOT Statement (also
Unsuccessfully)

```
DECLARE @colors TABLE
        (color_name VARCHAR(25));

INSERT INTO @colors
        (color_name)
VALUES ('Black'), ('Blue'), ('Grey'), ('Multi'), ('Red'), ('Silver'),
('Silver/Black'), ('White'), ('Yellow');

SELECT
        *
FROM
(       SELECT
                PRODUCT.Name AS product_name,
                PRODUCT.Color AS product_color,
                PRODUCT.ReorderPoint,
                PRODUCT_INVENTORY.Quantity AS product_quantity
        FROM Production.Product PRODUCT
    LEFT JOIN Production.ProductInventory PRODUCT_INVENTORY
    ON PRODUCT.ProductID = PRODUCT_INVENTORY.ProductID
) PRODUCT_DATA
PIVOT
(       SUM(product_quantity)
        FOR product_color IN (SELECT color_name FROM @colors)
) PIVOT_DATA;
```

Both examples are logical attempts to incorporate more customizable inputs into our query. In the first example, we try to feed in all colors from `Production.Product`. If this worked, we could always use PIVOT for all values in a column, without the need to hard code them ahead of time. The second attempt uses a table variable to store a set of colors prior to executing the PIVOT statement. If this worked, we could then customize a color list prior to runtime using input from an application or person.

Unfortunately, neither syntax works, and will generate similar error messages:

```
Msg 156, Level 15, State 1, Line 50
Incorrect syntax near the keyword 'SELECT'.
Msg 102, Level 15, State 1, Line 50
Incorrect syntax near ')'.
```

These messages are not terribly helpful, but do imply that our syntax is incorrect. Our slick attempt at solving a problem didn't work, but there is another way to get past this limitation in the syntax of PIVOT: dynamic SQL! The column name list must be present in our TSQL prior to runtime, and that can be accomplished by building a command string with the column list details added in when the string is built. This will allow us to have a dynamic column list available from any source we choose. Here is a new version of our PIVOT where we use a table variable to store a list of colors, and feed it into dynamic SQL to output to a column list that we specify at runtime.

Listing 9-5. Use of Dynamic SQL and a Table Variable to Create a Variable Column List at Runtime

```
DECLARE @colors TABLE
        (color_name VARCHAR(25));

INSERT INTO @colors
        (color_name)
VALUES ('Black'), ('Grey'), ('Silver/Black'), ('White');

DECLARE @sql_command NVARCHAR(MAX);
SELECT @sql_command = '
SELECT
        *

FROM
```

```
(       SELECT
                PRODUCT.Name AS product_name,
                PRODUCT.Color AS product_color,
                PRODUCT.ReorderPoint,
                PRODUCT_INVENTORY.Quantity AS product_quantity
        FROM Production.Product PRODUCT
    LEFT JOIN Production.ProductInventory PRODUCT_INVENTORY
    ON PRODUCT.ProductID = PRODUCT_INVENTORY.ProductID
) PRODUCT_DATA
PIVOT
(       SUM(product_quantity)
        FOR product_color IN (';

SELECT @sql_command = @sql_command + '[' + color_name + '], '
FROM @colors;

SELECT @sql_command = SUBSTRING(@sql_command, 1, LEN(@sql_command) - 1);

SELECT @sql_command = @sql_command + ' )) PIVOT_DATA
';

EXEC sp_executesql @sql_command;
```

The PIVOT TSQL above is exactly the same as it was before, but we incorporate several dynamic SQL methods from earlier in this book in order to accomplish our goal. First, we generate a dynamic list of colors and add it to our command string:

```
SELECT @sql_command = @sql_command + '[' + color_name + '], '
FROM @colors;

SELECT @sql_command = SUBSTRING(@sql_command, 1, LEN(@sql_command) - 1);
```

For any number of colors in our table variable, this will append them to our command string, contained in brackets and delimited by commas. The additional SELECT statement removes the trailing comma that remains from the list generation.

Once the list of colors has been appended, we can complete the command string and execute it to get our result set.

	product_name	ReorderPoint	Black	Grey	Silver/Black	White
1	All-Purpose Bike Stand	3	NULL	NULL	NULL	NULL
2	AWC Logo Cap	3	NULL	NULL	NULL	NULL
3	Bike Wash - Dissolver	3	NULL	NULL	NULL	NULL
4	Cable Lock	3	NULL	NULL	NULL	NULL
5	Classic Vest, L	3	NULL	NULL	NULL	NULL
6	Classic Vest, M	3	NULL	NULL	NULL	NULL
7	Classic Vest, S	3	NULL	NULL	NULL	NULL
8	Fender Set - Mountain	3	NULL	NULL	NULL	NULL
9	Full-Finger Gloves, L	3	144	NULL	NULL	NULL
10	Full-Finger Gloves, M	3	108	NULL	NULL	NULL

Figure 9-3. Results of the Dynamic PIVOT in Listing 9-5

Note that columns only exist for the colors that we included in the table variable. Any products for which the color is not given in a column header will have NULLs for all new columns added by the PIVOT operation.

With this framework in place, we can tackle scenarios that were previously impossible. First, let's rewrite the previous query so that it includes ALL colors, regardless of which are added or removed in the underlying data over time. To accomplish this, all we need to do is replace the INSERT into the table variable to use a query of `Production.Product`, rather than a static list of values, as shown in Listing 9-6.

Listing 9-6. Dynamic PIVOT that Uses All Color Values in Production.Product

```
DECLARE @colors TABLE
        (color_name VARCHAR(25));

INSERT INTO @colors
        (color_name)
SELECT DISTINCT
        Product.Color
FROM Production.Product
WHERE Product.Color IS NOT NULL;

DECLARE @sql_command NVARCHAR(MAX);
SELECT  @sql_command = '
SELECT
        *
```

```
FROM
(       SELECT
                PRODUCT.Name AS product_name,
                PRODUCT.Color AS product_color,
                PRODUCT.ReorderPoint,
                PRODUCT_INVENTORY.Quantity AS product_quantity
        FROM Production.Product PRODUCT
    LEFT JOIN Production.ProductInventory PRODUCT_INVENTORY
    ON PRODUCT.ProductID = PRODUCT_INVENTORY.ProductID
) PRODUCT_DATA
PIVOT
(       SUM(product_quantity)
        FOR product_color IN (';

SELECT @sql_command = @sql_command + '[' + color_name + '], '
FROM @colors;

SELECT  @sql_command = SUBSTRING(@sql_command, 1, LEN(@sql_command) - 1);

SELECT  @sql_command = @sql_command + '         )) PIVOT_DATA
';

PRINT @sql_command;
EXEC sp_executesql @sql_command;
```

The text of the command string prior to execution shows that it looks identical to our original hard-coded PIVOT query earlier:

```
SELECT
        *
FROM
(       SELECT
                PRODUCT.Name AS product_name,
                PRODUCT.Color AS product_color,
                PRODUCT.ReorderPoint,
                PRODUCT_INVENTORY.Quantity AS product_quantity
        FROM Production.Product PRODUCT
    LEFT JOIN Production.ProductInventory PRODUCT_INVENTORY
    ON PRODUCT.ProductID = PRODUCT_INVENTORY.ProductID
```

```
) PRODUCT_DATA
PIVOT
(       SUM(product_quantity)
        FOR product_color IN ([Black], [Blue], [Grey], [Multi], [Red],
        [Silver], [Silver/Black], [White], [Yellow])) PIVOT_DATA
```

Our ultimate test is to add a few colors to Production.Product and see what happens to our command string and output when we run the dynamic PIVOT again:

```
UPDATE Production.Product
SET Product.Color = 'Fuschia'
WHERE Product.ProductID = 325 -- Decal 1
UPDATE Production.Product
SET Product.Color = 'Aquamarine'
WHERE Product.ProductID = 326 -- Decal 2
```

Here, we update two products to use new colors that were not present in AdventureWorks originally: Fuchsia and Aquamarine. With these colors added, let's run the dynamic PIVOT and review the new command string:

```
SELECT
        *
FROM
(       SELECT
                PRODUCT.Name AS product_name,
                PRODUCT.Color AS product_color,
                PRODUCT.ReorderPoint,
                PRODUCT_INVENTORY.Quantity AS product_quantity
        FROM Production.Product PRODUCT
    LEFT JOIN Production.ProductInventory PRODUCT_INVENTORY
    ON PRODUCT.ProductID = PRODUCT_INVENTORY.ProductID
) PRODUCT_DATA
PIVOT
(       SUM(product_quantity)
        FOR product_color IN ([Aquamarine], [Black], [Blue], [Fuschia],
        [Grey], [Multi], [Red], [Silver], [Silver/Black], [White],
        [Yellow] )) PIVOT_DATA
```

Note that the new colors that we added are now present in the PIVOT. Reviewing the output in Figure 9-4, we can confirm that the columns are in the result set and correctly populated based on the changes we made.

	product_name	ReorderPoint	Aquamarine	Black	Blue	Fuschia	Grey	Multi	Red	Silver	Silver/Black	White	Yellow
349	Adjustable Race	750	NULL	NULL	NULL	NULL	NULL	NULL	NULL	NULL	NULL	NULL	NULL
350	Bearing Ball	750	NULL	NULL	NULL	NULL	NULL	NULL	NULL	NULL	NULL	NULL	NULL
351	Chain Stays	750	NULL	NULL	NULL	NULL	NULL	NULL	NULL	NULL	NULL	NULL	NULL
352	Chainring	750	NULL	1684	NULL	NULL	NULL	NULL	NULL	NULL	NULL	NULL	NULL
353	Chainring Bolts	750	NULL	NULL	NULL	NULL	NULL	NULL	NULL	1136	NULL	NULL	NULL
354	Chainring Nut	750	NULL	NULL	NULL	NULL	NULL	NULL	NULL	1750	NULL	NULL	NULL
355	Cone-Shaped Race	750	NULL	NULL	NULL	NULL	NULL	NULL	NULL	NULL	NULL	NULL	NULL
356	Crown Race	750	NULL	NULL	NULL	NULL	NULL	NULL	NULL	NULL	NULL	NULL	NULL
357	Cup-Shaped Race	750	NULL	NULL	NULL	NULL	NULL	NULL	NULL	NULL	NULL	NULL	NULL
358	Decal 1	750	NULL	NULL	NULL	1750	NULL	NULL	NULL	NULL	NULL	NULL	NULL
359	Decal 2	750	1684	NULL	NULL	NULL	NULL	NULL	NULL	NULL	NULL	NULL	NULL
360	External Lock Washer 1	750	NULL	NULL	NULL	NULL	NULL	NULL	NULL	NULL	NULL	NULL	NULL

Figure 9-4. *Dynamic PIVOT with the inclusion of two new colors*

With the preceding syntax, we can make any PIVOT dynamic and supply a list of values from user input, a TSQL query, or anywhere that data can be queried from in SQL Server. This reduces the need to hard code specific column headings into stored procedure, thereby reducing maintenance costs over time. The last thing we want to worry about is adjusting TSQL or application code whenever a new color bike is added to the product inventory!

The following TSQL will clean up our changes and remove the new colors used, returning them to NULL as they originally were set:

```
UPDATE Production.Product
SET Product.Color = NULL
WHERE Product.ProductID = 325 -- Decal 1
UPDATE Production.Product
SET Product.Color = NULL
WHERE Product.ProductID = 326 -- Decal 2
```

UNPIVOT

PIVOT has its counterpart in UNPIVOT, which takes a query with a column list and reconstructs it into row data. To demonstrate this using familiar data, we will output the results of our previous example into a table for use in this section using the TSQL in Listing 9-7.

Listing 9-7. Query to Store Data for Use in a Dynamic UNPIVOT Demonstration

```
DECLARE  @sql_command NVARCHAR(MAX);
SELECT  @sql_command = '
SELECT
      *

INTO dbo.Products_By_Color
FROM
(      SELECT
              PRODUCT.Name AS product_name,
              PRODUCT.Color AS product_color,
              PRODUCT.ReorderPoint,
              PRODUCT_INVENTORY.Quantity AS product_quantity
      FROM Production.Product PRODUCT
   LEFT JOIN Production.ProductInventory PRODUCT_INVENTORY
   ON PRODUCT.ProductID = PRODUCT_INVENTORY.ProductID
) PRODUCT_DATA
PIVOT
(      SUM(product_quantity)
      FOR product_color IN ([Black], [Blue], [Grey], [Multi], [Red],
      [Silver], [Silver/Black], [White], [Yellow])) PIVOT_DATA';
Exec Sp_executesql @sql_command;
```

By adding an INTO to the SELECT, the output we reviewed will be stored in the table dbo.Products_By_Color, which will be used in our UNPIVOT testing below.

The syntax for UNPIVOT mirrors that of PIVOT and involves the use of a similar column list, with the exception that the data will be reverted to rows, removing all additional columns listed. This can be seen in Listing 9-8.

Listing 9-8. Using UNPIVOT to Revert Column Headers into Row Data

```
SELECT
      *
FROM
   (SELECT
              *
```

```
      FROM dbo.Products_By_Color) AS PRODUCTS_BY_COLOR
UNPIVOT
   (product_quantity FOR Color IN
      ([Black], [Blue], [Grey], [Multi], [Red], [Silver], [Silver/Black],
      [White], [Yellow])
) AS UNPIVOT_DATA;
```

Figure 9-5 shows a subset of the output from the preceding statement.

	product_name	ReorderPoint	product_quantity	Color
1	AWC Logo Cap	3	288	Multi
2	Classic Vest, L	3	252	Blue
3	Classic Vest, M	3	216	Blue
4	Classic Vest, S	3	180	Blue
5	Full-Finger Gloves, L	3	144	Black
6	Full-Finger Gloves, M	3	108	Black
7	Full-Finger Gloves, S	3	72	Black
8	Half-Finger Gloves, L	3	36	Black
9	Half-Finger Gloves, M	3	0	Black
10	Half-Finger Gloves, S	3	324	Black
11	Hydration Pack - 70 oz.	3	108	Silver
12	Long-Sleeve Logo Jersey, L	3	216	Multi
13	Long-Sleeve Logo Jersey, M	3	180	Multi
14	Long-Sleeve Logo Jersey, S	3	144	Multi
15	Long-Sleeve Logo Jersey, XL	3	252	Multi
16	Men's Bib-Shorts, L	3	144	Multi
17	Men's Bib-Shorts, M	3	108	Multi
18	Men's Bib-Shorts, S	3	72	Multi

Figure 9-5. Output from the UNPIVOT statement in Listing 9-8

All of the new columns that we introduced in the last section have been removed and their corresponding names inserted into the new Color column. The syntax for UNPIVOT involves three additional bits of syntax that are worth describing in detail:

1. A new column for the unpivoted quantity data. In this case, we called the new column `product_quantity`, though any name could be used. When using UNPIVOT, there is no need to provide an aggregation, as all values are moved into this column whether duplicated or not.

2. The new column that will contain the previous multitude of pivoted column names must be provided. In this example, we name it "Color."

3. A column list must be provided, similar to when we wrote a PIVOT statement. Each column in this list will be included within rows of the result set. Any omitted column names will not be represented in the result set.

The results from this query are not the same as our original data. It is important to emphasize that UNPIVOT is not simply the opposite of PIVOT, and that applying one after the other will rarely result in identical sets of data. In the preceding example, there are two important differences between this data and what we began with at the start of the chapter.

First, NULLs have been eliminated. Any product with no color defined was dropped out of the result set. The results show all product-color combinations for which a color in the list we provided was present and had a quantity defined. The second difference involves the quantities themselves. When we apply PIVOT to a set of data, we supply an aggregate to process multiple rows with the same value. Once quantities have been summed, there is no way for us to "un-sum" them. The results of the UNPIVOT contain product quantity totals that represent multiple products from the original data in `production.Product`.

Now that we have addressed the important differences between PIVOT, UNPIVOT, and the ways in which data is handled by each, we can work on making UNPIVOT more flexible.

As before, we want to be able to apply UNPIVOT from a dynamic list of column names, and not be forced to supply values ahead of time in our code. This allows us to make data or schema changes at will without having to adjust UNPIVOT code each and every time. Our first challenge is to generate a list of colors given a group of columns in a table, rather than row data. To get all of the columns, there are a few options available to us. The first would be to go back to `Production.Product` and use the colors from that table to fuel this query, as seen in Listing 9-9.

Listing 9-9. A Dynamic UNPIVOT, Using Original Row Data to Supply Color Names

```
DECLARE @colors TABLE
        (color_name VARCHAR(25));

INSERT INTO @colors
        (color_name)
SELECT DISTINCT
        Product.Color
FROM Production.Product
WHERE Product.Color IS NOT NULL;

DECLARE @sql_command NVARCHAR(MAX);
SELECT  @sql_command = '
SELECT
        *
FROM
   (SELECT
                *
        FROM dbo.Products_By_Color) AS PRODUCTS_BY_COLOR
UNPIVOT
   (product_quantity FOR Color IN
        (';

SELECT @sql_command = @sql_command + '[' + color_name + '], '
FROM @colors;

SELECT  @sql_command = SUBSTRING(@sql_command, 1, LEN(@sql_command) - 1);

SELECT  @sql_command = @sql_command + '        )) AS UNPIVOT_DATA;
';

EXEC sp_executesql @sql_command;
```

This approach works and will provide the same output as earlier, but has a distinct limitation in that our color list from earlier may not apply here. If it doesn't, then we need to collect column name data from the table schema itself and use that to power our UNPIVOT. This can be accomplished by querying the **sys.tables** and **sys.columns** system views, which provide information about the structure and names of our tables and columns. There are other system objects available that can provide similar data, such as INFORMATION_SCHEMA.COLUMNS, but for our example here we'll stick to the two aforementioned views, which reference data in sys.objects. This can be seen in Listing 9-10.

Listing 9-10. A Dynamic UNPIVOT, Using Schema Metadata to Supply Color Names

```
DECLARE @colors TABLE
        (color_name VARCHAR(25));

INSERT INTO @colors
        (color_name)
SELECT
        columns.name
FROM sys.tables
INNER JOIN sys.columns
ON columns.object_id = tables.object_id
WHERE tables.name = 'Products_By_Color'
AND columns.name NOT IN ('product_name', 'ReorderPoint');

DECLARE @sql_command NVARCHAR(MAX);
SELECT  @sql_command = '
SELECT
        *
FROM
   (SELECT
              *
      FROM dbo.Products_By_Color) AS PRODUCTS_BY_COLOR
UNPIVOT
    (product_quantity FOR Color IN
       (';

SELECT @sql_command = @sql_command + '[' + color_name + '], '
FROM @colors;

SELECT  @sql_command = SUBSTRING(@sql_command, 1, LEN(@sql_command) - 1);
```

```
SELECT  @sql_command = @sql_command + '          )) AS UNPIVOT_DATA;
';
```

```
EXEC sp_executesql @sql_command;
```

Everything in this example is the same as the previous one, except for the collection of color data, which uses the column names for the table dbo.Products_By_Color as provided by sys.columns. Note that we need to provide an exceptions list here that includes any columns that we do not wish to UNPIVOT. In this example, there are two additional columns that are not colors and that we do not wish to convert into row data: product_name and ReorderPoint. If we forget these exceptions, we might get unexpected output, or an error message such as this:

```
Msg 8167, Level 16, State 1, Line 329
The type of column "ReorderPoint" conflicts with the type of other columns
specified in the UNPIVOT list.
```

In this case, we included columns of different data types in the UNPIVOT. While the quantities listed under the color columns are all of type INT, ReorderPoint is a SMALLINT and product_name is NVARCHAR(50). The exceptions can be hard coded as we have done previously, or passed in as variables into wherever the TSQL for the UNPIVOT runs from.

Additional Examples

The functionality demonstrated above was perfect for teaching the basics of PIVOT and UNPIVOT, as well as integrating dynamic SQL into their usage. A very common real-world use of these operators is to produce accounting data that is distributed by month, quarter, or year in column headers. For example, what if we wanted to return sales data with column headings per quarter? We can integrate PIVOT into a common table expression, which allows us to set up financial data that we can then transform into columnar data for reporting or further analysis. This example can be seen in Listing 9-11.

Listing 9-11. Using PIVOT to Group Sales Data by Quarter

```
WITH CTE_SALES AS (
        SELECT
                DATEPART(QUARTER, OrderDate) AS order_quarter,
```

```
                DATEPART(YEAR, OrderDate) AS order_year,
                TotalDue
        FROM Sales.SalesOrderHeader)
SELECT
        *
FROM
(       SELECT
                *
        FROM CTE_SALES
) PRODUCT_DATA
PIVOT
(       SUM(TotalDue)
        FOR order_quarter IN ([1], [2], [3], [4])
) PIVOT_DATA
ORDER BY order_year ASC;
```

The result of the query in Listing 9-11 can be seen in the small result set in Figure 9-6.

	order_year	1	2	3	4
1	2011	NULL	1074117.4188	5647550.6633	7434031.4429
2	2012	9443736.8161	9935495.1729	10164406.8281	8132061.4949
3	2013	8771886.3577	12225061.383	14339319.1851	13629621.0374
4	2014	14373277.4766	8046220.8391	NULL	NULL

Figure 9-6. *Using PIVOT to obtain sales by quarter*

Each quarter is given its own column, with sales totals aggregated in each row below. Instances of NULL represent scenarios where there was no data in the underlying for those specific time periods. We could also write the PIVOT query to return all quarters, including year, as a column header, as seen in Listing 9-12.

Listing 9-12. Using PIVOT to Group Sales Data by Quarter and Year in a Single Result Row

```
WITH CTE_SALES AS (
        SELECT
                'Totals' AS Totals,
                'Q' + CAST(DATEPART(QUARTER, OrderDate) AS VARCHAR(1)) + '-' +
```

```
                    CAST(DATEPART(YEAR, OrderDate) AS VARCHAR(4)) AS
                    quarter_and_year,
              TotalDue
        FROM Sales.SalesOrderHeader)
SELECT
        *
FROM
(       SELECT
               *
        FROM CTE_SALES
) PRODUCT_DATA
PIVOT
(       SUM(TotalDue)
        FOR quarter_and_year IN ([Q2-2011], [Q3-2011], [Q4-2011], [Q1-2012],
                                 [Q2-2012], [Q3-2012], [Q4-2012], [Q1-2013],
                                 [Q2-2013], [Q3-2013], [Q4-2013], [Q1-2014],
                                 [Q2-2014])
) PIVOT_DATA
```

By combining quarter and year into a single string, we can condense our data into a single row with one column per quarter, including the year. The column Totals is included so that we have some sort of row header, but it is not necessary to successfully retrieve our result set.

This syntax introduces the same problem we had earlier, though, in that we were forced to hard code a list of quarters into the TSQL. If new data is added, then our query will not account for it and the result set will be incomplete. Dynamic SQL can rescue us again, by allowing us to declare a list of quarters ahead of time and then integrate it into a command string that will use PIVOT to crunch our source data appropriately, regardless of the dates that are included. This is shown in Listing 9-13.

Listing 9-13. Dynamic PIVOT Used to Return any Number of Quarters of Financial Data

```
DECLARE @quarters TABLE
        (quarter_and_year NVARCHAR(7));

INSERT INTO @quarters
        (quarter_and_year)
```

```sql
SELECT DISTINCT
        'Q' + CAST(DATEPART(QUARTER, OrderDate) AS VARCHAR(1)) + '-' +
                CAST(DATEPART(YEAR, OrderDate) AS VARCHAR(4))
FROM Sales.SalesOrderHeader

DECLARE @sql_command NVARCHAR(MAX);

SELECT @sql_command = '
WITH CTE_SALES AS (
        SELECT
                "Totals" AS Totals,
                "Q" + CAST(DATEPART(QUARTER, OrderDate) AS VARCHAR(1)) + "-" +
                        CAST(DATEPART(YEAR, OrderDate) AS VARCHAR(4)) AS
                        quarter_and_year,
                TotalDue
        FROM Sales.SalesOrderHeader)
SELECT
        *
FROM
(       SELECT
                *
        FROM CTE_SALES
) PRODUCT_DATA
PIVOT
(       SUM(TotalDue)
        FOR quarter_and_year IN ('

SELECT @sql_command = @sql_command + '[' + quarter_and_year + '], '
FROM @quarters;

SELECT  @sql_command = SUBSTRING(@sql_command, 1, LEN(@sql_command) - 1);

SELECT  @sql_command = @sql_command + '         )) PIVOT_DATA
';

PRINT @sql_command;
EXEC sp_executesql @sql_command;
```

Multiple PIVOT Operators

For our next example, we'll illustrate a more advanced usage of PIVOT. Whereas previously we only used PIVOT to operate on a single column, it is possible to apply this operator to multiple columns of distinct values. Let's say that we wanted to crunch our product data by color and by safety stock level? This can be done using a single query, as follows in Listing 9-14.

Listing 9-14. Using Multiple PIVOT Operators in a Single TSQL Statement

```
SELECT
        *
FROM
(       SELECT
                PRODUCT.Name AS product_name,
                PRODUCT.Color AS product_color,
                PRODUCT.ReorderPoint,
                PRODUCT_INVENTORY.Quantity AS product_quantity,
                PRODUCT.SafetyStockLevel
        FROM Production.Product PRODUCT
    LEFT JOIN Production.ProductInventory PRODUCT_INVENTORY
    ON PRODUCT.ProductID = PRODUCT_INVENTORY.ProductID
) PRODUCT_DATA
PIVOT
(       SUM(product_quantity)
        FOR product_color IN ([Black], [Blue], [Grey], [Multi], [Red],
        [Silver], [Silver/Black], [White], [Yellow])
) PIVOT_DATA_COLOR
PIVOT
(       COUNT(SafetyStockLevel)
        FOR SafetyStockLevel IN ([4], [60], [100], [500], [800], [1000])
) PIVOT_DATA_LEVEL
```

The query above will return the results shown in figure 9-7.

	product_name	ReorderPoint	Black	Blue	Grey	Multi	Red	Silver	Silver/Black	White	Yellow	4	60	100	500	800	1000
1	Adjustable Race	750	NULL	NULL	NULL	NULL	NULL	NULL	NULL	NULL	NULL	0	0	0	0	0	1
2	All-Purpose Bike Stand	3	NULL	NULL	NULL	NULL	NULL	NULL	NULL	NULL	NULL	1	0	0	0	0	0
3	AWC Logo Cap	3	NULL	NULL	NULL	288	NULL	NULL	NULL	NULL	NULL	1	0	0	0	0	0
4	BB Ball Bearing	600	NULL	NULL	NULL	NULL	NULL	NULL	NULL	NULL	NULL	0	0	0	0	1	0
5	Bearing Ball	750	NULL	NULL	NULL	NULL	NULL	NULL	NULL	NULL	NULL	0	0	0	0	0	1
6	Bike Wash - Dissolver	3	NULL	NULL	NULL	NULL	NULL	NULL	NULL	NULL	NULL	1	0	0	0	0	0
7	Blade	600	NULL	NULL	NULL	NULL	NULL	NULL	NULL	NULL	NULL	0	0	0	0	1	0
8	Cable Lock	3	NULL	NULL	NULL	NULL	NULL	NULL	NULL	NULL	NULL	1	0	0	0	0	0
9	Chain	375	NULL	NULL	NULL	NULL	NULL	589	NULL	NULL	NULL	0	0	0	1	0	0
10	Chain Stays	750	NULL	NULL	NULL	NULL	NULL	NULL	NULL	NULL	NULL	0	0	0	0	0	1

***Figure 9-7.** Results of a query that uses two PIVOT operators for data aggregation*

A new set of columns has been added to our result set with the number of times a particular SafetyStockLevel value matches the ones provided in our list. This can be a very handy trick if we want to report on multiple metrics side by side and wish to do so in a single query, rather than joining multiple result sets together.

We can implement dynamic SQL just as we did before to ensure that all list values for both metrics are correctly accounted for. When we do this, we will need to include a separate table variable for SafetyStockLevel values, in addition to those for Color, as shown in Listing 9-15.

***Listing 9-15.** Using Multiple PIVOT Operators with Dynamic SQL*

```
DECLARE @colors TABLE
        (color_name VARCHAR(25));

INSERT INTO @colors
        (color_name)
SELECT DISTINCT
        Product.Color
FROM Production.Product
WHERE Product.Color IS NOT NULL;

DECLARE @stock_levels TABLE
        (safety_stock_level SMALLINT);

INSERT INTO @stock_levels
SELECT DISTINCT
        Product.SafetyStockLevel
FROM Production.Product;
DECLARE @sql_command NVARCHAR(MAX);
```

```
SELECT  @sql_command = '
SELECT
      *
FROM
(       SELECT
              PRODUCT.Name AS product_name,
              PRODUCT.Color AS product_color,
              PRODUCT.ReorderPoint,
              PRODUCT_INVENTORY.Quantity AS product_quantity,
              PRODUCT.SafetyStockLevel
      FROM Production.Product PRODUCT
   LEFT JOIN Production.ProductInventory PRODUCT_INVENTORY
   ON PRODUCT.ProductID = PRODUCT_INVENTORY.ProductID
) PRODUCT_DATA
PIVOT
(       SUM(product_quantity)
      FOR product_color IN (';

SELECT @sql_command = @sql_command + '[' + color_name + '], '
FROM @colors;

SELECT  @sql_command = SUBSTRING(@sql_command, 1, LEN(@sql_command) - 1);

SELECT  @sql_command = @sql_command + '          )) PIVOT_DATA_COLOR
PIVOT
(       COUNT(SafetyStockLevel)
      FOR SafetyStockLevel IN (';

SELECT @sql_command = @sql_command + '[' + CAST(safety_stock_level AS
NVARCHAR) + '], '
FROM @stock_levels;

SELECT  @sql_command = SUBSTRING(@sql_command, 1, LEN(@sql_command) - 1);

SELECT  @sql_command = @sql_command + '          )) PIVOT_DATA_LEVEL
';
PRINT @sql_command;
EXEC sp_executesql @sql_command;
```

The result set is exactly the same as it was previously. We can verify that we didn't make any mistakes by reviewing the text of the command string:

```
SELECT
        *
FROM
(        SELECT
                PRODUCT.Name AS product_name,
                PRODUCT.Color AS product_color,
                PRODUCT.ReorderPoint,
                PRODUCT_INVENTORY.Quantity AS product_quantity,
                PRODUCT.SafetyStockLevel
        FROM Production.Product PRODUCT
    LEFT JOIN Production.ProductInventory PRODUCT_INVENTORY
    ON PRODUCT.ProductID = PRODUCT_INVENTORY.ProductID
) PRODUCT_DATA
PIVOT
(        SUM(product_quantity)
        FOR product_color IN ([Black], [Blue], [Grey], [Multi], [Red],
        [Silver], [Silver/Black], [White], [Yellow])) PIVOT_DATA_COLOR
PIVOT
(        COUNT(SafetyStockLevel)
        FOR SafetyStockLevel IN ([4], [60], [100], [500], [800], [1000]))
        PIVOT_DATA_LEVEL
```

Combining multiple PIVOT operators with dynamic SQL provides an immense amount of flexibility when generating columnar data given the contents of multiple columns. By producing a result set in a single query, we ensure relational integrity and that we didn't make any mistakes when outputting data to intermediate locations. The syntax is the same as it was for a single PIVOT, and does not become much more complex as we add further instances of it.

Multiple UNPIVOT Operators

For the final example of this chapter, we'll build on our work thus far to UNPIVOT the result set from before. This will be accomplished using multiple UNPIVOT operators. Keep in mind that the result set for this operation will not be the same as the original input data from the start of the last example. While the results of the UNPIVOT will be meaningful, it is important to remember that applying PIVOT and UNPIVOT to a data set is unlikely to return equivalent results as the original data set. Granularity is often lost and cannot be reconstituted, regardless of how fancy we get with our TSQL skills!

Our first step is to take the data from the last example and store it in a table to reuse it in our UNPIVOT:

```
SELECT
        *
INTO dbo.Products_By_Color_and_Stock_Level
FROM
(       SELECT
                PRODUCT.Name AS product_name,
                PRODUCT.Color AS product_color,
                PRODUCT.ReorderPoint,
                PRODUCT_INVENTORY.Quantity AS product_quantity,
                PRODUCT.SafetyStockLevel
        FROM Production.Product PRODUCT
    LEFT JOIN Production.ProductInventory PRODUCT_INVENTORY
    ON PRODUCT.ProductID = PRODUCT_INVENTORY.ProductID
) PRODUCT_DATA
PIVOT
(       SUM(product_quantity)
        FOR product_color IN ([Black], [Blue], [Grey], [Multi], [Red],
        [Silver], [Silver/Black], [White], [Yellow])) PIVOT_DATA_COLOR
PIVOT
(       COUNT(SafetyStockLevel)
        FOR SafetyStockLevel IN ([4], [60], [100], [500], [800], [1000]))
        PIVOT_DATA_LEVEL;
```

The table Products_By_Color_and_Stock_Level is created to store the pivoted output that we will work with for the duration of this chapter. Our first attempt at an UNPIVOT is shown in Listing 9-16.

Listing 9-16. First Attempt at Using Two UNPIVOT Operators in a Single
Statement

```
SELECT
      *
FROM
   (SELECT
              *
      FROM dbo.Products_By_Color_and_Stock_Level) AS PRODUCTS_BY_COLOR_
      AND_STOCK_LEVEL
UNPIVOT
   (product_quantity FOR Color IN
      ([Black], [Blue], [Grey], [Multi], [Red], [Silver], [Silver/Black],
      [White], [Yellow])
) AS UNPIVOT_DATA_COLOR
UNPIVOT
   (safety_stock_level FOR SafetyStockLevel IN
      ([4], [60], [100], [500], [800], [1000])
) AS UNPIVOT_DATA_STOCK_LEVEL;
```

The preceding query returns results but they are a bit suspect, as seen in the result
set in Figure 9-8.

	product_name	ReorderPoint	product_quantity	Color	safety_stock_level	SafetyStockLevel
1	AWC Logo Cap	3	288	Multi	1	4
2	AWC Logo Cap	3	288	Multi	0	60
3	AWC Logo Cap	3	288	Multi	0	100
4	AWC Logo Cap	3	288	Multi	0	500
5	AWC Logo Cap	3	288	Multi	0	800
6	AWC Logo Cap	3	288	Multi	0	1000
7	Chain	375	589	Silver	0	4
8	Chain	375	589	Silver	0	60
9	Chain	375	589	Silver	0	100
10	Chain	375	589	Silver	1	500
11	Chain	375	589	Silver	0	800
12	Chain	375	589	Silver	0	1000
13	Chainring	750	1684	Black	0	4

Figure 9-8. *Results from an improperly constructed query with two UNPIVOT
operators*

Note that we receive six rows back for each product. Since the safety stock levels were defined as non-NULL counts, the UNPIVOT operation sees all as valid values and returns rows for each. Ideally we want the column names pivoted into row values for both colors and stock levels, but with the assumption that zero values are omitted for all stock levels. There are a variety of ways to fix this, and we will do so using an additional WHERE clause to remove the zeroes altogether, as shown in Listing 9-17.

Listing 9-17. UNPIVOT Example, with Zero Values Removed

```
SELECT
        product_name,
        ReorderPoint,
        product_quantity,
        Color,
        SafetyStockLevel
FROM
    (SELECT
                *
        FROM dbo.Products_By_Color_and_Stock_Level) AS PRODUCTS_BY_COLOR_
        AND_STOCK_LEVEL
UNPIVOT
    (product_quantity FOR Color IN
        ([Black], [Blue], [Grey], [Multi], [Red], [Silver], [Silver/Black],
        [White], [Yellow])
) AS UNPIVOT_DATA_COLOR
UNPIVOT
    (safety_stock_level FOR SafetyStockLevel IN
        ([4], [60], [100], [500], [800], [1000])
) AS UNPIVOT_DATA_STOCK_LEVEL
WHERE safety_stock_level <> 0;
```

By filtering on safety_stock_level <> 0, we remove the zeroes. In addition, we explicitly choose the columns for the output set such that safety_stock_level is not included, as its contents are no longer important to the result set and will only contain ones. The results now look cleaner and more like what we expected the first time.

	product_name	ReorderPoint	product_quantity	Color	SafetyStockLevel
1	AWC Logo Cap	3	288	Multi	4
2	Chain	375	589	Silver	500
3	Chainring	750	1684	Black	1000
4	Chainring Bolts	750	1136	Silver	1000
5	Chainring Nut	750	1750	Silver	1000
6	Classic Vest, L	3	252	Blue	4
7	Classic Vest, M	3	216	Blue	4
8	Classic Vest, S	3	180	Blue	4
9	Freewheel	375	844	Silver	500
10	Front Brakes	375	767	Silver	500
11	Front Derailleur	375	853	Silver	500

Figure 9-9. *Results from the corrected UNPIVOT query in Listing 9-17*

Each column is now populated with meaningful values, removing zero values and the extra placeholder `safety_stock_level` column.

Now that we have a working query with multiple UNPIVOT operators, we can apply dynamic SQL to it to return results for any values of Color or `SafetyStockLevel` found in the `Products_By_Color_and_Stock_Level` table previously created. This fun query can be found in Listing 9-18.

Listing 9-18. Dynamic SQL Used in Conjunction with Multiple UNPIVOT Operators

```
DECLARE @colors TABLE
        (color_name VARCHAR(25));

INSERT INTO @colors
        (color_name)
SELECT
        columns.name
FROM sys.tables
INNER JOIN sys.columns
ON columns.object_id = tables.object_id
WHERE tables.name = 'Products_By_Color_and_Stock_Level'
AND columns.name NOT IN ('product_name', 'ReorderPoint')
AND ISNUMERIC(columns.name) = 0;
```

```sql
DECLARE @stock_levels TABLE
        (safety_stock_level SMALLINT);

INSERT INTO @stock_levels
SELECT
        columns.name
FROM sys.tables
INNER JOIN sys.columns
ON columns.object_id = tables.object_id
WHERE tables.name = 'Products_By_Color_and_Stock_Level'
AND columns.name NOT IN ('product_name', 'ReorderPoint')
AND ISNUMERIC(columns.name) = 1;

DECLARE @sql_command NVARCHAR(MAX);
SELECT  @sql_command = '
SELECT
        product_name,
        ReorderPoint,
        product_quantity,
        Color,
        SafetyStockLevel
FROM
   (SELECT
                *
        FROM dbo.Products_By_Color_and_Stock_Level) AS PRODUCTS_BY_COLOR_
        AND_STOCK_LEVEL
UNPIVOT
   (product_quantity FOR Color IN
      (';
SELECT @sql_command = @sql_command + '[' + color_name + '], '
FROM @colors;

SELECT  @sql_command = SUBSTRING(@sql_command, 1, LEN(@sql_command) - 1);

SELECT  @sql_command = @sql_command + '          )) AS UNPIVOT_DATA_COLOR
UNPIVOT
   (safety_stock_level FOR SafetyStockLevel IN
      ('
```

```
SELECT @sql_command = @sql_command + '[' + CAST(safety_stock_level  AS
NVARCHAR) + '], '
FROM @stock_levels;

SELECT  @sql_command = SUBSTRING(@sql_command, 1, LEN(@sql_command) - 1);

SELECT  @sql_command = @sql_command + '         )) AS UNPIVOT_DATA_STOCK_
LEVEL
WHERE safety_stock_level <> 0;';
PRINT @sql_command;
EXEC sp_executesql @sql_command;
```

The first challenge is parsing the column names into each table variable for use later on. In this case we are fortunate in that the colors are all string data, whereas the stock levels are all numeric. By checking whether the column name is numeric, we can split the column names into two meaningful lists. In the event that the column names could not easily be separated, we could separate the initial data into multiple holding tables, rather than putting it all into Products_By_Color_and_Stock_Level.

In an effort to avoid adding more complexity, a potentially better way to divide the columns would be to tag each with a meaningful name. For the preceding example, colors could be prefixed with "*Color:*" and stock levels prefixed with "*StockLevel:*." When we filter column names for each table variable of possible values, the prefixes could be easily checked instead. Since we determine the structure of those prefixes, we can ensure they are unique, meaningful, and allow us to maintain our data in a single holding table.

The command string for the preceding UNPIVOT operation will look like this:

```
SELECT
        product_name,
        ReorderPoint,
        product_quantity,
        Color,
        SafetyStockLevel
FROM
    (SELECT
            *
        FROM dbo.Products_By_Color_and_Stock_Level) AS PRODUCTS_BY_COLOR_
        AND_STOCK_LEVEL
```

```
UNPIVOT
    (product_quantity FOR Color IN
      ([Black], [Blue], [Grey], [Multi], [Red], [Silver], [Silver/Black],
      [White], [Yellow]         )) AS UNPIVOT_DATA_COLOR
UNPIVOT
    (safety_stock_level FOR SafetyStockLevel IN
      ([4], [60], [100], [500], [800], [1000])) AS UNPIVOT_DATA_STOCK_LEVEL
      WHERE safety_stock_level <> 0;
```

This TSQL, with minor formatting differences, is identical to the statement that we tested before, in which dynamic SQL was not used. The result set is also identical to what we returned previously. Note the row count of the results that we have generated, as seen in Figure 9-10.

Figure 9-10. *Row count from the UNPIVOT query in Listing 9-18*

There were a total of 184 rows returned, which is far smaller than the size of the original data set that we worked with. Our original data, taken from Production.Product and Production.ProductInventory, contained 1,141 rows. The results of the PIVOT operations reduced that count to 504 rows. With each operation, the granularity of our data set is reduced as we aggregate the results. As such, it is important to remember that PIVOT and UNPIVOT, even when used one after the other, will generally not restore a data set into its original form. Therefore, use these transformations as methods to acquire reporting data efficiently, but not to reconstruct or validate data. While it is possible to build sequences of PIVOT and UNPIVOT operations that can reverse data into its original structure and contents, it is unlikely to be a useful exercise.

Utilizing multiple UNPIVOT operations can allow a complex reporting data set to be reverted into summary data for use in further reports or as a way to input columnar data into a transactional system as row data. Utilizing dynamic SQL allows for all possible column values to be efficiently accounted for, even if the set of columns can change over time!

Classification Using PIVOT and CASE

Pivot can be used to organize data, taking a range of values and sorting them into groups that be reported on as needed. This allows us to dynamically generate a list of categories and apply rules to our data to populate those categories. Consider the example in Listing 9-19.

Listing 9-19. Using CASE to Group Categories Prior to the PIVOT Operation

```
DECLARE @colors TABLE
        (color_name VARCHAR(25));

INSERT INTO @colors
        (color_name)
VALUES
        ('Standard Color'),
        ('Other'),
        ('Undefined');

DECLARE @sql_command NVARCHAR(MAX);
SELECT @sql_command = '
SELECT
        *
FROM
(        SELECT
                PRODUCT.Name AS product_name,
                CASE WHEN PRODUCT.Color IS NULL THEN "Undefined"
                        WHEN PRODUCT.Color IN ("White", "Black", "Grey",
                        "Silver/Black") THEN "Other"
                        ELSE "Standard Color"
                END AS product_color,
                PRODUCT.ReorderPoint,
                PRODUCT_INVENTORY.Quantity AS product_quantity
        FROM Production.Product PRODUCT
    LEFT JOIN Production.ProductInventory PRODUCT_INVENTORY
    ON PRODUCT.ProductID = PRODUCT_INVENTORY.ProductID
) PRODUCT_DATA
```

```
PIVOT
(       SUM(product_quantity)
       FOR product_color IN (';
SELECT @sql_command = @sql_command + '[' + color_name + '], '
FROM @colors;

SELECT @sql_command = SUBSTRING(@sql_command, 1, LEN(@sql_command) - 1);

SELECT @sql_command = @sql_command + ' )) PIVOT_DATA
';

EXEC sp_executesql @sql_command;
```

In this script, we defined a set of categories up front, rather than a full list of colors. These categories discern between monochromatic colors, other colors, and undefined colors (that have NULL for Color). By applying PIVOT to a CASE statement, we can easily organize the results into a customized set of categories of our choosing. The results of this categorization are shown in Figure 9-11.

	product_name	ReorderPoint	Standard Color	Other	Undefined
1	All-Purpose Bike Stand	3	NULL	NULL	144
2	AWC Logo Cap	3	288	NULL	NULL
3	Bike Wash - Dissolver	3	NULL	NULL	36
4	Cable Lock	3	NULL	NULL	252
5	Classic Vest, L	3	252	NULL	NULL
6	Classic Vest, M	3	216	NULL	NULL
7	Classic Vest, S	3	180	NULL	NULL
8	Fender Set - Mountain	3	NULL	NULL	108

Figure 9-11. *Results of categorization using PIVOT over a CASE statement*

Instead of getting a result set with a column per color, the colors are aggregated into the categories we supplied. In this example, we hard coded a set of three categories, but they could just as easily be supplied by a query that pulls categories from a relevant metadata table.

This allows us to crunch meaningful results from our data prior to the creation of columns. In addition to saving us time later, we can get a more predictable result set.

This is especially valuable if there is a large number of possible colors. We may not want a result set with a hundred columns, but a more organized set of sixteen standard ones would be acceptable.

The subquery that we PIVOT can have any operators applied to it. CASE is one example, but we could apply any functions to our input data to stage it for processing. Data functions, string manipulation, and mathematical operators can be applied as needed, as well as CAST/CONVERT to turn our data set into exactly what we want prior to converting row data into columnar data. Ultimately, this will save us time and effort, as we will have far less work to do with our results because they will already be in a friendly and easy-to-consume format.

Conclusion

PIVOT and UNPIVOT are often seen as advanced or finicky operators to be avoided whenever possible. For the use cases presented, though, they can provide large amounts of data quickly in an atomic and set-based approach. As a performance bonus, there is no need to implement loops, cursors, or other iterative solutions that could run slowly or be resource intensive on larger volumes of data.

The biggest challenge with these operators is that column lists must be explicitly provided prior to runtime. Hard coding these values greatly increases related technical debt by forcing us to keep track of and update these values whenever related application or database changes occur. This maintenance cost is high and presents opportunities for software bugs to manifest themselves that would be difficult to avoid and frustrating to diagnose.

Implementing dynamic SQL in conjunction with PIVOT or UNPIVOT allows us to generate column lists at runtime based on whatever criteria the developer chooses to apply. So long as this logic is relevant, there will be no need to adjust stored procedures or code when new values are added or old ones removed.

CHAPTER 10

Solving Common Problems

Dynamic SQL presents a unique opportunity to take common database problems or limitations and solve them quickly. Oftentimes we run into frustrating situations where we are managing different databases, schemas, or settings, and there is no easy way to make changes to a mixed set of objects. This chapter provides an opportunity to explore some examples of situations where dynamic SQL can resolve complex situations. In addition, we will provide general guidelines and techniques that could apply to any similar database problem.

Collation Conflicts

Database collations in SQL Server provide a set of rules that are used when sorting or comparing data. The following rules may be applied to data when a collation is specified:

- *Case sensitivity*: When selected, lowercase letters will always sort ahead of capital letters, otherwise they will be the same, for sorting and filtering purposes.

- *Accent sensitivity*: When this option is selected, accented characters are treated distinctly from unaccented characters when sorted or compared.

- *Width sensitivity*: This option specifies whether full-width and half-width characters are treated equally when sorted or compared.

- *Kana sensitivity*: In Japanese, Hiragana and Katakana characters will be sorted and compared as different characters when this option is selected.

- *Variation-selector-sensitivity*: In Japanese, allows different ideographic variation selectors to be differentiated between.

© Edward Pollack 2019
E. Pollack, *Dynamic SQL*, https://doi.org/10.1007/978-1-4842-4318-3_10

Different applications may require different collations to manage their data effectively. It is less expensive to specify an accurate collection in the database than to constantly sort and check rules in the application. For example, if case sensitivity is required on all strings, using a case sensitive collation will be more efficient than an application validating the case of characters in all strings it reads.

Collations may be used to manage multiple languages or character sets in applications that are used worldwide. This ensures that all users have a positive experience when reading data. Imagine a scenario in which a sorted list of names had the letter K before the letter C. This problem is common in other languages when we do not properly manage sorting via a collation (or some other method).

The Problem

SQL Server will prevent direct assignments or comparisons between string data of different collations. This is by design, as comparing two different rule sets without a conversion has no obvious resolution, and SQL Server would prefer to prevent this than make assumptions that could be incorrect. If we are working with data in multiple collations, we must account for the differences to ensure that we act on it according to the correct business logic.

To test collations, we will create a new database, a new table within it, and populate it with data from AdventureWorks, as seen in Listing 10-1.

Listing 10-1. Building a Test Database for Collation Testing

```
IF EXISTS (SELECT * FROM sys.databases WHERE name = 'Collation_Test')
BEGIN
        DROP DATABASE Collation_Test;
END
GO

CREATE DATABASE Collation_Test COLLATE Traditional_Spanish_CI_AS;
GO
USE Collation_Test;
GO
```

```
CREATE TABLE dbo.Spanish_Employees
(       BusinessEntityID INT NOT NULL,
        NationalIDNumber NVARCHAR(15) NOT NULL,
        LoginID NVARCHAR(256) NOT NULL,
        OrganizationNode HIERARCHYID NULL,
        OrganizationLevel SMALLINT NULL,
        JobTitle NVARCHAR(50) NOT NULL,
        BirthDate DATE NOT NULL,
        MaritalStatus NCHAR(1) NOT NULL,
        Gender NCHAR(1) NOT NULL,
        HireDate DATE NOT NULL,
        SalariedFlag BIT NOT NULL,
        VacationHours SMALLINT NOT NULL,
        SickLeaveHours SMALLINT NOT NULL,
        CurrentFlag BIT NOT NULL,
        rowguid UNIQUEIDENTIFIER ROWGUIDCOL NOT NULL,
        ModifiedDate DATETIME NOT NULL,);
GO

INSERT INTO Collation_Test.dbo.Spanish_Employees
SELECT
        *
FROM AdventureWorks2016CTP3.HumanResources.Employee;
```

Note that when we created the database Collation_Test, it was explicitly given the collation Traditional_Spanish_CI_AS. All strings in this database will, by default, be stored and sorted in this new collation, rather than the instance default or the settings found on other databases. On my SQL Server, the default collation is SQL_Latin1_General_CP1_CI_AS. This can be verified in the server properties in the GUI, as shown in Figure 10-1.

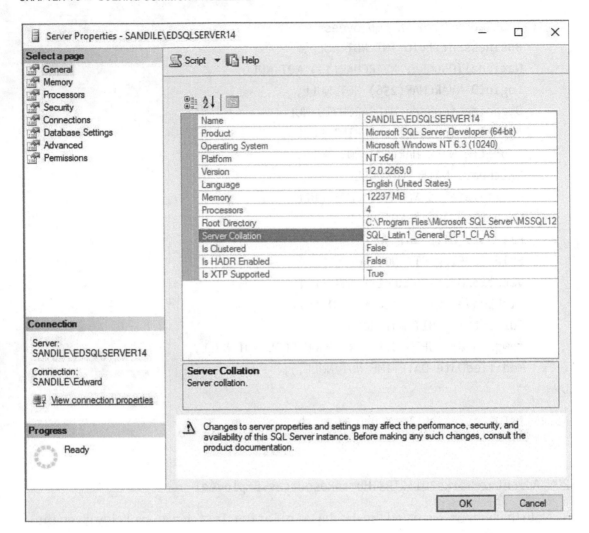

Figure 10-1. *Default server collation, as seen in the SQL Server Properties window*

Under "Server Collation," the default for my server can be found. This is the collation that will be used on any new database that is created in which another collation is not supplied. This can also be verified with TSQL:

```
SELECT SERVERPROPERTY('Collation') AS ServerDefaultCollation;
```

The resulting collation is the same as seen previously in the GUI and can be verified in Figure 10-2.

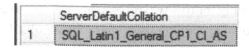

	ServerDefaultCollation
1	SQL_Latin1_General_CP1_CI_AS

Figure 10-2. *The default collation on my test server*

To illustrate one of the differences between different collations, we will look at the
`HumanResources.Employee` table, focusing on the `JobTitle` column within the original
table and the newly created one that is collated using Traditional Spanish. Listing 10-2
shows each of these queries.

Listing 10-2. Two Test Queries, Illustrating Differences in Two Distinct Collations

```
SELECT
      *
FROM AdventureWorks2016CTP3.HumanResources.Employee
WHERE JobTitle LIKE 'C%'
ORDER BY JobTitle;

SELECT
      *
FROM Collation_Test.dbo.Spanish_Employees
WHERE JobTitle LIKE 'C%'
ORDER BY JobTitle;
```

The results of the preceding queries are a bit unusual, and indicate that there are
significant differences between each collation.

	BusinessEntityID	NationalIDNumber	LoginID	OrganizationNode	OrganizationLevel	JobTitle	BirthDate	
1	1	295847284	adventure-works\ken0	NULL	NULL	Chief Executive Officer	1969-01-29	
2	234	184188301	adventure-works\laura1	0x84	1	Chief Financial Officer	1976-01-06	
3	218	540688287	adventure-works\tengiz0	0x7B5AB0	4	Control Specialist	1990-04-28	
4	221	260805477	adventure-works\chris1	0x7B5B08	4	Control Specialist	1987-05-26	

	BusinessEntityID	NationalIDNumber	LoginID	OrganizationNode	OrganizationLevel	JobTitle	BirthDate	Marital
1	218	540688287	adventure-works\tengiz0	0x7B5AB0	4	Control Specialist	1990-04-28	S
2	221	260805477	adventure-works\chris1	0x7B5B08	4	Control Specialist	1987-05-26	M

Figure 10-3. *Different collations result in the same query providing different
results*

The second result set only returns two rows, whereas the original AdventureWorks table includes two additional executives. Why were the results different? It turns out that in traditional Spanish, the letters *"CH"* are considered a separate letter of the alphabet. We can view those rows of data for which the job title begins in those characters like this:

```
SELECT
      *
FROM Collation_Test.dbo.Spanish_Employees
WHERE JobTitle LIKE 'CH%'
ORDER BY JobTitle;
```

This query returns the results in Figure 10-4.

	BusinessEntityID	NationalIDNumber	LoginID	OrganizationNode	OrganizationLevel	JobTitle	BirthDate
1	1	295847284	adventure-works\ken0	NULL	NULL	Chief Executive Officer	1969-01-29
2	234	184188301	adventure-works\laura1	0x84	1	Chief Financial Officer	1976-01-06

Figure 10-4. *Illustration of the difference between "C" and "CH" in a Spanish collation*

Because of the language differences, the filter "C%" does not include the results that are returned by the filter "CH%." In addition, these letters will not sort as they normally would in a Latin collation:

```
SELECT
      *
FROM Collation_Test.dbo.Spanish_Employees
WHERE JobTitle BETWEEN 'C' AND 'D'
ORDER BY JobTitle;
```

This query returns all four results from the first part of Figure 10-3, as seen in Figure 10-5.

	BusinessEntityID	NationalIDNumber	LoginID	OrganizationNode	OrganizationLevel	JobTitle	BirthDate
1	218	540688287	adventure-works\tengiz0	0x7B5AB0	4	Control Specialist	1990-04-28
2	221	260805477	adventure-works\chris1	0x7B5B08	4	Control Specialist	1987-05-26
3	1	295847284	adventure-works\ken0	NULL	NULL	Chief Executive Officer	1969-01-29
4	234	184188301	adventure-works\laura1	0x84	1	Chief Financial Officer	1976-01-06

Figure 10-5. *Sorting differences in the traditional Spanish collation*

In this collation, "*C*" comes before "*CH*" in the alphabet. This may seem like a minor difference, but for a user running a web search, these results could easily lead to incorrect assumptions. For example, the user searches as we did, returns two results, and never realizes that there are two additional employees they may have been looking for in the table.

It is possible to force collations on any result set, as shown in Listing 10-3.

Listing 10-3. Forcing a Specific Collation on Filters and Sorts in a Result Set

```
SELECT
     *
FROM Collation_Test.dbo.Spanish_Employees
WHERE JobTitle COLLATE SQL_Latin1_General_CP1_CI_AS LIKE 'C%'
ORDER BY JobTitle COLLATE SQL_Latin1_General_CP1_CI_AS;

SELECT
     *
FROM Collation_Test.dbo.Spanish_Employees
WHERE JobTitle COLLATE SQL_Latin1_General_CP1_CI_AS BETWEEN 'C' AND 'D'
ORDER BY JobTitle COLLATE SQL_Latin1_General_CP1_CI_AS;
```

The results of the preceding queries return the data we would typically expect, as seen in Figure 10-6.

	BusinessEntityID	NationalIDNumber	LoginID	OrganizationNode	OrganizationLevel	JobTitle
1	1	295847284	adventure-works\ken0	NULL	NULL	Chief Executive Officer
2	234	184188301	adventure-works\laura1	0x84	1	Chief Financial Officer
3	218	540688287	adventure-works\tengiz0	0x7B5AB0	4	Control Specialist
4	221	260805477	adventure-works\chris1	0x7B5B08	4	Control Specialist

	BusinessEntityID	NationalIDNumber	LoginID	OrganizationNode	OrganizationLevel	JobTitle
1	1	295847284	adventure-works\ken0	NULL	NULL	Chief Executive Officer
2	234	184188301	adventure-works\laura1	0x84	1	Chief Financial Officer
3	218	540688287	adventure-works\tengiz0	0x7B5AB0	4	Control Specialist
4	221	260805477	adventure-works\chris1	0x7B5B08	4	Control Specialist

Figure 10-6. *Forcing a collation to return desired results*

One final example of collation conflict occurs when we try to directly compare columns from any one collation with another:

```
SELECT
        *
FROM Collation_Test.dbo.Spanish_Employees
INNER JOIN AdventureWorks2016CTP3.HumanResources.Employee
ON Spanish_Employees.LoginID = Employee.LoginID;
```

The preceding query will result in an error:

```
Msg 468, Level 16, State 9, Line 94
Cannot resolve the collation conflict between "SQL_Latin1_General_CP1_CI_AS"
and "Traditional_Spanish_CI_AS" in the equal to operation.
```

To make this query work, we must force the collation of one join column to match the other involved. Which collation we convert depends on our use case, but without changing one of them, we will be unable to join, filter on, or compare results from either data set:

```
SELECT
        *
FROM Collation_Test.dbo.Spanish_Employees
INNER JOIN AdventureWorks2016CTP3.HumanResources.Employee
ON Spanish_Employees.LoginID = Employee.LoginID COLLATE Traditional_
Spanish_CI_AS
```

By forcing a collation onto the join predicate, we can ensure that each column can be compared to the other and results properly returned. Alternatively, we can use the DATABASE_DEFAULT clause to automatically adjust the column collation on-the-fly, which can be extremely useful when working with varied data sets, or those guided by dynamic SQL:

```
SELECT
        *
FROM Collation_Test.dbo.Spanish_Employees
INNER JOIN AdventureWorks2016CTP3.HumanResources.Employee
ON Spanish_Employees.LoginID = Employee.LoginID COLLATE DATABASE_DEFAULT;
```

Note that if we want to collate text into the server's default, then this would not be the correct solution, but for maintaining consistency within a database, it's a quick and easy solution!

The Solution

Forcing a specific collation works when we know exactly what collations to expect when running queries. What if we are working with many different collations and do not know until runtime exactly which we want to sort by? If we manage many servers and databases, each with a different default collation, then we cannot make assumptions when converting collations at runtime. In addition, forcing all columns to a specific collation may affect the output in ways that users or applications would be intolerant of.

Dynamic SQL can help us turn a six-page problem into a one-page solution! By returning the default collation of the server or database as we did above, we can always return or compare data in the correct collation. The script in Listing 10-4 will result in a collation conflict error.

Listing 10-4. Collation Conflict Example Using a Table Variable

```
USE AdventureWorks2016CTP3
GO

DECLARE @temp_employees TABLE
(       id INT NOT NULL IDENTITY(1,1),
        LoginID NVARCHAR(256) NOT NULL);

INSERT INTO @temp_employees
        (LoginID)
SELECT TOP 50
        LoginID
FROM AdventureWorks2016CTP3.HumanResources.Employee
ORDER BY Employee.JobTitle;

SELECT
        Spanish_Employees.NationalIDNumber,
        Spanish_Employees.LoginID,
        Spanish_Employees.JobTitle,
```

```
        Spanish_Employees.BirthDate,
        Spanish_Employees.HireDate
FROM Collation_Test.dbo.Spanish_Employees
WHERE Spanish_Employees.LoginID IN
        (SELECT LoginID FROM @temp_employees);
```

Temporary tables and table variables are created using the collation of the TempDB database, which will typically match the server's default collation. In this case, the table variable is created in the Latin collation, whereas the LoginID we are checking is in the Spanish collation. This can be corrected permanently the dynamic SQL in Listing 10-5.

Listing 10-5. Resolving a Collation Conflict with Dynamic SQL

```
USE AdventureWorks2016CTP3
GO

DECLARE @sql_command NVARCHAR(MAX);
DECLARE @server_collation NVARCHAR(50);
SELECT @server_collation = CAST(SERVERPROPERTY('Collation') AS NVARCHAR(50));

SELECT @sql_command = '

DECLARE @temp_employees TABLE
(       id INT NOT NULL IDENTITY(1,1),
        LoginID NVARCHAR(256) NOT NULL);

INSERT INTO @temp_employees
        (LoginID)
SELECT TOP 50
        LoginID
FROM AdventureWorks2016CTP3.HumanResources.Employee
ORDER BY Employee.JobTitle;

SELECT
        Spanish_Employees.NationalIDNumber,
        Spanish_Employees.LoginID,
        Spanish_Employees.JobTitle,
        Spanish_Employees.BirthDate,
        Spanish_Employees.HireDate
```

```
FROM Collation_Test.dbo.Spanish_Employees
WHERE Spanish_Employees.LoginID IN
        (SELECT LoginID COLLATE ' + @server_collation + ' FROM @temp_employees);'
EXEC sp_executesql @sql_command;
```

The method indicated can be reversed to work with data using the collation of a specific database. The script in Listing 10-6 will return data using the default collation of our test database, rather than the server collation.

Listing 10-6. Using Dynamic SQL to Collate Data into a Specific Database's Default Collation

```
USE master
GO
DECLARE @sql_command NVARCHAR(MAX);
DECLARE @database_name NVARCHAR(128) = 'Collation_Test';

DECLARE @collation_name NVARCHAR(50);
SELECT @collation_name = collation_name
FROM sys.databases WHERE databases.name = @database_name;

SELECT @sql_command = '
SELECT
        Spanish_Employees.NationalIDNumber,
        Spanish_Employees.LoginID,
        Spanish_Employees.JobTitle,
        Spanish_Employees.BirthDate,
        Spanish_Employees.HireDate
FROM Collation_Test.dbo.Spanish_Employees
WHERE Spanish_Employees.LoginID IN
        (SELECT TOP 50 LoginID COLLATE ' + @collation_name + '
         FROM AdventureWorks2016CTP3.HumanResources.Employee ORDER BY
         LoginID COLLATE ' + @collation_name + ')';

EXEC sp_executesql @sql_command;
```

This example how to return a database's default collation from sys.databases and use that data to quickly resolve what would otherwise be a collation conflict. This method could similarly be employed to return a server's default collation and apply that instead.

Organizing and Archiving Data

When working with the archival or movement of data, we may want to name objects such as tables, databases, or schemas with a customized name based on the date, time, or application. This allows objects to be meaningfully tagged on an ongoing basis, without the need for any human intervention. Using standard TSQL, this would be difficult without some complex application code to manage the process for us.

The Problem

What if we have a log table that grows very quickly, but where we never need data older than a week? Partitioning the table such that the current week is isolated into a single partition is one solution, but was only available in Enterprise edition prior to SQL Server 2016 SP1. In addition, we might want to move the old data to a different server or storage environment. If this or any similar situations are involved, then managing the process ourselves may be an easier and more portable solution.

To begin this example, we will populate a table with a variety of data based on date and time, as seen in Listing 10-7.

Listing 10-7. Create Database Log Data for an Archiving Demonstration

```
USE AdventureWorks2016CTP3;
CREATE TABLE dbo.Database_Log
      (log_id INT NOT NULL IDENTITY(1,1) CONSTRAINT PK_Database_Log
      PRIMARY KEY CLUSTERED,
       Log_Time DATETIME,
       Log_Data NVARCHAR(1000));

DECLARE @datetime DATETIME = CURRENT_TIMESTAMP;
DECLARE @datediff TABLE
      (previous_hour SMALLINT);
DECLARE @count SMALLINT = 0;
WHILE @count <= 360
BEGIN
      INSERT INTO @datediff
            (previous_hour)
      SELECT @count;
```

```
        SELECT @count = @count + 1
END

SELECT @count = 0;
WHILE @count <= 1000
BEGIN
        INSERT INTO Database_Log
                (Log_Time, Log_Data)
        SELECT
                DATEADD(HOUR, -1 * previous_hour, CURRENT_TIMESTAMP),
                CAST(DATEADD(HOUR, -1 * previous_hour, CURRENT_TIMESTAMP) AS
                NVARCHAR)
        FROM @datediff;

        SELECT @count = @count + 1;
END
```

This script will create a table called Database_Log and populate it with 361,361 rows of data containing a variety of log times, and the string conversion of those times. The data looks like Figure 10-7.

log_id	Log_Time	Log_Data
67069	2015-11-15 13:30:10.707	Nov 15 2015 1:30PM
67070	2015-11-15 12:30:10.707	Nov 15 2015 12:30PM
67071	2015-11-15 11:30:10.707	Nov 15 2015 11:30AM
67072	2015-11-15 10:30:10.707	Nov 15 2015 10:30AM
67073	2015-11-15 09:30:10.707	Nov 15 2015 9:30AM
67074	2015-11-15 08:30:10.707	Nov 15 2015 8:30AM
67075	2015-11-15 07:30:10.707	Nov 15 2015 7:30AM
67076	2015-11-15 06:30:10.707	Nov 15 2015 6:30AM
67077	2015-11-15 05:30:10.707	Nov 15 2015 5:30AM
67078	2015-11-15 04:30:10.707	Nov 15 2015 4:30AM
67079	2015-11-15 03:30:10.707	Nov 15 2015 3:30AM
67080	2015-11-15 02:30:10.707	Nov 15 2015 2:30AM

Figure 10-7. Sample of Database Log Data Created in Listing 10-7

Let's say we want to archive data every week into a new table that contains a week's worth of data. This would normally require quite a bit of manual labor to manage table names correctly. What if we also wanted to separate data into databases by year, such that each calendar year was given its own unique database? This may seem like an unusual use case, but the need to move large volumes of data around by a time slice is very common. Dynamic SQL techniques can be applied to any similar problem, regardless of the specific objects or business rules.

To provide some older data that will be archived into additional databases, we'll run one more data population script to increase our data size even further, as seen in Listing 10-8.

Listing 10-8. Script to Increase the Size of Data in the Database_Log Table

```
DECLARE @year_offset TINYINT = 5;

WHILE @year_offset > 0
BEGIN
        INSERT INTO dbo.Database_Log
                (Log_Time, Log_Data)
        SELECT TOP 10000
                DATEADD(YEAR, -1 * @year_offset, Log_Time),
                CAST(DATEADD(YEAR, -1 * @year_offset, Log_Time) AS NVARCHAR)
        FROM Database_Log
        SELECT @year_offset = @year_offset - 1;
END
```

Now we have an additional 50,000 rows of data from up to 5 years ago, which will allow us to easily demonstrate the problem outlined above.

The Solution

To process this data correctly, we need to perform the following tasks:

1. Read data from the log table by time period.

2. Create new database or table objects (if they do not already exist).

3. Insert the data into those objects.

4. Delete the archived data from the log table.

The script in Listing 10-9 will accomplish the tasks as outlined.

Listing 10-9. Using Dynamic SQL to Archive Data into Dynamically Named Tables

```
DECLARE @sql_command NVARCHAR(MAX);
DECLARE @parameter_list NVARCHAR(MAX) = '@start_of_week DATETIME, @end_of_
week DATETIME';
DECLARE @min_datetime DATETIME;
SELECT @min_datetime = MIN(Log_Time) FROM Database_Log;
DECLARE @previous_min_time DATETIME = '1/1/1900';
DECLARE @start_of_week DATETIME = CAST(DATEADD(dd, -1 * (DATEPART(dw,
@min_datetime) - 1), @min_datetime) AS DATE);
DECLARE @end_of_week DATETIME = DATEADD(WEEK, 1, @start_of_week);
DECLARE @current_year SMALLINT;
DECLARE @current_week TINYINT;
DECLARE @database_name NVARCHAR(128);
DECLARE @table_name NVARCHAR(128);

WHILE (@previous_min_time <> @min_datetime)
BEGIN
        SELECT @current_year = DATEPART(YEAR, @start_of_week);
        SELECT @current_week = DATEPART(WEEK, @start_of_week);
        SELECT @database_name = 'Database_Log_' + CAST(@current_year AS
        NVARCHAR);
        SELECT @table_name = 'Database_Log_' + CAST(@current_year AS
        NVARCHAR) + '_' + CAST(@current_week AS NVARCHAR)
        -- Create the yearly database if it does not already exist.
        IF NOT EXISTS (SELECT * FROM sys.databases WHERE databases.name =
        @database_name)
        BEGIN
                SELECT @sql_command = 'CREATE DATABASE [' + @database_name + ']';
                EXEC sp_executesql @sql_command;
        END
        -- Create the weekly table if it does not already exist.
        SELECT @sql_command = '
        USE [' + @database_name + '];
```

```
        IF NOT EXISTS (SELECT * FROM sys.tables WHERE tables.name = "' +
        @table_name + "')
        BEGIN
                CREATE TABLE [dbo].[' + @table_name + ']
                (Log_Id INT NOT NULL CONSTRAINT PK_Database_Log_' + CAST
                (@current_year AS NVARCHAR) + '_' + CAST(@current_week
                AS NVARCHAR) + ' PRIMARY KEY CLUSTERED,
                 Log_Time DATETIME,
                 Log_Data NVARCHAR(1000));
        END'
        EXEC sp_executesql @sql_command;

        SELECT @sql_command = '
        INSERT INTO [' + @database_name + '].[dbo].[' + @table_name + ']
                (Log_Id, Log_Time, Log_Data)
        SELECT
                Log_Id,
                Log_Time,
                Log_Data
        FROM AdventureWorks2016CTP3.dbo.Database_Log
        WHERE Log_Time >= @start_of_week
        AND Log_Time <= @end_of_week
        AND Log_Time < DATEADD(WEEK, -1, CURRENT_TIMESTAMP);
        DELETE
        FROM AdventureWorks2016CTP3.dbo.Database_Log
        WHERE Log_Time >= @start_of_week
        AND Log_Time <= @end_of_week
        AND Log_Time < DATEADD(WEEK, -1, CURRENT_TIMESTAMP);'

        EXEC sp_executesql @sql_command, @parameter_list, @start_of_week,
        @end_of_week

        SELECT @previous_min_time = @min_datetime;
        SELECT @min_datetime = MIN(Log_Time) FROM Database_Log;
```

```
SELECT @start_of_week = CAST(DATEADD(dd, -1 * (DATEPART(dw,
@min_datetime) - 1), @min_datetime) AS DATE);
SELECT @end_of_week = DATEADD(WEEK, 1, @start_of_week);
END
```

When the preceding script completes running, we'll be able to view some new databases on our server, as seen in Figure 10-8.

Figure 10-8. *New databases created when the script in Listing 10-9 is executed*

For each year represented by the Log_Time within Database_Log, a new database was created. In addition, tables were created in those databases for each week represented within that data, as seen in Figure 10-9.

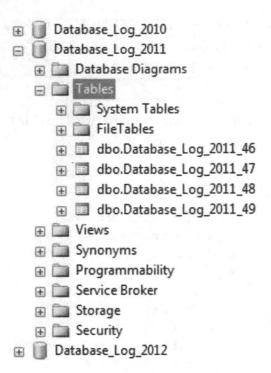

Figure 10-9. *New tables created when the script in Listing 10-9 is executed*

The guts of the logic that we employed revolve around creating databases and tables dynamically based on the date and time provided by Log_Time. Once those objects are created, data is inserted into them and then deleted from the source table. We can review the data in a single table to verify that this script did exactly what we intended it to, as seen in Figure 10-10.

```
SELECT
        *
FROM Database_Log_2011.dbo.Database_Log_2011_48
```

	Log_Id	Log_Time	Log_Data
1	371372	2011-11-26 23:41:40.400	Nov 26 2011 11:41PM
2	371373	2011-11-26 22:41:40.400	Nov 26 2011 10:41PM
3	371374	2011-11-26 21:41:40.400	Nov 26 2011 9:41PM
4	371375	2011-11-26 20:41:40.400	Nov 26 2011 8:41PM
5	371376	2011-11-26 19:41:40.400	Nov 26 2011 7:41PM
6	371377	2011-11-26 18:41:40.400	Nov 26 2011 6:41PM
7	371378	2011-11-26 17:41:40.400	Nov 26 2011 5:41PM
8	371379	2011-11-26 16:41:40.400	Nov 26 2011 4:41PM
9	371380	2011-11-26 15:41:40.400	Nov 26 2011 3:41PM
10	371381	2011-11-26 14:41:40.400	Nov 26 2011 2:41PM
11	371382	2011-11-26 13:41:40.400	Nov 26 2011 1:41PM
12	371383	2011-11-26 12:41:40.400	Nov 26 2011 12:41PM

Figure 10-10. *Sample data from a weekly log table*

All data within this new table is identical to how it appeared in the original `Database_Log` table, including the `Log_Id`. The only difference is the new database and table location of the data.

Reorganizing data when the reference points change over time can be a complex task. Dynamic SQL allows data to be organized, moved, and new objects created with relatively simple logic. In fewer than one hundred lines of TSQL, we were able to take all old data from a log table and move it to any number of new database objects that were created at runtime based on the age of that data.

Every use case for reorganizing, archiving, or moving data will be different, but the general technique illustrated above can be extremely useful when we want to minimize the complexity and size of an important archiving process. Always consider how the archived data will be used prior to building a new process. Whether it is moved to separate databases, tables, or partitions, we now have the luxury of being able to index it uniquely based on its new purpose. By treating it as an archive repository, and not transactional data, we gain the flexibility to optimize it based on its new purpose.

Dynamic SQL can be used to manage additional indexes, constraints, keys, views, and stored procedures that all can allow the new data to be accessed efficiently and conveniently. Creating those objects would be as easy as adding to our command string in the same way as the primary keys were created above.

Customized Database Objects

The ability to create highly flexible custom objects is not a simple task unless some sort of dynamic code or TSQL is implemented. Our needs in this area can be very specific, but generalized techniques can be used to get exactly what we want every time.

The Problem

Sometimes we want to create objects with specific use cases, but where the tables or columns involved may not always be the same. Generating a stored procedure, function, or view given those variables would normally be a manually intensive process. We can implement dynamic SQL to create or modify existing objects in ways that are both scalable and reliable.

In Chapter 9, we introduced using dynamic SQL to PIVOT or UNPIVOT data when the column lists were not known until runtime. What if we wanted to summarize the table data output by those processes into a view, which would provide a convenient data source for an application to access? Once a view is created, we can consider additional options, such as schemabinding to improve schema integrity.

Let's consider a scenario where we want to provide insight into employee hire dates based on job titles. For a specific company, this is data that is requested so often that a request is made for a more permanent data structure based on it. There would be a number of ways to approach this, including a custom table, view, or an ETL process to manage report data based on these needs. These processes could be managed via triggers, stored procedures, or a variety of other methods.

The Solution

For the scenario just outlined, we'll provide an example solution using a schemabound view, though other methods could be used if the report or data requirements were different. The following TSQL in Listing 10-10 will return the raw data that we are looking for.

Listing 10-10. Dynamic Pivot that Returns a Count of Hire Year by Job Title

```
DECLARE @hire_date_years TABLE
        (hire_date_year NVARCHAR(50));

INSERT INTO @hire_date_years
        (hire_date_year)
SELECT DISTINCT
        DATEPART(YEAR, Employee.HireDate)
FROM HumanResources.Employee;

DECLARE @sql_command NVARCHAR(MAX);
SELECT @sql_command = '
SELECT
        *
FROM
(       SELECT
                Employee.BusinessEntityID,
                Employee.JobTitle,
                DATEPART(YEAR, Employee.HireDate) AS HireDate_Year
        FROM HumanResources.Employee
) EMPLOYEE_DATA
PIVOT
(       COUNT(BusinessEntityID)
        FOR HireDate_Year IN (';

SELECT @sql_command = @sql_command + '[' + hire_date_year + '], '
FROM @hire_date_years;

SELECT  @sql_command = SUBSTRING(@sql_command, 1, LEN(@sql_command) - 1);

SELECT  @sql_command = @sql_command + ')) PIVOT_DATA';

PRINT @sql_command;
EXEC sp_executesql @sql_command;
```

The output of the query returns a data set similar to that in Figure 10-11.

	JobTitle	2006	2007	2008	2009	2010	2011	2012	2013
4	Accounts Receivable Specialist	0	0	1	2	0	0	0	0
5	Application Specialist	0	0	1	3	0	0	0	0
6	Assistant to the Chief Financial Officer	0	0	0	1	0	0	0	0
7	Benefits Specialist	0	0	1	0	0	0	0	0
8	Buyer	0	0	0	3	6	0	0	0
9	Chief Executive Officer	0	0	0	1	0	0	0	0
10	Chief Financial Officer	0	0	0	1	0	0	0	0
11	Control Specialist	0	0	1	1	0	0	0	0
12	Database Administrator	0	0	0	2	0	0	0	0
13	Design Engineer	0	0	2	0	0	1	0	0
14	Document Control Assistant	0	0	0	2	0	0	0	0
15	Document Control Manager	0	0	0	1	0	0	0	0
16	Engineering Manager	0	1	0	0	0	0	0	0
17	European Sales Manager	0	0	0	0	0	0	1	0
18	Facilities Administrative Assistant	0	0	0	1	0	0	0	0

Figure 10-11. *Hire data returned by the dynamic PIVOT query in Listing 10-10*

Each job title is listed as the first column followed by a list of columns for each hire date year present in the Employee table. If employees are added or removed from the underlying table, then columns may be added or removed from this data set as hire dates are added or removed.

Now that we have a query that returns the results we want in the columnar format that we are looking for; we can move this data into a customized view. One technicality that we need to overcome is that when we create a schemabound view, we cannot include * in the column list. If we take the preceding TSQL and add a CREATE VIEW... WITH SCHEMABINDING to the query, we will get the following error:

```
Msg 1054, Level 15, State 6, Procedure v_job_title_year_summary, Line 6
Syntax '*' is not allowed in schema-bound objects.
Msg 102, Level 15, State 1, Procedure v_job_title_year_summary, Line 13
Incorrect syntax near 'EMPLOYEE_DATA'.
```

To make this syntax work, we will need to make the column list dynamic, in addition to the PIVOT details. The TSQL in Listing 10-11 is the view creation script, with that alteration included.

Listing 10-11. Dynamic SQL Used to Create a Customized View with a Variable Column List

```
IF EXISTS (SELECT * FROM sys.views WHERE views.name = 'v_job_title_year_
summary')
BEGIN
      DROP VIEW v_job_title_year_summary
END
GO

DECLARE @hire_date_years TABLE
      (hire_date_year NVARCHAR(50));

INSERT INTO @hire_date_years
      (hire_date_year)
SELECT DISTINCT
      DATEPART(YEAR, Employee.HireDate)
FROM HumanResources.Employee;

DECLARE @sql_command NVARCHAR(MAX);
SELECT @sql_command = '
CREATE VIEW dbo.v_job_title_year_summary
WITH SCHEMABINDING
AS
SELECT
      JobTitle,'

SELECT @sql_command = @sql_command + '
[' + hire_date_year + '], '
FROM @hire_date_years;

SELECT @sql_command = SUBSTRING(@sql_command, 1, LEN(@sql_command) - 1);
SELECT @sql_command = @sql_command + '
FROM
(      SELECT
            Employee.BusinessEntityID,
            Employee.JobTitle,
            DATEPART(YEAR, Employee.HireDate) AS HireDate_Year
      FROM HumanResources.Employee
```

```
) EMPLOYEE_DATA
PIVOT
(      COUNT(BusinessEntityID)
       FOR HireDate_Year IN (';

SELECT @sql_command = @sql_command + '[' + hire_date_year + '], '
FROM @hire_date_years;

SELECT @sql_command = SUBSTRING(@sql_command, 1, LEN(@sql_command) - 1);

SELECT @sql_command = @sql_command + ')) PIVOT_DATA';

PRINT @sql_command;
EXEC sp_executesql @sql_command;
```

Once this script is run, we can look in our views list to quickly verify that the new view was created and that it contains the correct columns, as seen in Figure 10-12.

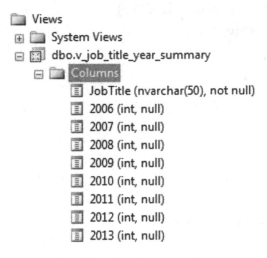

Figure 10-12. *Columns contained in the custom view created in Listing 10-11*

The view definition will not update automatically as data is updated, but since the underlying data is not likely to change constantly, we can manage this update daily (or at whatever interval is deemed necessary). Let's say that we update a few hire dates to years that are not included in the current underlying employee data:

```
UPDATE HumanResources.Employee
SET HireDate = '1/1/2015'
WHERE BusinessEntityID = 282
```

```
UPDATE HumanResources.Employee
SET HireDate = '1/1/2014'
WHERE BusinessEntityID IN (260, 285)
```

Now, if we select data from the view, we'll notice that 2014 and 2015 have not been added to it, as seen in Figure 10-13.

```
SELECT
        *

FROM dbo.v_job_title_year_summary
```

	Job Title	2006	2007	2008	2009	2010	2011	2012	2013
1	Accountant	0	0	0	2	0	0	0	0
2	Accounts Manager	0	0	0	1	0	0	0	0
3	Accounts Payable Specialist	0	0	0	2	0	0	0	0
4	Accounts Receivable Specialist	0	0	1	2	0	0	0	0
5	Application Specialist	0	0	1	3	0	0	0	0
6	Assistant to the Chief Financial Officer	0	0	0	1	0	0	0	0
7	Benefits Specialist	0	0	1	0	0	0	0	0
8	Buyer	0	0	0	3	6	0	0	0
9	Chief Executive Officer	0	0	0	1	0	0	0	0
10	Chief Financial Officer	0	0	0	1	0	0	0	0

Figure 10-13. *Without refreshing the view, 2014 and 2015 columns will not be returned*

For additional columns to be added to the view, it must be refreshed or recreated. In order to recreate it easily, we'll encapsulate the TSQL view creation from earlier into a stored procedure, as shown in Listing 10-12.

Listing 10-12. Stored Procedure Used to Create a Dynamically Generated View

```
IF EXISTS (SELECT * FROM sys.procedures WHERE procedures.name = 'create_v_
job_title_year_summary')
BEGIN
        DROP PROCEDURE dbo.create_v_job_title_year_summary;
END
GO
CREATE PROCEDURE dbo.create_v_job_title_year_summary
```

```
AS
BEGIN
        IF EXISTS (SELECT * FROM sys.views WHERE views.name = 'v_job_title_
        year_summary')
        BEGIN
                DROP VIEW v_job_title_year_summary;
        END

        DECLARE @hire_date_years TABLE
                (hire_date_year NVARCHAR(50));

        INSERT INTO @hire_date_years
                (hire_date_year)
        SELECT DISTINCT
                DATEPART(YEAR, Employee.HireDate)
        FROM HumanResources.Employee;

        DECLARE @sql_command NVARCHAR(MAX);
        SELECT @sql_command = '
        CREATE VIEW dbo.v_job_title_year_summary
        WITH SCHEMABINDING
        AS
        SELECT
                JobTitle,'
        SELECT @sql_command = @sql_command + '
        [' + hire_date_year + '], '
        FROM @hire_date_years;

        SELECT @sql_command = SUBSTRING(@sql_command, 1, LEN(@sql_command) - 1);

        SELECT @sql_command = @sql_command + '
        FROM
        (SELECT
                Employee.BusinessEntityID,
                Employee.JobTitle,
                DATEPART(YEAR, Employee.HireDate) AS HireDate_Year
          FROM HumanResources.Employee
        ) EMPLOYEE_DATA
```

```
        PIVOT
        (COUNT(BusinessEntityID)
              FOR HireDate_Year IN (';

        SELECT @sql_command = @sql_command + '[' + hire_date_year + '], '
        FROM @hire_date_years;

        SELECT @sql_command = SUBSTRING(@sql_command, 1, LEN(@sql_command) - 1);

        SELECT @sql_command = @sql_command + ')) PIVOT_DATA';

        PRINT @sql_command;
        EXEC sp_executesql @sql_command;
END
```

With this stored procedure, we can now recreate our dynamic view with ease:

```
EXEC dbo.create_v_job_title_year_summary;
```

When we check the contents of the view, we can verify that it has been appropriately updated:

```
SELECT
        *
FROM dbo.v_job_title_year_summary
```

	Job Title	2006	2007	2008	2009	2010	2011	2012	2013	2014	2015
45	Production Technician - WC40	0	0	7	14	5	0	0	0	0	0
46	Production Technician - WC45	0	0	5	10	0	0	0	0	0	0
47	Production Technician - WC50	0	0	8	18	0	0	0	0	0	0
48	Production Technician - WC60	1	0	5	15	5	0	0	0	0	0
49	Purchasing Assistant	0	0	0	0	1	0	0	0	1	0
50	Purchasing Manager	0	0	0	0	0	1	0	0	0	0
51	Quality Assurance Manager	0	0	0	1	0	0	0	0	0	0
52	Quality Assurance Supervisor	0	0	1	0	0	0	0	0	0	0
53	Quality Assurance Technician	0	0	1	2	1	0	0	0	0	0
54	Recruiter	0	0	1	1	0	0	0	0	0	0
55	Research and Development Engineer	0	0	1	1	0	0	0	0	0	0
56	Research and Development Manager	0	0	0	2	0	0	0	0	0	0
57	Sales Representative	0	0	0	0	0	8	3	2	0	1

Figure 10-14. New data for 2014 and 2015 has been included in the view, once refreshed

Columns have been added for 2014 and 2015 data and would have been added in order to encompass any other years that were added or removed since the last time the view was created. Note that a view that is based on a PIVOT cannot be indexed, but dynamically generated views can be indexed normally, so long as they do not include PIVOT or UNPIVOT and are schema-bound.

Generating schema using dynamic SQL can be a very convenient way to create objects when knowledge of the underlying data structures may not be complete until runtime. It can also allow for complex business logic to be summarized into database objects using relatively simple TSQL syntax. The ability to greatly simplify application or report code can sometimes be more important than the burden of creating a new database object.

As with creating any new objects, always ensure that they are needed and that there is not a more efficient method available. Oftentimes, new SQL Server versions, application releases, or business changes can allow for new methods to be implemented for efficiently retrieving data.

A Note on System Tables

SQL Server has a handful of system databases that provide important functionality and are necessary for its normal operation. TempDB, master, model, and msdb all are used by various processes to manage metadata about our server. The following is a quick synopsis on the effects of different collations on system database usage.

Temporary tables are created and stored in TempDB, a system database in SQL Server that is used for the creation and persistence of temporary objects. Like all other databases, TempDB has a collation associated with it. By default, TempDB will have whatever collation was specified at the time that SQL Server was installed, which typically will be the server default.

When temp tables are created, they will be assigned the collation of TempDB, even if that collation is different than the database you are currently working in. If data within the temp table is joined, grouped, aggregated, or compared with data in the database that is of a different collation, then an error will be thrown similar to those seen earlier in this chapter.

Msdb is used to manage information about internal SQL Server processes, such as backups and SQL Server Agent processes. Because it will be in the system default collation, care should be taken when working with this data if it is to be used by a database with a different collation.

Master is the repository for important system information, such as logins, configuration settings, and database metadata and will also share the system default collation. If there is a need to retrieve any string data from the master database, be sure to collate it appropriately prior to comparing or storing it elsewhere on the server.

Model is a potentially tricky system database to manage with regard to collation. New databases are created as a copy of model and will share its data and configuration, including collection. On a server with multiple collations, it will be necessary to specify a collation whenever creating a new database to ensure that the default is not used, if a different collation is needed. Most organizations will create new databases based on existing databases or backup files, which will curtail this challenge. Any scenario in which model is used will need to be monitored to make sure that the resulting database is configured with the correct collection for the target application.

Because of the behavior of system databases, collation management may be necessary on any SQL Server with database collations that differ from the system defaults. In general, it is a best practice to not maintain servers with mixed collations. This eliminates the need for custom code that manages different collations. It also reduces the risk that third-party software or maintenance applications will break as a result of not being prepared to deal with a server with mixed collations.

Conclusion

In this chapter, we reviewed a handful of dynamic SQL applications that allowed us to add flexibility to processes that are normally not tolerant of changes at runtime. Many more applications exist, with the only limitation being your imagination.

When creating any new schema, whether dynamically generated or not, always consider the impact and efficiency of doing so. All database objects must be maintained, and that cumulative upkeep must be considered when contemplating the creation of new objects. The goal of using dynamic SQL is to either allow for processes that would otherwise not be easily possible, or to decrease complexity in those that might require a manual or resource-intensive component.

The usage of dynamic SQL for these purposes will be dictated by your own business logic, database server version, and the rules and policies used by your development team. While some solutions will be useful to a wide audience, others may prove to be the savior of one specific development environment. Regardless of how universal the solution is, keeping this tool in mind will allow for difficult database challenges to be solved in creative ways that otherwise could be costly and time-consuming to resolve.

CHAPTER 11

Applications of Dynamic SQL

Once we have established the idea that dynamic SQL can solve a wide variety of challenges, we can begin to apply it to larger and more complex problems. Our goal is to leave you with a variety of practical scripts that can be brought into any database environment and tailored to a unique use. There are many real-world challenges for which dynamic SQL is an efficient solution and where we can accomplish a great deal of work in compact, reusable code.

Database Backups

Another necessary database maintenance task is to ensure that all important data is backed up on a regular basis. Maintenance plans are often used for this task, but they lack flexibility and can become very complex if we wish to customize them for a variety of use cases. If we are managing many database servers, all of which have different backup needs, the result can be dozens (or more) of different maintenance plans. Each of these will require the same level of care and maintenance, and hence the same level of technical debt to ensure normal operation over time.

What can often be preferable is to create a backup script tailored to an environment that is capable of being expanded, customized, and adjusted as needed over time. We'll cover the three common needs of a backup plan: full backups, differential backups, and transaction log backups. A common configuration is to run full backups once a week, differentials each other day, and transaction log backups intermittently throughout the day. Larger backups (full & differential) should be run during off-hours when the system is less used, as backup operations can require significant IO to process. Alternatively, backups can be offloaded to an AlwaysOn Availability Group, or some other secondary data source.

391

© Edward Pollack 2019

E. Pollack, *Dynamic SQL*, https://doi.org/10.1007/978-1-4842-4318-3_11

This stored procedure will execute as often as we want transaction log backups
to run. When it is run at the time of day corresponding to `@differential_and_full_`
`backup_time`, then one of those will be run instead. `@full_backup_day` indicates which
day of the week the full backup should be taken. `@backup_location` provides the
location on disk where backups should be saved. Last, `@print_output_only` determines
if backups should be taken or if the command string should be printed out instead. This
stored procedure can be seen in Listing 11-1.

Listing 11-1. Database Backup Stored Procedure Using Dynamic SQL

```
IF EXISTS (SELECT * FROM sys.procedures WHERE procedures.name =
'backup_plan')
BEGIN
        DROP PROCEDURE dbo.backup_plan;
END
GO

CREATE PROCEDURE dbo.backup_plan
        @differential_and_full_backup_time TIME = '00:00:00', -- Default to
        midnight.
        @full_backup_day TINYINT = 1, -- Default to Sunday.
        @backup_location NVARCHAR(MAX) = 'E:\SQLBackups\', -- Default to my
        backup folder.
        @print_output_only BIT = 1
AS
BEGIN
        SET NOCOUNT ON;
        DECLARE @current_time TIME = CAST(CURRENT_TIMESTAMP AS TIME);
        DECLARE @current_day TINYINT = DATEPART(DW, CURRENT_TIMESTAMP);
        DECLARE @datetime_string NVARCHAR(MAX) = FORMAT(CURRENT_TIMESTAMP ,
        'MMddyyyyHHmmss');
        DECLARE @sql_command NVARCHAR(MAX) = '';

        DECLARE @database_list TABLE
                (database_name NVARCHAR(MAX) NOT NULL, recovery_model_desc
                NVARCHAR(MAX));

        INSERT INTO @database_list
```

```
            (database_name, recovery_model_desc)
SELECT
        name,
        recovery_model_desc
FROM sys.databases
WHERE databases.name NOT IN ('msdb', 'master', 'TempDB', 'model');

-- Check if a full backup is to be taken now.
IF (@current_day = @full_backup_day) AND (@current_time BETWEEN
@differential_and_full_backup_time AND DATEADD(MINUTE, 10,
@differential_and_full_backup_time))
BEGIN
        SELECT @sql_command = @sql_command +
        '
        BACKUP DATABASE [' + database_name + ']
        TO DISK = "' + @backup_location + database_name + '_' +
        @datetime_string + '.bak";
        '
        FROM @database_list;

        IF @print_output_only = 1
                PRINT @sql_command;
        ELSE
                EXEC sp_executesql @sql_command;
END
ELSE -- Check if a differential backup is to be taken now.
IF (@current_day <> @full_backup_day) AND (@current_time BETWEEN
@differential_and_full_backup_time AND DATEADD(MINUTE, 10,
@differential_and_full_backup_time))
BEGIN
SELECT @sql_command = '';
        SELECT @sql_command = @sql_command +
        '
        BACKUP DATABASE [' + database_name + ']
        TO DISK = "' + @backup_location + database_name + '_' +
        @datetime_string + '.dif"
```

```
            WITH DIFFERENTIAL;
            '

            FROM @database_list;

            IF @print_output_only = 1
                    PRINT @sql_command;
            ELSE
                    EXEC sp_executesql @sql_command;
    END
    ELSE -- If neither full or differential, then take a transaction log
    backup.
    BEGIN
  SELECT @sql_command = '';
            SELECT @sql_command = @sql_command +
            '

            BACKUP LOG [' + database_name + ']
            TO DISK = "' + @backup_location + database_name + '_' +
            @datetime_string + '.trn"
            '

            FROM @database_list
            WHERE recovery_model_desc = 'FULL';

            IF @print_output_only = 1
                    PRINT @sql_command;
            ELSE
                    EXEC sp_executesql @sql_command;
      END
END
```

This script will perform backups on all databases except for msdb, tempdb, master, and model. As was the case in all previous scripts, the database list can easily be adjusted to cater to any custom needs. This script can be executed on any schedule and will perform transaction log backups of the database except when it is the allotted time and date for a differential backup or full backup. If the current time is 7:53pm on Tuesday, we can test the script for each backup use case:

```
EXEC dbo.backup_plan @differential_and_full_backup_time = '19:50:00', @full_
backup_day = 3, @backup_location = 'E:\SQLBackups\', @print_output_only = 1;
```

This will perform a full backup, as the current time is within 10 minutes of the designated full backup time, the full backup day has been set to Tuesday (3, and the backup statements will be printed rather than executed. The command string output is as follows:

```
BACKUP DATABASE [AdventureWorks2012]
TO DISK = 'E:\SQLBackups\AdventureWorks2012_12012015195529.bak';

BACKUP DATABASE [AdventureWorks2014]
TO DISK = 'E:\SQLBackups\AdventureWorks2014_12012015195529.bak';

BACKUP DATABASE [AdventureWorksDW2012]
TO DISK = 'E:\SQLBackups\AdventureWorksDW2012_12012015195529.bak';

BACKUP DATABASE [AdventureWorksDW2014]
TO DISK = 'E:\SQLBackups\AdventureWorksDW2014_12012015195529.bak';
```

If we change @print_output_only to zero and execute the stored procedure again, we can verify the backup files in the directory they are expected to be output to.

Name	Date modified	Type	Size
Old	12/1/2015 7:28 PM	File folder	
AdventureWorks2012_12012015195509.bak	12/1/2015 7:55 PM	BAK File	19.
AdventureWorks2014_12012015195509.bak	12/1/2015 7:55 PM	BAK File	19.
AdventureWorksDW2012_12012015195509.bak	12/1/2015 7:55 PM	BAK File	12.
AdventureWorksDW2014_12012015195509.bak	12/1/2015 7:55 PM	BAK File	9.

Figure 11-1. *Full backup files created in the dynamic backup script in Listing 11-1*

All four full backups are there, with the names that we assigned. Now, let's execute the stored procedure for a differential backup situation:

```
EXEC dbo.backup_plan @differential_and_full_backup_time = '19:50:00',
@full_backup_day = 3, @backup_location = 'E:\SQLBackups\', @print_output_
only = 1;
```

The resulting command string is as follows:

```
BACKUP DATABASE [AdventureWorks2012]
TO DISK = 'E:\SQLBackups\AdventureWorks2012_12012015200242.dif'
```

```
WITH DIFFERENTIAL;

BACKUP DATABASE [AdventureWorks2014]
TO DISK = 'E:\SQLBackups\AdventureWorks2014_12012015200242.dif'
WITH DIFFERENTIAL;

BACKUP DATABASE [AdventureWorksDW2012]
TO DISK = 'E:\SQLBackups\AdventureWorksDW2012_12012015200242.dif'
WITH DIFFERENTIAL;

BACKUP DATABASE [AdventureWorksDW2014]
TO DISK = 'E:\SQLBackups\AdventureWorksDW2014_12012015200242.dif'
WITH DIFFERENTIAL;
```

In this case, today is not the correct day for a full backup, but it is time for a differential backup. If we execute this with `@print_output_only` set to zero, we can verify that the backup files were correctly generated in Figure 11-2.

Name	Date modified	Type	Size
Old	12/1/2015 7:28 PM	File folder	
AdventureWorks2012_12012015195509.bak	12/1/2015 7:55 PM	BAK File	19
AdventureWorks2012_12012015200230.dif	12/1/2015 8:02 PM	DIF File	
AdventureWorks2014_12012015195509.bak	12/1/2015 7:55 PM	BAK File	19
AdventureWorks2014_12012015200230.dif	12/1/2015 8:02 PM	DIF File	
AdventureWorksDW2012_12012015195509.bak	12/1/2015 7:55 PM	BAK File	12
AdventureWorksDW2012_12012015200230.dif	12/1/2015 8:02 PM	DIF File	
AdventureWorksDW2014_12012015195509.bak	12/1/2015 7:55 PM	BAK File	9
AdventureWorksDW2014_12012015200230.dif	12/1/2015 8:02 PM	DIF File	

Figure 11-2. *Differential backup files created in the dynamic backup script in Listing 11-1*

In addition to the four full backups created earlier, we can now confirm that four differential backups have also been created in the same folder. Last, let's run a command that will trigger a transaction log backup:

```
EXEC dbo.backup_plan @differential_and_full_backup_time = '00:00:00',
@full_backup_day = 1, @backup_location = 'E:\SQLBackups\', @print_output_
only = 1;
```

Here, the full backup day is Sunday and the full/differential backup time is midnight. Since it is currently none of these times, a transaction log backup is taken instead. The resulting command string is as follows:

```
BACKUP LOG [AdventureWorks2014]
TO DISK = 'E:\SQLBackups\AdventureWorks2014_12012015200631.trn'
```

Note that only a single database is getting backed up. This may at first glance appear to be an error, since we explicitly told this stored procedure to run backups against four databases, but in fact is correct. We cannot run transaction log backups on any database in the simple recovery mode. On my server, three of the four databases included in this backup plan are in simple recovery and were therefore explicitly omitted from that step. We can verify this with the following query:

```
SELECT
      name,
      recovery_model_desc
from sys.databases
WHERE name IN ('AdventureWorks2012', 'AdventureWorks2014',
'AdventureWorksDW2012', 'AdventureWorksDW2014');
```

The results of this query confirm this finding, as seen in Figure 11-3.

	name	recovery_model_desc
1	AdventureWorks2012	SIMPLE
2	AdventureWorks2014	FULL
3	AdventureWorksDW2012	SIMPLE
4	AdventureWorksDW2014	SIMPLE

Figure 11-3. *Verifying the recovery model for a specific set of databases*

Production databases should be set to the full recovery mode or given unique treatment so that important data is backed up as frequently as necessary!

When we execute the stored proc with @print_output_only set to zero, the output folder can be inspected and the appropriate results verified in Figure 11-4.

Name	Date modified	Type	Size
Old	12/1/2015 7:28 PM	File folder	
AdventureWorks2012_12012015195509.bak	12/1/2015 7:55 PM	BAK File	19
AdventureWorks2012_12012015200230.dif	12/1/2015 8:02 PM	DIF File	
AdventureWorks2014_12012015195509.bak	12/1/2015 7:55 PM	BAK File	19
AdventureWorks2014_12012015200230.dif	12/1/2015 8:02 PM	DIF File	
AdventureWorks2014_12012015200435.trn	12/1/2015 8:04 PM	TRN File	
AdventureWorksDW2012_12012015195509.bak	12/1/2015 7:55 PM	BAK File	12
AdventureWorksDW2012_12012015200230.dif	12/1/2015 8:02 PM	DIF File	
AdventureWorksDW2014_12012015195509.bak	12/1/2015 7:55 PM	BAK File	9
AdventureWorksDW2014_12012015200230.dif	12/1/2015 8:02 PM	DIF File	

Figure 11-4. *Additional transaction log backup taken with the script in Listing 11-1*

A single new file was added: a transaction log backup for AdventureWorks2014, which happens to be in the FULL recovery mode, as shown previously.

This stored procedure illustrates a basic framework for building your own customized backup plan, providing complete control over the details. As a bonus, you can accomplish your tasks using a single job and stored procedure, rather than potentially many maintenance plans and/or maintenance plan tasks.

Some additional possibilities for additional functionality include the following:

1. Logging of backup time and duration for each operation

2. Cleanup of old backup records in MSDB

3. Cleanup of old backup files from the output location

4. Customized alerts if backups fail or take longer than a specific time limit

5. Try/catch blocks to manage any errors in the stored procedure

6. Store proc parameters as metadata in a table, so that it can be freely modified for any database, set of databases, or server.

There are certainly many other options available for your consideration. In this example, all databases (except for a handful of system ones) were backed up, but we could just as easily have omitted the WHERE clause or adjusted it so that we backed up a specific set of databases on the server. Additionally, system databases could be managed separately if they had a unique set of rules to follow.

The backup times for this stored procedure were determined by the job run time, but could also be built in as stored proc parameters as well. Both scenarios work, and which you use would depend on how you prefer to manage that data. An additional option that would go well with parameters would be to store metadata in a permanent control table. This would provide information about databases to back up, frequency, and type, and could easily be customized to fit the needs of your environment.

If running a stored procedure in SQL Server seems limiting for the operations you are considering, then PowerShell or SSIS may be used to provide better access to the file system and Windows functionality. As with much of our work thus far, the limits to your success with this model are primarily time and creativity.

Saving Generated Scripts

Dynamic SQL can be written as part of stored procedures to execute as needed by an application, but it also be saved for later. Dynamic SQL can be used to generate a command string that is then saved to a file or new stored procedure to be executed at a future time or as part of another application.

This flexibility can be convenient when there is a process with many steps in which certain ones must execute on a rigid schedule. For example, we may wish to generate a script based on the schema in a database at midnight, but not return the data itself until a data load completes at 4AM. Alternatively, we may wish to review the SQL file or save it elsewhere for posterity, prior to or in addition to executing it. One other way to accomplish this, and avoid moving data into the operating system, would be to store it in a table.

Saving Scripts to a Table

The simplest method of saving a command string would be to insert it into a table. This allows for additional flexibility in that we could add timestamps to commands or save old commands. To facilitate this process, we will create a table to store the command data, as shown in Listing 11-2.

Listing 11-2. Table to Store Dynamic SQL Output.

```
CREATE TABLE dbo.sql_command
(       command_id INT NOT NULL IDENTITY(1,1) CONSTRAINT PK_sql_commands
        PRIMARY KEY CLUSTERED,
        sql_command NVARCHAR(MAX) NOT NULL,
        time_stamp DATETIME NOT NULL CONSTRAINT DF_sql_commands_time_stamp
        DEFAULT (CURRENT_TIMESTAMP));
```

Note that there is an additional column that stores a default timestamp. This ensures that any TSQL that is saved can be associated easily with the time it was generated. To demonstrate using this table, let's modify the backup stored procedure from earlier to insert to it, rather than print to the GUI, as seen in Listing 11-3.

Listing 11-3. Backup Stored Procedure with an Output-to-Table Option.

```
IF EXISTS (SELECT * FROM sys.procedures WHERE procedures.name = 'backup_
plan_output')
BEGIN
        DROP PROCEDURE dbo.backup_plan_output;
END
GO

CREATE PROCEDURE dbo.backup_plan_output
        @differential_and_full_backup_time TIME = '00:00:00', -- Default to
        midnight.
        @full_backup_day TINYINT = 1, -- Default to Sunday.
        @backup_location NVARCHAR(MAX) = 'E:\SQLBackups\', -- Default to my
        backup folder.
        @output_results_to_table BIT = 1
AS
BEGIN
        SET NOCOUNT ON;
        DECLARE @current_time TIME = CAST(CURRENT_TIMESTAMP AS TIME);
        DECLARE @current_day TINYINT = DATEPART(DW, CURRENT_TIMESTAMP);
        DECLARE @datetime_string NVARCHAR(MAX) = FORMAT(CURRENT_TIMESTAMP ,
        'MMddyyyyHHmmss');
        DECLARE @sql_command NVARCHAR(MAX) = '';
```

```
DECLARE @database_list TABLE
        (database_name NVARCHAR(MAX) NOT NULL, recovery_model_desc
        NVARCHAR(MAX));

INSERT INTO @database_list
        (database_name, recovery_model_desc)
SELECT
        name,
        recovery_model_desc
FROM sys.databases
WHERE databases.name NOT IN ('msdb', 'master', 'TempDB', 'model');

-- Check if a full backup is to be taken now.
IF (@current_day = @full_backup_day) AND (@current_time BETWEEN
@differential_and_full_backup_time AND DATEADD(MINUTE, 10,
@differential_and_full_backup_time))
BEGIN
        SELECT @sql_command = @sql_command +
        '
        BACKUP DATABASE [' + database_name + ']
        TO DISK = "' + @backup_location + database_name + '_' +
        @datetime_string + '.bak";
        '
        FROM @database_list;

        IF @output_results_to_table = 1
        BEGIN
                INSERT INTO dbo.sql_command
                        (sql_command)
                SELECT @sql_command
        END
        ELSE
        BEGIN
                EXEC sp_executesql @sql_command;
        END
END
ELSE -- Check if a differential backup is to be taken now.
```

```
IF (@current_day <> @full_backup_day) AND (@current_time BETWEEN
@differential_and_full_backup_time AND DATEADD(MINUTE, 10,
@differential_and_full_backup_time))
 BEGIN
SELECT @sql_command = '';
        SELECT @sql_command = @sql_command +
        '
        BACKUP DATABASE [' + database_name + ']
        TO DISK = "' + @backup_location + database_name + '_' +
        @datetime_string + '.dif"
        WITH DIFFERENTIAL;
        '
        FROM @database_list;

        IF @output_results_to_table = 1
        BEGIN
                INSERT INTO dbo.sql_command
                        (sql_command)
                SELECT @sql_command
        END
        ELSE
        BEGIN
                EXEC sp_executesql @sql_command;
        END
 END
 ELSE -- If neither full or differential, then take a transaction log
 backup.
 BEGIN
SELECT @sql_command = '';
        SELECT @sql_command = @sql_command +
        '
        BACKUP LOG [' + database_name + ']
        TO DISK = "' + @backup_location + database_name + '_' +
        @datetime_string + '.trn"
        '
        FROM @database_list
```

```
        WHERE recovery_model_desc = 'FULL';

        IF @output_results_to_table = 1
        BEGIN
                INSERT INTO dbo.sql_command
                        (sql_command)
                SELECT @sql_command
        END
        ELSE
        BEGIN
                EXEC sp_executesql @sql_command;
        END
    END
END
```

Note that the only difference, aside from renaming a few variables, is to perform an INSERT to dbo.sql_command rather than print the output. Let's execute the stored procedure a few times, and then review the contents of the table:

```
EXEC dbo.backup_plan_output @differential_and_full_backup_time =
'19:50:00', @full_backup_day = 3, @backup_location = 'E:\SQLBackups\',
@output_results_to_table = 1;
EXEC dbo.backup_plan_output @differential_and_full_backup_time =
'00:00:00', @full_backup_day = 1, @backup_location = 'E:\SQLBackups\',
@output_results_to_table = 1;
EXEC dbo.backup_plan_output @differential_and_full_backup_time =
'13:40:00', @full_backup_day = 2, @backup_location = 'E:\SQLBackups\',
@output_results_to_table = 1;
```

These all pass different values for the parameters, but otherwise are the same. Reviewing the new table reveals that our command strings were saved as expected, along with time stamps, as seen in Figure 11-5.

	command_id	sql_command	time_stamp
1	1	BACKUP LOG [Test] TO DISK = 'E:\SQLBackups\Test_10012...	2018-10-01 13:45:22.253
2	2	BACKUP LOG [Test] TO DISK = 'E:\SQLBackups\Test_10012...	2018-10-01 13:45:22.253
3	3	BACKUP DATABASE [Test] TO DISK = 'E:\SQLBackups\Test...	2018-10-01 13:45:22.260

Figure 11-5. BACKUP statements created by the script in Listing 11-3

Once here, they could be executed at any time in the future or reviewed by a DBA or developer to ensure that the command strings are being generated correctly. In addition to delaying execution, this tactic can be excellent for debugging problematic dynamic SQL, or simply allowing for command strings to be logged prior to execution. The following script in Listing 11-4 is another adaption of the backup script from earlier, which will write the generated command strings to a physical SQL file.

Listing 11-4. Backup Maintenance Script, which Outputs the Command String to a File

```
IF EXISTS (SELECT * FROM sys.procedures WHERE procedures.name = 'backup_
plan_output')
BEGIN
        DROP PROCEDURE dbo.backup_plan_output;
END
GO

CREATE PROCEDURE dbo.backup_plan_output
        @differential_and_full_backup_time TIME = '00:00:00', -- Default to
        midnight.
        @full_backup_day TINYINT = 1, -- Default to Sunday.
        @backup_location NVARCHAR(MAX) = 'E:\SQLBackups\', -- Default to my
        backup folder.
        @sql_data_location NVARCHAR(MAX) = 'E:\SQLData\', -- Default to my
        SQL data file folder.
        @sql_server_name NVARCHAR(MAX) = 'SSANDILE\EDSQLSERVER14', -- Server
        name to operate on.
        @print_output_to_file_only BIT = 1
AS
BEGIN
        SET NOCOUNT ON;
        DECLARE @current_time TIME = CAST(CURRENT_TIMESTAMP AS TIME);
        DECLARE @current_day TINYINT = DATEPART(DW, CURRENT_TIMESTAMP);
        DECLARE @datetime_string NVARCHAR(MAX) = FORMAT(CURRENT_TIMESTAMP ,
         'MMddyyyyHHmmss');
        DECLARE @sql_command NVARCHAR(MAX) = ";
        DECLARE @bcp_command VARCHAR(4000);
```

```
DECLARE @database_list TABLE
       (database_name NVARCHAR(MAX) NOT NULL, recovery_model_desc
       NVARCHAR(MAX));

INSERT INTO @database_list
       (database_name, recovery_model_desc)
SELECT
       name,
       recovery_model_desc
FROM sys.databases
WHERE databases.name NOT IN ('msdb', 'master', 'TempDB', 'model');

-- Check if a full backup is to be taken now.
IF (@current_day = @full_backup_day) AND (@current_time BETWEEN
@differential_and_full_backup_time AND DATEADD(MINUTE, 10,
@differential_and_full_backup_time))
BEGIN
       SELECT @sql_command = @sql_command +
       'BACKUP DATABASE [' + database_name + '] TO DISK = ""' +
       @backup_location + database_name + '_' + @datetime_string +
       '.bak"";'
       FROM @database_list;

       IF @print_output_to_file_only = 1
               BEGIN
                       SELECT @bcp_command =
                       'bcp "SELECT "' + @sql_command + '"" queryout
                        ' + @sql_data_location + 'TempOutput.
                        sql -c -T -S' + @sql_server_name + '
                        -dAdventureWorks2014';
                       EXEC xp_cmdshell @bcp_command;
                       SELECT @bcp_command = 'type "' + @sql_data_
                       location + 'TempOutput.sql" >> "' + @sql_data_
                       location + 'QueryOutput.sql"';
                       EXEC xp_cmdshell @bcp_command;
               END
       ELSE
```

```
                    EXEC sp_executesql @sql_command;
END
ELSE -- Check if a differential backup is to be taken now.
IF (@current_day <> @full_backup_day) AND (@current_time BETWEEN
@differential_and_full_backup_time AND DATEADD(MINUTE, 10,
@differential_and_full_backup_time))
BEGIN
        SELECT @sql_command = '';
        SELECT @sql_command = @sql_command +
        'BACKUP DATABASE [' + database_name + '] TO DISK = '''' +
        @backup_location + database_name + '_' + @datetime_string +
        '.dif'''' WITH DIFFERENTIAL;'
        FROM @database_list;

        IF @print_output_to_file_only = 1
                BEGIN
                        SELECT @bcp_command =
                        'bcp "SELECT ''' + @sql_command + '''" queryout
                        ' + @sql_data_location + 'TempOutput.
                        sql -c -T -S' + @sql_server_name + '
                        -dAdventureWorks2014';
                        EXEC xp_cmdshell @bcp_command;
                        SELECT @bcp_command = 'type "' + @sql_data_
                        location + 'TempOutput.sql" >> "' + @sql_data_
                        location + 'QueryOutput.sql"';
                        EXEC xp_cmdshell @bcp_command;
                END
        ELSE
                EXEC sp_executesql @sql_command;
END
ELSE -- If neither full or differential, then take a transaction log
backup.
BEGIN
        SELECT @sql_command = '';
        SELECT @sql_command = @sql_command +
```

```
                'BACKUP LOG [' + database_name + '] TO DISK = ""' + @backup_
                location + database_name + '_' + @datetime_string + '.trn""'
                FROM @database_list
                WHERE recovery_model_desc = 'FULL';

                IF @print_output_to_file_only = 1
                        BEGIN
                                SELECT @bcp_command =
                                'bcp "SELECT "' + @sql_command + ""' queryout '
                                + @sql_data_location + 'TempOutput.sql -c
                                -T -S' + @sql_server_name + '
                                -dAdventureWorks2014';
                                EXEC xp_cmdshell @bcp_command;
                                SELECT @bcp_command = 'type "' + @sql_data_
                                location + 'TempOutput.sql" >> "' + @sql_data_
                                location + '\QueryOutput.sql"';
                                EXEC xp_cmdshell @bcp_command;
                        END
                ELSE
                        EXEC sp_executesql @sql_command;
        END
END
```

Instead of printing the command string, it outputs it to a file. Note that since BCP will by default overwrite the destination file, we must insert each new command string to an intermediary file, TempOutput.sql, prior to appending the output to its final destination, QueryOutput.sql. File paths and the server name have been parameterized to make this proc more versatile. Let's run some examples from earlier:

```
EXEC dbo.backup_plan_output @differential_and_full_backup_time =
'13:55:00', @full_backup_day = 3, @backup_location = 'E:\SQLBackups\',
        @sql_data_location = 'E:\SQLData\', @sql_server_name = 'SANDILE\
        EDSQLSERVER14', @print_output_to_file_only = 1;
EXEC dbo.backup_plan_output @differential_and_full_backup_time =
'13:55:00', @full_backup_day = 1, @backup_location = 'E:\SQLBackups\',
        @sql_data_location = 'E:\SQLData\', @sql_server_name = 'SANDILE\
        EDSQLSERVER14', @print_output_to_file_only = 1;
```

```
EXEC dbo.backup_plan_output @differential_and_full_backup_time =
'10:00:00', @full_backup_day = 1, @backup_location = 'E:\SQLBackups\',
        @sql_data_location = 'E:\SQLData\', @sql_server_name = 'SANDILE\
        EDSQLSERVER14', @print_output_to_file_only = 1;
```

When run, no backups are taken. Instead, the command strings are sent to the text files indicated. The following are the contents of QueryOutput.sql:

```
BACKUP DATABASE [AdventureWorks2012] TO DISK = 'e:\SQLBackups\
AdventureWorks2012_12062015140236.dif' WITH DIFFERENTIAL;BACKUP
DATABASE [AdventureWorks2014] TO DISK = 'e:\SQLBackups\
AdventureWorks2014_12062015140236.dif' WITH DIFFERENTIAL;BACKUP
DATABASE [AdventureWorksDW2012] TO DISK = 'e:\SQLBackups\
AdventureWorksDW2012_12062015140236.dif' WITH DIFFERENTIAL;BACKUP
DATABASE [AdventureWorksDW2014] TO DISK = 'e:\SQLBackups\
AdventureWorksDW2014_12062015140236.dif' WITH DIFFERENTIAL;


BACKUP DATABASE [AdventureWorks2012] TO DISK = 'e:\SQLBackups\
AdventureWorks2012_12062015140236.bak';BACKUP DATABASE [AdventureWorks2014]
TO DISK = 'e:\SQLBackups\AdventureWorks2014_12062015140236.
bak';BACKUP DATABASE [AdventureWorksDW2012] TO DISK = 'e:\
SQLBackups\AdventureWorksDW2012_12062015140236.bak';BACKUP
DATABASE [AdventureWorksDW2014] TO DISK = 'e:\SQLBackups\
AdventureWorksDW2014_12062015140236.bak';


BACKUP LOG [AdventureWorks2014] TO DISK = 'e:\SQLBackups\
AdventureWorks2014_12062015140236.trn'
```

The output file lacks spacing, as BCP works best with single-line TSQL queries. If we wanted to improve the spacing, we could easily add additional intermediary steps into the BCP commands to insert new lines into the file. Regardless, the output is functionally correct and will perform the requested backups to the output folder specified.

Please note the use of xp_cmdshell in the stored procedure. This is typically used when it is necessary to run file operations or OS commands form within SQL Server. Typically, this is only used in restricted or private environments, as it can be a security threat when allowed on a public server. Consider your use case carefully before implementing it, and if your server is in a public environment, use SSIS, PowerShell, or another tool instead.

By default, `xp_cmdshell` is disabled, but you can enable it with the TSQL in Listing 11-5.

Listing 11-5. Enabling xp_cmdshell

```
EXEC sp_configure 'show advanced options', 1
GO
RECONFIGURE
GO
EXEC sp_configure 'xp_cmdshell', 1
GO
RECONFIGURE
GO
```

For more information on the pros and cons of `xp_cmdshell`, see Chapters 2 and 4, which cover SQL Injection and security, respectively. Alternatively, PowerShell can be used to control OS operations to avoid its use.

Executing TSQL on Other Servers

When managing multiple servers, there often are times when we need to execute TSQL from our current server that will run remotely on another SQL Server. While these TSQL statements are not being executed with dynamic SQL, the statement creation and execution is very similar and worth a short demonstration.

Let's consider a scenario where we have a centralized reporting server where we wish to pull data from the local server, in addition to others that we have on-site. We would want to loop through each server, retrieving data from each and returning it to the target data store locally. First, let's create a simple log table for the next example:

```
CREATE TABLE dbo.recent_product_counts
     (     count_id INT NOT NULL IDENTITY(1,1) CONSTRAINT PK_recent_
     product_counts PRIMARY KEY CLUSTERED,
          product_count INT NOT NULL,
          server_name NVARCHAR(128),
```

```
        sample_time DATETIME NOT NULL CONSTRAINT DF_recent_product_
        counts DEFAULT (CURRENT_TIMESTAMP));
```

With a place to store our results, we'll create a stored procedure that illustrates using OPENQUERY in order to return a specific row count from a remote server and store the results in this table. This can be seen in Listing 11-6.

Listing 11-6. Using Dynamic SQL and OPENQUERY to Retrieve Data from Remove Servers

```
IF EXISTS (SELECT * FROM sys.procedures WHERE procedures.name = 'get_
product_count_all_servers')
BEGIN
        DROP PROCEDURE dbo.get_product_count_all_servers;
END
GO

CREATE PROCEDURE dbo.get_product_count_all_servers
AS
BEGIN
        SET NOCOUNT ON;
        DECLARE @sql_command NVARCHAR(MAX) = '';

        SELECT
                name AS server_name
        INTO #servers
        FROM sys.servers;

        SELECT @sql_command = @sql_command + '
        INSERT INTO AdventureWorks2014.dbo.recent_product_counts
                (product_count, server_name)
        SELECT
                product_count,
                "' + server_name + '"
        FROM OPENQUERY([' + server_name + '], "SELECT COUNT(*) AS product_
        count FROM AdventureWorks2014.Production.Product WHERE ModifiedDate
        >= ""2/8/2014""");'
        FROM #servers
```

```
    WHERE server_name <> @@SERVERNAME;

    SELECT @sql_command = @sql_command + '
    INSERT INTO AdventureWorks2014.dbo.recent_product_counts
        (product_count, server_name)
    SELECT
        COUNT(*),
        @@SERVERNAME
    FROM AdventureWorks2014.Production.Product WHERE ModifiedDate >=
    "2/8/2014"';

    EXEC sp_executesql @sql_command;

    DROP TABLE #servers;
END
```

There are two sections in this stored procedure: the first will generate TSQL to access all servers in sys.servers that are not the local server. The second manages the local server only, as the syntax to access it does not require OPENQUERY. After running this query twice, the contents of recent_product_counts are as follows in Figure 11-6.

count_id	product_count	server_name	sample_time
1	504	SANDILE\EDSQLSERVER2016	2015-12-06 14:50:22.927
2	504	SANDILE\EDSQLSERVER14	2015-12-06 14:50:22.927
3	504	SANDILE\EDSQLSERVER2016	2015-12-06 14:52:09.200
4	504	SANDILE\EDSQLSERVER14	2015-12-06 14:52:09.203

Figure 11-6. Product counts collected from multiple servers, using the proc in Listing 11-6

In the case of my computer there is only one other server available to query, but if there were more, then each would be included in the result set. The ModifiedDate used in the stored procedure would typically be a current day, week, or month of interest based on the current date and time, but since the data in AdventureWorks is static, we need to look back a bit further to collect meaningful counts.

It is not necessary to query all SQL Servers in sys.servers, either. A custom list could be created, or a server table could be created and accessed to manage any number of local or remove servers. Also note the use of many apostrophes in the command string text. Since OPENQUERY requires an apostrophe-delimited string, as does sp_executesql, we need to double the number of apostrophes used. This ensures that we maintain the correct number of string delimiters when the final queries are passed to each other SQL Server for execution.

Debug often when nesting strings in a manner like this to ensure that you get the apostrophe count correct. Printing the command string prior to execution will help to ensure that the output is as expected. When in doubt, start from scratch and build the statement up one level at a time, until it is complete. In the preceding code, the number of apostrophes is doubled because the entire TSQL statement is nested in another string, but different applications of dynamic SQL may result in slightly different results.

The rewards for writing this sort of dynamic SQL carefully will outweigh any of the complexities of nesting strings within each other. Being able to efficiently retrieve important data from other servers without loops, maintenance plans, or SSIS packages can be beneficial when looking for a simple solution to a data access need such as this.

Generating Schema from Metadata

There are times, especially in reporting and analytics, when the ability to create dimension or lookup tables automatically can be extremely useful and time-saving. This is often necessary when supporting an application such as Tableau or Power BI, which may require a predefined set of lookup tables for all dimensions to be reported on.

Manually built processes to accomplish this task are time-consuming, complex, and error-prone. Automating it will save resources while greatly improving the quality of the result.

Building a Solution

Consider a table that we wish to report on, but need a corresponding dimension for each lookup column in that table. Most common ways to accomplish this involve either purchasing third-party tools or building a hard-coded solution that builds specific schema for specific columns.

Our goal here will be to accomplish the same task without spending money and by eliminating the need for stored procedures that include specific table, schema, or column references. Instead, we will move all metadata describing our reporting table into a single metadata table that can be easily read or modified as needed. By centralizing this information, we greatly reduce the lines of code that require maintenance and make changing this data trivially easy!

For this example, we will create a reporting table and populate it with data, as seen in Listing 11-7.

Listing 11-7. Create a Test Reporting Table for Use in a Schema Generation Demo

```
USE AdventureworksDW2016CTP3;
GO

CREATE TABLE dbo.fact_customer_metrics_hourly
(       fact_customer_metrics_hourly_id BIGINT NOT NULL IDENTITY(1,1)
CONSTRAINT PK_fact_customer_metrics_hourly PRIMARY KEY CLUSTERED,
        start_time_hour SMALLDATETIME NOT NULL,
        dim_customer_name VARCHAR(50) NOT NULL,
        dim_customer_type VARCHAR(10) NOT NULL,
        dim_customer_status VARCHAR(10) NOT NULL,
        api_call_count INT NOT NULL,
        development_request_count SMALLINT NOT NULL,
        data_sent_gb INT NOT NULL);
GO

INSERT INTO dbo.fact_customer_metrics_hourly
        (start_time_hour, dim_customer_name, dim_customer_type, dim_
        customer_status, api_call_count, development_request_count, data_
        sent_gb)
VALUES
        ('9/14/2018 8:00', 'T-Rex Development', 'Developer', 'Active', 500,
         3, 1000),
        ('9/14/2018 8:00', 'Ed"s QA Shop', 'QA', 'Active', 0, 17, 2),
        ('9/14/2018 8:00', 'Seventeen Corp.', 'Design', 'Inactive', 0, 1, 0),
        ('9/14/2018 8:00', 'Team #2', 'Developer', 'Active', 0, 1, 2500),
        ('9/14/2018 9:00', 'T-Rex Development', 'Developer', 'Active',
         500, 3, 1000),
        ('9/14/2018 9:00', 'Ed"s QA Shop', 'QA', 'Active', 500, 3, 1000),
```

```
('9/14/2018 9:00', 'Seventeen Corp.', 'Design', 'Inactive', 0, 2, 0),
('9/14/2018 10:00', 'T-Rex Development', 'Developer', 'Active', 500,
  3, 1000),
('9/14/2018 10:00', 'Ed"s QA Shop', 'QA', 'Active', 500, 3, 1000),
('9/14/2018 11:00', 'T-Rex Development', 'Developer', 'Active', 500,
  3, 1000),
('9/14/2018 12:00', 'Ed"s QA Shop', 'QA', 'Active', 500, 3, 1000);
GO
```

Note that some of the dimensions are explicitly maintained within fact data. This is sometimes done to simplify reporting, fine-tune performance, or made the data more readable. What is missing here, though, are dimension tables that pair with each dimension column.

Our solution will be to implement a stored procedure that consumes dimension metadata and generates tables using that information. To start this process, we'll create a metadata table that contains basic information about each column that we would like to report on. This data can be populated manually or automatically and managed in whatever manner is deemed most efficient. This table creation and population can be seen in Listing 11-8.

Listing 11-8. Create and Populate a Dimension Metadata Table

```
IF NOT EXISTS (SELECT * FROM sys.tables WHERE tables.name = 'Dimension_
Table_Metadata')
BEGIN
       CREATE TABLE dbo.Dimension_Table_Metadata
       (      Dimension_ID SMALLINT IDENTITY(1,1) NOT NULL CONSTRAINT
              PK_Dimension_Table_Metadata PRIMARY KEY CLUSTERED,
              Target_Dimension_Table_Name VARCHAR(50) NOT NULL,
              Source_Fact_Schema_Name VARCHAR(128) NOT NULL,
              Source_Fact_Table_Name VARCHAR(128) NOT NULL,
              Source_Fact_Column_Name VARCHAR(50) NOT NULL
       );
END
GO

INSERT INTO dbo.Dimension_Table_Metadata
```

```
(Target_Dimension_Table_Name, Source_Fact_Schema_Name, Source_Fact_
Table_Name, Source_Fact_Column_Name)
VALUES
        ('dim_customer_name', 'dbo', 'fact_customer_metrics_hourly',
        'dim_customer_name'),
        ('dim_customer_type', 'dbo', 'fact_customer_metrics_hourly',
        'dim_customer_type'),
        ('dim_customer_status', 'dbo', 'fact_customer_metrics_hourly',
        'dim_customer_status');
GO
```

We now have a representation of three dimension columns and how we would like to consolidate that data, as seen in Figure 11-7.

	Dimension_ID	Target_Dimension_Table_Name	Source_Fact_Schema_Name	Source_Fact_Table_Name	Source_Fact_Column_Name
1	1	dim_customer_name	dbo	fact_customer_metrics_hourly	dim_customer_name
2	2	dim_customer_type	dbo	fact_customer_metrics_hourly	dim_customer_type
3	3	dim_customer_status	dbo	fact_customer_metrics_hourly	dim_customer_status

Figure 11-7. *Dimension attributes stored as metadata in our newly created table*

Each column has been defined by its schema, table, and column name. We have also assigned a target table that dimension data can be loaded into when we are ready to do so.

With this metadata defined, the next step is to create a stored procedure that can use this data to read fact tables and generate dimension tables. The following is a stored procedure that does exactly that, as seen in Listing 11-9.

Listing 11-9. Stored Procedure that Consolidates Dimension Data Using Previously Created Metadata

```
IF EXISTS (SELECT * FROM sys.procedures WHERE procedures.name = 'Generate_
Dimension_Tables')
BEGIN
        DROP PROCEDURE dbo.Generate_Dimension_Tables
END
GO
```

```
CREATE PROCEDURE dbo.Generate_Dimension_Tables
AS
BEGIN
        SET NOCOUNT ON;

        DECLARE @Sql_Command NVARCHAR(MAX) = '';
        SELECT @Sql_Command = @Sql_Command + '
            USE AdventureWorksDW2016CTP3;

            IF EXISTS (SELECT * FROM sys.tables INNER JOIN sys.schemas ON
            schemas.schema_id = tables.schema_id WHERE tables.name = ''
            + Dimension_Table_Metadata.Target_Dimension_Table_Name + ''
            AND schemas.name = '' + Dimension_Table_Metadata.Source_Fact_
            Schema_Name + ''')
            BEGIN
                    DROP TABLE [' + Dimension_Table_Metadata.Source_Fact_
                    Schema_Name + '].[' + Dimension_Table_Metadata.Target_
                    Dimension_Table_Name + '];
            END

            CREATE TABLE [' + Dimension_Table_Metadata.Source_Fact_
            Schema_Name + '].[' + Dimension_Table_Metadata.Target_
            Dimension_Table_Name + ']
            ([' + Dimension_Table_Metadata.Target_Dimension_Table_Name
            + '_Id] INT NOT NULL IDENTITY(1,1) CONSTRAINT [PK_' +
            Dimension_Table_Metadata.Target_Dimension_Table_Name + ']
            PRIMARY KEY CLUSTERED,
                    [' + Dimension_Table_Metadata.Source_Fact_Column_Name
                    + '] ' + USERDATATYPE.name +
                    CASE WHEN USERDATATYPE.name IN ('char', 'nchar',
                    'nvarchar', 'varchar') THEN
                            '(' +
                                CASE WHEN columns.max_length = -1 THEN
                                'MAX'
                                    WHEN USERDATATYPE.name IN ('char',
                                    'varchar') THEN CAST(columns.max_
                                    length AS VARCHAR(MAX))
```

```
                              ELSE CAST(columns.max_length / 2
                                   AS VARCHAR(MAX))
                         END + ')'
              ELSE '' END + ' NOT NULL);

       INSERT INTO [' + Dimension_Table_Metadata.Source_Fact_Schema_
       Name + '].[' + Dimension_Table_Metadata.Target_Dimension_
       Table_Name + ']
           ([' + Dimension_Table_Metadata.Source_Fact_Column_Name + '])
       SELECT DISTINCT
               ' + Dimension_Table_Metadata.Source_Fact_Table_Name +
               '.' + Dimension_Table_Metadata.Source_Fact_Column_
               Name + '
       FROM [' + Dimension_Table_Metadata.Source_Fact_Schema_Name +
       '].[' + Dimension_Table_Metadata.Source_Fact_Table_Name + ']
       WHERE ' + Dimension_Table_Metadata.Source_Fact_Table_Name +
       '.' + Dimension_Table_Metadata.Source_Fact_Column_Name + ' IS
       NOT NULL;'
FROM dbo.Dimension_Table_Metadata
INNER JOIN sys.tables
ON tables.name = Dimension_Table_Metadata.Source_Fact_Table_Name
INNER JOIN sys.columns
ON tables.object_id = columns.object_id
AND columns.name COLLATE database_default = Dimension_Table_
Metadata.Source_Fact_Column_Name
INNER JOIN sys.schemas
ON schemas.schema_id = tables.schema_id
AND schemas.name = Dimension_Table_Metadata.Source_Fact_Schema_Name
INNER JOIN sys.types USERDATATYPE
ON columns.user_type_id = USERDATATYPE.user_type_id
INNER JOIN sys.types SYSTEMDATATYPE
ON SYSTEMDATATYPE.user_type_id = USERDATATYPE.system_type_id
WHERE (USERDATATYPE.name IN ('char', 'nchar', 'nvarchar', 'varchar')
        OR SYSTEMDATATYPE.name IN ('char', 'nchar', 'nvarchar',
        'varchar'));

EXEC sp_executesql @Sql_Command;
END
```

One key note on this stored procedure is that it is not long. At fewer than 50 lines of T-SQL, it illustrates how dynamic SQL can be used to simplify a complex process by generalizing processes. The steps to do this are as follows:

1. Drop the dimension table, if it exists.

2. Create a new dimension table.

3. Insert all dimension values into the newly created table.

Through each step, data types and sizes are preserved so that truncation is not an issue in the final table. With this complete, we can execute it and inspect the results:

```
EXEC dbo.Generate_Dimension_Tables;
GO
```

The resulting three tables can be viewed in Figure 11-8.

	dim_customer_name_Id	dim_customer_name
1	1	Ed's QA Shop
2	2	Seventeen Corp.
3	3	T-Rex Development
4	4	Team #2

	dim_customer_status_Id	dim_customer_status
1	1	Active
2	2	Inactive

	dim_customer_type_Id	dim_customer_type
1	1	Design
2	2	Developer
3	3	QA

Figure 11-8. Resulting dimension tables and their contents

Each row in `Dimension_Table_Metadata` has been used to load data from our fact table and turn it into dimension data. The resulting tables can be used to feed reporting processes and provide a distinct list of lookup columns for aggregation, sorting, or other operations.

The biggest benefit of an approach such as this is scalability. Adding a new table only requires that we add a single row of metadata to `Dimension_Table_Metadata`. If any objects change, those updates can be made centrally to this one location and the stored procedure will continue to operate normally using the new metadata.

This process is relatively simple and is intended to demonstrate one way we can convert data and metadata into schema and that it can be done with very little code, complexity, or maintainability. Its simplicity begs for customization, as many of the real-world applications of this would need to be modified to accommodate differing use cases. Here are some different ways in which we could tweak this code to provide additional capabilities:

- Limit the amount of fact data to load if there is no need to read all historical data. This would reduce reads and speed up the process greatly. If the fact table is very large, then this would be necessary to prevent the stored procedure from taking an unacceptably long time.

- Remove the hard-coded database name from the stored procedure. Alternatively, this could be made dynamic to operate on any database, if more than one is involved.

- Use a MERGE statement instead of a drop/create on the target dimension table. This will reduce work and allow for a slow, additive data load over time. It will also maintain a consistent primary key ID column, if needed.

- Add support for more data types, such as numeric, GUID, or custom data types. This could be a way to enumerate other less-common data types in the same fashion as with string data.

- Add additional columns to the resulting dimension tables to add ordering, tags, or additional metadata that could be used to better understand the data and what it means.

By using dynamic SQL, we were able to enumerate large amounts of metadata and data using very little code. Centralizing metadata into a single, easy-to-maintain location greatly improves the cost of data maintenance over time while allowing for processes to consume it to generate new data, schema, or data insights. This approach can be applied to many applications, whether they are as simple as this demonstration or far more complex.

Conclusion

In this chapter we presented a variety of applications that used many of the techniques presented in this book. Many of these scripts were very open-ended, allowing for a great deal of customization as they are built and implemented. List generation allowed for the avoidance of cursors and loops when building command strings, making execution very efficient.

There are countless other tasks that will present themselves over time in which dynamic SQL or many of its related topics will be invaluable for solving. Even when not developing new applications, knowledge of these tools allows us to be vigilant when reviewing others' work or when troubleshooting performance or application problems.

Be creative and willing to write something new, even if little content is available to get you started. Many great tools have been built because of the question, "Why hasn't anyone done this yet?!" This book has provided a starting point, but as new versions of SQL Server and other database tools are released, and as the complexity of software applications increases with time, the opportunity for novel solutions increases.

Even if you think an idea may be a dead end, explore it anyway, and doubly so if it is someone else claiming it's a dead end. I would wager that more than half of the "brilliant solutions" I've come up with over the years have led to absolutely nothing of use, but the remainder were what have kept me optimistic about database development and optimization throughout my career.

CHAPTER 12

Index Usage and Maintenance

For our final chapter, we will apply dynamic SQL to one of its most fitting applications: the care and maintenance of our SQL Servers and databases. These tasks are all too often associated with hard-coded, hacked, messy T-SQL that is written to be forgotten. Of all the places where a developer might copy and paste code from a dubious source, this is the most common.

Our goal is to create a set of scripts that can perform important tasks and do so in a scalable, reusable, and maintainable fashion. We want tools that are easy to use and simple to customize. Each application presented in this chapter will be a self-contained way to solve a problem. Use this code to take control of server maintenance and get better insights out of your databases!

Indexes are central to performance. For most queries to perform optimally, they require an index to select data from efficiently. Alternatively, unused indexes waste resource, consuming disk space and slowing down writes on associated objects. Heavily fragmented indexes can waste disk space and memory as they become overwhelmed with unused space and disorganized data.

The following section outlines a variety of common indexing problems along with solutions that can be customized and applied to any database environment.

Index Defragmentation

One of the most immediate questions that we ask when reviewing a poorly performing query is if the correct indexes are in place and if they are adequate. An additional question that should not need to be asked is if those indexes are being properly maintained. Over time as an index is inserted to, updated, and deleted from, the

© Edward Pollack 2019
E. Pollack, *Dynamic SQL*, https://doi.org/10.1007/978-1-4842-4318-3_12

B-tree that it is built on becomes fragmented. The more time that passes, the worse the situation gets and the more time it takes to traverse the B-tree effectively and return the data requested by your queries.

Running jobs regularly that check for index fragmentation and take action as necessary will ensure that this situation never becomes detrimental to application performance. As a bonus, index usage metrics teach us about table usage as we learn which are read-heavy, write-heavy, or both. Our first task toward achieving this goal is to identify how fragmented our indexes are, and to do so on any set of databases on our server.

This information can be found in the `sys.dm_db_index_physical_stats` dynamic management view. The following query in Listing 12-1 joins data from this view into a handful of system views to include the name of the database, table, and indexes involved.

Listing 12-1. Query to Determine Index Fragmentation for All Indexes in a Given Database

```
USE AdventureWorks2016CTP3
DECLARE @database_name VARCHAR(100) = 'AdventureWorks2016CTP3';

SELECT
        SD.name AS database_name,
        SO.name AS object_name,
        SI.name AS index_name,
        IPS.index_type_desc,
        IPS.page_count,
        IPS.avg_fragmentation_in_percent -- Be sure to filter as much as
        possible...this can return a lot of data if you don't filter by
        database and table.
FROM sys.dm_db_index_physical_stats(NULL, NULL, NULL, NULL , NULL) IPS
INNER JOIN sys.databases SD
ON SD.database_id = IPS.database_id
INNER JOIN sys.indexes SI
ON SI.index_id = IPS.index_id
INNER JOIN sys.objects SO
ON SO.object_id = SI.object_id
AND IPS.object_id = SO.object_id
```

```
WHERE alloc_unit_type_desc = 'IN_ROW_DATA'
AND index_level = 0
AND SD.name = @database_name
ORDER BY IPS.avg_fragmentation_in_percent DESC;
```

This query specifically targets one database in the filter (based on the parameter declared at the top), but could be adjusted to check any or all user databases on a server. The results in Figure 12-1 show each index, ordered by fragmentation, along with some additional useful information.

	database_name	object_name	index_name	index_type_desc	page_count	avg_fragmentation_in_percent
1	AdventureWorks2014	DatabaseLog	PK_DatabaseLog_DatabaseLogID	NONCLUSTERED INDEX	4	75
2	AdventureWorks2014	BusinessEntityContact	AK_BusinessEntityContact_rowguid	NONCLUSTERED INDEX	4	75
3	AdventureWorks2014	BusinessEntityContact	IX_BusinessEntityContact_PersonID	NONCLUSTERED INDEX	3	66.6666666666667
4	AdventureWorks2014	BusinessEntityContact	IX_BusinessEntityContact_ContactTypeID	NONCLUSTERED INDEX	3	66.6666666666667
5	AdventureWorks2014	ProductReview	IX_ProductReview_ProductID_Name	NONCLUSTERED INDEX	3	66.6666666666667
6	AdventureWorks2014	ProductCostHistory	PK_ProductCostHistory_ProductID_StartDate	CLUSTERED INDEX	3	66.6666666666667
7	AdventureWorks2014	Store	AK_Store_rowguid	NONCLUSTERED INDEX	3	66.6666666666667
8	AdventureWorks2014	ProductDescription	AK_ProductDescription_rowguid	NONCLUSTERED INDEX	3	66.6666666666667
9	AdventureWorks2014	SpecialOfferProduct	PK_SpecialOfferProduct_SpecialOfferID_ProductID	CLUSTERED INDEX	3	66.6666666666667
10	AdventureWorks2014	ProductListPriceHistory	PK_ProductListPriceHistory_ProductID_StartDate	CLUSTERED INDEX	3	66.6666666666667
11	AdventureWorks2014	Employee	AK_Employee_LoginID	NONCLUSTERED INDEX	3	66.6666666666667

Figure 12-1. *Index fragmentation results from the query in Listing 12-1*

Now that we have identified our most fragmented tables, we need to figure out the best way to address them. We have two options available to us:

Index Rebuild

When an index is rebuilt, it is completely replaced with a new copy of the index, built from scratch as though it were just newly created. In SQL Server Standard edition, this is an offline operation, meaning that it can cause contention while running. When rebuilding indexes in Standard edition, use caution to schedule them at a time when that interruption is tolerable. In Enterprise edition, rebuilds can be run online, allowing them to operate while other transactions occur at the same time. Regardless of edition, rebuilding indexes is a resource-intensive operation and should be done during off hours when the server has extra resources to spare.

In SQL Server 2017, resumable online index rebuilds were introduced, allowing a rebuild to continue where it left off if it were interrupted. Prior to this feature, canceling an index rebuild would cause the entire operation to roll back, which can also be time-consuming and resource intensive.

Index Reorganization

Reorganizing an index results in cleanup at the leaf level, reordering pages and reapplying the fill-factor as necessary. This operation is always online, regardless of the edition of SQL Server you are running, and can be interrupted at any time with no ill effects.

Despite being a somewhat simpler process, an index reorg can potentially take as long as an index rebuild for a very wide index. Keeping track of these times can allow you to periodically review index maintenance tasks and ensure they are running acceptably fast.

Creating an Index Maintenance Solution

We now know what the problem is and what tools are available to solve it, so now we can step through a sample of a solution. The need for dynamic SQL is immediate: we have multiple databases, tables, indexes, and potential operations. This is a scenario where the dynamic TSQL will be simpler and easier to implement than a long, procedural solution.

Let's start with a stored procedure that checks the fragmentation level and will choose whether to reorganize or rebuild based on user input. For this example, we'll choose 10% for a reorg and 35% for a rebuild, as well as use those numbers as default parameter values. It will have a `@print_only` flag that determines if we should print the results for review or execute them. The proc will include all databases on the instance, except for `model`, `master`, `msdb`, and `tempdb`. This can easily be customized to act on any set of databases, though. One last addition is the inclusion of the schema name, so that we can support databases with multiple schemas aside from `dbo`. This new script can be viewed in its entirety in Listing 12-2.

Listing 12-2. Simple Index Maintenance Solution Using Dynamic SQL

```
IF EXISTS (SELECT * FROM sys.procedures WHERE procedures.name = 'index_
maintenance_demo')
BEGIN
        DROP PROCEDURE dbo.index_maintenance_demo;
END
GO
```

```
CREATE PROCEDURE dbo.index_maintenance_demo
      @reorganization_percentage TINYINT = 10,
      @rebuild_percentage TINYINT = 35,
      @print_results_only BIT = 1
AS
BEGIN
      SET NOCOUNT ON;
      DECLARE @sql_command NVARCHAR(MAX) = '';
      DECLARE @parameter_list NVARCHAR(MAX) = '@reorganization_percentage
TINYINT, @rebuild_percentage TINYINT'
      DECLARE @database_name NVARCHAR(MAX);
      DECLARE @database_list TABLE
            (database_name NVARCHAR(MAX) NOT NULL);

      INSERT INTO @database_list
            (database_name)
      SELECT
            name
      FROM sys.databases
      WHERE databases.name NOT IN ('msdb', 'master', 'TempDB', 'model');

      CREATE TABLE #index_maintenance
      (     database_name NVARCHAR(MAX),
            schema_name NVARCHAR(MAX),
            object_name NVARCHAR(MAX),
            index_name NVARCHAR(MAX),
            index_type_desc NVARCHAR(MAX),
            page_count BIGINT,
            avg_fragmentation_in_percent FLOAT,
            index_operation NVARCHAR(MAX));

      SELECT @sql_command = @sql_command + '
      USE [' + database_name + ']

      INSERT INTO #index_maintenance
            (database_name, schema_name, object_name, index_name,
            index_type_desc, page_count, avg_fragmentation_in_percent,
            index_operation)
```

```
SELECT
        CAST(SD.name AS NVARCHAR(MAX)) AS database_name,
        CAST(SS.name AS NVARCHAR(MAX)) AS schema_name,
        CAST(SO.name AS NVARCHAR(MAX)) AS object_name,
        CAST(SI.name AS NVARCHAR(MAX)) AS index_name,
        IPS.index_type_desc,
        IPS.page_count,
        IPS.avg_fragmentation_in_percent, -- Be sure to filter as much
        as possible...this can return a lot of data if you dont filter
        by database and table.
        CAST(CASE
                WHEN IPS.avg_fragmentation_in_percent >= @rebuild_
                percentage THEN "REBUILD"
                WHEN IPS.avg_fragmentation_in_percent >=
                @reorganization_percentage THEN "REORGANIZE"
        END AS NVARCHAR(MAX)) AS index_operation
FROM sys.dm_db_index_physical_stats(NULL, NULL, NULL, NULL , NULL) IPS
INNER JOIN sys.databases SD
ON SD.database_id = IPS.database_id
INNER JOIN sys.indexes SI
ON SI.index_id = IPS.index_id
INNER JOIN sys.objects SO
ON SO.object_id = SI.object_id
AND IPS.object_id = SO.object_id
INNER JOIN sys.schemas SS
ON SS.schema_id = SO.schema_id
WHERE alloc_unit_type_desc = "IN_ROW_DATA"
AND index_level = 0
AND SD.name = "' + database_name + "'
AND IPS.avg_fragmentation_in_percent >= @reorganization_percentage
AND SI.name IS NOT NULL -- Only review index, not heap data.
AND SO.is_ms_shipped = 0 -- Do not perform maintenance on system
objects.
ORDER BY SD.name ASC;'
FROM @database_list
WHERE database_name IN (SELECT name FROM sys.databases);
```

```
    EXEC sp_executesql @sql_command, @parameter_list, @reorganization_
    percentage, @rebuild_percentage;

    SELECT @sql_command = '';
    SELECT @sql_command = @sql_command +
    '       USE [' + database_name + ']
            ALTER INDEX [' + index_name + '] ON [' + schema_name + '].
            [' + object_name + ']
            ' + index_operation + ';
    '
    FROM #index_maintenance;

    SELECT * FROM #index_maintenance
    ORDER BY avg_fragmentation_in_percent DESC;

    IF @print_results_only = 1
            PRINT @sql_command;
    ELSE
            EXEC sp_executesql @sql_command;

    DROP TABLE #index_maintenance;
END
```

Note that a maintenance stored procedure such as this can exist anywhere, but ideally could be included in a user-defined maintenance/support database. This provides us control over our schema and leaves system databases as untouched as possible.

This script builds a long command string from a sequence of index rebuild or reorg operations. Note that each set of dynamic SQL operations builds strings using a dynamically generated list prior to execution. This avoids the need for loops or cursors and accomplishes our tasks very quickly and efficiently. Let's execute this for the default parameters:

```
EXEC dbo.index_maintenance_demo @reorganization_percentage = 10, @rebuild_
percentage = 35, @print_results_only = 1;
```

Since `@print_results_only` is set to 1, no index actions will be taken. The command string will be printed out at the end of the stored procedure, prior to dropping the temporary table. Here is a subset of the results that printed on my server:

```
USE [AdventureWorks2014]
        ALTER INDEX [IX_vProductAndDescription] ON [Production].
        [vProductAndDescription]
        REORGANIZE;
USE [AdventureWorks2014]
        ALTER INDEX [IX_vStateProvinceCountryRegion] ON [Person].
        [vStateProvinceCountryRegion]
        REBUILD;
USE [AdventureWorks2016CTP3]
        ALTER INDEX [PK_ProductCostHistory_ProductID_StartDate] ON
        [Production].[ProductCostHistory]
        REBUILD;
USE [AdventureWorks2016CTP3]
        ALTER INDEX [AK_ProductDescription_rowguid] ON [Production].
        [ProductDescription]
        REBUILD;
USE [AdventureWorks2016CTP3]
        ALTER INDEX [PK_DatabaseLog_DatabaseLogID] ON [dbo].[DatabaseLog]
        REBUILD;
USE [AdventureWorks2016CTP3]
        ALTER INDEX [PK_ProductInventory_ProductID_LocationID] ON
        [Production].[ProductInventory]
        REORGANIZE;
```

Note that results for a variety of databases were returned and will vary accordingly on your test machine. When working with long command strings, beware of truncation, either in the string itself or by Management Studio's results pane when printing sample output. As a precaution against this, I've cast all strings in the temporary table as NVARCHAR(MAX), to ensure that the command string is not converted to any of the smaller string data types.

It is also important to note that dynamic SQL was used to gather index fragmentation data as some of the views, such as `sys.tables` or `dm_db_index_physical_stats` are database-specific. To collect all data for each database, it was necessary to USE each database and then check the views within them independently of each other. Similarly, to perform index maintenance, it is necessary to USE the appropriate database first before running a rebuild or reorganize statement.

The contents of the temporary table are also output, so we can further review the data returned, as seen in Figure 12-2.

	database_name	schema_name	object_name	index_name	index_type_desc	page_count	avg_fragmentation_in_percent	index_operation
1	AdventureWorks2014	Production	ProductCostHistory	PK_ProductCostHistory_ProductID_StartDate	CLUSTERED INDEX	3	66.6666666666667	REBUILD
2	AdventureWorks2014	Production	ProductDescription	AK_ProductDescription_rowguid	NONCLUSTERED INDEX	3	66.6666666666667	REBUILD
3	AdventureWorks2014	dbo	DatabaseLog	PK_DatabaseLog_DatabaseLogID	NONCLUSTERED INDEX	3	75	REBUILD
4	AdventureWorks2014	Production	ProductInventory	PK_ProductInventory_ProductID_LocationID	CLUSTERED INDEX	7	57.1428571428571	REBUILD
5	AdventureWorks2014	Production	ProductListPriceHistory	PK_ProductListPriceHistory_ProductID_StartDate	CLUSTERED INDEX	3	66.6666666666667	REBUILD
6	AdventureWorks2014	Sales	SpecialOfferProduct	PK_SpecialOfferProduct_SpecialOfferID_ProductID	CLUSTERED INDEX	3	66.6666666666667	REBUILD
7	AdventureWorks2014	Sales	SpecialOfferProduct	AK_SpecialOfferProduct_rowguid	NONCLUSTERED INDEX	2	50	REBUILD
8	AdventureWorks2014	Person	StateProvince	PK_StateProvince_StateProvinceID	CLUSTERED INDEX	2	50	REBUILD
9	AdventureWorks2014	Production	ProductModelProduc...	PK_ProductModelProductDescriptionCulture_Prod...	CLUSTERED INDEX	4	50	REBUILD
10	AdventureWorks2014	Production	BillOfMaterials	AK_BillOfMaterials_ProductAssemblyID_Compone...	CLUSTERED INDEX	20	15	REORGANIZE
11	AdventureWorks2014	Production	BillOfMaterials	PK_BillOfMaterials_BillOfMaterialsID	NONCLUSTERED INDEX	9	33.3333333333333	REORGANIZE
12	AdventureWorks2014	Production	BillOfMaterials	IX_BillOfMaterials_UnitMeasureCode	NONCLUSTERED INDEX	10	30	REORGANIZE

Figure 12-2. *Full fragmentation results, as returned from the query in Listing 12-2*

Here we can review each index, its fragmentation level, and the operation that was chosen based on our inputs. If we are confident that this stored procedure does exactly what we want it to, then we can allow it to execute the entire command string and clean up all indexes in these databases:

```
EXEC dbo.index_maintenance_demo @reorganization_percentage = 10, @rebuild_
percentage = 35, @print_results_only = 0;
```

After about 30 seconds of waiting, the script completes successfully and our index maintenance is complete! We can add additional options and continue to customize this script to our heart's content. Some features to consider adding:

- Add WITH (ONLINE = ON) to rebuild operations so they can run online (Enterprise edition only)

- Add WITH (SORT_IN_TEMP = ON) to rebuild operations so they can sort intermediary rebuild results in TempDB, which can speed up operations. Keep in mind that enough space must be available in TempDB for this to work.

- Adjust the fill factor on an index, if one besides the default is needed.

- Check the size of the index and take actions differently based on that information.

- Add logging so that you can review the commands executed, as well as the time needed to complete them.

- Exceptions for tables that are write-heavy and are not worth the effort to perform maintenance against. Similarly, we can omit databases that do not require maintenance to avoid unnecessary work.

Use this script as a starting point and tailor it to your environment's needs, regardless of how they may differ from what we have presented here. There are an infinite number of ways to customize and improve upon this concept, with your imagination being the only barrier between you and the perfect index maintenance solution!

Index Usage Statistics

Knowing which indexes are used, unused, or misused provides valuable information that can be used to effectively manage performance. Collecting this data and trending it over time allows us to accomplish some important tasks:

- Unused indexes can be removed to reclaim wasted space and speed up writes.

- Write-heavy indexes may be able to be removed.

- Indexes with many scans and lookups may suggest missing or inadequate indexing on the table.

- Duplicate indexes may be removed.

SQL Server stores all index usage data in `sys.dm_db_index_usage_stats`. The query in Listing 12-3 shows how we can use this view to learn about our index usage.

Listing 12-3. Viewing Index Usage Statistics Using dm_db_index_usage_stats

```
SELECT
        schemas.name AS SchemaName,
        tables.name AS TableName,
        indexes.name AS IndexName,
```

```
        indexes.type_desc AS IndexType,
        dm_db_index_usage_stats.*
FROM sys.dm_db_index_usage_stats
INNER JOIN sys.indexes
ON indexes.object_id = dm_db_index_usage_stats.object_id
AND indexes.index_id = dm_db_index_usage_stats.index_id
INNER JOIN sys.tables
ON tables.object_id = indexes.object_id
INNER JOIN sys.schemas
ON schemas.schema_id = tables.schema_id
WHERE dm_db_index_usage_stats.database_id = DB_ID()
AND indexes.name IS NOT NULL;
```

The results of this query show any index usage that has occurred on my local SQL Server within the database that I ran it, as seen in Figure 12-3.

	SchemaName	TableName	IndexName	IndexType	database_id	object_id	index_id	user_seeks	user_scans	user_lookups	user_updates	last_user_seek
1	Sales	SalesOrderDetail	PK_SalesOrderDetail_SalesOrderID_SalesOrderDet...	CLUSTERED	8	1474104292	1	0	1	0	0	NULL
2	Production	UnitMeasure	PK_UnitMeasure_UnitMeasureCode	CLUSTERED	8	1054626800	1	0	4	0	0	NULL
3	Sales	SalesOrderHeader	PK_SalesOrderHeader_SalesOrderID	CLUSTERED	8	1586104691	1	0	1	0	0	NULL
4	Person	Person	IX_Person_LastName_FirstName_MiddleName	NONCLUSTERED	8	2085582468	3	0	52	0	0	NULL
5	Person	Person	PK_Person_BusinessEntityID	CLUSTERED	8	2085582468	1	10	0	52	0	2018-09-18 07:27:45.947
6	Production	Product	AK_Product_Name	NONCLUSTERED	8	146099561	3	14	0	0	0	2018-09-18 07:27:46.250

Figure 12-3. *Index usage statistics from my AdventureWorks database*

Included in our data is the schema name, table name, index name, index type, and a variety of metrics counting seeks, scans, and more. Before continuing, we must consider a handful of caveats to this data that will influence how we use it:

- All index usage data is reset when SQL Server is restarted.

- Prior to SQL Server 2012SP2CU12, 2012SP3CU3 and SQL Server 2014SP2, index rebuilds also reset index usage stats.

- Completely unused indexes are not included in dm_db_index_ usage_stats. A new row is added for an index when it is first read or written to.

These details mean that we need to capture data regularly to not lose it upon a restart or rebuild. We also need to account for unused indexes that never receive any reads or writes, as they will not be populated in our result set at all.

To attack this problem, we will start by creating tables to store these stats. Listing 12-4 shows the creation of tables that will store index usage stats detail data, summary data, and daily usage data.

Listing 12-4. Tables to Store Index Usage Statistics

```
CREATE TABLE dbo.index_usage_stats_detail
(       index_usage_stats_detail_Id INT NOT NULL IDENTITY(1,1) CONSTRAINT
        PK_index_usage_stats_detail PRIMARY KEY CLUSTERED,
        index_usage_stats_detail_create_datetime DATETIME NOT NULL,
        [database_name] SYSNAME,
        [schema_name] SYSNAME,
        table_name SYSNAME,
        index_name SYSNAME,
        user_seek_count BIGINT,
        user_scan_count BIGINT,
        user_lookup_count BIGINT,
        user_update_count BIGINT,
        last_user_seek DATETIME,
        last_user_scan DATETIME,
        last_user_lookup DATETIME,
        last_user_update DATETIME,
        is_primary_key BIT NOT NULL,
        is_clustered_index BIT NOT NULL
);

CREATE NONCLUSTERED INDEX IX_index_usage_stats_detail_index_usage_stats_
detail_create_datetime ON dbo.index_usage_stats_detail (index_usage_stats_
detail_create_datetime);
GO

CREATE TABLE dbo.index_usage_daily_stats
(       index_usage_daily_stats_id INT NOT NULL IDENTITY(1,1) CONSTRAINT
PK_index_usage_daily_stats PRIMARY KEY CLUSTERED,
        index_usage_daily_stats_date DATE NOT NULL,
        [database_name] SYSNAME,
```

```
        [schema_name] SYSNAME,
        table_name SYSNAME,
        index_name SYSNAME,
        user_seek_count_daily BIGINT,
        user_scan_count_daily BIGINT,
        user_lookup_count_daily BIGINT,
        user_update_count_daily BIGINT,
        last_user_seek DATETIME,
        last_user_scan DATETIME,
        last_user_lookup DATETIME,
        last_user_update DATETIME,
        user_seek_count_last_update BIGINT,
        user_scan_count_last_update BIGINT,
        user_lookup_count_last_update BIGINT,
        user_update_count_last_update BIGINT,
        is_primary_key BIT NOT NULL,
        is_clustered_index BIT NOT NULL,
        index_usage_daily_stats_Last_Update_Datetime DATETIME NOT NULL
);

CREATE NONCLUSTERED INDEX IX_index_usage_daily_stats_index_usage_daily_
stats_date ON dbo.index_usage_daily_stats (index_usage_daily_stats_date);

CREATE NONCLUSTERED INDEX IX_index_usage_daily_stats_database_name_schema_
name_table_name_index_name ON dbo.index_usage_daily_stats ([database_name],
[schema_name], table_name, index_name);
GO
```

These two tables provide us with different ways to store and manage usage metrics:

- Index_usage_stats_detail will contain stats directly from dm_
  db_index_usage_stats with no aggregation or transformations
  against it.

- Index_usage_daily_stats will roll up data from a given date so that
  we can easily trend usage over time or over any custom time period.

With tables created to store index usage data, we can now create a stored procedure to collect that data and store it in those tables. The process to do so is relatively straightforward:

1. Compile a list of nonsystem databases.

2. Iterate through each database and:

    a. Collect a list of all indexes in the database.

    b. Collect index stats detail for each index.

3. Calculate index usage daily stats based on the detailed data collected and the previous day's metrics.

4. Add daily metrics for completely unused indexes not present in dm_db_index_usage_stats.

With this basic process defined, let's create our collection proc, execute it, and examine the results. The stored procedure definition can be seen in Listing 12-5.

Listing 12-5. Stored Procedure to Populate Index Usage Statistics Tables

```
CREATE PROCEDURE dbo.populate_index_usage_stats
       @detail_data_retention_days TINYINT = 20,
       @daily_data_retention_days TINYINT = 120,
       @aggregate_database_data BIT = 0
AS
BEGIN
       SET NOCOUNT ON;

       DELETE index_usage_stats_detail
       FROM dbo.index_usage_stats_detail
       WHERE index_usage_stats_detail.index_usage_stats_detail_create_
       datetime < DATEADD(DAY, -1 * @detail_data_retention_days, CURRENT_
       TIMESTAMP);

       DELETE index_usage_daily_stats
       FROM dbo.index_usage_daily_stats
       WHERE index_usage_daily_stats.index_usage_daily_stats_date <
       DATEADD(DAY, -1 * @daily_data_retention_days, CURRENT_TIMESTAMP);
```

```
DECLARE @index_collection_timestamp DATETIME = CURRENT_TIMESTAMP;
DECLARE @index_collection_date DATE = CAST(CURRENT_TIMESTAMP AS
DATE);

CREATE TABLE #database_list
        (       [database_name] SYSNAME NOT NULL PRIMARY KEY CLUSTERED,
                is_processed BIT NOT NULL);

DECLARE @sql_command NVARCHAR(MAX);
DECLARE @current_database_name SYSNAME;

INSERT INTO #database_list
        ([database_name], is_processed)
SELECT
        databases.name AS [database_name],
        0 AS is_processed
FROM sys.databases
WHERE databases.name NOT IN ('master', 'msdb', 'model', 'tempdb',
'ReportServerTempDB', 'ReportServer')
AND databases.state_desc = 'ONLINE';

CREATE TABLE #index_usage_stats_detail
(       index_usage_stats_detail_create_datetime DATETIME NOT NULL,
        [database_name] SYSNAME,
        [schema_name] SYSNAME,
        table_name SYSNAME,
        index_name SYSNAME,
        user_seek_count BIGINT,
        user_scan_count BIGINT,
        user_lookup_count BIGINT,
        user_update_count BIGINT,
        last_user_seek DATETIME,
        last_user_scan DATETIME,
        last_user_lookup DATETIME,
        last_user_update DATETIME,
        is_primary_key BIT NOT NULL,
        is_clustered_index BIT NOT NULL    );
```

```
CREATE TABLE #all_indexes
(     all_indexes_id INT NOT NULL IDENTITY(1,1) PRIMARY KEY CLUSTERED,
      [database_name] SYSNAME NOT NULL,
      [schema_name] SYSNAME NOT NULL,
      table_name SYSNAME NOT NULL,
      index_name SYSNAME NOT NULL,
      is_primary_key BIT NOT NULL,
      is_clustered_index BIT NOT NULL    );

WHILE EXISTS (SELECT * FROM #database_list database_list WHERE
database_list.is_processed = 0)
BEGIN
      SELECT TOP 1
            @current_database_name = database_list.[database_name]
      FROM #database_list database_list
      WHERE database_list.is_processed = 0;

      SELECT
            @sql_command =
            '      USE [' + @current_database_name + ']
                  INSERT INTO #index_usage_stats_detail
                        (index_usage_stats_detail_create_
                        datetime, [database_name], [schema_name],
                        table_name, index_name, user_seek_count,
                         user_scan_count, user_lookup_count,
                         user_update_count, last_user_seek, last_
                         user_scan, last_user_lookup, last_user_
                         update,
                         is_primary_key, is_clustered_index)
                  SELECT
                        "' + CAST(@index_collection_timestamp AS
                        NVARCHAR(MAX)) + "' AS index_usage_stats_
                        detail_create_datetime,
                        "' + REPLACE(@current_database_name,
                        "", """) + "' AS [database_name],
                        schemas.name AS [schema_name],
```

```
            tables.name AS table_name,
            indexes.name AS index_name,
            dm_db_index_usage_stats.user_seeks
            AS user_seek_count,
            dm_db_index_usage_stats.user_scans
            AS user_scan_count,
            dm_db_index_usage_stats.user_lookups
            AS user_lookup_count,
            dm_db_index_usage_stats.user_updates
            AS user_update_count,
            dm_db_index_usage_stats.last_user_seek
            AS last_user_seek,
            dm_db_index_usage_stats.last_user_scan
            AS last_user_scan,
            dm_db_index_usage_stats.last_user_lookup
            AS last_user_lookup,
            dm_db_index_usage_stats.last_user_update
            AS last_user_update,
            ISNULL(indexes.is_primary_key, 0) AS is_
            primary_key,
            ISNULL(CASE WHEN indexes.type_desc =
            "CLUSTERED" THEN 1 ELSE 0 END, 0) AS is_
            clustered_index
FROM [' + @current_database_name + '].sys.dm_db_
index_usage_stats
INNER JOIN [' + @current_database_name + '].sys.
indexes
ON indexes.object_id = dm_db_index_usage_stats.
object_id
AND indexes.index_id = dm_db_index_usage_stats.
index_id
INNER JOIN [' + @current_database_name + '].sys.
tables
ON tables.object_id = indexes.object_id
INNER JOIN [' + @current_database_name + '].sys.
schemas
```

```
                    ON schemas.schema_id = tables.schema_id
                    WHERE dm_db_index_usage_stats.database_id =
                    (SELECT DB_ID("' + REPLACE(@current_database_
                    name, "", """) + "'))
                    AND indexes.name IS NOT NULL;

                    INSERT INTO #all_indexes
                            ([database_name], [schema_name], table_
                            name, index_name, is_primary_key, is_
                            clustered_index)
                    SELECT
                            "' + REPLACE(@current_database_name,
                            "", """) + "' AS [database_name],
                            schemas.name COLLATE DATABASE_DEFAULT AS
                            [schema_name],
                            tables.name COLLATE DATABASE_DEFAULT AS
                            table_name,
                            indexes.name COLLATE DATABASE_DEFAULT
                            AS index_name,
                            ISNULL(indexes.is_primary_key, 0) AS is_
                            primary_key,
                            ISNULL(CASE WHEN indexes.type_desc =
                            "CLUSTERED" THEN 1 ELSE 0 END, 0) AS is_
                            clustered_index
                    FROM [' + @current_database_name + '].sys.
                    indexes
                    INNER JOIN [' + @current_database_name + '].sys.
                    tables
                    ON indexes.object_id = tables.object_id
                    INNER JOIN [' + @current_database_name + '].sys.
                    schemas
                    ON schemas.schema_id = tables.schema_id
                    WHERE indexes.name IS NOT NULL;';

        EXEC sp_executesql @sql_command;
```

```
        UPDATE database_list
                SET is_processed = 1
        FROM #database_list database_list
        WHERE [database_name] = @current_database_name;
    END

    INSERT INTO dbo.index_usage_stats_detail
            (       index_usage_stats_detail_create_datetime, [database_
                    name], [schema_name], table_name, index_name, user_
                    seek_count,
                    user_scan_count, user_lookup_count, user_update_count,
                    last_user_seek, last_user_scan, last_user_lookup, last_
                    user_update,
                    is_primary_key, is_clustered_index      )
    SELECT
            index_usage_stats_detail_create_datetime,
            [database_name],
            [schema_name],
            table_name,
            index_name,
            user_seek_count,
            user_scan_count,
            user_lookup_count,
            user_update_count,
            last_user_seek,
            last_user_scan,
            last_user_lookup,
            last_user_update,
            is_primary_key,
            is_clustered_index
    FROM #index_usage_stats_detail;
```

```
IF @aggregate_database_data = 0
BEGIN
      MERGE INTO dbo.index_usage_daily_stats AS utilization_target
      USING (          SELECT
                            @index_collection_date AS index_usage_
                            stats_detail_Create_Date,
                            index_usage_stats_detail.[database_name],
                            index_usage_stats_detail.[schema_name],
                            index_usage_stats_detail.table_name,
                            index_usage_stats_detail.index_name,
                            index_usage_stats_detail.user_seek_count,
                            index_usage_stats_detail.user_scan_count,
                            index_usage_stats_detail.user_lookup_
                            count,
                            index_usage_stats_detail.user_update_
                            count,
                            index_usage_stats_detail.last_user_seek,
                            index_usage_stats_detail.last_user_scan,
                            index_usage_stats_detail.last_user_
                            lookup,
                            index_usage_stats_detail.last_user_
                            update,
                            index_usage_stats_detail.is_primary_key,
                            index_usage_stats_detail.is_clustered_
                            index,
                            index_usage_daily_stats.user_seek_count_
                            last_update,
                            index_usage_daily_stats.user_scan_count_
                            last_update,
                            index_usage_daily_stats.user_lookup_
                            count_last_update,
                            index_usage_daily_stats.user_update_
                            count_last_update
```

```
                        FROM #index_usage_stats_detail index_usage_
                        stats_detail
                        LEFT JOIN dbo.index_usage_daily_stats
                        ON index_usage_stats_detail.[database_name] =
                        index_usage_daily_stats.[database_name]
                        AND index_usage_stats_detail.[schema_name] =
                        index_usage_daily_stats.[schema_name]
                        AND index_usage_stats_detail.table_name = index_
                        usage_daily_stats.table_name
                        AND index_usage_stats_detail.index_name = index_
                        usage_daily_stats.index_name
                        AND index_usage_daily_stats.index_usage_daily_
                        stats_date = DATEADD(DAY, -1, @index_collection_
                        date)) AS utilization_source
        ON (   utilization_target.[database_name] = utilization_source.
               [database_name]
                        AND utilization_target.[schema_name] =
                        utilization_source.[schema_name]
                        AND utilization_target.table_name = utilization_
                        source.table_name
                        AND utilization_target.index_name = utilization_
                        source.index_name
                        AND utilization_target.index_usage_daily_stats_
                        date = @index_collection_date   )
    WHEN MATCHED
        THEN UPDATE
                SET user_seek_count_daily = CASE
                                WHEN utilization_source.user_
                                seek_count >= utilization_target.
                                user_seek_count_last_update
                                    THEN utilization_source.user_
                                    seek_count - utilization_
                                    target.user_seek_count_last_
                                    update + utilization_target.
                                    user_seek_count_daily
```

441

```
                                    WHEN utilization_source.user_
                                    seek_count < utilization_target.
                                    user_seek_count_last_update
                                        THEN utilization_source.user_
                                        seek_count + utilization_
                                        target.user_seek_count_daily
                                                        END,
                    user_scan_count_daily = CASE
                                    WHEN utilization_source.user_
                                    scan_count >= utilization_target.
                                    user_scan_count_last_update
                                        THEN utilization_source.user_
                                        scan_count - utilization_
                                        target.user_scan_count_last_
                                        update + utilization_target.
                                        user_scan_count_daily
                                    WHEN utilization_source.user_
                                    scan_count < utilization_target.
                                    user_scan_count_last_update
                                        THEN utilization_source.user_
                                        scan_count + utilization_
                                        target.user_scan_count_daily
                                                        END,
                    user_lookup_count_daily = CASE
                                    WHEN utilization_source.user_
                                    lookup_count >= utilization_
                                    target.user_lookup_count_last_
                                    update
                                        THEN utilization_source.
                                        user_lookup_count -
                                        utilization_target.user_
                                        lookup_count_last_update
                                        + utilization_target.user_
                                        lookup_count_daily
```

```
        WHEN utilization_source.user_
        lookup_count < utilization_
        target.user_lookup_count_last_
        update
            THEN utilization_source.user_
            lookup_count + utilization_
            target.user_lookup_count_daily
                            END,
user_update_count_daily = CASE
        WHEN utilization_source.user_
        update_count >= utilization_
        target.user_update_count_last_
        update
            THEN utilization_source.
            user_update_count -
            utilization_target.user_
            update_count_last_update +
            utilization_target.user_
            update_count_daily
        WHEN utilization_source.user_
        update_count < utilization_
        target.user_update_count_last_
        update
            THEN utilization_source.user_
            update_count + utilization_
            target.user_update_count_daily
                            END,
last_user_seek = CASE
        WHEN utilization_source.
        last_user_seek IS NULL THEN
        utilization_target.last_user_seek
        WHEN utilization_target.
        last_user_seek IS NULL THEN
        utilization_source.last_
        user_seek
```

```
            WHEN utilization_source.last_
            user_seek < utilization_target.
            last_user_seek
                THEN utilization_target.last_
                user_seek
            ELSE utilization_source.last_
            user_seek
                                    END,
last_user_scan = CASE
            WHEN utilization_source.last_
            user_scan IS NULL
                THEN utilization_target.last_
                user_scan
            WHEN utilization_target.last_
            user_scan IS NULL
                THEN utilization_source.last_
                user_scan
            WHEN utilization_source.last_
            user_scan < utilization_target.
            last_user_scan
                THEN utilization_target.last_
                user_scan
            ELSE utilization_source.last_
            user_scan
                                    END,
last_user_lookup = CASE
            WHEN utilization_source.last_
            user_lookup IS NULL
                THEN utilization_target.last_
                user_lookup
            WHEN utilization_target.last_
            user_lookup IS NULL
                THEN utilization_source.last_
                user_lookup
```

```
                              WHEN utilization_source.last_
                              user_lookup < utilization_target.
                              last_user_lookup THEN utilization_
                              target.last_user_lookup
                              ELSE utilization_source.last_
                              user_lookup
                                                  END,
                last_user_update = CASE
                              WHEN utilization_source.last_
                              user_update IS NULL
                              THEN utilization_target.last_
                              user_update
                              WHEN utilization_target.
                              last_user_update IS NULL THEN
                              utilization_source.last_user_
                              update
                              WHEN utilization_source.
                              last_user_update < utilization_
                              target.last_user_update THEN
                              utilization_target.last_user_
                              update
                              ELSE utilization_source.last_
                              user_update
                                                  END,
                user_seek_count_last_update = utilization_
                source.user_seek_count,
                user_scan_count_last_update = utilization_
                source.user_scan_count,
                user_lookup_count_last_update =
                utilization_source.user_lookup_count,
                user_update_count_last_update =
                utilization_source.user_update_count,
                index_usage_daily_stats_Last_Update_
                Datetime = CURRENT_TIMESTAMP
WHEN NOT MATCHED BY TARGET
```

```
                THEN INSERT
                      (         index_usage_daily_stats_date, [database_
                                name], [schema_name], table_name, index_
                                name, user_seek_count_daily, user_scan_
                                count_daily, user_lookup_count_daily,
                                user_update_count_daily,
                                last_user_seek, last_user_scan, last_
                                user_lookup, last_user_update, user_seek_
                                count_last_update, user_scan_count_last_
                                update, user_lookup_count_last_update,
                                user_update_count_last_update, is_
                                primary_key, is_clustered_index,
                                index_usage_daily_stats_Last_Update_
                                Datetime    )
                VALUES
                      (         @index_collection_date,
                                utilization_source.[database_name],
                                utilization_source.[schema_name],
                                utilization_source.table_name,
                                utilization_source.index_name,
                                CASE WHEN utilization_source.user_seek_
                                count_last_update IS NULL
                                        THEN ISNULL(utilization_
                                        source.user_seek_count, 0)
                                    WHEN utilization_source.user_seek_
                                    count >= utilization_source.user_
                                    seek_count_last_update
                                        THEN utilization_source.
                                        user_seek_count -
                                        utilization_source.user_
                                        seek_count_last_update
                                  ELSE utilization_source.user_seek_count
                                END,
                                CASE WHEN utilization_source.user_scan_
                                count_last_update IS NULL
```

```
                THEN ISNULL(utilization_
                source.user_scan_count, 0)
            WHEN utilization_source.user_scan_
            count >= utilization_source.user_
            scan_count_last_update
                THEN utilization_source.user_
                scan_count - utilization_source.
                user_scan_count_last_update
                ELSE utilization_source.user_
                scan_count
        END,
        CASE WHEN utilization_source.user_lookup_
        count_last_update IS NULL
                THEN ISNULL(utilization_source.
                user_lookup_count, 0)
                WHEN utilization_source.user_
                lookup_count >= utilization_
                source.user_lookup_count_last_
                update
                THEN utilization_source.user_
                lookup_count - utilization_
                source.user_lookup_count_last_
                update
                ELSE utilization_source.user_
                lookup_count
        END,
        CASE WHEN utilization_source.user_update_
        count_last_update IS NULL
                THEN ISNULL(utilization_source.
                user_update_count, 0)
                WHEN utilization_source.user_
                update_count >= utilization_
                source.user_update_count_last_
                update
                THEN utilization_source.user_
                update_count - utilization_
```

```
                                    source.user_update_count_last_
                                    update
                                    ELSE utilization_source.user_
                                    update_count
                       END,
                       utilization_source.last_user_seek,
                       utilization_source.last_user_scan,
                       utilization_source.last_user_lookup,
                       utilization_source.last_user_update,
                       ISNULL(utilization_source.user_seek_
                       count, 0),
                       ISNULL(utilization_source.user_scan_
                       count, 0),
                       ISNULL(utilization_source.user_lookup_
                       count, 0),
                       ISNULL(utilization_source.user_update_
                       count, 0),
                       utilization_source.is_primary_key,
                       utilization_source.is_clustered_index,
                       CURRENT_TIMESTAMP    );
    END
    ELSE -- If data is to be pre-aggregated by index, then do so here.
    BEGIN
          MERGE INTO dbo.index_usage_daily_stats AS utilization_target
          USING (        SELECT
                                @index_collection_date AS index_usage_
                                stats_detail_Create_Date,
                                'ALL' AS [database_name],
                                index_usage_stats_detail.[schema_name],
                                index_usage_stats_detail.table_name,
                                index_usage_stats_detail.index_name,
                                SUM(index_usage_stats_detail.user_seek_
                                count) AS user_seek_count,
                                SUM(index_usage_stats_detail.user_scan_
                                count) AS user_scan_count,
```

```
                    SUM(index_usage_stats_detail.user_lookup_
                    count) AS user_lookup_count,
                    SUM(index_usage_stats_detail.user_update_
                    count) AS user_update_count,
                    MAX(index_usage_stats_detail.last_user_
                    seek) AS last_user_seek,
                    MAX(index_usage_stats_detail.last_user_
                    scan) AS last_user_scan,
                    MAX(index_usage_stats_detail.last_user_
                    lookup) AS last_user_lookup,
                    MAX(index_usage_stats_detail.last_user_
                    update) AS last_user_update,
                    MAX(CAST(index_usage_stats_detail.is_
                    primary_key AS TINYINT)) AS is_primary_
                    key,
                    MAX(CAST(index_usage_stats_detail.
                    is_clustered_index AS TINYINT)) AS is_
                    clustered_index,
                    index_usage_daily_stats.user_seek_count_
                    last_update,
                    index_usage_daily_stats.user_scan_count_
                    last_update,
                    index_usage_daily_stats.user_lookup_
                    count_last_update,
                    index_usage_daily_stats.user_update_
                    count_last_update
FROM #index_usage_stats_detail index_usage_
stats_detail
LEFT JOIN dbo.index_usage_daily_stats
ON index_usage_stats_detail.[schema_name] =
index_usage_daily_stats.[schema_name]
AND index_usage_stats_detail.table_name = index_
usage_daily_stats.table_name
AND index_usage_stats_detail.index_name = index_
usage_daily_stats.index_name
```

```
                        AND index_usage_daily_stats.index_usage_daily_
                        stats_date = DATEADD(DAY, -1, @index_collection_
                        date)
                        AND index_usage_daily_stats.[database_name] =
                        'ALL'
                        GROUP BY index_usage_stats_detail.[schema_name],
                        index_usage_stats_detail.table_name, index_
                        usage_stats_detail.index_name,
                            index_usage_daily_stats.user_seek_count_
                            last_update, index_usage_daily_stats.
                            user_scan_count_last_update, index_usage_
                            daily_stats.user_lookup_count_last_
                            update,
                            index_usage_daily_stats.user_update_
                            count_last_update) AS utilization_source
            ON (    utilization_target.[database_name] = 'ALL'
                        AND utilization_target.[schema_name] =
                        utilization_source.[schema_name]
                        AND utilization_target.table_name = utilization_
                        source.table_name
                        AND utilization_target.index_name = utilization_
                        source.index_name
                        AND utilization_target.index_usage_daily_stats_
                        date = @index_collection_date    )
        WHEN MATCHED
            THEN UPDATE
                    SET user_seek_count_daily = CASE
                                WHEN utilization_source.user_
                                seek_count >= utilization_target.
                                user_seek_count_last_update
                                THEN utilization_source.user_
                                seek_count - utilization_target.
                                user_seek_count_last_update +
                                utilization_target.user_seek_
                                count_daily
```

```
            WHEN utilization_source.user_
            seek_count < utilization_target.
            user_seek_count_last_update
            THEN utilization_source.user_
            seek_count + utilization_target.
            user_seek_count_daily
                                    END,
user_scan_count_daily = CASE
            WHEN utilization_source.user_
            scan_count >= utilization_target.
            user_scan_count_last_update
            THEN utilization_source.user_
            scan_count - utilization_target.
            user_scan_count_last_update +
            utilization_target.user_scan_
            count_daily
            WHEN utilization_source.user_
            scan_count < utilization_target.
            user_scan_count_last_update
            THEN utilization_source.user_
            scan_count + utilization_target.
            user_scan_count_daily
                                    END,
user_lookup_count_daily = CASE
            WHEN utilization_source.user_
            lookup_count >= utilization_
            target.user_lookup_count_last_
            update
            THEN utilization_source.user_
            lookup_count - utilization_
            target.user_lookup_count_last_
            update + utilization_target.
            user_lookup_count_daily
            WHEN utilization_source.user_
            lookup_count < utilization_
```

```
                                           target.user_lookup_count_last_
                                           update
                                           THEN utilization_source.user_
                                           lookup_count + utilization_
                                           target.user_lookup_count_daily
                                                               END,
                    user_update_count_daily = CASE
                                           WHEN utilization_source.user_
                                           update_count >= utilization_
                                           target.user_update_count_last_
                                           update
                                           THEN utilization_source.user_
                                           update_count - utilization_
                                           target.user_update_count_last_
                                           update + utilization_target.
                                           user_update_count_daily
                                           WHEN utilization_source.user_
                                           update_count < utilization_
                                           target.user_update_count_last_
                                           update
                                           THEN utilization_source.user_
                                           update_count + utilization_
                                           target.user_update_count_daily
                                                               END,
                    last_user_seek = CASE
                                           WHEN utilization_source.
                                           last_user_seek IS NULL THEN
                                           utilization_target.last_user_seek
                                           WHEN utilization_target.
                                           last_user_seek IS NULL THEN
                                           utilization_source.last_user_seek
                                           WHEN utilization_source.last_
                                           user_seek < utilization_target.
                                           last_user_seek THEN utilization_
                                           target.last_user_seek
```

```
                         ELSE utilization_source.last_
                         user_seek
                                             END,
        last_user_scan = CASE
                         WHEN utilization_source.
                         last_user_scan IS NULL THEN
                         utilization_target.last_user_scan
                         WHEN utilization_target.
                         last_user_scan IS NULL THEN
                         utilization_source.last_user_scan
                         WHEN utilization_source.last_
                         user_scan < utilization_target.
                         last_user_scan THEN utilization_
                         target.last_user_scan
                         ELSE utilization_source.last_
                         user_scan
                                             END,
        last_user_lookup = CASE
                         WHEN utilization_source.last_user_
                         lookup IS NULL THEN utilization_
                         target.last_user_lookup
                         WHEN utilization_target.
                         last_user_lookup IS NULL THEN
                         utilization_source.last_user_
                         lookup
                         WHEN utilization_source.
                         last_user_lookup < utilization_
                         target.last_user_lookup THEN
                         utilization_target.last_user_
                         lookup
                         ELSE utilization_source.last_
                         user_lookup
                                             END,
        last_user_update = CASE
```

```
                          WHEN utilization_source.
                          last_user_update IS NULL THEN
                          utilization_target.last_user_
                          update
                          WHEN utilization_target.
                          last_user_update IS NULL THEN
                          utilization_source.last_user_
                          update
                          WHEN utilization_source.
                          last_user_update < utilization_
                          target.last_user_update THEN
                          utilization_target.last_user_
                          update
              ELSE utilization_source.last_user_update
                                              END,
                user_seek_count_last_update = utilization_
                source.user_seek_count,
                user_scan_count_last_update = utilization_
                source.user_scan_count,
                user_lookup_count_last_update =
                utilization_source.user_lookup_count,
                user_update_count_last_update =
                utilization_source.user_update_count,
                index_usage_daily_stats_Last_Update_
                Datetime = CURRENT_TIMESTAMP
    WHEN NOT MATCHED BY TARGET
        THEN INSERT
            (    index_usage_daily_stats_date, [database_
                name], [schema_name], table_name, index_
                name, user_seek_count_daily, user_scan_
                count_daily, user_lookup_count_daily,
                user_update_count_daily,
                last_user_seek, last_user_scan, last_user_
                lookup, last_user_update, user_seek_count_
```

```
                last_update, user_scan_count_last_update,
                user_lookup_count_last_update,
                user_update_count_last_update, is_primary_
                key, is_clustered_index, index_usage_daily_
                stats_Last_Update_Datetime  )
VALUES
        (    @index_collection_date,
             'ALL',
             utilization_source.[schema_name],
             utilization_source.table_name,
             utilization_source.index_name,
             CASE WHEN utilization_source.user_seek_
             count_last_update IS NULL
                     THEN ISNULL(utilization_source.
                     user_seek_count, 0)
                     WHEN utilization_source.user_
                     seek_count >= utilization_source.
                     user_seek_count_last_update
                     THEN utilization_source.user_
                     seek_count - utilization_source.
                     user_seek_count_last_update
                     ELSE utilization_source.user_
                     seek_count
             END,
             CASE WHEN utilization_source.user_scan_
             count_last_update IS NULL
                     THEN ISNULL(utilization_source.
                     user_scan_count, 0)
                     WHEN utilization_source.user_
                     scan_count >= utilization_source.
                     user_scan_count_last_update
                     THEN utilization_source.user_
                     scan_count - utilization_source.
                     user_scan_count_last_update
```

455

```
                                ELSE utilization_source.user_
                                scan_count
                END,
                                CASE WHEN utilization_source.
                                user_lookup_count_last_update IS
                                NULL
                                THEN ISNULL(utilization_source.
                                user_lookup_count, 0)
                            WHEN utilization_source.user_lookup_
                            count >= utilization_source.user_
                            lookup_count_last_update
                                THEN utilization_source.user_
                                lookup_count - utilization_source.
                                user_lookup_count_last_update
                            ELSE utilization_source.user_lookup_
                            count
                END,
                CASE WHEN utilization_source.user_update_
                count_last_update IS NULL
                                THEN ISNULL(utilization_source.
                                user_update_count, 0)
                            WHEN utilization_source.user_update_
                            count >= utilization_source.user_
                            update_count_last_update
                                THEN utilization_source.user_
                                update_count - utilization_
                                source.user_update_count_last_
                                update
                            ELSE utilization_source.user_update_
                            count
                END,
                utilization_source.last_user_seek,
                utilization_source.last_user_scan,
                utilization_source.last_user_lookup,
                utilization_source.last_user_update,
                ISNULL(utilization_source.user_seek_count, 0),
```

```
                       ISNULL(utilization_source.user_scan_count, 0),
                       ISNULL(utilization_source.user_lookup_
                       count, 0),
                       ISNULL(utilization_source.user_update_
                       count, 0),
                       utilization_source.is_primary_key,
                       utilization_source.is_clustered_index,
                       CURRENT_TIMESTAMP   );
END

-- Check for any indexes that are completely unused, and therefore
   do not appear in any index stats usage DMV data.
-- Update summary and daily stats data as needed based on this data.
IF @aggregate_database_data = 0
BEGIN
     INSERT INTO dbo.index_usage_daily_stats
     (      index_usage_daily_stats_date, [database_name], [schema_
            name], table_name, index_name, user_seek_count_daily,
            user_scan_count_daily, user_lookup_count_daily, user_
            update_count_daily,
            last_user_seek, last_user_scan, last_user_lookup, last_
            user_update, user_seek_count_last_update, user_scan_
            count_last_update, user_lookup_count_last_update,
            user_update_count_last_update, is_primary_key, is_
            clustered_index, index_usage_daily_stats_Last_Update_
            Datetime   )
     SELECT
            @index_collection_date,
            all_index_data.[database_name],
            all_index_data.[schema_name],
            all_index_data.table_name,
            all_index_data.index_name,
            0 AS user_seek_count_daily,
            0 AS user_scan_count_daily,
            0 AS user_lookup_count_daily,
            0 AS user_update_count_daily,
```

```
                    NULL AS last_user_seek,
                    NULL AS last_user_scan,
                    NULL AS last_user_lookup,
                    NULL AS last_user_update,
                    0 AS user_seek_count_last_update,
                    0 AS user_scan_count_last_update,
                    0 AS user_lookup_count_last_update,
                    0 AS user_update_count_last_update,
                    all_index_data.is_primary_key,
                    all_index_data.is_clustered_index,
                    CURRENT_TIMESTAMP AS index_usage_daily_stats_Last_
                    Update_Datetime
            FROM #all_indexes all_index_data
            LEFT JOIN dbo.index_usage_daily_stats
            ON all_index_data.[database_name] = index_usage_daily_stats.
            [database_name]
            AND all_index_data.[schema_name] = index_usage_daily_stats.
            [schema_name]
            AND all_index_data.table_name = index_usage_daily_stats.
            table_name
            AND all_index_data.index_name = index_usage_daily_stats.
            index_name
            AND index_usage_daily_stats.index_usage_daily_stats_date =
            @index_collection_date
            WHERE index_usage_daily_stats.index_usage_daily_stats_id
            IS NULL;
        END
        ELSE -- If we are aggregating all database data together, then
              do so here.
        BEGIN
            INSERT INTO dbo.index_usage_daily_stats
            (       index_usage_daily_stats_date, [database_name], [schema_
                    name], table_name, index_name, user_seek_count_daily,
                    user_scan_count_daily, user_lookup_count_daily, user_
                    update_count_daily,
```

```
            last_user_seek, last_user_scan, last_user_lookup, last_
            user_update, user_seek_count_last_update, user_scan_
            count_last_update, user_lookup_count_last_update,
            user_update_count_last_update, is_primary_key, is_
            clustered_index, index_usage_daily_stats_Last_Update_
            Datetime  )
SELECT
            @index_collection_date,
            'ALL' AS [database_name],
            all_index_data.[schema_name],
            all_index_data.table_name,
            all_index_data.index_name,
            0 AS user_seek_count_daily,
            0 AS user_scan_count_daily,
            0 AS user_lookup_count_daily,
            0 AS user_update_count_daily,
            NULL AS last_user_seek,
            NULL AS last_user_scan,
            NULL AS last_user_lookup,
            NULL AS last_user_update,
            0 AS user_seek_count_last_update,
            0 AS user_scan_count_last_update,
            0 AS user_lookup_count_last_update,
            0 AS user_update_count_last_update,
            MAX(CAST(all_index_data.is_primary_key AS TINYINT)),
            MAX(CAST(all_index_data.is_clustered_index AS TINYINT)),
            CURRENT_TIMESTAMP AS index_usage_daily_stats_Last_
            Update_Datetime
FROM #all_indexes all_index_data
LEFT JOIN dbo.index_usage_daily_stats
ON index_usage_daily_stats.[database_name] = 'ALL'
AND all_index_data.[schema_name] = index_usage_daily_stats.
[schema_name]
```

```
            AND all_index_data.table_name = index_usage_daily_stats.
            table_name
            AND all_index_data.index_name = index_usage_daily_stats.
            index_name
            AND index_usage_daily_stats.index_usage_daily_stats_date =
            @index_collection_date
            WHERE index_usage_daily_stats.index_usage_daily_stats_id
            IS NULL
            GROUP BY all_index_data.[schema_name], all_index_data.
            table_name, all_index_data.index_name;
    END

    DROP TABLE #all_indexes;
    DROP TABLE #index_usage_stats_detail;
    DROP TABLE #database_list;
END
```

Note the parameters that are passed into the stored procedure:

- `@detail_data_retention_days`: This instructs the proc to remove any detail data older than this number of days. The default is 20, but can be changed to any amount, depending on the amount of history you'd like and resources available to store it.

- `@daily_data_retention_days`: This instructs the proc to remove any daily reporting data older than this number of days. The default is 120, but can be changed to any amount, depending on how far back you'd like to report on index usage.

- `@aggregate_database_data`: When set to 1, indexes will be aggregated by name across all databases. This is useful in a scenario when an SQL Server has many databases with the same schema, and you would want index stats to be combined across all databases. This will result in a single row per index on each server with the database name set to "ALL."

This stored procedure uses dynamic SQL to iterate through databases and construct custom T-SQL to execute and collect index metrics. Let's run a test execution of this process using the default parameter values:

```
EXEC dbo.populate_index_usage_stats;
```

With our initial population complete, let's view the contents of index_usage_stats_ detail in Figure 12-4.

index_usage_stats_detail_id	index_usage_stats_detail_create_datetime	database_name	schema_name	table_name	index_name	user_seek_count	user_scan_count	user_lookup_count	user_update_count	last_user_seek
1	2018-09-18 09:22:00.000	AdventureWorks2016CTP3	Sales	SalesOrderDetail	PK_SalesOrderDetail_SalesOrderID_SalesOrderDetailID	0	1	0	0	NULL
2	2018-09-18 09:22:00.000	AdventureWorks2016CTP3	Production	UnitMeasure	PK_UnitMeasure_UnitMeasureCode	0	4	0	0	NULL
3	2018-09-18 09:22:00.000	AdventureWorks2016CTP3	Sales	SalesOrderHeader	PK_SalesOrderHeader_SalesOrderID	0	1	0	0	NULL
4	2018-09-18 09:22:00.000	AdventureWorks2016CTP3	Person	Person	IX_Person_LastName_FirstName_MiddleName	0	52	0	0	NULL
5	2018-09-18 09:22:00.000	AdventureWorks2016CTP3	Person	Person	PK_Person_BusinessEntityID	10	0	52	0	2018-09-18 07:27:45
6	2018-09-18 09:22:00.000	AdventureWorks2016CTP3	dbo	index_usage_stats_detail	IX_index_usage_stats_detail_index_usage_stats_detail_...	1	0	0	1	2018-09-18 09:22:10
7	2018-09-18 09:22:00.000	AdventureWorks2016CTP3	dbo	index_usage_stats_detail	PK_index_usage_stats_detail	0	1	0	1	NULL
8	2018-09-18 09:22:00.000	AdventureWorks2016CTP3	dbo	index_usage_daily_stats	IX_index_usage_daily_stats_index_usage_daily_stats_d...	1	0	0	1	2018-09-18 09:22:10
9	2018-09-18 09:22:00.000	AdventureWorks2016CTP3	dbo	index_usage_daily_stats	PK_index_usage_daily_stats	0	1	0	1	NULL
10	2018-09-18 09:22:00.000	AdventureWorks2016CTP3	dbo	index_usage_daily_stats	IX_index_usage_daily_stats_database_name_schema_...	0	0	0	1	NULL

Figure 12-4. *Detailed index usage stats*

Each row contains data for every index in every user database on my SQL Server that happens to have any usage recorded in dm_db_index_usage_stats. Figure 12-5 shows what the aggregate data in index_usage_daily_stats looks like.

index_usage_daily_stats_id	index_usage_daily_stats_date	database_name	schema_name	table_name	index_name	user_seek_count_daily	user_scan_count_daily	user_lookup_count_daily	user_update_count_daily
1	2018-09-18	AdventureWorks2016CTP3	Sales	SalesOrderDetail	PK_SalesOrderDetail_SalesOrderID_SalesOrderDetailID	0	1	0	0
2	2018-09-18	AdventureWorks2016CTP3	Production	UnitMeasure	PK_UnitMeasure_UnitMeasureCode	0	4	0	0
3	2018-09-18	AdventureWorks2016CTP3	Sales	SalesOrderHeader	PK_SalesOrderHeader_SalesOrderID	0	1	0	0
4	2018-09-18	AdventureWorks2016CTP3	Person	Person	IX_Person_LastName_FirstName_MiddleName	0	52	0	0
5	2018-09-18	AdventureWorks2016CTP3	Person	Person	PK_Person_BusinessEntityID	10	0	52	0
6	2018-09-18	AdventureWorks2016CTP3	dbo	index_usage_stats_detail	IX_index_usage_stats_detail_index_usage_stats_detail_...	1	0	0	1
7	2018-09-18	AdventureWorks2016CTP3	dbo	index_usage_stats_detail	PK_index_usage_stats_detail	0	1	0	1
8	2018-09-18	AdventureWorks2016CTP3	dbo	index_usage_daily_stats	IX_index_usage_daily_stats_index_usage_daily_stats_d...	1	0	0	1
9	2018-09-18	AdventureWorks2016CTP3	dbo	index_usage_daily_stats	PK_index_usage_daily_stats	0	1	0	1
10	2018-09-18	AdventureWorks2016CTP3	dbo	index_usage_daily_stats	IX_index_usage_daily_stats_database_name_schema_...	0	0	0	1

Figure 12-5. *Aggregated daily index usage stats*

The data looks similar, but we only get a single row per day per index. Over time, this allows us to sample more often and still be able to report on a consistent set of data, regardless of when the collection process runs.

Let's use this data to compile a list of unused indexes over the past 90 days, as seen in Listing 12-6.

Listing 12-6. List of Unused Indexes

```
SELECT
        index_usage_daily_stats.[database_name],
        index_usage_daily_stats.[schema_name],
        index_usage_daily_stats.table_name,
        index_usage_daily_stats.index_name,
        index_usage_daily_stats.is_primary_key,
        index_usage_daily_stats.is_clustered_index
FROM dbo.index_usage_daily_stats
WHERE index_usage_daily_stats.index_usage_daily_stats_date >= DATEADD
(DAY, -90, GETUTCDATE())
```

```
GROUP BY index_usage_daily_stats.[database_name], index_usage_daily_stats.
[schema_name], index_usage_daily_stats.table_name, index_usage_daily_stats.
index_name,
index_usage_daily_stats.is_primary_key, index_usage_daily_stats.is_
clustered_index
HAVING SUM(index_usage_daily_stats.user_seek_count_daily) = 0
AND SUM(index_usage_daily_stats.user_scan_count_last_update) = 0
AND SUM(index_usage_daily_stats.user_lookup_count_last_update) = 0;
```

Figure 12-6 shows the resulting list of unused indexes.

	database_name	schema_name	table_name	index_name	is_primary_key	is_clustered_index
1	AdventureWorks2016CTP3	dbo	AWBuildVersion	PK_AWBuildVersion_SystemInformationID	1	1
2	AdventureWorks2016CTP3	dbo	DatabaseLog	PK_DatabaseLog_DatabaseLogID	1	0
3	AdventureWorks2016CTP3	dbo	employee_login	PK_employee	1	1
4	AdventureWorks2016CTP3	dbo	ErrorLog	PK_ErrorLog_ErrorLogID	1	1
5	AdventureWorks2016CTP3	dbo	index_usage_daily_stats	IX_index_usage_daily_stats_database_name_schema_...	0	0
6	AdventureWorks2016CTP3	Demo	DemoSalesOrderDetailSeed	IX_OrderID	0	0
7	AdventureWorks2016CTP3	Demo	DemoSalesOrderDetailSeed	PK__DemoSale__499359DA37DC4424	1	0
8	AdventureWorks2016CTP3	Demo	DemoSalesOrderHeaderSeed	PK__DemoSale__499359DA31897820	1	0
9	AdventureWorks2016CTP3	HumanResources	Department	AK_Department_Name	0	0
10	AdventureWorks2016CTP3	HumanResources	Department	PK_Department_DepartmentID	1	1

Figure 12-6. *List of completely unused indexes*

Using this information, we can target our cleanup efforts to these indexes first. An index should not be dropped without sufficient research. It is possible that the index provides an important unique constraint on the database, or that it may be used infrequently for a quarterly or annual report that will time out without it. Either way, we can begin to paint a picture of how frequently indexes are read and if any have zero use since our collection process started.

Let's consider that we have run the preceding query and isolated unused indexes and dealt with them appropriately. What's next? We can look at indexes that are underused, as seen in Listing 12-7. That is, indexes that have usage, but are mostly writes, rather than reads. These indexes may be important, but are likely candidates to consider dropping or altering after the unused indexes are fully researched.

Listing 12-7. List of Underused Indexes

```
SELECT
        index_usage_daily_stats.[database_name],
        index_usage_daily_stats.[schema_name],
```

```
    index_usage_daily_stats.table_name,
    index_usage_daily_stats.index_name,
    SUM(index_usage_daily_stats.user_seek_count_daily) AS user_seek_
    count,
    SUM(index_usage_daily_stats.user_scan_count_daily) AS user_scan_
    count,
    SUM(index_usage_daily_stats.user_lookup_count_daily) AS user_lookup_
    count,
    SUM(index_usage_daily_stats.user_update_count_daily) AS user_update_
    count,
    MAX(index_usage_daily_stats.last_user_seek) AS last_user_seek,
    MAX(index_usage_daily_stats.last_user_scan) AS last_user_scan,
    MAX(index_usage_daily_stats.last_user_lookup) AS last_user_lookup,
    MAX(index_usage_daily_stats.last_user_update) AS last_user_update,
    index_usage_daily_stats.is_primary_key,
    index_usage_daily_stats.is_clustered_index
FROM dbo.index_usage_daily_stats
WHERE index_usage_daily_stats.index_usage_daily_stats_date>=DATEADD(DAY,-90,
GETUTCDATE())
GROUP BY index_usage_daily_stats.[database_name], index_usage_daily_stats.
[schema_name], index_usage_daily_stats.table_name, index_usage_daily_stats.
index_name,
index_usage_daily_stats.is_primary_key, index_usage_daily_stats.is_
clustered_index
HAVING (SUM(index_usage_daily_stats.user_seek_count_daily) + SUM(index_
usage_daily_stats.user_scan_count_daily) + SUM(index_usage_daily_stats.
user_lookup_count_daily)) /
        (CASE WHEN SUM(index_usage_daily_stats.user_seek_count_daily) +
        SUM(index_usage_daily_stats.user_scan_count_daily) + SUM(index_
        usage_daily_stats.user_lookup_count_daily) + SUM(index_usage_
        daily_stats.user_update_count_daily) = 0 THEN 0.00001 ELSE
        SUM(index_usage_daily_stats.user_seek_count_daily) + SUM(index_
        usage_daily_stats.user_scan_count_daily) + SUM(index_usage_daily_
        stats.user_lookup_count_daily) + SUM(index_usage_daily_stats.
        user_update_count_daily) END) <= 0.1;
```

We can also consider indexes that are mostly used for scans and lookups, rather than seeks. These indexes present opportunities for research. An index with a very high number of lookups might benefit from additional include columns or a new index to supplement its usage. An index with a high number of scans may indicate suboptimal queries or a missing index that could greatly improve performance. Listing 12-8 provides a query that will only return indexes where the ratio of scans to seeks is greater than 90%, or when the ratio of lookups to seeks is greater than 90%.

Listing 12-8. Query to List Indexes that Are Used Primarily for Scans or Lookups

```
SELECT
        index_usage_daily_stats.[database_name],
        index_usage_daily_stats.[schema_name],
        index_usage_daily_stats.table_name,
        index_usage_daily_stats.index_name,
        SUM(index_usage_daily_stats.user_seek_count_daily) AS user_seek_
        count,
        SUM(index_usage_daily_stats.user_scan_count_daily) AS user_scan_
        count,
        SUM(index_usage_daily_stats.user_lookup_count_daily) AS user_lookup_
        count,
        SUM(index_usage_daily_stats.user_update_count_daily) AS user_update_
        count,
        MAX(index_usage_daily_stats.last_user_seek) AS last_user_seek,
        MAX(index_usage_daily_stats.last_user_scan) AS last_user_scan,
        MAX(index_usage_daily_stats.last_user_lookup) AS last_user_lookup,
        MAX(index_usage_daily_stats.last_user_update) AS last_user_update,
        index_usage_daily_stats.is_primary_key,
        index_usage_daily_stats.is_clustered_index
FROM dbo.index_usage_daily_stats
WHERE index_usage_daily_stats.index_usage_daily_stats_date >= DATEADD(DAY,
-90, GETUTCDATE())
GROUP BY index_usage_daily_stats.[database_name], index_usage_daily_stats.
[schema_name], index_usage_daily_stats.table_name, index_usage_daily_stats.
index_name,
```

```
index_usage_daily_stats.is_primary_key, index_usage_daily_stats.is_
clustered_index
HAVING SUM(index_usage_daily_stats.user_scan_count_daily) /
          (CASE WHEN SUM(index_usage_daily_stats.user_scan_count_daily) +
          SUM(index_usage_daily_stats.user_seek_count_daily) + SUM(index_
          usage_daily_stats.user_lookup_count_daily) = 0 THEN 0.00001 ELSE
          SUM(index_usage_daily_stats.user_scan_count_daily) + SUM(index_
          usage_daily_stats.user_seek_count_daily) + SUM(index_usage_daily_
          stats.user_lookup_count_daily) END) > 0.9
          OR SUM(index_usage_daily_stats.user_lookup_count_daily) /
          (CASE WHEN SUM(index_usage_daily_stats.user_scan_count_daily) +
          SUM(index_usage_daily_stats.user_seek_count_daily) + SUM(index_
          usage_daily_stats.user_lookup_count_daily) = 0 THEN 0.00001 ELSE
          SUM(index_usage_daily_stats.user_scan_count_daily) + SUM(index_
          usage_daily_stats.user_seek_count_daily) + SUM(index_usage_daily_
          stats.user_lookup_count_daily) END) > 0.9;
```

This query returns an interesting set of results, as seen in Figure 12-7.

	database_name	schema_name	table_name	index_name	user_seek_count	user_scan_count	user_lookup_count	user_update_count
1	AdventureWorks2016CTP3	dbo	index_usage_daily_stats	PK_index_usage_daily_stats	0	17	0	4
2	AdventureWorks2016CTP3	dbo	index_usage_stats_detail	PK_index_usage_stats_detail	0	4	0	3
3	AdventureWorks2016CTP3	Person	Person	IX_Person_LastName_FirstName_MiddleName	0	52	0	0
4	AdventureWorks2016CTP3	Production	UnitMeasure	PK_UnitMeasure_UnitMeasureCode	0	10	0	0
5	AdventureWorks2016CTP3	Sales	SalesOrderDetail	PK_SalesOrderDetail_SalesOrderID_SalesOrderDetailD	0	1	0	0
6	AdventureWorks2016CTP3	Sales	SalesOrderHeader	PK_SalesOrderHeader_SalesOrderID	0	1	0	0
7	AdventureworksDW2016CTP3	dbo	dim_customer_name	PK_dim_customer_name	0	2	0	1
8	AdventureworksDW2016CTP3	dbo	dim_customer_status	PK_dim_customer_status	0	2	0	1
9	AdventureworksDW2016CTP3	dbo	dim_customer_type	PK_dim_customer_type	0	2	0	1
10	AdventureworksDW2016CTP3	dbo	Dimension_Table_Metadata	PK_Dimension_Table_Metadata	0	3	0	1
11	AdventureworksDW2016CTP3	dbo	DimOrganization	PK_DimOrganization	0	1	0	0
12	AdventureworksDW2016CTP3	dbo	fact_customer_metrics_hourly	PK_fact_customer_metrics_hourly	0	3	0	1
13	AdventureworksDW2016CTP3	dbo	FactInternetSalesReason	PK_FactInternetSalesReason_SalesOrderNumber_Sales...	0	1	0	0
14	AdventureworksDW2016CTP3	dbo	FactProductInventory	PK_FactProductInventory	0	1	0	0

Figure 12-7. *List of indexes used primarily for scans or lookups*

The results show an assortment of indexes with high scan counts that might be worth investigating. Those with the highest scan counts are most likely to be problematic, whereas those with a few can likely be ignored.

With an index usage stats collection process, we can schedule a job to pull this data regularly and report on it to return meaningful results on a regular basis. This is required as data is not persisted indefinitely by SQL Server, and reporting on data without sufficient history will result in bad indexing decisions that may do more harm than good.

Automate the reporting and alerting, and we can only hear about problems when they become relevant. This will allow us to evolve our indexing to meet the needs of changing applications without relying on performance complaints as our primary source of feedback.

Missing Index Statistics

When we review an execution plan, we may see a missing index suggestion, as seen in Figure 12-8.

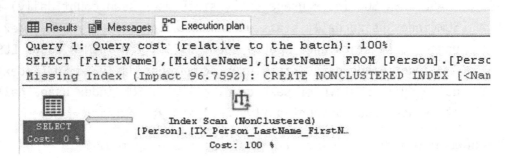

Figure 12-8. *An execution plan that shows a typical missing index warning*

We can click on the missing index and drill into the details, learning about what columns are recommended and the impact the index would have. The data used to generate a missing index suggestion is stored in dynamic management views within SQL Server. This allows us to track missing indexes without having to interactively run queries in Management Studio and look for missing index details. This allows us to respond to poorly performing queries before users complain about latency or administrators become concerned over excessive resource consumption.

Not all missing indexes are good suggestions. Some may not have a significant impact. Others may cover far too many columns, making the performance improvement not worth the cost. Once collected, though, we can sift through this data programmatically and ensure that the best index suggestions are reported on, whereas the less effective ones are either ignored or put to the bottom of the list.

The views involved in missing indexes are a bit more complex than with index usage data, as there is more organization required to group index information, as well as the need to separate index metadata from index statistics. The query in Listing 12-9 joins these views to familiar system views to create a set of missing indexes with the details we need to make sense of them.

Listing 12-9. Query to Return the Set of Missing Indexes in the Current Database

```
SELECT
        databases.name AS [Database_Name],
        schemas.name AS [Schema_Name],
        tables.name AS Table_Name,
        dm_db_missing_index_details.Equality_Columns,
        dm_db_missing_index_details.Inequality_Columns,
        dm_db_missing_index_details.Included_Columns AS Include_Columns,
        dm_db_missing_index_group_stats.Last_User_Seek,
        dm_db_missing_index_group_stats.Avg_Total_User_Cost,
        dm_db_missing_index_group_stats.Avg_User_Impact,
        dm_db_missing_index_group_stats.User_Seeks,
        dm_db_missing_index_groups.Index_Group_Handle,
        dm_db_missing_index_groups.Index_Handle
FROM sys.dm_db_missing_index_groups
INNER JOIN sys.dm_db_missing_index_group_stats
ON dm_db_missing_index_group_stats.group_handle = dm_db_missing_index_
groups.index_group_handle
INNER JOIN sys.dm_db_missing_index_details
ON dm_db_missing_index_groups.index_handle = dm_db_missing_index_details.
index_handle
INNER JOIN sys.databases
ON databases.database_id = dm_db_missing_index_details.database_id
INNER JOIN sys.tables
ON tables.[object_id] = dm_db_missing_index_details.[object_id]
INNER JOIN sys.schemas
ON schemas.[schema_id] = tables.[schema_id]
WHERE databases.name =  DB_NAME();
```

When executed, we get a set of missing indexes that include the database, schema, table, index definition, and some statistics on how it would help future query executions, as seen in Figure 12-9.

Database_Name	Schema_Name	Table_Name	Equality_Columns	Inequality_Columns	Include_Columns	Last_User_Seek	Avg_Total_User_Cost	Avg_User_Impact	User_Seeks
AdventureWorks2016CTP3	Person	Person	NULL	[FirstName]	[Title]	2018-09-19 13:16:48.893	0.874662779160763	93.38	53
AdventureWorks2016CTP3	Sales	SalesOrderHeader	[Status]	NULL	[RevisionNumber], [SalesOrderNumber], [CustomerID]	2018-09-13 06:53:40.833	0.571141551851852	71.83	1
AdventureWorks2016CTP3	Sales	SalesOrderDetail	NULL	[OrderQty]	[CarrierTrackingNumber]	2018-09-13 06:53:50.223	1.11718508222222	83.21	1
AdventureWorks2016CTP3	Person	Person	[FirstName]	NULL	NULL	2018-09-19 13:31:28.940	0.119282204444444	96.76	1

Figure 12-9. *A list of missing indexes generated from the missing index views*

The data returned is quite specific, providing enough detail to understand the impact an index would have on a given system. Some notes on the metrics returned:

- Equality columns are those needed to satisfy an equality query, such as equals or IN.

- Inequality columns are needed by queries utilizing operators such as NOT IN, not equals, greater than, or less than.

- The average user impact is the percentage improvement a query cost would experience if the index were used.

- User seeks is the number of times the missing index would have been used, had it existed.

- Last user seek is the most recent time the index was suggested by the query optimizer.

The rules around the maintenance of this data are the same as index usage stats. This means that the data from these views is temporary and will be removed when SQL Server restarts. As a result, we need to regularly collect, store, and trend it to draw meaningful conclusions.

We will start this project similarly to our collection process for index usage stats, by creating tables to store our data long term. Listing 12-10 contains code for the creation of these two new tables.

Listing 12-10. Creation of Tables to Store Missing Index Metrics

```
CREATE TABLE dbo.missing_index_stats_detail
(       missing_index_stats_detail_Id INT NOT NULL IDENTITY(1,1) CONSTRAINT
        PK_missing_index_stats_detail PRIMARY KEY CLUSTERED,
        missing_index_stats_detail_create_datetime DATETIME NOT NULL,
        [database_name] SYSNAME NOT NULL,
        [schema_name] SYSNAME NOT NULL,
        table_name VARCHAR(256) NOT NULL,
```

```
        equality_columns VARCHAR(MAX) NULL,
        inequality_columns VARCHAR(MAX) NULL,
        include_columns VARCHAR(MAX) NULL,
        last_user_seek DATETIME NOT NULL,
        avg_total_user_cost FLOAT NOT NULL,
        avg_user_impact FLOAT NOT NULL,
        user_seeks BIGINT NOT NULL,
        index_group_handle INT NOT NULL,
        index_handle INT NOT NULL
);

CREATE NONCLUSTERED INDEX IX_missing_index_stats_detail_last_user_seek ON
dbo.missing_index_stats_detail(last_user_seek);
GO

CREATE TABLE dbo.missing_index_stats_summary
(       missing_index_stats_summary_Id INT NOT NULL IDENTITY(1,1)
CONSTRAINT PK_missing_index_stats_summary
PRIMARY KEY CLUSTERED,
        [database_name] SYSNAME NOT NULL,
        [schema_name] SYSNAME NOT NULL,
        table_name VARCHAR(256) NOT NULL,
        equality_columns VARCHAR(MAX) NOT NULL,
        inequality_columns VARCHAR(MAX) NOT NULL,
        include_columns VARCHAR(MAX) NOT NULL,
        first_index_suggestion_time DATETIME NOT NULL,
        last_user_seek DATETIME NOT NULL,
        avg_total_user_cost FLOAT NOT NULL,
        avg_user_impact FLOAT NOT NULL,
        user_seeks BIGINT NOT NULL,
        user_seeks_last_update BIGINT NOT NULL
);

CREATE NONCLUSTERED INDEX IX_missing_index_stats_summary_last_user_seek ON dbo.
missing_index_stats_summary(last_user_seek);
CREATE NONCLUSTERED INDEX IX_missing_index_stats_summary_database_name_
table_name ON dbo.missing_index_stats_summary([database_name], table_name);
GO
```

`missing_index_stats_detail` will contain the raw data pulled from the missing index views, whereas `missing_index_stats_summary` will contain long-term running totals for these metrics. This will allow us to track both short-term and long-term trends with ease.

Before continuing, let's define a basic list of steps that we will want to follow to collect and store missing index metrics:

1. Create and populate a list of all nonsystem databases on the SQL Server.

2. Iterate through each database and collect missing index stats detail data.

3. Merge the detail data into summary data, adding new missing indexes and incrementing existing metrics as needed.

This process is relatively simple, and the T-SQL to accomplish these tasks is far less lengthy than that needed to collect index usage metrics. Listing 12-11 is a stored procedure that will follow the process defined earlier.

Listing 12-11. Stored Procedure to Collect Missing Index Metrics

```
CREATE PROCEDURE dbo.populate_missing_index_data
        @retention_period_for_detail_data_days SMALLINT = 30,
        @delete_all_summary_data BIT = 0,
        @aggregate_all_database_data BIT = 0
AS
BEGIN
        SET NOCOUNT ON;

        DELETE missing_index_stats_detail
        FROM dbo.missing_index_stats_detail
        WHERE missing_index_stats_detail.last_user_seek < DATEADD(DAY,
        -1 * @retention_period_for_detail_data_days, CURRENT_TIMESTAMP);

        IF @delete_all_summary_data = 1
        BEGIN
                TRUNCATE TABLE dbo.missing_index_stats_summary;
        END
```

```
DECLARE @Last_Seek_Time DATETIME;
SELECT
    @Last_Seek_Time = MAX(missing_index_stats_detail.last_user_seek)
FROM dbo.missing_index_stats_detail;
IF @Last_Seek_Time IS NULL
BEGIN
    SELECT @Last_Seek_Time = DATEADD(WEEK, -1, CURRENT_TIMESTAMP);
END

-- Generate a database list so that we collect data from all
   databases on the server.
DECLARE @Database_List TABLE
    (     [database_name] SYSNAME NOT NULL,
          Is_Processed BIT NOT NULL);

DECLARE @Sql_Command NVARCHAR(MAX);
DECLARE @Current_database_name SYSNAME;

INSERT INTO @Database_List
    ([database_name], Is_Processed)
SELECT
    databases.name AS [database_name],
    0 AS Is_Processed
FROM sys.databases
WHERE databases.name NOT IN ('master', 'msdb', 'model', 'tempdb',
'ReportServerTempDB', 'ReportServer')
AND databases.state_desc = 'ONLINE';

CREATE TABLE #missing_index_stats_detail
(    missing_index_stats_detail_Id INT IDENTITY(1,1) NOT NULL
     PRIMARY KEY CLUSTERED,
     [database_name] SYSNAME,
     [schema_name] SYSNAME,
     table_name SYSNAME,
     equality_columns VARCHAR(MAX),
     inequality_columns VARCHAR(MAX),
     include_columns VARCHAR(MAX),
```

```
                last_user_seek DATETIME,
                avg_total_user_cost FLOAT,
                avg_user_impact FLOAT,
                user_seeks BIGINT,
                index_group_handle INT,
                index_handle INT);

    -- Loop through each database and collect missing index stats for each.
    WHILE EXISTS (SELECT * FROM @Database_List Database_List WHERE
    Database_List.Is_Processed = 0)
    BEGIN
                SELECT TOP 1
                        @Current_database_name = Database_List.[database_name]
                FROM @Database_List Database_List
                WHERE Database_List.Is_Processed = 0;

                SELECT @Sql_Command = '
                USE [' + @Current_database_name + '];

                INSERT INTO #missing_index_stats_detail
                        ([database_name], [schema_name], table_name, equality_
                        columns, inequality_columns, include_columns, last_
                        user_seek,
                         avg_total_user_cost, avg_user_impact, user_seeks,
                         index_group_handle, index_handle)
                SELECT
                        databases.name AS [database_name],
                        schemas.name AS [schema_name],
                        tables.name AS table_name,
                        dm_db_missing_index_details.equality_columns,
                        dm_db_missing_index_details.inequality_columns,
                        dm_db_missing_index_details.Included_Columns AS
                        include_columns,
                        dm_db_missing_index_group_stats.last_user_seek,
                        dm_db_missing_index_group_stats.avg_total_user_cost,
                        dm_db_missing_index_group_stats.avg_user_impact,
```

```
                dm_db_missing_index_group_stats.user_seeks,
                dm_db_missing_index_groups.index_group_handle,
                dm_db_missing_index_groups.index_handle
        FROM sys.dm_db_missing_index_groups
        INNER JOIN sys.dm_db_missing_index_group_stats
        ON dm_db_missing_index_group_stats.group_handle = dm_db_
        missing_index_groups.index_group_handle
        INNER JOIN sys.dm_db_missing_index_details
        ON dm_db_missing_index_groups.index_handle = dm_db_missing_
        index_details.index_handle
        INNER JOIN sys.databases
        ON databases.database_id = dm_db_missing_index_details.
        database_id
        INNER JOIN sys.tables
        ON tables.[object_id] = dm_db_missing_index_details.[object_id]
        INNER JOIN sys.schemas
        ON schemas.[schema_id] = tables.[schema_id]
        WHERE databases.name = "' + @Current_database_name + "'
        AND dm_db_missing_index_group_stats.last_user_seek > "' +
        CAST(@Last_Seek_Time AS NVARCHAR(MAX)) + "';';

        EXEC sp_executesql @Sql_Command;

        UPDATE Database_List
                SET Is_Processed = 1
        FROM @Database_List Database_List
        WHERE [database_name] = @Current_database_name;
END

INSERT INTO dbo.missing_index_stats_detail
        (missing_index_stats_detail_Create_Datetime, [database_name],
        [schema_name], table_name, equality_columns, inequality_
        columns, include_columns,
         last_user_seek, avg_total_user_cost, avg_user_impact, user_
         seeks, index_group_handle, index_handle)
```

```
SELECT DISTINCT
    CURRENT_TIMESTAMP AS missing_index_stats_detail_Create_Datetime,
        [database_name],
        [schema_name],
        table_name,
        equality_columns,
        inequality_columns,
        include_columns,
        last_user_seek,
        avg_total_user_cost,
        avg_user_impact,
        user_seeks,
        index_group_handle,
        index_handle
FROM #missing_index_stats_detail;

IF @aggregate_all_database_data = 0
BEGIN
    MERGE INTO dbo.missing_index_stats_summary AS Index_Summary_Target
    USING (SELECT [database_name], [schema_name], table_name,
    ISNULL(equality_columns, ") AS equality_columns,
    ISNULL(inequality_columns, ") AS inequality_columns,
    ISNULL(include_columns, ") AS include_columns,
                        MAX(last_user_seek) AS last_user_seek,
                        AVG(avg_total_user_cost) AS avg_total_
                        user_cost, AVG(avg_user_impact) AS
                        avg_user_impact, SUM(user_seeks) AS
                        user_seeks
                        FROM #missing_index_stats_detail
                        GROUP BY [database_name], [schema_
                        name], table_name, equality_columns,
                        inequality_columns, include_columns) AS
                        Index_Summary_Source
        ON (Index_Summary_Source.[database_name] = Index_Summary_
        Target.[database_name]
```

```
            AND Index_Summary_Source.[schema_name] = Index_Summary_
            Target.[schema_name]
            AND Index_Summary_Source.table_name = Index_Summary_
            Target.table_name
            AND Index_Summary_Source.equality_columns = Index_
            Summary_Target.equality_columns
            AND Index_Summary_Source.inequality_columns = Index_
            Summary_Target.inequality_columns
            AND Index_Summary_Source.include_columns = Index_
            Summary_Target.include_columns)
WHEN MATCHED
        THEN UPDATE
                SET last_user_seek = Index_Summary_Source.last_
                user_seek,
                        user_seeks = CASE
                                WHEN Index_Summary_Source.user_
                                seeks = Index_Summary_Target.
                                user_seeks_last_update
                                    THEN Index_Summary_Target.
                                    user_seeks
                                WHEN Index_Summary_Source.user_
                                seeks >= Index_Summary_Target.
                                user_seeks
                                    THEN Index_Summary_Source.
                                    user_seeks + Index_Summary_
                                    Target.user_seeks - Index_
                                    Summary_Target.user_seeks_
                                    last_update
                                WHEN Index_Summary_Source.user_
                                seeks < Index_Summary_Target.
                                user_seeks
                                AND Index_Summary_Source.user_
                                seeks < Index_Summary_Target.
                                user_seeks_last_update
                                    THEN Index_Summary_Target.
                                    user_seeks + Index_Summary_
                                    Source.user_seeks
```

```
                              WHEN Index_Summary_Source.user_
                              seeks < Index_Summary_Target.
                              user_seeks
                              AND Index_Summary_Source.user_
                              seeks > Index_Summary_Target.
                              user_seeks_last_update
                                  THEN Index_Summary_Source.
                                  user_seeks + Index_Summary_
                                  Target.user_seeks - Index_
                                  Summary_Target.user_seeks_
                                  last_update
                                         END,
                      user_seeks_last_update = Index_Summary_
                      Source.user_seeks,
                      avg_total_user_cost = Index_Summary_
                      Source.avg_total_user_cost,
                      avg_user_impact = Index_Summary_Source.
                      avg_user_impact
        WHEN NOT MATCHED BY TARGET
            THEN INSERT
                  VALUES (Index_Summary_Source.[database_name],
                  Index_Summary_Source.[schema_name], Index_
                  Summary_Source.table_name, Index_Summary_Source.
                  equality_columns,
                              Index_Summary_Source.inequality_
                              columns, Index_Summary_Source.
                              include_columns, CURRENT_
                              TIMESTAMP, Index_Summary_Source.
                              last_user_seek,
                              Index_Summary_Source.avg_total_
                              user_cost, Index_Summary_Source.
                              avg_user_impact, Index_Summary_
                              Source.user_seeks, Index_
                              Summary_Source.user_seeks);

        END
```

```
ELSE
BEGIN
    MERGE INTO dbo.missing_index_stats_summary AS Index_Summary_
    Target
    USING (SELECT 'ALL' AS [database_name], [schema_name],
    table_name, ISNULL(equality_columns, '') AS equality_columns,
    ISNULL(inequality_columns, '') AS inequality_columns,
    ISNULL(include_columns, '') AS include_columns,
                        MAX(last_user_seek) AS last_user_seek,
                        AVG(avg_total_user_cost) AS avg_total_
                        user_cost, AVG(avg_user_impact) AS avg_
                        user_impact, SUM(user_seeks) AS user_seeks
                        FROM #missing_index_stats_detail GROUP
                        BY [schema_name], table_name, equality_
                        columns, inequality_columns, include_
                        columns) AS Index_Summary_Source
    ON (Index_Summary_Target.[database_name] = 'ALL'
        AND Index_Summary_Source.[schema_name] = Index_Summary_
        Target.[schema_name]
        AND Index_Summary_Source.table_name = Index_Summary_
        Target.table_name
        AND Index_Summary_Source.equality_columns = Index_
        Summary_Target.equality_columns
        AND Index_Summary_Source.inequality_columns = Index_
        Summary_Target.inequality_columns
        AND Index_Summary_Source.include_columns = Index_
        Summary_Target.include_columns)
    WHEN MATCHED
            THEN UPDATE
                    SET last_user_seek = Index_Summary_Source.last_
                    user_seek,
                        user_seeks = CASE
                                WHEN Index_Summary_Source.user_
                                seeks = Index_Summary_Target.
                                user_seeks_last_update
```

```
                                    THEN Index_Summary_Target.
                                    user_seeks
                              WHEN Index_Summary_Source.user_
                              seeks >= Index_Summary_Target.
                              user_seeks
                                    THEN Index_Summary_Source.
                                    user_seeks + Index_Summary_
                                    Target.user_seeks - Index_
                                    Summary_Target.user_seeks_
                                    last_update
                              WHEN Index_Summary_Source.user_
                              seeks < Index_Summary_Target.
                              user_seeks
                              AND Index_Summary_Source.user_
                              seeks < Index_Summary_Target.
                              user_seeks_last_update
                                    THEN Index_Summary_Target.
                                    user_seeks + Index_Summary_
                                    Source.user_seeks
                              WHEN Index_Summary_Source.user_
                              seeks < Index_Summary_Target.
                              user_seeks
                              AND Index_Summary_Source.user_
                              seeks > Index_Summary_Target.
                              user_seeks_last_update
                                    THEN Index_Summary_Source.
                                    user_seeks + Index_Summary_
                                    Target.user_seeks - Index_
                                    Summary_Target.user_seeks_
                                    last_update
                                        END,
                  user_seeks_last_update = Index_Summary_
                  Source.user_seeks,
                  avg_total_user_cost = Index_Summary_
                  Source.avg_total_user_cost,
                  avg_user_impact = Index_Summary_Source.
                  avg_user_impact
```

```
            WHEN NOT MATCHED BY TARGET
                THEN INSERT
                    VALUES ('ALL', Index_Summary_Source.[schema_
                    name], Index_Summary_Source.table_name, Index_
                    Summary_Source.equality_columns,
                            Index_Summary_Source.inequality_
                            columns, Index_Summary_Source.include_
                            columns, CURRENT_TIMESTAMP, Index_
                            Summary_Source.last_user_seek,
                            Index_Summary_Source.avg_total_
                            user_cost, Index_Summary_Source.
                            avg_user_impact, Index_Summary_Source.
                            user_seeks, Index_Summary_Source.
                            user_seeks);
        END

        DROP TABLE #missing_index_stats_detail;
END
```

Note the three parameters defined within the stored procedure:

- `@retention_period_for_detail_data_days`: How many days of detail data to retain. This will vary based on available storage and the amount of missing index data that is generated regularly. Here, we default this to 30 days of retention.

- `@delete_all_summary_data`: When set to 1, will clear out all summary data. This is useful after a major server or software change might render older data irrelevant. Alternatively, you can filter by `last_user_seek` to remove out-of-date index suggestions while retaining historical data.

- `@aggregate_all_database_data`: For a server with many databases that contain the same schema, this option will combine index suggestions between all databases, using "ALL" as the database name. This can save space and allow for more intelligent decisions on multitenant servers with a large quantity of similar databases.

Let's execute this stored procedure and review the results in each table:

```
EXEC populate_missing_index_data;
SELECT * FROM dbo.missing_index_stats_detail;
SELECT * FROM dbo.missing_index_stats_summary
```

Figure 12-10 shows what the results look like on my local server.

	missing_index_stats_detail_Id	missing_index_stats_detail_create_datetime	database_name	schema_name	table_name	equality_columns	inequality_columns	include_columns	
1	1	2018-09-20 07:59:08.687	AdventureWorks2016CTP3	Person	Person	NULL	[FirstName]	[Title]	
2	2	2018-09-20 07:59:08.687	AdventureWorks2016CTP3	Sales	SalesOrderDetail	NULL	[OrderQty]	[CarrierTrackingNumber]	
3	3	2018-09-20 07:59:08.687	AdventureWorks2016CTP3	Sales	SalesOrderHeader	[Status]	NULL	[RevisionNumber], [SalesOrderNumber], [CustomerID]	

	missing_index_stats_summary_Id	database_name	schema_name	table_name	equality_columns	inequality_columns	include_columns	first_index_suggestion_time	last_user_see
1	1	AdventureWorks2016CTP3	Person	Person		[FirstName]	[Title]	2018-09-20 07:59:08.700	2018-09-20 (
2	2	AdventureWorks2016CTP3	Sales	SalesOrderDetail		[OrderQty]	[CarrierTrackingNumber]	2018-09-20 07:59:08.700	2018-09-20 (
3	3	AdventureWorks2016CTP3	Sales	SalesOrderHeader	[Status]		[RevisionNumber], [SalesOrderNumber], [CustomerID]	2018-09-20 07:59:08.700	2018-09-20 (

Figure 12-10. *Missing index metrics collected by the stored procedure*

The first result set is the raw data from the missing index dynamic management views, which will contain a row per index per execution. The second is the aggregate data, which will only return a single row per index.

We can make this process easier by adding views on top of these tables that build an index creation statement for each index. Also useful would be a more usable long-term improvement measure that takes into account query cost, number of seeks, and the average user impact. This would provide a better objective metric for evaluating which indexes are more useful than others. Listing 12-12 contains the CREATE statements for these views.

Listing 12-12. Views that Add Additional Insights to Our Missing Index Metrics

```
CREATE VIEW dbo.v_missing_index_stats_detail
AS
SELECT
      missing_index_stats_detail_create_datetime,
      [database_name],
      [schema_name],
      table_name,
      'CREATE NONCLUSTERED INDEX [missing_index_' + CONVERT (VARCHAR,
      missing_index_stats_detail.index_group_handle) + '_' + CONVERT
      (VARCHAR, missing_index_stats_detail.index_handle) + '_' +
```

```
        table_name + ']' + ' ON [' + table_name + ']
        (' + ISNULL(missing_index_stats_detail.equality_columns, '') +
        CASE WHEN missing_index_stats_detail.equality_columns IS NOT
        NULL
                                    AND missing_index_stats_detail.
                                    inequality_columns IS NOT NULL
                                    THEN ','
                                    ELSE ''
                                    END +
        ISNULL(missing_index_stats_detail.inequality_columns, '') + ')'
        + ISNULL(' INCLUDE (' + missing_index_stats_detail.include_
        columns + ')', '') AS index_creation_statement,
    missing_index_stats_detail.avg_total_user_cost * (missing_index_
    stats_detail.avg_user_impact / 100.0) * missing_index_stats_detail.
    user_seeks AS improvement_measure,
    equality_columns,
    inequality_columns,
    include_columns,
    ISNULL(LEN(missing_index_stats_detail.equality_columns) -
    LEN(REPLACE(missing_index_stats_detail.equality_columns, '[', '')),
    0) AS equality_column_count,
    ISNULL(LEN(missing_index_stats_detail.inequality_columns) -
    LEN(REPLACE(missing_index_stats_detail.inequality_columns, '[', '')),
    0) AS inequality_column_count,
    ISNULL(LEN(missing_index_stats_detail.include_columns) -
    LEN(REPLACE(missing_index_stats_detail.include_columns, '[', '')), 0)
    AS included_column_count,
    last_user_seek,
    user_seeks,
    index_group_handle,
    index_handle
FROM dbo.missing_index_stats_detail;
GO
```

```
CREATE VIEW dbo.v_missing_index_stats_summary
AS
SELECT
        [database_name],
        [schema_name],
        table_name,
        'CREATE NONCLUSTERED INDEX [missing_index_' + CONVERT (VARCHAR,
        missing_index_stats_summary.missing_index_stats_summary_Id) + '_' +
                table_name + ']' + ' ON [' + table_name + ']
                (' + missing_index_stats_summary.equality_columns + CASE WHEN
                missing_index_stats_summary.equality_columns <> ''
                                        AND missing_index_stats_summary.
                                        inequality_columns <> ''
                                        THEN ','
                                        ELSE ''
                                        END +
        missing_index_stats_summary.inequality_columns + ')' + CASE
        WHEN missing_index_stats_summary.include_columns = ''
                                        THEN ''
                                        ELSE ' INCLUDE (' + missing_
                                        index_stats_summary.include_
                                        columns + ')'
                                        END AS index_creation_statement,
        missing_index_stats_summary.avg_total_user_cost * (missing_index_
        stats_summary.avg_user_impact / 100.0) * missing_index_stats_
        summary.user_seeks AS improvement_measure,
        missing_index_stats_summary.equality_columns,
        missing_index_stats_summary.inequality_columns,
        missing_index_stats_summary.include_columns,
        ISNULL(LEN(missing_index_stats_summary.equality_columns) -
LEN(REPLACE(missing_index_stats_summary.equality_columns, '[', '')), 0)
AS equality_column_count,
        ISNULL(LEN(missing_index_stats_summary.inequality_columns) -
LEN(REPLACE(missing_index_stats_summary.inequality_columns, '[', '')), 0)
AS inequality_column_count,
```

```
    ISNULL(LEN(missing_index_stats_summary.include_columns) -
    LEN(REPLACE(missing_index_stats_summary.include_columns, '[', ")), 0)
    AS included_column_count,
    missing_index_stats_summary.first_index_suggestion_time,
    missing_index_stats_summary.last_user_seek,
    missing_index_stats_summary.user_seeks
FROM dbo.missing_index_stats_summary;
```

These views add the following new columns to our metrics:

- Index creation statement for the given index. Note that the name is arbitrary and likely should be changed.

- Improvement measure, which is defined as: Cost * Impact% * Seeks. This unitless number provides a way to evaluate indexes against each other to determine which are the most worthwhile to consider first.

- Equality column count

- Inequality column count

- Include column count

Let's run the collection stored procedure again and select from these new views:

```
EXEC populate_missing_index_data;
SELECT * FROM dbo.v_missing_index_stats_detail;
SELECT * FROM dbo.v_missing_index_stats_summary;
```

The results show a new-and-improved set of missing index metrics, as seen in Figure 12-11.

	missing_index_stats_detail_create_datetime	database_name	schema_name	table_name	index_creation_statement	improvement_measure
1	2018-09-20 07:59:08.687	AdventureWorks2016CTP3	Person	Person	CREATE NONCLUSTERED INDEX [missing_index_2_1_Per...	41.6547652621963
2	2018-09-20 07:59:08.687	AdventureWorks2016CTP3	Sales	SalesOrderDetail	CREATE NONCLUSTERED INDEX [missing_index_6_5_Sal...	0.929609706917111
3	2018-09-20 07:59:08.687	AdventureWorks2016CTP3	Sales	SalesOrderHeader	CREATE NONCLUSTERED INDEX [missing_index_4_3_Sal...	0.410250976695185
4	2018-09-20 08:43:26.060	AdventureWorks2016CTP3	Person	Person	CREATE NONCLUSTERED INDEX [missing_index_2_1_Per...	41.6547652621963
5	2018-09-20 08:43:26.060	AdventureWorks2016CTP3	Sales	SalesOrderDetail	CREATE NONCLUSTERED INDEX [missing_index_6_5_Sal...	0.929609706917111
6	2018-09-20 08:43:26.060	AdventureWorks2016CTP3	Sales	SalesOrderHeader	CREATE NONCLUSTERED INDEX [missing_index_4_3_Sal...	0.410250976695185

	database_name	schema_name	table_name	index_creation_statement	improvement_measure	equality_columns	inequality_columns	inclu
1	AdventureWorks2016CTP3	Person	Person	CREATE NONCLUSTERED INDEX [missing_index_1_Perso...	41.6547652621963		[FirstName]	[Title
2	AdventureWorks2016CTP3	Sales	SalesOrderDetail	CREATE NONCLUSTERED INDEX [missing_index_2_Sales...	0.929609706917111		[OrderQty]	[Carr
3	AdventureWorks2016CTP3	Sales	SalesOrderHeader	CREATE NONCLUSTERED INDEX [missing_index_3_Sales...	0.410250976695185	[Status]		[Rev

Figure 12-11. *Missing index metrics from the missing index views*

The first result set shows that data has now been collected twice, once at 7:59 and again at 8:43. The second set of results shows a single row per index, with metrics aggregated over time based on continued usage. If we were to evaluate these indexes, then the first one on `Person.Person` would be the one we'd consider first, as it has the highest improvement measure.

From this point, we can order, filter, and curate the results to provide only what we want to see. The following are a handful of filters that could be useful in reducing the indexes to consider:

- Only include indexes with more than a certain number of user seeks. We probably don't want to add an index that will only ever be used once or twice.

- Filter out indexes that have not had a seek in the past week. If an index suggestion is no longer relevant, then there may be no need to consider it.

- Only include indexes with an improvement measure greater than an arbitrary number. This filters out those that will not have enough impact to be useful.

- Avoid recommending indexes that are very similar to existing indexes. Alternatively, add a warning of this so that we know that they may need to be compared prior to making any final indexing decisions.

Keep in mind that infrequent or low impact indexes may still be worth considering in special circumstances, such as in a reporting environment. The preceding filters are a good way to prioritize what to consider first and what can wait a little while for our attention.

Last, not all index suggestions are necessarily worth the effort. An index suggestion with 35 include columns may be overkill, and leaving out the includes may still provide a worthwhile index. Always test and verify indexes prior to implementing them, to be certain they help performance and justify the costs associated with more indexes.

This process provides a way to use dynamic SQL to iterate through databases and generate T-SQL that collects missing index metrics and stores them for long-term trending and planning. This helps us overcome the limitations of the built-in dynamic management views while organizing this data in a far more user-friendly format.

Conclusion

In this chapter, we applied dynamic SQL to the challenge of index maintenance. These processes allowed us to tackle index fragmentation, index usage statistics, and missing index tracking. While fully functional as-is, each of these processes can be further customized to provide additional functionality or to better fit a specific application environment.

Use the tactics provided here as a template for building and customizing other maintenance processes. Doing so can allow seamless execution of queries across multiple databases, servers, or database objects. Indexing is one common maintenance challenge, but our careers will be filled with many others. The flexibility of dynamic SQL can help solve these problems with less code and complexity than a more hard-coded solution would.

Index

A

Accent sensitivity, 361
Advantages
    configuration data, 9
    ORM, 8
    performance, 8
    reduce operator intervention, 9
    search boxes, 7
    WHERE clauses, 7
AdventureWorks, 303, 328, 336, 366
Aggregate function, 329
Application traffic, scanning, 54
Archiving/movement of data
    database log data, 372–373
    data size, increase, 374
    dynamic SQL, 374–376
    Log_Time, 377–378
    new databases, 377
    new tables, 378
    reference points, 379
    tasks, 374
    TSQL, 372
Auditing users and logins
    list, mappings, 146
    object-level permissions, 144
    script, user-created securables, 144
    server logins and roles, 142
    TSQL to return relationships, 145
Audit password policies, 126

B

Backup software, 105
BACKUP statements, 403
Batched command
    string creation, 151–153
Blind SQL injection attacks, 51–52
Built in function, 41
Bushy query tree, 306
BusinessEntityContact table, 135
Business logic, complex, 388

C

Cardinality
    back to dynamic SQL, 246–247
    statistics (*see* Statistics)
    sys.dm_db_stats_properties, 244–245
    trace flag 2371, 245–246
Case sensitivity, 361
CAST/CONVERT, 360
CH% filter, 366
Classic parameter sniffing, 307
Cleanup, 138
COALESCE statement, 80
Code review, 55
Collation_Test database, 363
Command string,
    dynamic SQL, 44, 47, 50, 147
Common table expression (CTE), 81

© Edward Pollack 2019
E. Pollack, *Dynamic SQL*, https://doi.org/10.1007/978-1-4842-4318-3

INDEX

Revisiting Security
  IO statistics, 269
  list-building SELECT statement, 273
  parameters, 270–271
  quality assurance, 274
  SQL injection, 272–273
  stored procedure, 267–269
@row_count_to_return, 85
Row level security
  customizing, options, 158
  employee login table,
      creation, 153–154
  epollack, 156
  security policy, creation, 155
  SELECT against
      employee_login, 156–157
  table-valued function, creation, 155

S

SafetyStockLevel value, 348
SalesOrderDetail, 217
SalesOrderHeader, 217
Saving generated scripts, 399
Saving scripts, table
  backup maintenance script, 404–407
  BACKUP statements, 403
  dbo.sql_command, 403
  dynamic SQL, 400
  QueryOutput.sql, 407–408
  stored procedure, 400–402
  xp_cmdshell, 408–409
Scalability, 419
Schema generation demo, 413–414
Schema Name, 48–49
Schema search
  execution output
      full table name, 136

primary key name, 136
    table name, 135
  stored procedure, 128–129, 131–134
Scope
  command strings, 169
  definitions, 165
  important aspect, 168–169
  manage, 169–170
  parameters, 167
  SELECT statement, 165
  stored procedure, 166–168
  TSQL statement, 165
Search grid
  blank searches, 80
  conditional paging, 83–85
  data paging, 80, 82
  input-based, 87, 89–91
  limitations, 86
  result row count (see Result row count)
Security context, changing
  object/execution, 112
  ownership chaining, 112, 119
  permissions, 112–114
    GRANT EXECUTE, 120
    VeryLimitedUser, 120
  results, executing dynamic SQL, 119
  REVERT command, 113
  stored procedure
    dynamic SQL, 117–118
    EXECUTE AS CALLER, 116–117
    EXECUTE AS OWNER, 115–116
  user by using EXECUTE AS, 112
  WITH NO REVERT, 114
Security disaster, 120
Security login and user usage, 140–141
Security testing, 53–54
SELECT statement, 333
Server logins and roles, 143

494